Studies in Renaissance Literature

Volume 2

DOCTRINE AND DEVOTION IN SEVENTEENTH-CENTURY POETRY

STUDIES IN DONNE, HERBERT, CRASHAW, AND VAUGHAN

This book offers a comprehensive account of the literary and theological background to English devotional poetry of the seventeenth century, concentrating on four major poets, Donne, Herbert, Vaughan and Crashaw. In so doing, it challenges both Protestant poetics and postmodernism, the prevailing critical approaches to Renaissance literature. By reading the poetry in the light of Continental devotional literature and theology, the author demonstrates that religious poetry in seventeenth-century England was not rigidly or exclusively Protestant in its doctrinal and liturgical orientation. He argues that poetic genres and devices that have been ascribed to strict Reformation influence are equally prominent in the Catholic poetry of Spain and France, and that dogmatic stances often associated with Luther and Calvin are part of the broader Christian tradition reaffirmed by the Counter-Reformation, thus establishing the conception of the Church of England as via media between Rome and Geneva more firmly. The book also argues that postmodernist anxiety about subjective identity and the capacity of language for signification is in fact a concern of such landmark Christian thinkers as Augustine and Aquinas, and appears in devotional poetry in the Christian tradition.

Professor R. V. YOUNG teaches at North Carolina State University.

Studies in Renaissance Literature

ISSN 1465–6310

General editors
John T. Shawcross
Graham Parry

Editorial board
John T. Shawcross
Helen E. Wilcox
John N. King
Graham Parry

Volume 1: The Theology of John Donne
Jeffrey Johnson

Studies in Renaissance Literature offers investigations of topics both spanning the sixteenth and seventeenth centuries and growing out of medieval concerns, up to the Restoration period. Particularly encouraged are new examinations of the interplay between the literature of the English Renaissance and its culural history.

Proposals or queries may be sent directly to the editors at the addresses given below; all submissions will receive prompt and informed consideration.

Professor John T. Shawcross, Department of English, University of Kentucky, Lexington, Kentucky 40506, USA

Professor Helen E. Wilcox, Rijksuniversiteit Groningen, Broerstraat 5, POB 72,9700 AB, Groningen, The Netherelands

Dr John N. King, Department of English, the Ohio State University, Columbus, Ohio 43210, USA

Professor Graham Parry, Department of English, University of York, Heslington, York YO1 5DD, UK

DOCTRINE AND DEVOTION IN SEVENTEENTH-CENTURY POETRY

STUDIES IN DONNE, HERBERT, CRASHAW, AND VAUGHAN

R. V. Young

D. S. BREWER

First published 2000
D. S. Brewer, Cambridge

ISBN 0 85991 569 7

D. S. Brewer is an imprint of Boydell & Brewer Ltd
PO Box 9, Woodbridge, Suffolk IP12 3DF, UK
and of Boydell & Brewer Inc.
PO Box 41026, Rochester, NY 14604–4126, USA
website: http://www.boydell.co.uk

A catalogue record for this book is available
from the British Library

Library of Congress Catalog Card Number: 99–042064

This publication is printed on acid-free paper

Printed in Great Britain by
St Edmundsbury Press Ltd, Bury St Edmunds, Suffolk

CONTENTS

For Louis Martz – most reverend head, to whom I owe
All that I am in arts, all that I know.

LIST OF ILLUSTRATIONS

ABBREVIATIONS

BJJ	*Ben Jonson Journal*
BNYPL	*Bulletin of the New York Public Library*
ELH	*English Literary History*
ELR	*English Literary Renaissance*
GHJ	*George Herbert Journal*
JEGP	*Journal of English and Germanic Philology*
JDJ	*John Donne Journal*
MLN	*Modern Language Notes*
MLQ	*Modern Language Quarterly*
MP	*Modern Philology*
PL	*Patrologia Latina*
PLL	*Papers in Language and Literature*
PQ	*Philological Quarterly*
RES	*Review of English Studies*
SEL	*Studies in English Literature*
SP	*Studies in Philology*
TSLL	*Texas Studies in Language and Literature*

ACKNOWLEDEGMENTS

This book began with a series of papers delivered at learned conferences over the past fifteen years: a Dearborn Renaissance Conference, several John Donne Society Conferences, and a celebration of the Herbert quatercentenary at the University of Groningen. I am grateful to the organizers of these gatherings for including me in their programs and to the original audiences for their responses, which were usually both perceptively critical and encouraging. Briefer, earlier versions of some sections of the book have appeared in three volumes published by the University of Missouri Press: "Bright Shootes of Everlastingnesse": The Seventeenth-Century Religious Lyric, ed. Claude J. Summers and Ted-Larry Pebworth (1987); New Perspectives on the Life and Art of Richard Crashaw, ed. John R. Roberts (1990); and New Perspectives on the Seventeenth-Century Devotional Poets, ed. John R. Roberts (1994). Earlier versions of some sections also appeared in a special Herbert issue of Renascence (1993) and in the proceedings of the Groningen Herbert conference, George Herbert: Sacred and Profane, ed. Helen Wilcox and Richard Todd (VU University Press, 1995). I am grateful for the opportunity to republish this material in thoroughly revised form here. I also wish to express my thanks to the American Council of Learned Societies for financial support during a year's leave of absence, and to the English Department of North Carolina State University for release time, which provided opportunities for undistracted research and writing.

My colleague Tom Hester and Tony Low of New York University both read an early draft of the manuscript in its entirety, and the book has benefitted immeasurably from their wisdom. Stan Stewart, Joseph Schwarz, Phoebe Spinrad, and Richard Harp have also provided invaluable intellectual and moral support for many years. Series editor John Shawcross and a second anonymous reader saved me from a number of errors and helped me to a better understanding of my own work. Any remaining defects or infelicities are a result of my invincible ignorance, not their counsel.

The editorial staff at Boydell & Brewer has been unfailingly courteous and helpful: I thank especially Vanda Andrews, Pru Harrison, and Caroline Palmer for their patience and professional care. Sue Dykstra-Poel, of the firm's American office, first suggested the series to me: I am grateful for this encouragement and for years of friendship.

Acknowlededgments

The dedication to Louis Martz is a humble attempt to acknowledge an immense intellectual and personal debt.

R.V.Y., 1 October 1999

Part I

THE PRESENCE OF GRACE IN
SEVENTEENTH-CENTURY POETRY

Visible form not only "points" to an invisible, unfathomable mystery; form is the apparition of this mystery, and reveals it while, naturally at the same time, protecting and veiling it. – Hans Urs von Balthasar[1]

T HE persistence of the Christian poetry of the seventeenth century as a focus of controversy is an extraordinary feature of the generally secularized academic culture of the present. The energies both of traditional historical scholars and the proponents of esoteric theories and earnest ideological programs are engaged in determining the nature and significance of this poetry. Such continuing interest is still more extraordinary insofar as it involves a preoccupation with grace – a concept central to the Christian explanation of salvation, but bafflingly elusive both as an ideal and as an experience. An understanding of how the devotional poets of the seventeenth century dealt with the desire for an attainment of grace ought to furnish a unique insight into a culture shaped by a vision of reality very different from our own. That the religion of this culture yet retains the power to fascinate contemporary minds of largely secular outlook may reveal important elements of the relationship between past and present. Struggles of the intellect and spirit are never finally won or lost – at least not in the campaigns of this world – and perhaps in the current controversies of postmodernist theory the true shape of the modern era's formative stages may at last become visible. In her magisterial account of the Thirty Years' War, C. V. Wedgwood remarks that the contestants in that mammoth but futile encounter never had a view of their real enemy: "The fundamental issue was between revealed and rationalized belief, but the sense of danger was not strong enough to bring the Churches together. The lesser issue between Catholic and Protestant obscured the greater, and the Churches had already set the scene for their own destruction."[2] This study proposes, then, an investigation of the doctrinal

---

[1] *The Glory of the Lord: A Theological Aesthetics*, vol. I; *Seeing the Form*, trans. Erasmo Leiva-Merikakis, ed. Joseph Fessio, S.J., and John Riches (San Francisco: Ignatius Press, 1982), p. 151.
[2] *The Thirty Years' War* (1938; rpt. Garden City, NY: Doubleday & Co., 1961), p. 22. For the

1

and devotional foundations of the seventeenth-century religious lyric. What emerges is a view of poetry striving to capture in the spell of verbal form a sense of the mystery that was rapidly being banished from the world.

The flowering of the English devotional lyric, long treated as an Anglican phenomenon with Catholic overtones distinct from Puritanism, is now widely regarded as unambiguously Protestant, with negligible debts to continental Catholicism. Many scholars have claimed a distinctively Protestant poetics to be the source of the English tradition of devotional poetry.[3] Happily conforming clergymen of the Church of England, like George Herbert and Thomas Traherne, and the bitterly anti-Puritan physician, Henry Vaughan, are melded together with such poets as Andrew Marvell, George Wither and the American Puritan minister, Edward Taylor, into a broad Protestant "consensus." Even Donne's Holy Sonnets and Hymns are not infrequently smuggled into the Reformation schema. Once seen as examples of the influence of Ignatian meditation on Anglican poetry, the Holy Sonnets are now more often interpreted as an expression of the final crisis in the poet's conversion from his boyhood Catholic recusancy to a Calvinism consistent with Anglican orthodoxy.

This new school of seventeenth-century scholarship has not gone unchallenged by defenders of the older view;[4] however, the most vociferous

subtle but ineluctable undermining of the Christian world view among early, nominally pious scientists, see Richard S. Westfall, *Science and Religion in Seventeenth-Century England* (1958; rpt. Ann Arbor: University of Michigan Press, 1973).

[3] For the formative books of the "Anglican" perspective, see especially Helen C. White, *The Metaphysical Poets* (1936; rpt. New York: Collier Books, 1962); Helen Gardner, ed., *John Donne: The Divine Poems*, 2nd ed. (Oxford: Clarendon Press, 1978); Louis L. Martz, *The Poetry of Meditation* 2nd ed. (New Haven: Yale University Press, 1962); and Rosemond Tuve, *A Reading of George Herbert* (Chicago: University of Chicago Press, 1952). These books, all *first* published by the early 1950s, were not regarded as especially "Anglican" or "Anglo-Catholic" in orientation until the issue was raised in these terms some two decades later. Among the most important contributions to the emergence of "Protestant poetics" are William Halewood, *The Poetry of Grace: Reformation Themes in English Seventeenth-Century Poetry* (New Haven: Yale University Press, 1970); Barbara Lewalski, *Donne's Anniversaries and the Poetry of Praise* (Princeton: Princeton University Press, 1973); Andrew Weiner, *Sir Philip Sidney and the Poetics of Protestantism* (Minneapolis: University of Minnesota Press, 1978); and the definitive work of the school, Lewalski's *Protestant Poetics and the Seventeenth-Century Religious Lyric* (Princeton: Princeton University Press, 1979). The importance of the trend was recognized by a special session on Protestant poetics at the 1983 MLA convention in New York, and the stream of books and articles continues unabated.

[4] The most important single work in this vein is Anthony Low, *Love's Architecture: Devotional Modes in Seventeenth-Century English Poetry* (New York: New York University Press, 1978). Anthony Raspa, *The Emotive Image: Jesuit Poetics in the English Renaissance* (Fort Worth: Texas Christian University Press, 1983) makes radical claims for Catholic influence. In addition there are recent books on Herbert – who in the 1980s became the focus of the controversy – which explicitly deny his having Puritan or Calvinist leanings: Heather A. R. Asals, *Equivocal Predication: George Herbert's Way to God* (Toronto: University of Toronto Press, 1981); Diana Benet, *The Secretary of Praise: The Poetic Vocation of George Herbert*

alternative to "Protestant poetics" has been the application of a mélange of postmodernist strategies to the devotional poets, who are thus reassessed in the light of contemporary secular preoccupations.[5] The heroic labors of Stanley Fish among seventeenth-century catechisms notwithstanding, the "new readers" are often accused of inadequate attention to history. Of course the issue is often precisely what counts as an historical interpretation of a text: is it an investigation of the author's intentions in the light of conscious literary and religious traditions, or is it a probing of the socio-economic matrix that (supposedly) produced the author? Or, from a deconstructionist perspective, is it possible to distinguish either an author or social institution from the texts for which they are putatively responsible? The parties to the

(Columbia: University of Missouri Press, 1984); Stanley Stewart, *George Herbert*, Twayne's English Authors Series No. 428 (Boston: G. K. Hall, 1986); and Terry G. Sherwood, *Herbert's Prayerful Art* (Toronto: University of Toronto Press, 1989). See Sherwood also for an expressly "Anglican" reading of Donne: *Fulfilling the Circle: A Study of John Donne's Thought* (Toronto: University of Toronto Press, 1984). For an attempt to mediate between the new "Cavaliers" and "Roundheads" from a decidedly "Roundhead" perspective, see Gene Edward Veith, "The Religious Wars in George Herbert Criticism: Reinterpreting Seventeenth-Century Anglicanism," *GHJ* 11, No. 2 (1988) 19–35. Edward W. Tayler, *Donne's Idea of Woman: Structure and Meaning in* The Anniversaries (New York: Columbia University Press, 1991), esp. pp. 12–18, 78–79, replies not only to Lewalski's reading of the *Anniversaries* as an example of Protestant poetics, but also to postmodernist anachronisms in reading pre-Enlightenment poetry.

[5] Notes 3 and 4 are inadequate; this one impossible; still, I shall attempt to sketch the kind of work I have in mind. The seminal work applying the new historicism to Renaissance literature (though it deals with none of the poets in this study) is Stephen Greenblatt, *Renaissance Self-Fashioning: From More to Shakespeare* (Chicago: University of Chicago Press, 1980). Greenblatt's method and outlook, with more emphatic recourse to both Derrida and Foucault, is applied to Donne, Herbert and Marvell (among others) by Jonathan Goldberg, *James I and the Politics of Literature: Jonson, Shakespeare, Donne, and Their Contemporaries* (Baltimore: Johns Hopkins University Press, 1983); and *Voice Terminal Echo: Postmodernism and English Renaissance Texts* (London: Methuen, 1986). There are acrid new historicist overtones in John Carey, *John Donne: Life Mind and Art* (New York: Oxford University Press, 1981); and the new historicism is explicit in Arthur Marotti, *John Donne: Coterie Poet* (Madison: University of Wisconsin Press, 1986). Herbert is again a central figure: Stanley Fish applies his own unique style of postmodernist commentary in "Letting Go: The Dialectic of the Self in Herbert's Poetry," in *Self-Consuming Artifacts: The Experience of Seventeenth-Century Literature* (Berkeley: University of California Press, 1972), pp. 156–223 (this volume contains a less interesting section on Donne, pp. 43–77); and in *The Living Temple: George Herbert and Catechizing* (Berkeley: University of California Press, 1978); and his influence, as well as that of Greenblatt, Foucault and Derrida, is evident in Barbara Leah Harman, *Costly Monuments: Representations of the Self in George Herbert's Poetry* (Cambridge: Harvard University Press, 1982). Michael C. Schoenfeldt, *Prayer and Power: George Herbert and Renaissance Courtship* (Chicago: University of Chicago Press, 1991) is another new-historicist reading; and although Helen Vendler, *The Poetry of George Herbert* (Cambridge: Harvard University Press, 1975) is rather old-fashioned in method, it fits in with this group because of its resolute secularism. Debora K. Shuger, *Habits of Thought in the English Renaissance: Religion, Politics and the Dominant Culture* (Berkeley: University of California Press, 1990) gives a novel twist to the new-historicist project.

controversy seem to compose a lopsided triangle. The argument between "Anglican" and "Puritan" interpretations of the seventeenth-century devotional poetry is an argument over the true meanings of poems; the various postmodernists introduce the question of what constitutes meaning itself, or whether meaning is even possible. The nature of this poetry, intimately personal as well as formally religious, is peculiarly provocative of such controversy because it necessarily poses problems of intention, voice, and personal presence; and the verbal resonance and resilience of the best of it resists its most dogged interpreters.

Despite the broad acceptance it now enjoys, Protestant poetics is in several ways a flawed view of the devotional poets. First, it is based on a simplistic and inaccurate view of the doctrinal issues of the Reformation era. Secondly, it sets out to establish the existence of an exclusively Protestant mode of poetry without determining whether the same features of theme and style might not be available in contemporaneous Catholic poetry. Finally, it often forces the poetry into doctrinal frames that neglect the paradoxical richness and play of wit generated by the tension between the poetic evocation of spiritual experience and a doctrinal or theological proposition. The new-historicist and deconstructionist approaches can be even more reductive: poems and poets alike vanish either into a wasteland of ideological imperatives or an abyss of floating signifiers – or, more commonly, both. The work of the poet is denied the very integrity of argument that the theorist implicitly claims for his own text.

The contribution of the contending parties has, nevertheless, been valuable. If Protestant poetics often tends to be merely doctrinaire in seeking to be doctrinal, it has restored at least some sense of the force with which doctrine was felt and believed in the seventeenth century. To this development in the study of the Christian poetry of the era, the aggressively non-Christian approach of most contemporary theory adds another important perspective. While it is improbable that most critics who labor to prove that Herbert was a Calvinist (or a Laudian) are themselves Calvinists (or Laudians), the critic who deconstructs "Affliction (I)" or who finds in the image of God in Donne's Holy Sonnets a sublimation of royal absolutism is quite likely to prefer his own understanding of reality as a more adequate account than any of the seventeenth-century versions of Christianity. Hence in a surprising way, poets like Donne and Herbert are honored by the very effort to subject their works to the hermeneutic demands of twentieth-century ideologies. What appears to be dismissive skepticism is covert acknowledgment of a text's power to resist appropriation, and it ought to endow with poignant immediacy our deliberations over the relative weight of Protestant and Catholic teachings and practices in the devotional poetry of the past.

The poems of Donne and Herbert, of Crashaw and Vaughan, are something more than so many carcasses spread out on a table for dissection; they are part of the intellectual and spiritual drama of the seventeenth century.

Although these poets may seem to have been losers in their struggle against the secularization of the mind of Western man, the contest is, perhaps, altogether played out. Insofar as the Reformation is a crucial episode in the development of the modern world,[6] Protestant poetics is an attempt to accommodate the devotional poets to the secularism increasingly pervasive during the past four centuries. Because it emphasizes the shattering of the unity of Christendom and of the continuity of Christian culture, Protestant poetics becomes the (possibly inadvertent) ally of postmodernism. What the latter does overtly to poems from the past is done somewhat equivocally by the former, but the ultimate result is the same: texts that sit uneasily with characteristic contemporary attitudes are rewoven to provide a comfortable fit. What is finally at stake in our interpretation of the poetry of our ancestors is, then, the judgment that we pass on ourselves.

The theology of grace provides an effective point of departure, for the very concept of grace is antithetical to what may be taken as the typical modern *Weltanschauung*, with its strains of Marxist materialism, Nietzschean nihilism and Freudian *Schadenfreude*. Underlying the notion of grace is the conviction that behind what is visible, beyond what can be articulated, there is not nothing, but something – the unexpected gift, the unmerited favor.[7]

i

A recurrent preoccupation of Protestant poetics is the Reformation teaching that man's justification begins with *prevenient grace*. William Halewood quotes one of Donne's sermons on this point: "He is as precise as Taylor in his use of the nomenclature of Reformation theology," Halewood writes. "The grace which provokes the faith which leads to justification is *preventing* or *prevenient*: 'no man can prepare that worke, no man can begin it, no man can proceed in it of himselfe. The desire and the actual beginning is from the

---

[6] See Anthony Kemp, *The Estrangement of the Past: A Study of the Origins of Modern Historical Consciousness* (New York/Oxford: Oxford University Press, 1991), esp. pp. 66–104, for the general historical thesis. For the English Reformation specifically as a disruption of traditional medieval culture imposed from above as a radical ideology, see J. J. Scarisbrick, *The Reformation and the English People* (Oxford: Basil Blackwell, 1984); David Cressy, *Bonfires and Bells: National Memory and the Protestant Calendar in Elizabethan and Stuart England* (Berkeley and Los Angeles: University of California Press, 1989); and Eamon Duffy. *The Stripping of the Altars: Traditional Religion in England, 1400–1580* (New Haven and London: Yale University Press, 1992).

[7] Devotional poetry, in its apprehension of grace, constitutes a paradigm of a view of literature opposite to that intimated in a discussion of Rousseau by Paul de Man, "Criticism and Crisis," in *Blindness and Insight*, ed. Wlad Godzich, 2nd ed. (Minneapolis: University of Minnesota Press, 1983), p. 18: "here, the consciousness does not result from the absence of something, but consists of the presence of a nothingness. Poetic language names this void with ever renewed understanding and, like Rousseau's longing, it never tires of naming it again. This persistent naming is what we call literature."

preventing grace of God' (*Sermons*, 2: 305)."[8] Barbara Lewalski is even more emphatic:

> Because man's natural state is so desperate, there can be no question (as in some Roman Catholic formulations) of man's preparing himself through moral virtue for the reception of grace, or of performing works good and meritorious in themselves; everything that he does himself is necessarily evil and corrupt. As the tenth of the Thirty-nine Articles of the established church put it, "The condition of man, after the fall of Adam is such that he cannot turne, and prepare himselfe by his owne naturall strength, and good workes, to faith, and calling upon God, wherefore we have no power to doe good workes pleasant, and acceptable to God, without the grace of God preventing us, that we may have a good will, and working with us when we have that good will."[9]

Now this is all very puzzling. "Prevenient grace" hardly qualifies as a decisive example of "the nomenclature of Reformation theology," since the term figures prominently in the Council of Trent's *Decree on Justification* (1547), a document that states quite explicitly that the work of salvation begins not with man's efforts, but with the unmerited grace of God:

> [The Council] declares further that the beginning of this same justification in adults must be received from the prevenient grace of God through Christ Jesus; that is, from his call, by which they are called for no existing merit of their own, in order that those who have by sins turned away from God, might be disposed through his awakening and help to turn to their own justification, by freely assenting to and cooperating with that grace. Thus as God touches the human heart with the light of the Holy Spirit, the man himself is not wholly inactive, inasmuch as he might cast it aside. Nonetheless, without God's grace he cannot move himself toward justice in God's sight by his own free will. Hence when it is said in Sacred Scripture, "Turn toward me and I shall turn toward you" (Zach. 1.3), we are reminded of our freedom; and when we respond, "Convert us, Lord, to you and we shall be converted" (Lam. 5.21), we confess that we are anticipated by God's grace.[10]

---

[8] *The Poetry of Grace*, pp. 62–63.

[9] *Protestant Poetics*, pp. 15–16.

[10] Henr. Denzinger and Clem. Bannwart, S.J., ed., *Enchiridion Symbolorum, Definitionum et Declarationum de Rebus Fidei et Morum*, 17th ed. (Fribourg: Herder, 1928), No. 797: "Declarat praeterea, ipsius iustificationis exordium in adultis a Dei per Christum Iesum praeveniente gratia sumendum esse, hoc est, ab eius vocatione, qua nullis eorum exsistentibus meritis vocantur, ut qui per peccata a Deo aversi erant, per eius excitantem atque adiuvantem gratiam ad convertendum se ad suam ipsorum iustificationem, eidem gratiae libere assentiendo et cooperando, disponantur, ita ut tangente Deo cor hominis per Spiritus Sancti illuminationem neque homo ipse nihil omnino agat, inspirationem illam recipiens, quippe qui illam et abicere potest, neque tamen sine gratia Dei movere se ad iustitiam coram illo libera sua voluntate possit. Unde in sacris litteris cum dicitur: *Convertimini ad me, et ego convertar ad vos* (Zach. 1.3), libertatis nostrae admonemur; cum respondemus: *Converte nos, Domine, ad te, et convertemur* (Thr. 5.21), Dei nos gratia praeveniri confitemur."

This teaching is not a Tridentine novelty. St. Thomas Aquinas makes it clear that the "preparation for grace" attributed by Lewalski (without citation) to "some Roman Catholic formulations" can only come after and as a result of God's prior gift of grace: "But if we speak of grace as it signifies a help from God moving us to good, no preparation is required on man's part anticipating, as it were, the divine help, but rather, every preparation in man must be by the help of God moving the soul to good."[11] Or as the mystic, San Juan de la Cruz, succinctly puts it, "Without his grace one is unable to merit his grace."[12]

The principal Catholic controversialist of the age, Robert Bellarmine, observes that God's "special help is owed to no cause, but is bestowed out of a certain new and infinite liberality of God, particularly if we speak of the first grace anticipating [*praeveniente*] and rousing man; hence the name of grace is more properly applied to special help than to general, just as the habits of faith, hope, and charity are more properly called gifts of grace than faculties of willing and understanding."[13] Although he insists that grace does not remove free choice, he still maintains that "the Saints after the fall of Adam have grace not only by which they are able to merit well and persevere if they will, but they have grace in a measure much more powerful, by which it is brought about that they can will."[14] Bellarmine is typical of the Catholic Reformation in his concern to find a way of reconciling the dogma of God's gracious predestination of the elect with the dogma of human free choice; that is, he seeks to affirm both the dignity of human reason and the mysterious presence of divine Providence in human life. This commitment is underscored by his efforts to mediate the controversy over divine foreknowledge and human free will that raged around the turn of the seventeenth century between Domingo Bañez and the Dominicans, and Luis de Molina and the

[11] *Summa Theologiae* I–II.112. 2: "Sed si loquamur de gratia secundum quod significat auxilium Dei moventis ad bonum, sic nulla praeparatio requiritur ex parte hominis quasi praeveniens divinum auxilium; sed potius quaecumque praeparatio in homine esse potest, est ex auxilio Dei moventis animam ad bonum." The Latin text of the *Summa* is quoted throughout from the edition Cura Fratrum Ordinis Praedicatorum, 5 vols. (Madrid: Biblioteca de Autores Cristianos, 1955).

[12] *Cántico espiritual* 32.5: "Sin su gracia no se puede merecer su gracia." *Vida y obras completas de San Juan de La Cruz*, ed. Crisógono de Jesús, O.C.D., Matías del Niño Jesús, O.C.D., and Lucinio del SS. Sacramento, O.C.D., 5th ed. (Madrid: Biblioteca de Autores Cristianos, 1964), p. 718.

[13] *De Gratia & libero arbitrio* I. ii, *Opera Roberti Bellarmini Politiani, S.J.*, 7 vols. (Venice, 1721–28), IV. 213: "Speciale autem nulla ratione est debitum, sed ex nova quadam & infinita Dei liberalitate donatur, praesertim si loquamur de prima gratia hominem praeveniente & excitante: quare nomen gratiae magis proprie convenit auxilio speciali, quam generali, sicut etiam magis proprie habitus fidei, spei & charitatis, quam intelligendi, volendique facultates, dona gratiae nominantur."

[14] *De Gratia primi hominis* I. vii. *Opera* IV. 12: "Sancti vero post lapsum Adae, non habent solum gratiam, qua possint bene mereri, & perseverare, si velint, sed habent gratiam quandam potentiorem, qua fit, ut velint."

Jesuits. Critics who accept at face value the Protestant accusation that Catholicism is a religion of works have failed to notice that Molina, the champion of the role of the will in justification, was for the most part on the defensive, and that he was himself deeply concerned about safeguarding doctrinal integrity regarding God's foreknowledge.[15]

There are certainly significant differences between Protestant and Catholic versions of justification; the insistence of the Council of Trent and Catholic theologians on the cooperation of man's free will with God's grace is an example of particular importance. But there is no basis for suggesting that the concept of prevenient grace was a discovery, or even a rediscovery, of the Reformation; and this understanding of grace makes a difference in the interpretation of seventeenth-century devotional poetry. At times it appears that the proponents of Protestant poetics have derived their conception of Catholic doctrine wholly from Reformation polemics: accordingly they read the devotional poems as expositions of an exclusively Protestant, indeed a Calvinist, view of election and grace. Donne's Holy Sonnets, with their anxious attention to the final destiny of the speaker's soul, have provided fertile ground for such expositions. According to one critic, they "yield more fully to an analysis of their biblical motifs, their anguished Pauline speaker, their presentation of states of soul attendant upon the Protestant drama of regeneration, than they do to any other meditative scheme," and the first of these sonnets, "As due by many titles," is thus designated a treatment of "the problem of election."[16]

Here and there in the Holy Sonnets there are explicitly Calvinist terms, as well as passages that suggest a Calvinist theology of grace – the phrase "Impute me righteous" in Sonnet 3 ("This is my playes last scene"), for instance, or the famous paradox that closes "Batter my heart," the tenth sonnet. But neither the first sonnet, "As due by many titles," nor the Holy Sonnets as a group should be read as a specifically Calvinist, or even Protestant, exposition of election and grace. In fact, the persona of the Holy Sonnets seems to be trying out different versions of grace in order to arrive at a theologically moderate position. We know from his letters that Donne inclined this way. Writing to Henry Goodyer within a year of the date he is believed to have composed the Holy Sonnets, he praises his own verse litany, "That neither the Roman Church need call it defective, because it abhors not the particular mention of the blessed Triumphers in heaven; nor

---

[15] See Alfred J. Freddoso, "Preface" and "Introduction" to Luis de Molina, *On Divine Foreknowledge: Part IV of the Concordia*, trans. Freddoso (Ithaca, New York: Cornell University Press, 1988), esp. pp. vii–viii, 2–8; and James Broderick, S.J., *Robert Bellarmine: Saint and Scholar* (Westminster, Maryland: Newman Press, 1961), pp. 189–216.

[16] Lewalski, *Protestant Poetics*, pp. 265–66. Unlike Lewalski, I follow the 1633 order of the first twelve sonnets as given by the Gardner edition of the *Divine Poems*, which seems to have been vindicated by Patrick F. O'Connell, "The Successive Arrangements of Donne's 'Holy Sonnets'," *PQ* 60 (1981) 323–42, esp. 334.

the Reformed can discreetly accuse it, of attributing more than a rectified devotion ought to doe"; and in another letter to Goodyer, written about the same time, he says of Catholic and Protestant churches, "The channels of Gods mercies run through both fields; and they are sister teats of his graces, yet both diseased and infected, but not both alike."[17] This is hardly the tone of militant Calvinism.

Donne's "ecumenical" predisposition is further developed in his *Essays in Divinity*, probably composed during the three or four years before his ordination in 1614/15. As Evelyn Simpson observes, this work would scarcely have commended Donne to Anglican orthodoxy, as represented by the Calvinist Archbishop of Canterbury, George Abbot, "a narrow-minded man, bitterly hostile to the Church of Rome."[18] In the *Essays* Donne maintains, to the contrary, that despite sharp differences between the Anglican and Roman communions, they share the same foundation: "Yet though we branch out *East* and *West*, that Church concurs with us in the root, and sucks her vegetation from one and the same ground, *Christ Jesus*." Donne continues, "So Synagogue and Church is the same thing, and of the Church, *Roman* and *Reformed*, and all other distinctions of place, Discipline, or Person, but one Church, journying to one *Hierusalem*, and directed by one guide, Christ Jesus." Most remarkable, Donne even goes so far as to prefer a unity based on the form of *any* of the principal churches – Roman, Genevan, or Anglican – to the disunity prevailing in his day:

> And though to all my thanksgivings to God, I ever humbly acknowledg, as one of his greatest Mercies to me, that he gave me my Pasture in this Park, and my milk from the brests of this Church, yet out of a fervent, and (I hope) not inordinate affection, even to such an Unity, I do zealously wish, that the whole catholick Church, were reduced to such Unity and agreement, in the form and profession Established, in any one of these Churches (though ours were principally to be wished) which have not by any additions destroyed the foundation and possibility of salvation in Christ Jesus; That then the Church,

---

[17] *Letters to Several Persons of Honour* (1651), intro. M. Thomas Hester (fac. rpt.; New York: Delmar, 1977), pp. 34, 102. Hester gives as the dates of these letters 1608 and 1609 respectively, in the schedule, pp. xviii–xxii.

[18] "Introduction," to John Donne, *Essays in Divinity*, ed. Evelyn M. Simpson (Oxford: Clarendon Press, 1952), p. xi. Recent scholarship has noted that Donne was friendly with Abbot in the 1620s and shared some of the Bishop's negative views regarding the Arminianism emerging in the Church of England under the influence of Laud. To be friendly with a Calvinist, however, does not make one a Calvinist, and to oppose ecclesiastical ambitions of an imprudent man like Laud does not mean one accepts all the doctrinal positions of his opponents. For examples of this line of argument see Joshua Scodel, "John Donne and the Religious Politics of the Mean," in *John Donne's Religious Imagination: Essays in Honor of John T. Shawcross*, ed. Raymond-Jean Frontain and Frances M. Malpezi (UCA Press: Conway, AR, 1995), esp. pp. 63–70; and Jeanne Shami, "'The Stars in their Order Fought Against Sisera': John Donne and the Pulpit Crisis of 1622," *John Donne Journal* 14 (1995) 1–58.

discharged of disputations, and misapprehensions, and this defensive warr, might contemplate Christ clearly and uniformely.[19]

Again, this is not the tone of Calvinist rigor, and the emphasis on the corporate unity of the Church seems incompatible with the stress on individual election urged by Calvin and his more implacable English followers. Hence when Donne plainly repudiates Calvin on the specific matter of grace in a subsequent passage of the *Essays in Divinity*, his theology is perfectly consistent.

Calvin, in his reply to Cardinal Sadoleto, names "justification by faith, the first and keenest subject of controversy between us,"[20] but his own *Antidote to the Council of Trent* clearly establishes that the central theological issue of the Protestant Reformation was freedom of the will. Calvin says "amen" to the Council's first three canons on justification, which stipulate respectively that man cannot be justified by his own human works or the law without the grace of Christ; that this grace does not merely make salvation easier, but is absolutely necessary; and that prevenient grace is requisite even to dispose man to desire salvation. Calvin only begins to take exception with the fourth canon, which says, "If anyone say that the free will of man, moved and excited by God, in no way cooperates by assenting to God's stimulus and call, by which it disposes and prepares itself for receiving the grace of justification, and that it is unable to resist, if it would, but that as a thing inanimate it is able to do nothing and is held merely passive, let him be anathema."[21] Calvin's rejoinder is, "that the efficacy of divine grace is such, that all opposition is beaten down, and we who were unwilling are made obedient, it is not we who assent, but the Lord by the Prophet, when he promises that he will make us to walk in his precepts."[22] Calvin raises similar objections to canons V through VII, which assert that Adam's sin did not obliterate free will; that man does evil only on his own with God's permissive will and not His own proper consenting; and that man is not utterly incapable of doing good before justification.

When Donne meditates on God's mercy in the *Essays in Divinity*, his discussion of grace and nature is Thomistic, his view of the human will far more Tridentine than Calvinist: "In our repentances and reconciliations, though the first grace proceed only from God, yet we concurr so, as there is an union of two Hypostases, *Grace* and *Nature*. Which, (as the incarnation of

---

[19] *Essays in Divinity*, pp. 50, 51, 51–52.

[20] *John Calvin: Selections from His Writings*, ed. John Dillenberger (Garden City, New York: Doubleday, 1971), p. 95.

[21] Denzinger, no. 814: "Si quis dixerit, liberum hominis arbitrium a Deo motum et exercitatum nihil cooperari assentiendo Deo excitanti atque vocanti, quo ad obtinendam iustificationis gratiam se disponat ac praeparet, neque posse dissentire, si velit, sed velut inanime quoddam nihil omnino agere mereque passive se habere: anathema sit."

[22] Dillenberger, p. 194.

our Blessed Saviour himself was) is conceived in us of the Holy Ghost, without father; but fed and produced by us; that is, by our will first enabled and illumined. For neither God nor man determines mans will; (for that must imply either a necessiting therof from God, or else *Pelagianisme*) but they condetermine it." Above all, Donne denies Calvin's notion of irresistible grace by which "all opposition is beaten down": "And yet we may not say, but that God begins many things which we frustrate; and calls when we come not."[23] The issue would not go away for Donne, even after his ordination. To be sure, he had to be far more cautious in his very public sermons than in his letters or *Essays*, which were not published during his lifetime, and it is to be expected, therefore, that Donne would always speak respectfully of Calvin, whose role in the international Reformation was not unlike that of Lenin in international Marxism, both as theorist and successful practical tactician. It is, likewise, to be expected, as Paul Sellin urges, that Donne, as an official representative of James I on the continent in 1619–20, would not preach in such a way as to offend the Calvinist convictions of England's Dutch and German allies or directly contradict any of the articles of the recently concluded and severely Calvinist Synod of Dort (1618–19).[24] But in fact the passage quoted above from *Essays in Divinity* plainly contradicts Calvin and his followers at the Synod, who condemn those "that teach, that *God, in regenerating a man, doth not employ that omnipotent strength, whereby he may powerfully & infallibly bow and bend his will unto faith, and conversion: but that all the gracious operations (which God useth for our conversion) beeing accomplished, nevertheless man can withstand God, and his holy Spirit, intending that mans conversion, yea and oftentimes doth make actuall resistance, to the utter defeating of his owne regeneration: so that it lieth in mans power to bee, or not to be, regenerate.*"[25] Donne clung to the contrary belief in freedom of the will. In a sermon of 1626, for example, he affirms what seems to be a version of predestination consistent with Calvin: "Christ doth not now begin to make that man his, but now declares to us, that he hath been his from all eternity." But a few pages further, immediately after referring to "the Eternal Decree of my Election," he attacks what – for Calvin and the Synod of Dort – seems the necessary corollary, the doctrine of irresistible

---

[23] *Essays in Divinity*, pp. 80, 81.

[24] See the monograph by Paul R. Sellin, *John Donne and "Calvinist" Views of Grace* (Amsterdam: VU Boekhandel/Uitgerij, 1983); and *So Doth, So Is Religion: John Donne and Diplomatic Contexts in the Reformed Netherlands, 1619–1620* (Columbia: University of Missouri Press, 1988). Obviously, sermons delivered abroad to zealously Calvinist audiences by a man on a diplomatic mission will furnish little insight into Donne's personal view of Calvin's theology. On the elusiveness of such texts, see Annabel Patterson, *Censorship and Interpretation: The Conditions of Writing in Early Modern England* (Madison: University of Wisconsin Press, 1984).

[25] *The Judgement of the Synode Holden at Dort* (London, 1619; fac. rpt. Amsterdam, 1974), p. 39. I have expanded contractions, used modern "s," and modernized u/v usage.

grace (which Donne prudently attributes to "the later School"): "He came not to force and compel them, who would not be brought into the way: Christ saves no man against his will."[26] Like the fathers of the Council of Trent, Donne seeks to formulate the delicate balance between grace and nature, between predestination and free will. If his conclusions differ somewhat from theirs, he is further still from Calvin and the Synod of Dort.

Donne's concern to reconcile human free will with divine foreknowledge and predestination suggests a scholastic mentality at odds with the spirit of the doctrinal and ecclesiastical revolution begun by Luther and fostered by Calvin. Throughout the Middle Ages scholastic theologians struggled with the dilemma of free will and predestination, and by the end of the period the intellectual tension had become acute. A mental weariness and impatience with the effort of balancing the dual burden is manifest early in the fourteenth century in the way that William of Ockham frames the question:

> For I ask whether or not the determination of a created will necessarily follows the determination of the divine will. If it does, then the will necessarily acts [as it does], just as fire does, and so merit and demerit are done away with. If it does not, then the determination of a created will is required for knowing determinately one or the other part of a contradiction regarding those [future things that depend absolutely on a created will]. For the determination of the uncreated will does not suffice, because a created will can oppose the determination [of the uncreated will]. Therefore, since the determination of the [created] will was not from eternity, God did not have certain cognition of the things that remained [for a created will to determine].[27]

The crucial doctrinal innovation of the Protestant Reformation amounts to seizing one horn of the dilemma and ignoring the other. Thus Calvin writes, "God being pleased in this matter to act as a free dispenser and disposer, distinctly declares, that the only ground on which he will show mercy to one rather than to another is his sovereign pleasure; for when mercy is bestowed on him who asks it, though he indeed does not suffer a refusal, he however either anticipates or partly acquires a favour, the whole merit of which God claims for himself."[28] The created will here becomes negligible, and "so merit and demerit are done away with." In Calvin's version of predestination, the sole and absolute determinant of the fate of every individual of the human

---

[26] "A Sermon Preached to the Household at White-hall, April 30, 1626," in *The Sermons of John Donne*, ed. George R. Potter and E. M. Simpson, 10 vols. (Berkeley: University of California Press, 1953–62), VII.153, 156. Donne's sermons are quoted throughout from this edition, with references parenthetically cited in the text.

[27] *Predestination, God's Foreknowledge, and Future Contingents*, trans. Marilyn McCord Adams and Norman Kretzman, 2nd ed. (Indianapolis: Hackett, 1983), p. 49. The bracketed passages are interpolations by the translators in the interest of clarity.

[28] *Institutes of the Christian Religion*, III. xxii. 6, trans. Henry Beveridge (1845; rpt. Grand Rapids, Michigan: W. B. Eerdmans, 1957), II. 218.

race lies in the decree of God's will: "The decree, I admit, is dreadful," Calvin says, "and yet it is impossible to deny that God foreknew what the end of man was to be before he made him, and foreknew, because he had so ordained by his decree." A few lines further on he adds that it should not seem "absurd when I say that God not only foresaw the fall of the first man, and in him the ruin of his posterity; but also at his own pleasure arranged it."[29] Bellarmine cites this passage as evidence that Calvin makes God the author of sin: "Whereas Calvin teaches that God out of his own will alone, before he foresaw the decision of the free choice of the first man, decreed the fall of man, and since no one can resist the will of God, it follows that the first man was unable to escape that fall."[30] Bellarmine regards this implication of the denial of free will as blasphemy, but not the notions of predestination and election, which he defends and expounds. Counter-Reformation divines as a group return with renewed vigor to the resolution of the paradoxical dichotomy of free will and predestination, insisting always that our freedom is real and crucial, but not the cause of predestination.[31] The experience of this paradox is one of the principal themes not only of Donne's religious prose, but also of his devotional poems.

It is not surprising, therefore, to find many parallels to theological features in the Holy Sonnets in the devotional poems of Donne's Catholic contemporaries, who exhibit an equal concern with the problem of election and grace. A richer sense of what is at stake in the Holy Sonnets and in the entire spectrum of English devotional poems is made possible by a reading that takes into account comparable poets from the continent. A good example is furnished by Francisco de Quevedo (1580–1645) in his *Christian Heraclitus* (*Heráclito cristiano*, 1613). Like Donne's Holy Sonnets, this work is a collection of penitential lyrics that focus on the spiritual condition of the poetic persona. The parallels begin to emerge with the first poem of each set. The octave of Donne's "As due by many titles" establishes the misery of man's natural condition by seeing his situation as that of a debtor who tries to cancel his debts by inviting God to foreclose on his already hopelessly over-mortgaged self:

---

[29] *Institutes* III. xxiii. 7; II. 232.

[30] *De Amissione Gratiae et Statu Peccati* II. vi; *Opera* IV. 60: "Ubi docet Calvinus Deum ex sua sola voluntate, antequam determinationem liberi arbitrii primi hominis praevideret, decrevisse hominis lapsum, & quia Dei voluntati nemo resistere potest, sequitur, non potuisse primum hominem effugere lapsum illum."

[31] See, for example, Bellarmine, *De Gratia et Libero Arbitrio* II. x–xii; *Opera* IV. 246ff, which shows from divine letters, the tradition of the Church, reason, and Scripture that "Not any cause of Predestination is in us" ("Praedestinationis nullam esse causam in nobis"). See also one of Donne's favorite sources, St. Bernard of Clairvaux, *De gratia et libero arbitrio* 1.2, *PL* 182. 603: "Tolle liberum arbitrium, et non erit quod salvetur: tolle gratiam, non erit unde salvetur"[Take away free will, and there will not be anything to be saved: take away grace, and there will be no means of salvation]. This paradox is of course at the heart of Augustine's lifelong work.

As due by many titles I resigne
My selfe to thee, O God, first I was made
By thee, and for thee, and when I was decay'd
Thy blood bought that, the which before was thine,
I am thy sonne, made with the selfe to shine,
Thy servant, whose paines thou hast still repaid,
Thy sheepe, thine Image, and till I betray'd
My selfe, a temple of thy Spirit divine.[32]

The proliferation of metaphors, suggesting various relationships with God, is an indication of the speaker's uncertainty and the feebleness of his position. Hence the sestet dwells queasily on the prospect that the proffered self may not be worth the cost of refurbishing, that only the devil is still interested in asserting his claim to this property:

Why doth the devill then usurpe in mee?
Why doth he steale, nay ravish that's thy right?
Except thou rise and for thine owne worke fight,
Oh I shall soone despaire, when I doe see
That thou lov'st mankind well, yet wilt not chuse me.
And Satan hates mee, yet is loth to lose mee.

Like this first of the Holy Sonnets, the first poem of Quevedo's *Heráclito* is an intense reflection of the poet's fearful sense of his utter dependence on divine grace:

Un nuevo corazón, un hombre nuevo
ha menester, Señor, la ánima mía;
desnúdame de mí, que ser podría
que a tu piedad pagase lo que debo.
    Dudosos pies por ciega noche llevo,
que ya he llegado a aborrecer el día,
y temo que hallaré la muerte fría
envuelta en (bien que dulce) mortal cebo.
    Tu hacienda soy; tu imagen, Padre, he sido,
y, si no es tu interés en mí, no creo
que otra cosa defiende mi partido.[33]

[A new heart, a new man, Lord, are what my soul has need of; strip me of myself, for it could be that in your pity you might pay what I owe.

I take doubtful steps in the blind night, for already I have come to hate the day, and I fear that I shall find cold death wrapped in a deadly bait (although sweet).

---

[32] Donne's poetry is quoted throughout from John T. Shawcross, ed., *The Complete Poetry of John Donne* (Garden City, New York: Doubleday, 1967).

[33] Quevedo's poetry is quoted from Francisco de Quevedo, *Obras completas*, ed. José Manuel Blecua (Barcelona: Editorial Planeta, 1963), I. 20.

I am of your making; your image, Father, I have been, and, if you have no concern for me, I believe that nothing else will take my part.]

Donne describes himself as "due by many titles" to God; Quevedo mentions the debt that he "owes" God, and describes himself as of God's "making" and formerly His "image" until corrupted by sin. Donne says that he is God's "owne worke" and His "Image." Both emphasize that God must take their part and "fight for" or "defend" the sinner, who is helpless without such assistance. Indeed, the fundamental theme of both poems is the total hopelessness of the sinner's situation without divine intervention. Donne closes on the brink of despair, awaiting some sign that God will "chuse" him; Quevedo, fearfully identifying himself with those who hate the light or day (John 3:20), calls upon God to take decisive action on behalf of a sinner who turns away from from spiritual health:

> Haz lo que pide verme cual me veo,
> no lo que pido yo: pues, de perdido,
> recato mi salud de mi desco.

[Do what is demanded by the way I seem, not what I demand: for, like a profligate, I hide my salvation from my desire.]

There are Catholic poets of grace besides Quevedo, and not all are confined to Spain. For example, the Frenchman Jean de la Ceppède (1550–1622) closes one of his *Théorèmes Spirituels* with the plea of a hapless sinner for divine help: "Mais c'est a vous, Seigneur, de me rendre capable / D'avoir part en vos biens: car mon âme coupable / Ne sçauroit sans vostre aide, à vous reuoler."[34] [But it is for you, Lord, to make me capable of sharing in your riches: for my guilty soul does not know how, without your aid, to return to you.] The close of another of La Ceppède's sonnets recalls a figure frequently associated with Luther's view of justification: "O Christ, ô sainct Agneau, daigne toy de cacher / Tous mes rouges pechez (brindelles des abysmes) / Dans les sanglans replis du manteau de ta chair."[35] [Oh Christ, oh holy Lamb, deign to hide / All my scarlet sins (the kindling twigs of the abyss) / Within the bloody folds of the cloak of your flesh.] Hence there is little reason to find anything peculiarly Protestant toward the close of Donne's "Hymne to God my God, in my sicknesse":[36]

---

[34] *Les Théorèmes sur le Sacré Mystère de Notre Rédemption* I. 3. 56. Reproduction de l'édition de Toulouse de 1613–1622, Préface de Jean Rousset (Genève: Librairie Droz, 1966), p. 444.

[35] *Théorèmes* I. 2. 63, p. 297. See Luther's *Commentary on Galatians* in *Martin Luther: Selections from His Writings*, ed. John Dillenberger (Garden City, New York: Doubleday & Co., 1961), p. 129: "So we shroud ourselves under the covering of Christ's flesh . . . lest God should see our sin."

[36] Cf. Lewalski, *Protestant Poetics*, pp. 16–17; and Richard Strier, *Love Known: Theology and Experience in George Herbert's Poetry* (Chicago: University of Chicago Press, 1983), p. 130, 130n. On La Ceppède's deep commitment to the Counter-Reformation, see P. A. Chilton,

> Looke Lord, and finde both *Adams* met in me;
> As the first *Adams* sweat surrounds my face,
> May the last *Adams* blood my soule embrace.   (ll. 23–25)

Obviously here, as in the Holy Sonnets, Donne is concerned with the problem of grace, conceived in terms of Pauline typology; however, this is hardly a theme unique to the Protestant Reformation. As the examples of Quevedo and La Ceppède indicate, continental Catholic poets were equally sensitive to man's hopeless sinfulness before God and radical dependence on His grace. In all of these poems the expression of a spiritual experience that escapes theological formulation seems more important than scoring polemical points. This is not to say that doctrine was unimportant to any of these poets, only that doctrine in poetry is ancillary to the articulation of the soul's experience of God.

Even in those Holy Sonnets that seem to display most explicitly the peculiar severities of Calvinism, it is difficult to find in Donne an uncritical propounder of Reformation theology. At first glance the famous conclusion to Sonnet 10, "Batter my heart," suggests nothing so much as the effect of Calvinist irresistible grace:

> Take mee to you, imprison mee, for I
> Except you'enthrall mee, never shall be free,
> Nor ever chast, except you ravish mee.

But even the critic who has been most resolute in turning up Calvinism in the Holy Sonnets finds it hedged by important reservations. John Stachniewski writes that "the essential subject matter" of Sonnet 10 is "the conflict between [Donne's] personal integrity and the demands of a theology which brutalized self-esteem." Stachniewski concludes that Donne's Calvinism in the Holy Sonnets is a temporary phase in his transition from Catholic to high Anglican, arising from his sense of worldly disappointment at the time of the poems' composition: "Donne felt his dependence on God to resemble his dependence on secular patronage with its attendant frustration, humiliation, and despair."[37]

The Poetry of Jean de la Ceppède: A Study in Text and Context (Oxford: Oxford University Press, 1977), pp. 24, 50–52. Terence Cave, *Devotional Poetry in France, c. 1570–1613* (Cambridge: Cambridge University Press, 1969), pp. 22–23, observes that the differences between Catholic and Protestant poetry in France are largely negative; i.e., some subjects available to Catholics are not available to Protestants.

[37] "John Donne: The Despair of the 'Holy Sonnets'," *ELH* 48 (1981) 690, 702–03. Stachniewski is joined by a throng of critics who find increasingly distasteful sociopolitical overtones. See Wilbur Sanders, *John Donne's Poetry* (Cambridge: Cambridge University Press, 1971), pp. 120–31; David Aers and Gunther Kress, "Vexatious Contraries: A Reading of Donne's Poetry," in Aers, Bob Hodge and Kress, *Literature, Language and Society in England, 1580–1680* (Totowa, New Jersey: Barnes & Noble, 1981), pp. 65–74; Carey, *John Donne*, pp. 51–59; and Marotti, *John Donne*, pp. 253–61.

This voguish effort to turn the Holy Sonnets into a sublimated manifesta-tion of the poet's socio-economic frustration highlights the complexity arising from scattered suggestions of Calvinism. Rather than subjecting the mystery of grace to ideological demystification, however, it is more fruitful to allow the nuances of Donne's *text* to emerge from its *con*text of literary and religious convention. "Batter my heart" is precisely a prayer for grace that, if the irresistibility of grace be true, is essentially pointless. However inap-propriate or indecorous the sexually charged, quasi-mystical conceit at the poem's close may seem,[38] Hugh Richmond has pointed to a striking parallel in a sonnet by the French Catholic poet Pierre de Ronsard (1524–1585).[39] In any case, the opening of "Batter my heart" qualifies any interpretation of the startling conclusion. Donne's speaker pleads that God stop tinkering with him ("for, you / As yet but knocke, breathe, shine, and seeke to mend") and instead reforge him altogether: "That I may rise, and stand, o'erthrow mee,' and bend / Your force, to breake, blowe, burn and make me new"(1–4).[40] Some of this language is reminiscent of the passage quoted above from the articles of the Synod of Dort, which describes God's "*omnipotent strength, where by he may infallibly bow, and bend his* [man's] *will unto faith*"; but just as plausibly the demand to be remade can be taken as a plea for infused sanctifying grace (*gratia gratum faciens*) which, as Barbara Lewalski observes, is contrary to conventional Reformation teaching: "The Reformers were adamant in their insistence that this justification is only imputed to the sinner, not infused into him as the Roman Catholics held, so as actually to restore God's image in him; however, the imputed righteousness is really his because he is joined to Christ as body to head."[41] Donne's sonnet resists clear doctrinal resolution just because it is an expression of religious uncertainty on the part of a speaker who is groping for some sense of balance between divine power and his own will and identity.

A too precise theological categorizing of the Holy Sonnets and socio-political reductivism are equally likely to flatten out the wit and daring characteristic of Donne's poetry and to neglect the genuine relationship of these poems to the social realities of Donne's time – a relationship far more subtle than the current loosely Marxist strain of the new historicism allows.

---

[38] It is not as indecorous as Marotti, p. 259, supposes, finding in it a "homosexual fantasy," and thus neglecting the Christian tradition that the human soul, whether of a man or a woman, is feminine in relation to Christ as Bridegroom. See the subtle treatment of Donne's difficulties with the feminine rôle in Anthony Low, *The Reinvention of Love: Poetry, Politics and Culture from Sidney to Milton* (Cambridge: Cambridge University Press, 1993), pp. 65–86.

[39] See Gardner, *Divine Poems*, pp. 152–53.

[40] That God is imagined as a tinker in this opening lines was first suggested by J. C. Levenson, "Donne's *Holy Sonnets*, XIV," *Explicator* (March 1953), Item 31. For an excerpt from this item and a selection from the ensuing controversy, see A. L. Clements, ed., *John Donne's Poetry: Authoritative Texts and Criticism*, 2nd ed. (New York: W. W. Norton & Co., 1992), pp. 325–49.

[41] *Protestant Poetics*, p. 17.

The equivocal implications of the third of these sonnets, "This is my playes last scene," with its explicit references to imputed righteousness, furnishes a good example. The octave presents a traditional meditative theme, the deathbed:

> This is my playes last scene, here heavens appoint
> My pilgrimages last mile; and my race
> Idly, yet quickly runne, hath this last pace,
> My spans last inch, my minutes latest point,
> And gluttonous death, will instantly unjoynt
> My body,'and soule, and I shall sleepe a space,
> But my'ever-waking part shall see that face,
> Whose feare already shakes my every joynt.

Clearly this poem is based on the standard Ignatian meditative topos of the Four Last Things.[42] Even as the octave evokes death and judgment, so the sestet adds heaven and hell:

> Then, as my soule, to'heaven her first seate, takes flight,
> And earth-borne body, in the earth shall dwell,
> So, fall my sinnes, that all may have their right,
> To where they'are bred, and would presse me, to hell.
> Impute me righteous, thus purg'd of evill,
> For thus I leave the world, the flesh, and devill.

The closing couplet could be seen as turning the Ignatian meditation into something emphatically Calvinist. Yet this almost magical invocation of the Calvinist dogma has troubled more than one critic. Wilbur Sanders calls these lines "blatant theological sophistry," and adds that "the spiritual malady so obviously won't give way to the patent medicine applied to it, that it almost seems to be a part of the poetic strategy to make us aware of this fact." Similarly, Arthur Marotti is scandalized by "something intractably boastful and self-advertising about" this and the other Holy Sonnets, and about the way "Donne pridefully *over*dramatizes the self. As Barbara Lewalski and others have noticed, Donne legitimately employed the Protestant devotional technique of 'application to the self' in both his poems and sermons, but this

---

[42] *Spiritual Exercises* (*Ejercicios espirituales*), 1st week, 5th exercise, in *Obras completas de San Ignacio de Loyola*, ed. Ignacio Iparraguirre, S.J. (Madrid: Biblioteca de Autores Cristianos, 1963), pp. 214–16. Lewalski, *Protestant Poetics*, p. 268, argues that the use of the pilgrimage and race tropes in the opening lines of this sonnet make it Protestant in mood. But the notion of life as a pilgrimage is too familiar an idea in the Middle Ages to require illustration. In the Renaissance, St. Thomas More combines the theme of life as a pilgrimage with the contemplation of death in a Latin epigram, *Vita Ipsa cursus ad mortem est*, in Fred Nichols, ed., *An Anthology of Neo-Latin Poetry* (New Haven: Yale University Press, 1979), p. 462. See also M. Thomas Hester, "The *troubled wit* of John Donne's 'blacke Soule'," *Cithara* 31 (1991) 16–17, for the medieval sources of the pilgrimage motif in that poem.

Fig. 1. Diego Velàzquez (1599–1600), *Christ on the Cross* (reproduced by permission of the Prado, Madrid).

does not explain the impression of boastfulness some sonnets create."[43] However, there is no cause for Sanders to assume that the "blatant theological sophistry" is merely "almost" a part of the poet's strategy, and none for Marotti to accept uncritically the claim that Donne is manipulating, crudely and smugly, a supposedly Protestant "technique" of "application to the self." Even if one looks askance upon Donne's religious and political choices, given what is known of his intelligence and perspicacity, it is more likely that he is playing with theological concepts in a witty, dramatic fashion than that he is writing bad verse theology.

With this reflection in mind, it is instructive to consider two other references to "imputation" in the Donne canon. The first appears in Satyre III:

> . . . and shall thy fathers spirit
> Meete blinde philosophers in heaven, whose merit
> Of strict life may be'imputed faith, and heare
> Thee, whom hee taught so easie wayes and neare
> To follow, damn'd?   (11–15)

In raising the theme of the virtuous heathen – a lively topic in the Middle Ages and among Renaissance humanists – Donne simply stands Calvinism on its head: instead of Christ's righteousness imputed to a man on the basis of his faith, Donne speculates that faith might be imputed to virtuous pagans on the basis of their righteousness. This passage comes in a poem that questions equally a thoughtless adherence to Catholicism, Calvinism, Anglicanism or Separatism, as well as sheer indifference, on behalf of the sincere individual believer, who is exhorted to "doubt wisely"(77) in making his choice. Thus a severe Calvinist version of grace is subverted by a witty turn growing out of a moderate Erasmian attitude amidst the horrors of sixteenth-century religious strife.[44]

The Reformation concept of imputed righteousness is subjected to an especially extravagant outburst of Donne's wit in the Elegy, "Come, Madam, come" – the notorious "Going to Bed" – in which the poetic persona is occupied with getting his mistress undressed as quickly as possible:

> Like pictures or like books gay coverings made
> For lay-men, are all women thus array'd.
> Themselves are mystick books, which only wee
> (Whom their imputed grace will dignifie)
> Must see reveal'd.   (39–43)

[43] Sanders, *John Donne's Poetry*, p. 128; Marotti, *John Donne*, p. 256.

[44] Donne may have absorbed a pre-Tridentine Erasmian Catholicity from his eccentric Jesuit uncle, Jasper Heywood. See Dennis Flynn, "The '*Annales* School' and the Catholicism of Donne's Family," *JDJ* 2 (1983), No. 2, 1–9. See also Maureen Sabine, *Feminine Engendered Faith: The Poetry of John Donne and Richard Crashaw* (London: Macmillan, 1992), p. 48, for further speculation about Heywood's influence on Donne.

Fig. 2. Velàquez, *Christ after the Flagellation contemplated by the Christian Soul* (reproduced by permission of the National Gallery, London).

Like his principal classical model, Ovid, Donne uses the erotic elegy as a vehicle for ridiculing the most revered ideals and institutions of respectable society. Amatory tropes become quick thrusts in a perilous anti-establishment poetic game. Here, beneath a surface of outrageous wit and blasphemous sensuality, Donne indulges in a momentary gesture of theological satire. In a context of "imputed grace" and the removal of clothing, it is difficult not to recall how Luther explains God's imputation of righteousness to the sinner, in his *Commentary on Galatians*, by comparing it to *covering* sin by grace and thus *not seeing* the sinner's "nakedness."[45] For Donne's speaker the woman's "imputed grace" permits him to *uncover* (or *discover*) and *see*. The implication of the conceit emerges when it is reversed: the justification of the elect, an utterly inscrutable act of arbitrary divine power, according to the formulations of Luther and Calvin alike, makes God's work of election as frivolous and fickle as a loose woman's choice of the lovers admitted to her bed. Hence this risqué poem by a young law student and flamboyant dandy is also a sly send-up of the dominant theology of the Reformation. If Donne was a product, even a victim, of his social circumstances, he was an equally shrewd critic of his society and its conventional beliefs.

The Satyres and the Elegies, if the usual datings are reliable, were written more than ten years before the Holy Sonnets: when the latter were composed, Donne had already undertaken the labor of an Anglican polemicist, and the idea of entering orders in the Church of England had at least been broached to him. But the Holy Sonnets, like almost all of Donne's poetry, are private exercises, circulated for the most part among his friends. There are undeniable marks of the poet's Catholic upbringing in their themes and structures,[46] and the specifically Calvinist elements are handled tentatively, even with an air of provisionality. Sonnet 3, "This is my playes last scene," with its reference to imputed righteousness, a doctrine ridiculed by Donne in other poems, seems to ask, "Does this work? Will my sins simply drop away into hell as I am 'purg'd of evill' by imputation?" A negative answer is implied in the nine remaining sonnets of the set, which keep seeking different approaches to the problem of justification and grace.

This does not mean that the doctrines of the Reformation, especially Calvin's views of justification, had no bearing on the Holy Sonnets; but rather that the impact of Calvinism was oblique rather than direct. In fact there is often a Calvinist subtext, like a magnetic field, exerting a subtle but continuous force over the most unlikely of the Holy Sonnets. The ninth

[45] Dillenberger, *Luther: A Selection*, p. 129. See above n. 34.
[46] For a careful assessment of this continuing influence, see Dennis Flynn, "Donne's Catholicism," *Recusant History* 13 (1975–76) 1–17, 178–95. This material has been assimilated into Dennis Flynn, *John Donne and the Ancient Catholic Nobility* (Bloomington and Indianapolis: Indiana University Press, 1995). See also M. Thomas Hester, *Kinde Pitty and Brave Scorn: John Donne's Satyres* (Durham, North Carolina: Duke University Press, 1982), esp. pp. 73–97; and Sabine, *Feminine Engendered Faith*, pp. 5, 28–29, 106, passim.

Fig. 3. Velázquez, *Venus and Cupid* (*The Rokeby Venus*) (reproduced by permission of the National Gallery, London).

sonnet, for instance, "What if this present were the worlds last night?" discloses under scrutiny the spiritual strains generated by the terrifying yet fascinating concept of irresistible grace.

The octave of the poem is an extravagant sacred parody of a Petrarchan love sonnet, written in continental style. Donne's anguished meditator, recalling the counsel of Astrophil's muse, attempts to convince himself that he need only "looke in [his] heart and write."[47] What he sees there is a graphic image of the Crucifixion, suggesting a Spanish baroque painting:

> What if this present were the worlds last night?
> Marke in my heart, O Soule, where thou dost dwell,
> The picture of Christ crucified, and tell
> Whether that countenance can thee affright,
> Teares in his eyes quench the amasing light,
> Blood fills his frownes, which from his pierc'd head fell,
> And can that tongue adjudge thee unto hell,
> Which pray'd forgivenesse for his foes fierce spight?

Even as Astrophil assures "sleepe" that no better image of Stella is available than what is in his mind (*Astrophil and Stella* 39), so Donne's speaker seeks to assure himself by means of the image of Christ in his mind. Yet the octave ends, literally, with a question mark; and, although Christ "pray'd forgivenesse for his foes fierce spight," when He returns as Judge of the world, some at least will indeed be "adjudged unto hell."

The sestet undertakes a strengthening of the persona's assurance of salvation by encouragement of an emotional and aesthetic response to the interior image of Christ that he has evoked. Again the conventions of Petrarchan/Neo-Platonic love poetry are recalled and parodied:

> No, no; but as in my idolatrie
> I said to all my profane mistresses,
> Beauty, of pitty, foulnesse onely is
> A signe of rigour: so I say to thee,
> To wicked spirits are horrid shapes assign'd,
> This beauteous forme assures a pitious minde.

The very slyness of these lines is troubling. In a poem resonant with echoes of Sidney, one can hardly forget that "two Negatives affirme" according to the "Grammer rules" of *Astrophil and Stella* 63. Can Donne's "No, no," like Stella's, be construed as an implicit *yes*? The speaker of "What if this present" must fear a certain poetic justice, since as a youthful seducer he seems, like Astrophil, to have distorted the conventions. In the Neo-Platonic discourse ascribed to him in the *Book of the Courtier*, Pietro Bembo tells us that a

---

[47] *Astrophil and Stella* 1. Sidney is quoted here and below from *The Poems of Sir Philip Sidney*, ed. William A. Ringler, Jr. (Oxford: Clarendon Press, 1962).

"beauteous forme" is a "signe" not of "a pitious minde" but of a virtuous soul.[48] Samuel Daniel's Delia, after all, was "faire, and *thus* vnkinde" (emphasis added).[49] In view of the evident duplicity of the persona's addresses to his "profane mistresses" in the past, his present analogous address to his own soul – patently intended to be overheard by the divine lover – is at best questionable, and a dubious means of assuring oneself of salvation. As Anne Ferry points out, "This shocking conclusion of a poem of persuasion in a sonnet beginning as a meditation on Christ must be intended to raise questions about the nature of what is in the speaker's heart, and its relation to his language."[50]

In a Calvinist perspective this is a crucial issue, for interpretation of the "picture" in the persona's heart – is it a "marke" of election or condemnation? – is contingent upon the speaker's emotional response to Christ's countenance. A painting like the *Christ on the Cross* (Fig. 1) by Donne's younger Spanish contemporary, Diego Velázquez (1599–1660), furnishes a fitting visual analogue. To find such a tearful, bloody visage "beauteous" is not an obviously natural or spontaneous response. To appreciate it in a detached fashion as a work of art requires a trained, or at least an acquired, aesthetic sensibility; but such a separation between aesthetic appreciation and devotion is a subsequent development, resulting in part from Reformation iconoclasm. To submit one's imagination wholeheartedly to the reality behind such a representation of Christ's suffering requires the grace of charity. Since grace in Calvin's view is irresistible, it is no wonder that Calvinists were often iconoclasts: the confrontation with interior images would have been terrible enough in itself. The picture of the suffering Christ within will, for a Calvinist, be an image of beauty to the man who has faith, when faith means the subjective, unpremeditated realization that one is in fact saved. "We shall now have a full definition of faith," Calvin says in *The Institutes* (III. ii. 7), "if we say that it is a firm and sure knowledge of the divine favour toward us founded on the truth of a free promise in Christ, and revealed to our minds, and sealed in our hearts, by the Holy Spirit." Seeking a "signe" of "pitty" instead of "rigour," seeking, that is, the "marke" of his faith and election, a man has nothing to consult but his feelings; for as Calvin adds, in the next section of *The Institutes* (III. ii. 8), "that assent itself . . . is more a matter of the heart than the head, or of the affection than the

---

[48] Baldasarre Castiglione, *The Courtier* IV, trans. Sir Thomas Hoby, in *Three Renaissance Classics*, ed. Burton A. Milligan (New York: Charles Scribner's Sons, 1953), p. 599: "Whereupon doth very seldom an ill soule dwell in a beautifull bodie. And therefore is the outward beautie a true signe of the inwarde goodnesse."

[49] Samuel Daniel, *Delia* VI, in *Poems and a Defence of Ryme*, ed. Arthur Colby Sprague (1930; rpt. Chicago: University of Chicago Press, 1965): "O had she not been faire, and thus vnkind, / My Muse had slept, and none had knowne my minde."

[50] *The "Inward" Language: Sonnets of Wyatt, Sidney, Shakespeare, Donne* (Chicago: University of Chicago Press, 1983), p. 229. See p. 231 on Christ "overhearing."

intellect."[51] Donne's persona seems to be trying to stimulate in himself the appropriate feelings toward the image of the crucified Christ – a passionate affection at least as intense as that he once felt for his "profane mistresses." The manipulative insincerity of the erotic analogy, however, infects his expression of desire for Christ.

The dilemma of Donne's persona is graphically illustrated in two more paintings by Velázquez, at one time placed side by side on a wall of London's National Gallery.[52] *Christ after the Flagellation contemplated by the Christian Soul* (Fig. 2) represents the aim of the speaker in Donne's sonnet. "In this rendition of the Flagellation," writes Jonathan Brown, "the narrative elements in the Gospel have been eliminated and substituted by symbolic elements which point to a source in a still unidentified mystical text. Christ, battered and bloodied, lies on the ground, the weight of His body pulling against the rope which ties Him to the column. From His head a pinpoint of light radiates toward the Soul, symbolizing the ray of grace which Christ, through His sacrifice, makes available to believers."[53] Whatever specific text may lie behind the painting, it is an exact visual analogue to the Ignatian paradigm of meditation. The symbolism pointed out by Brown is realized with what Michael Wilson terms a "restrained naturalism,"[54] which mirrors the meditative method set forth by Donne's Jesuit contemporary, Edward Dawson (1576?–1624?):

> The houre of meditation being come, we may imagine our selves to be invited by our good Angell, or by some other Saint to whome we are particularly devoted, to appeare in the presence of God . . . The seconde [*Preludium*] is common to all Meditations, and is an imagination of seeing the places where the thinges we meditate on were wrought, by imagining our selves to be really present at those places; which we must endeavour to represent so lively, as though we saw them indeed, with our corporal eyes; which to performe well it will help us much to behould before-hande some Image wherein that mistery is well represented.[55]

What Dawson describes, and what Velázquez depicts, is what the persona of Donne's sonnet attempts: a meditation on the sufferings of Christ in order to stimulate Christian devotion.

The emotion of the sonnet veers off, however, in a carnal direction in the sestet, evoking a mood that finds its visual analogue in the second Velázquez

---

[51] *Institutes of the Christian Religion*, trans. Henry Beveridge (Grand Rapids, Michigan: Eerdmans Publishing Co., 1957), I. 475, 476.

[52] As I saw them in the spring of 1983.

[53] *Velázquez: Painter and Courtier* (New Haven: Yale University Press, 1986), pp. 67–68.

[54] *The National Gallery London* (London: Orbis Publishing, 1977), p. 87.

[55] *The Practical Methode of Meditation* (1614), in Louis L. Martz, ed., *The Anchor Anthology of Seventeenth-Century Verse* (Garden City, New York: Doubleday & Co., 1969), I. 500, 502.

painting on the same wall of the National Gallery, *Venus and Cupid* (Fig. 3). Brown comments on "the irresistible beauty of Venus' body" and notes how "the surface has a sensuous quality which enhances the sensual attraction of the subject," and, further, how "This heightened sense of reality subtly but definitely alters the relationship between the subject and the viewer by stimulating the imagination." Here is a "profane mistress" indeed! On the other hand, Brown also points out that Velázquez "deftly avoids excessive immodesty by arbitrarily altering the mirror image. Had he followed the laws of reflection, the mirror would have revealed another part of the anatomy than the face."[56] Scrutiny of this face, however, discloses a certain vapid complacency that undermines to some extent the ravishing allure of the figure. The *précieux* Cupid and the ribbon-draped mirror, traditional symbol of vanity, serve the same end. Irony, as much as modesty, plays a rôle in Velázquez's manipulation of the reflection: the painting unfolds a vision not unlike that of Donne's Elegies – sensual, but also sardonic and disillusioned. This juxtaposition of the two canvases thus illuminates the source of the tension in "What if this present": the speaker recognizes the ultimate emptiness and deceit of unfettered eroticism, but he cannot rid his mind – his habits of thought and imagination – of the furtive duplicity of self-absorbed desire.

The air of tentativeness, if not downright factitiousness, dramatized in Donne's sonnet becomes apparent when it is set beside another work of Spanish art, an anonymous sonnet of the same era, "A Cristo crucificado" ("To Christ Crucified"):

No me mueve, mi Dios, para quererte
el cielo que me tienes prometido;
ni mi mueve el infierno tan temido
para dejar por eso ofenderte.

Tú me mueves, Señor; muéveme el verte
clavado en una cruz y escarnecido;
muéveme ver tu cuerpo tan herido;
muéveme tus afrentas y tu muerte.

Muéveme, en fin, tu amor, y en tal manera,
que aunque no hubiera cielo, yo te amara,
y aunque no hubiera infierno, te temiera.

No tienes que me dar porque te quiera;
pues aunque cuanto espero no esperara,
lo mismo que te quiero te quisiera.[57]

---

[56] *Velázquez*, p. 182. A photographic reconstruction demonstrates that the painter has misrepresented the reflection.

[57] *An Anthology of Spanish Poetry, 1500–1700*, ed. Arthur Terry (Oxford: Pergamon Press, 1968), II. 96–97. The poem was first published in 1628, but, as Terry points out, it could have been written any time after the middle of the sixteenth century.

[I am not moved, my God, to love you by the heaven you have promised; nor am I moved by fear of hell to leave off offending you for this. You move me, Lord; I am moved to see you nailed to a cross and ridiculed; I am moved to see your body so wounded; I am moved by your mistreatment and your death. Your love, at last, moves me in such fashion that though there were no heaven, I would love you, and though there were no hell, I would fear you. You do not have to give me anything so that I would love you; for though I might not hope as I do hope, I would love you the same as I do love you.]

The paraphrase offered here – really little more than a trot – gives no hint of the calm limpidity of these lines. Everything about this poem bespeaks a guileless simplicity, a spontaneous and passionate longing for the crucified Christ through which, paradoxically, self-abandonment has forged a single-ness and integrity of self. The contrast with Donne's sonnet is striking. Although the Donne poem is in many ways compatible with baroque Catholicism and seems, at first, to engage the same theme as the anonymous sonnet, Donne introduces an element of uneasy self-consciousness. The Spanish poem addresses Christ on the cross; the speaker of the Donne sonnet addresses his "Soule" with Christ as an inferential overhearer. The speaker of the Spanish poem simply dismisses any consideration of salvation as irrelevant to his exalted love of Christ, while Donne's persona is obsessed with finding sufficient love in his heart to be assured of salvation. As the example of Quevedo makes plain, the appropriately anonymous Spanish sonnet is exceptionally serene even for the mystical culture of baroque Spain; but the spiritual turbulence of Donne's Holy Sonnets can only be accounted for as a result of the impact of Reformation doctrines on a gradually defecting Catholic. Calvinist notions of grace pervade the Holy Sonnets in this fashion: not as a principal theological inspiration, but as a lingering fear of faithless-ness haunting the background of poems that in most of their features resemble Catholic devotional poetry of the continent.

As John Carey observes, "The Catholic notes in Donne's religious poems are remarkably clear and full. They are the work of a man who has renounced a religion to some manifestations of which he is still, at a profound level, attached." At the same time, Carey continues, Donne was by no means prepared to shoulder the spiritual burden of Calvin's complete teaching: he was overcome by "a sense of his own isolation from the company of God's elect: he was outcast, a part of no whole." He tried to adapt the conscience of an anguished Catholic apostate to a theological scheme that focused obsessive scrutiny on the individual self, since saving faith is, under the impact of the Reformation, becoming a trust in one's own salvation: "Justification by faith meant, in effect, justification by state of mind."[58] Donne thus becomes, as a result of his particular circumstances, a

---

[58] *John Donne*, pp. 51, 52, 57. Of course Catholicism was also becoming more private and personal at this time, partly as a result of humanism's focus on the individual and partly in

paradigm case of the alienation endemic to the period of the Protestant and Catholic Reformations. As a Catholic who abandoned the bitterly held faith of his recusant family, Donne expresses an especially intense experience of a general loss of orientation during his age. What the Reformation put into dispute was the means and nature of grace; that is, of the accessibility of God's saving power. In the Christian understanding of things, what must be saved is man's soul – his very individuality or self. Original Sin is, therefore, the primordial identity crisis. The disintegrating persona of Donne's poetry is a compelling figure from a contemporary theoretical perspective, but an acknowledgment of an opposing tendency in Donne's poetry is often negelected. "The rôle of the courtier," observes Maureen Sabine, "is especially congenial to a post-structuralist reading of shifting, indeterminate identity. But the Catholic assertion of the individual's uniqueness with its maternal assurance that every child is, in some respect, exceptional was essential to Donne's poetic confidence."[59]

Since the sixteenth century witnessed a massive challenge to the Church's traditional understanding of grace, that essential element in the affirmation of personal identity, it is no wonder that Anne Ferry has been able to trace a deepening preoccupation with self – with the urge to articulate an "'inward' language" of the individual mind – in the English sonnet sequences of the century. In her chapter on Donne, she observes that *sincerity* is an issue in Donne's earliest and most liturgically oriented devotional poetry: "Reward my muses white sincerity," he cries in the first poem of *La Corona*, with "A crowne of Glory" (6, 8). Likewise, in one of the last of his devotional sonnets, "Show me deare Christ, thy spouse," he is still worrying the issue of the true Church and the individual's relation to it with a daring yet uneasy ribaldry:

> Betray kind husband thy spouse to our sights,
> And let myne amorous soule court thy mild Dove,
> Who is most trew, and pleasing to thee, then
> When she'is embrac'd and open to most men. (11–14)

The poet who offers to seduce Jesus in "What if this present" now offers to cuckold him. "Here he pushes the convention to its most shocking limits," Ferry comments, "by taking literally the Church as bride of Christ, and then persuading him to share her grace, understood as a euphemism for sexual favors, with the speaker."[60]

---

response to the Reformation. Devotions based on St. Ignatius' *Spiritual Exercises*, made so widely influential by the missionary and educational enterprises of the Jesuits, were designed to strengthen the inner spiritual resources of individuals cut off from communal worship. Catholic recusants in England were effectively forced by government authority to make their religion a private affair and used Jesuit meditative techniques accordingly.

[59] *Feminine Engendered Faith*, p. 34.

[60] *The "Inward" Language*, p. 232. See pp. 221–46 passim.

But Donne writes metaphorically, not literally: sexual "grace" is a metaphor for *grace* – the ineffable, inconceivable gift by which God grants eternal life, an ongoing existence and identity to the soul or self. The "shocking" metaphor is intended to startle us into recognition of how very *different* God's love is from our own. We talk about it in our terms (we have no others), but in such a way that these terms are dismantled in paradox: His Bride shows her love in *promiscuous fidelity*. In a rather acid commentary on Donne's funeral sermon for King James, Jonathan Goldberg remarks, "The text, composed of sliding signifiers, has its authority from something absent from it, the unmentioned Christ, the dead king." In Donne's text, Goldberg adds, God speaks only "through representatives: his son, the king, the church, the apostles – and the king's preacher."[61] But at least in one way, Donne has already pre-empted this deconstructive gambit in the Holy Sonnets. The disclosure of the absence – the emptiness of self – behind the manipulative stratagems of the speaker's voice is a central theme. In the Holy Sonnets, the failed courtier, the apostate Catholic, broken on the rack of frustrated ambition and fear of hell, discovers for himself the poignant wisdom of his favorite Church Father, St. Augustine: "And what is a man, any man, when only a man?"[62] Even in one of the late sonnets, Donne is vividly aware of the inconsistency and insubstantiality, not only of the poetic persona, but of the rôle of churchman and Christian:

> Oh, to vex me, contraryes meete in one:
> Inconstancy unnaturally hath begott
> A constant habit; that when I would not
> I change in vowes, and in devotion.   (1–4)

In the Christian vision of reality, sin is privation, creeping nothingness; the speaker of this sonnet cannot find in himself a sufficiently firm identity even to manage consistent prayer:

> I durst not view heaven yesterday; and to day
> In prayers, and flattering speaches I court God:
> To morrow'I quake with true feare of his rod.   (9–11)

Donne's preoccupation with the insubstantiality and instability of individual identity was such that during the years after his wife's death it became a theme of his sermons. In a sermon preached at Whitehall in 1620 he explains the meaning of Abel's name as an indication of the human condition:

> But therefore principally was he, and so may we be content with the name of vanity, that so acknowledging our selves to be but vanity, we may turn, for all

[61] *James I and the Politics of Literature*, pp. 216–17.
[62] *Confessiones* IV. 1 (Migne, *Patrologia Latina* 32. 693) "Et quis homo est quilibet homo, cum sit homo?"

30

our being, and all our well being, for our essence, and existence, and subsistence, upon God *in whom onely we live and move and have our being;* for take us at our best, make every one an *Abel,* and yet that is but *Evanescentia in nihilum,* a vanishing, an evapourating. (*Sermons* III: 50)

In a Lincoln's Inn sermon of the same year, he applies the concept explicitly to himself and his congregation:

> I am not all here, I am here now preaching upon this text, and I am at home in my Library considering whether *S. Gregory,* or *S. Hierome,* have said best of this text, before. I am here speaking to you, and yet I consider by the way, in the same instant, what it is likely you will say to one another, when I have done. You are not all here neither; you are here now, hearing me, and yet you are thinking that you have heard a better Sermon somewhere else, of this text before ... you are here, and you remember your selves that now yee think of it, this had been the fittest time, now, when every body else is at Church, to have made such and such a private visit; and because you would be there, you are there. (*Sermons* III: 110)

Donne was an effective preacher because his own personal experience of sin enabled him both to touch and to sympathize with the sense of sin in his flock.

But though Donne's persona is hag-ridden by doubts of his own sincerity and hence by doubts of the validity of his sense of grace, the Calvinist dynamic does not finally dominate the Holy Sonnets. The last line of "Oh, to vex me," Anne Ferry observes, leaves final judgment of the speaker's sincerity to God: "Those are my best dayes, when I shake with feare." "The sonnet leaves the final impression," Ferry continues, "that the speaker has 'here', in his poem and in his heart, inward experience that he cannot name."[63] God's grace makes possible in the soul of a man what his words cannot express and his works cannot enact. The faith/works dichotomy of the Reformation is finally subsumed in God's gracious love, which fills up the emptiness of the displaced human voice. Hence the last sonnet of the set of twelve, "Father, part of thy double interest," closes with the law of love – not faith – as the ultimate Christian obligation:

> Yet such are those laws, that men argue yet
> Whether a man those statutes can fulfill;
> None doth, but thy all-healing grace and Spirit,
> Revive againe what law and letter kill.
> Thy lawes abridgement, and thy last command
> Is all but love; Oh let that last Will stand! (9–14)

These lines are not notably Catholic or Protestant. Here Donne is not taking a position on the theology of justification and grace; he is praying for grace and

---

[63] *The "Inward" Language,* pp. 243, 245.

exhorting himself to love. Herein he is typical of the English devotional poets of the seventeenth century, who, though mostly Protestants, are not, *in their poetry*, so much militant proponents of the Reformation doctrine of grace as Christians confronting God and seeking to articulate the experience of grace (or its absence) in their lives.

Given his peculiar personal history and circumstances, the issue was especially acute for Donne; it seems that his important contribution to the development of the Anglican *via media* within the Church of England was the result of a residual Catholic conscience in a man who, whatever his reasons, felt compelled to conform to and, eventually, minister in England's established Protestant church. Although proponents of Protestant poetics may stress the fact that the earliest citation for *via media* in the *Oxford English Dictionary* is dated 1834, the concept is clearly there in Donne's *Essays in Divinity* and in his poetry early and late. In Satyre III the English church is at least implicitly placed between the faded fripperies of Rome's "ragges" and "her onely, who'at Geneva'is call'd / Religion, plaine, simple, sullen, yong, / Contemptuous yet unhansome" (45–52). In the late sonnet, "Showe me deare Christ, thy spouse," the Catholic Church, which "Goes richly painted" is set against the various versions of the Reformation, "which rob'd and tore / Laments and mournes in Germany and here" (2–4). The point of the poem is to cast doubt on the proposition that any single visible church is *the* one and only "spouse" of Christ:

> Sleepes she a thousand, then peepes up one yeare?
> Is she selfe truth and errs? now new, now'outwore?
> Doth she,'and did she, and shall she evermore
> On one, on seaven, or on no hill appeare?   (5–8)

The implicit answer to these rhetorical questions is, of course not! Unable to stay in the Church of his family, unable to accept wholeheartedly the teachings of Luther and Calvin, Donne must have felt compelled to find in the vagueness of the Thirty-nine Articles a space in between: the Church of England appealed to Donne precisely by virtue of its theological and liturgical imprecision – the demands that (he believed) it did *not* make on the conscience of the individual. In his mind at least, there was space within the English church for a man to "Keepe the'truth which thou hast found" (Satyre III: 89).

ii

What makes belief in the *via media* more than just a manifestation of Donne's eccentric personal predilections is that it was evidently shared by many English Christians not burdened with his troublesome predicament. The concept of the *via media* may well be an inadequate and finally unworkable view of the Christian Church, but it was not constructed out of whole cloth by Izaak

Walton. Neither was it a recondite fantasy of the Tractarians in the middle of the nineteenth century, nor a sly imposition on the unwitting world by T. S. Eliot in the twentieth. Recipients of Donne's letters, like Henry Goodyer, and the courtiers and aristocrats who composed the audience for his devotional poetry and prose pieces like *Essays in Divinity* (Magdalene Herbert for instance) were doubtless sympathetic to the irenic views he expressed in these pieces.[64] Then there is George Herbert, who is generally recognized as a definitive type of the piety of the Church of England. Wholly free of Donne's nagging recusant conscience, Herbert is, nonetheless, a wholehearted enthusiast for his church's medial position between Rome and Geneva. In the *Musae Responsoriae*, his rejoinder to the Scotsman Andrew Melville's attack on the practices of the established church, he ridicules the Puritans' "vain fears" ("Metus inanes") of the "Vatican She-wolf" (*"Vaticanae Lupae"*):

> Nos pari praeteruehi
> Illam Charybdim cautione nouimus
> Vestrámque Scyllam, acquis parati spiculis
> Britannicam in Vulpem, ínque Romanam Lupam.[65] (xxx. 3–6)

> [We know how, with equal caution, to sail past that Charybdis and your Scylla, equally armed with arrows against the British fox and the Roman she-wolf.]

In his poem to King James in the *Musae* (XXXIX: *Ad Seren. Regem*), Herbert maintains that Christ himself "Says that only England presents to me complete worship" (13: "Sola mihi plenos, ait, exhibet *Anglia* cultus"), and without actually using the term *via media*, describes the Church of England as a "mean" ("medium") between Puritanism and Catholicism:[66]

> Hâc ope munitus securior excipis vndas,
> Quas Latij Catharíque mouent, atque inter vtrasque
> Pastor agis proprios, medio tutissimus, agnos. (30–32)

> [Guarded by this strength, more fearlessly you sustain the waves, which Romans and Puritans stir up, and, as a shepherd, drive your own sheep between them, safest in the mean.]

This point of view is not the fancy of a youthful polemicist; "The British Church," which holds an honorable place in *The Temple* and is not in the early Williams manuscript, makes exactly the same point:

[64] There is a useful discussion of the audience for Donne's religious works by Marotti, *John Donne*, pp. 245–55, although it is marred somewhat by his tendency toward socio-economic reductivism.

[65] Throughout this study Herbert is quoted from *The Works of George Herbert*, ed. F. E. Hutchinson (Oxford: Clarendon Press, 1941).

[66] In *The Latin Poetry of George Herbert: A Bilingual Edition* (Athens: University of Ohio Press, 1965), p. 59, Mark McCloskey and Paul R. Murphy translate "medio tutissumus" as "safest in a *via media*."

> A fine aspect in fit aray,
> Neither too mean, nor yet too gay,
> Shows who is best.
> Outlandish looks may not compare:
> For all they either painted are
> Or else undrest.   (7–12)

The "medium" between the waves stirred up by Catholics and Puritans in *Musae* becomes, in "The British Church," "The mean, thy praise and glorie is" (26). In addition to the clear evidence of these poems, Stanley Stewart has marshalled a thorough and definitive historical argument that Herbert took an anti-Puritan stand on all the substantive religious controversies of his time, and that he maintained a distinctive position more favorable to the retention of important elements of traditional Catholicism in the worship of the Church of England than was approved by continental or British Calvinists.[67]

Given the undeniable divisions among English Protestants in the era of Donne and Herbert, the usual recourse of the proponents of a distinctive Protestant poetics has been to distinguish sharply between liturgy and church polity on the one hand, and dogma and theology on the other, as factors in the interpretation of seventeenth-century devotional verse. The differences between Herbert and his Puritan antagonists are deemed matters merely of church order and style of worship: a doctrinal consensus based on Luther's, and especially Calvin's, conception of predestination and justification by faith is taken to be normative not only for the Church of England but also for the English religious lyric.[68] Now the disputing parties themselves sometimes had tactical reasons for minimizing their differences by insisting that quarrels over ecclesiology and the form of worship had no doctrinal implications, but it is hard to conceive them so naive as to believe it. *Lex orandi, lex credendi* is a shrewd as well as venerable maxim. The way a clergyman dresses and

---

[67] Stanley Stewart, "Herbert and the 'Harmonies' of Little Gidding," *Cithara* 24, No. 1 (1984) 3–26; and *George Herbert*, which includes the *Cithara* article with much additional material. Stewart's Twayne book is a remarkable work: both a fine practical introduction to Herbert for students and an indispensable contribution for scholars.

[68] For the most complete statement, see Lewalski, *Protestant Poetics*, pp. 13–27. See also Halewood, pp. 33–70; Richard Strier, "History, Criticism, and Herbert: A Polemical Note," *PLL* 17 (1981) 347–52; and *Love Known*, p. xv; and Gene Edward Veith, *Reformation Spirituality: The Religion of George Herbert* (Lewisburg, PA: Bucknell University Press, 1985), pp. 11–20. The Protestant poetics critics have some difficulty forging a consensus among themselves. Lewalski and Halewood both include Donne in the Lutheran/Calvinist consensus, while Veith maintains that Herbert was a Calvinist, Donne an Arminian. According to Veith, Luther drew back from the predestinarian rigors of *sola fide* justification associated with Calvin. Strier, on the other hand, maintains that Luther was firmly committed to justification by faith alone and provides the best theological model for Herbert. In "John Donne Awry and Squint: The 'Holy Sonnets', 1608–1610," *MP* 86 (1989) 357–84, however, Strier seems to agree with the Veith position that Donne was not a true Calvinist (or Lutheran).

performs the sacraments cannot be without bearing on the rôle of the clergy and of the sacraments in the economy of salvation and the spiritual life of the faithful. Genuine Calvinism, with its stress on the unmediated subjective operation of grace, would understandably object to such appurtenances of "Popery" as an episcopal hierarchy, clerical vestments, and elaborate liturgical ritual. In his rejoinder to Melville, Herbert endorses every one of these features of the established church and others equally offensive to Puritans, Calvin's most enthusiastic followers in Britain. Although in this deliberately irenic poem (see *Musae Resp.* XXXVII.31ff.) he de-emphasizes the doctrinal implications of his differences with Melville, they emerge forcefully, if obliquely, in the lyrics of *The Temple*.

There are certainly no grounds for Christopher Hodgkins to equate Herbert's approval of two-thirds of Melville's poem with an approval of the latter's "basic Calvinist theology."[69] Herbert merely agrees with Melville's praise of "holy authors" and love of God:

> Ritibus vna Sacris opponitur; altera Sanctos
>   Praedicat autores; tertia plena Deo est.
> Postremis ambabus idem sentimus vterque;
>   Ipse pios laudo; Numen & ipse colo. (*Musae Resp.* IV. 3–6)

> [In the first part you oppose sacred rites; in the second you proclaim sacred authors; the third is full of God. About the latter two we both feel the same; I myself praise the pious; I myself also worship the Deity.]

To acknowledge an opponent's piety hardly amounts to an endorsement of his theology. By the same token, Hodgkin's assertion that "'The Watercourse' explicitly affirms double predestination"[70] cannot be sustained. Hodgkins dismisses Louis Martz's argument that the phrase "as he sees fit" (l. 10) suggests an element of human co-operation – of "fittingness" rather than sheer arbitrariness – in God's judgments. But even the balanced dichotomies of "life/strife" (l. 5) and "salvation/damnation" (l. 10) recall St. Thomas's dictum that predestination and free will can both, *simultaneously*, determine man's eternal destiny.[71]

As with Donne, the central issue in recent scholarship on Herbert's poetry is his conception of grace, but in Herbert's case there has been no hesitation in proclaiming him a convinced adherent of the most extreme Reformation tenets. Gene Edward Veith maintains that the poem "Grace" treats its theme "in identical terms" to the treatment in Luther's *Lectures on Galatians*, where

---

[69] *Authority, Church and Society in George Herbert: Return to the Middle Way* (Columbia: University of Missouri Press, 1993), p. 151.

[70] Ibid., p. 21.

[71] Louis L. Martz, "The Generous Ambiguity of Herbert's *Temple*," in *A Fine Tuning: Studies in the Religious Poetry of Herbert and Milton*, ed. Mary A. Maleski (Binghamton, NY: Medieval & Renaissance Texts & Studies, 1989), p. 39. See *Summa Theologiae* I. 23. 5, quoted infra n. 120.

grace is compared to rain falling as "a heavenly gift from above" on the "dry earth," which, without it, lies barren.[72] Barbara Lewalski assimilates the poem to what she regards as a set of Reformation poetic conventions. In a chapter on Protestant emblem literature, she cites Herbert's "Grace" as an example of the influence of "a number of emblems which variously embody a biblical metaphor . . . God as gardener and man as plant or tree." Thus "Herbert's speaker sees himself as a dead stock and begs for dews from above." In a subsequent chapter Lewalski says, "The speaker begs for the Savior's 'suppling grace' to counter the effects of sin in a hard heart 'void of love' (ll. 18–19)."[73]

The problem begins in both of these accounts with the tacit assumption that the image of grace descending as dew or rain on the parched garden of the soul is exclusively Protestant. In summarizing and extending landmark studies of Rosemond Tuve and Stanley Stewart, Frances Malpezzi has noted the extensive occurrence of the metaphor in Scripture and medieval liturgy,[74] and it is equally prominent in the devotional literature of continental Catholicism during the sixteenth and seventeenth centuries. The Spanish Scripture scholar, Fray Luis de León, who, unlike Luther, remained in the Order of St. Augustine, saw rain and dew, like Luther, as a symbol of God's grace: "God's sending rain upon dry earth," he writes, commenting on Job 5.10, "and fertilizing with it and dressing with beauty and fruits the wasted, barren ground, is like lifting up the fallen with his favor."[75]

Perhaps the most striking Catholic parallel to Herbert's vision of grace descending like rain or dew from the heavens comes from Santa Teresa de Jesús, the Carmelite mystic of the preceding century. In a famous passage of her autobiography (*Libro de la Vida*, 1588), she describes four stages or phases of prayer life, with the fourth culminating stage the prayer of union. The cultivation of a life of prayer, she says, requires "watering" the garden of the soul. The beginning is like drawing water from a well, the second stage like bringing water by means of an irrigation wheel or aqueduct, the third like having a river run through the garden, and the fourth, finally, like rain falling on the garden of the soul, now completely passive (*Vida* 11. 7, p. 59).[76] The soul begins as a garden "in very infertile land that bears many weeds." The

---

[72] *Reformation Spirituality*, p. 47.

[73] *Protestant Poetics*, pp. 199, 294.

[74] "The Withered Garden in Herbert's 'Grace'," *JDJ* 4 (1985) 35–47, esp. 38–42. Malpezzi is, of course, elaborating on the seminal work of Stanley Stewart, *The Enclosed Garden: The Tradition and the Image in Seventeenth-Century Poetry* (Madison, Milwaukee, London: University of Wisconsin Press, 1967).

[75] *Exposición del Libro de Job*, in *Obras completas castellanas*, ed. Félix García, O.S.A., 4th ed. (Madrid: Biblioteca de autores cristianos, 1957), II. 114. See also the comments on Job 37.4, p. 597.

[76] Santa Teresa's writings are cited from *Obras completas de Santa Teresa de Jesús*, ed. Efren de la Madre de Dios, O.C.D. and Otger Steggink, O.Carm., 2nd ed. (Madrid: Biblioteca de Autores Cristianos, 1957).

Lord must "pull up the weeds and set good plants" (*Vida* 11. 6, p. 59: "comienza a hacer un huerto en tierra muy infructuosa que lleva muy malas hiervas, para que se deleite el Señor. Su Majestad arranca las malas hiervas y ha de plantar las buenas"). In Teresa's complex extended metaphor, the soul is both gardener and garden, yet paradoxically the whole process of growth in prayer life is a matter of relinquishing activity, of allowing God to take over the work of "gardening": "The Lord wishes here to help the gardener in such fashion that He is almost the gardener and the one who does everything" (*Vida* 16. 1, p. 77: "Quiere el Señor aquí ayudar a el hortolano de manera que casi Él es el hortolano y el que hace todo"). What the "pauper of a soul" could not manage "perchance with twenty years' effort, the celestial gardener could do in a moment," making the fruit of the soul grow and mature (*Vida* 17. 2, p. 79: "y lo que la pobre de el alma con travajo por ventura de veinte años de cansar el entendimiento no ha podido acaudalar, hácelo este hortolano celestial en un punto, y crece la fruta y madúrala de manera que se puede sustentar de su huerto, quiriéndolo el Señor").

As Malpezzi observes, in Herbert's "Grace" also, "the speaker is more than the gardener; he is the garden itself."[77] Like Santa Teresa, Herbert expresses a frustration with human efforts at "gardening":

> My stock lies dead, and no increase
> Doth my dull husbandrie improve:
> O let thy graces without cease
>   Drop from above!   (1–4)

Herbert's poem handles the same paradox as Teresa's discussion of prayer: that we must long and strive for the grace that can only be a gift, an accession of God's favor that wholly transcends human activity and desire. The result is that this life is inevitably a state of tension, an alternation of spiritual fulfillments and disappointments. "Grace," a poem of longing, closes with a plea for a permanent sense of grace, of God's indwelling presence:

> O come! for thou dost know the way:
> Or if to me thou wilt not move,
> Remove me, where I need not say,
>   *Drop from above.*   (21–24)

The italicizing of the last line, the refrain, indicates that the poem has turned to comment reflexively on its own argument: the speaker prays that he need no longer beg for grace, that he be transported to final union. It is a theme to which Herbert returns in "The Flower," a poem of fulfillment coming much later in "The Church": "O that I once past changing were, / Fast in thy Paradise, where no flower can wither!" (22–23). Santa Teresa likewise knows

---

[77] "The Withered Garden," p. 39.

that the "prayer of union" – a foretaste of Paradise – is always "quite brief" (*Vida* 18. 12, p. 84), and she offers encouragement and consolation for the times when even "the well is dry" and "for many days there is only dryness, disgust, and distaste" (*Vida* 11.10–11, p. 60: "Y es Dios tan bueno que, cuando por lo que Su Majestad sabe – por ventura para gran provecho nuestro – quiere que esté seco el pozo . . . que en muchos días no hay sino sequedad, y desgusto ye dessabor").

Herbert's cry for grace implies a spiritual longing conceived in metaphorical terms very much like Santa Teresa's. In "The Odour. 2. Cor. 2.15," a poem coming after "The Flower" and very near the end of "The Church," he prays that by communing with the sweetness of Christ ("*My Master*, which alone is sweet," l. 21), he, too, might acquire a fragrance "not displeasing" (l. 24) to God:

> This breathing would with gains by sweetning me
>   (As sweet things traffick when they meet)
>   Return to thee.
>   And so this new commerce and sweet
> Should all my life employ and busie me.   (26–30)

Lewalski sees this project of "a developing commerce in such sweet breathings" as exemplary of a specifically Protestant view of the "Savior-redeemed relationship,"[78] but it is in fact difficult not to be reminded once again of Santa Teresa's garden imagery and its assimilation of biblical types:

> Ya, ya se abren las flores, ya comienzan a dar
> olor. Aquí querría el alma que todos la viesen y
> entendiesen su gloria para alabanzas de Dios, y
> que la ayudasen a ella, y darles parte de su
> gozo, porque no puede tanto gozar.   (*Vida* 16. 3, p. 77)

> [Now, now the flowers open, now they begin to give fragrance. Here the soul wishes that everyone might see her and understand her glory for the praises of God, and that they might help her, and take part in her joy, since she is unable to enjoy so much.]

Lying behind this passage is Canticles 4.16: "Arise, north wind! Come, south wind! blow upon my garden that its perfumes may spread abroad." Hence Teresa and Herbert are both recalling passages of Scripture in order to place intimate personal experience in a traditional context, and in fact the association of the experience of grace with the Canticles text is a commonplace. One finds it, for example, in a twelfth-century sequence once attributed to St. Bernard:

---

[78] *Protestant Poetics*, pp. 294–95.

Dulcis Jesu memoria
dans vera cordi gaudia:
sed super mel et omnia
ejus dulcis praesentia.[79]

[Jesus, sweet in memory giving the heart true joys: but surpassing honey and all things is his sweet presence.]

Imagery of fragrance and sweetness is similarly associated with the Name of Jesus in seventeenth-century poems, such as the hymns to the Holy Name by Crashaw and Lope de Vega.[80] The notable common feature in the poem of Herbert and the autobiography of Santa Teresa is how each emphasizes the pleasure taken by Christ in the soul He has sweetened by grace. Teresa is, of course, a very different writer from Herbert, and the latter would doubtless be skeptical, if not downright suspicious, of the Carmelite nun's bold forays into mystical union. For all that, both are, finally, using similar metaphors to express similar experiences of an intimate relationship with Christ by which the soul is in some sense transformed. But it is a transformation in which the soul does not merely retain its own identity but discovers, for the first time, its true identity and nature.

Herbert's conception of grace, then, cannot be exclusively Protestant – not, at least, as it is imaginatively realized in his poetry. The assertion of the contrary can only be maintained by means of a factitious version of Catholic teaching on grace. Richard Strier, for example, uses "The Glance" as an illustration of how Herbert rejects a Catholic, Thomistic conception in favor of a Reformation model based on Luther and Calvin:

> The reformers insisted that grace was not a quality or a substance imparted to the soul but rather the experience of a change in God's *attitude*. It was not to be spoken of in terms of "infusion" but in terms of relationship. It designated for the reformers, not a *qualitas* but a *voluntas*. Melanchthon stated the position in an aphorism – "Grace," he said, "is not medicine but favor." Like "Love"(III), "The Glance" is very much in this tradition. All the physicality of stanza 1, all the talk of grace as a surpassingly "sugared" and powerful "cordial," is mock physicality. Grace is cordial the way a person is, not the way a liqueur is.[81]

The trouble with this account of Herbert's view of grace is that it depends upon a puzzling presupposition of "physicality" in the Catholic view. In a footnote to the quoted passage, Strier cites the *Summa Theologiae* (I–II.110.

---

[79] "The Rosy Sequence," 1–4, *The Oxford Book of Medieval Latin Verse*, ed. Stephen Gaselee (Oxford: Clarendon Press, 1928), p. 111.

[80] See the discussion by R. V. Young, *Richard Crashaw and the Spanish Golden Age* (New Haven: Yale University Press, 1982), pp. 125–27. See also Louis L. Martz, *The Poetry of Meditation*, pp. 249–59 for a discussion of the relationship between Herbert and St. François de Sales, esp. p. 254, for the quotation from François, where the devout Christian is advised to "plant him in thy bosome like a sweet-smelling posie."

[81] *Love Known*, p. 139.

39

1–2) as his source for the normative Catholic position, supposedly repudiated by Herbert as well as Luther and Calvin; but more attention seems to have been accorded Luther's attack than St. Thomas' actual teaching. Strier suggests that "substance" and "quality" are basically the same, when in fact they are contraries in Scholastic terminology. As St. Thomas explains, grace as a *qualitas* dwells "in" the soul as an accident not as a substance. But even as a substance (in the Godhead) grace is not therefore "physical" or in any sense a material entity. Likewise, "infused" is a technical analogical term used to distinguish what is of divine or supernatural origin (the gift of sanctifying grace) from what is inherent in human nature. Theological virtues, for example, are "infused" in a man insofar as they are added to his nature (hence *super*natural). This does not mean that they are literally "poured in" or in any sense "physical," and neither is the grace that they presuppose.[82]

Once the confusion between literal and figurative is resolved, it is difficult to see how "The Glance" in any sense constitutes a repudiation of Thomist ideas about grace:

> When first thy sweet and gracious eye
> Vouchsaf'd ev'n in the midst of youth and night
> To look upon me, who before did lie
> > Weltring in sinne;
> > I felt a sugred strange delight,
> Passing all cordials made by any art,
> Bedew, embalme, and overrunne my heart,
> > And take it in.   (1–8)

---

[82] Here are the relevant passages from the *Summa Theologiae* I–II.110. 2: "Creaturis autem naturalibus sic providet ut non solum moveat eas ad actus naturales, sed etiam largiatur eis formas et virtutes quasdam, quae sunt principia actuum, ut secundum seipsas inclinentur ad huiusmodi motus. Et sic motus quibus a Deo moventur, fiunt creaturis connaturales et faciles; . . . Multo igitur magis illis quos movet ad consequendum bonum supernaturale aeternum, infundit aliquas formas seu qualitates supernaturales, secundum quas suaviter et prompte ab ipso moveantur ad bonum aeternum consequendum. Et sic donum gratiae qualitas quaedam est . . . gratia, secundum quod est qualitas, dicitur agere in animam non per modum causae efficientis, sed per modum causae formalis; sicut albedo facit album, et iustitia iustum . . . Et quia gratia est supra naturam humanam, non potest esse quod sit substantia aut forma substantialis; sed est forma accidentalis ipsius animae. Id enim quod substantialiter est in Deo, accidentaliter fit in anima participante divinam bonitatem: ut de scientia patet . . . Et secundum hoc etiam gratia dicitur creari ex eo quod homines secundum ipsam creantur, idest in novo esse constituuntur, ex nihilo, idest non ex meritis; secundum illud *Ad Ephes.*2, 9: *Creati in Christo Iesu in operibus bonis.*" In the introduction to the translation cited by Strier himself, A.M. Fairweather, trans. and ed., *Nature and Grace: Selections from the Summa Theologica of St. Thomas Aquinas*, Library of Christian Classics, Vol. XI (Philadelphia: Westminster Press, 1954), p. 30, it is observed that the phrase "infusion of grace" is misleading, and "not intended as implying any positive description of the inward nature of grace" as "something magical, if not physical." Fairweather goes on to point out that "Aquinas held no brief for the notion that salvation could be merited by good works," and to "wonder what would have happened at the time of the Reformation if

The "sugred strange delight" that surpasses "all cordials" is not "physicality" – "mock" or otherwise; it is a metaphor, even as mention of the Lord's "sweet and gracious eye" and His act of looking are metaphors using physical vehicles for spiritual tenors. "An attitude, a gracious glance," Strier continues, "can be spoken of as if it were a medicine or a 'cordial' because it can be as powerful and affecting as one – or more so."[83] But surely not even Luther or Calvin could truly believe that St. Thomas Aquinas or any other Catholic theologian ever supposed that grace was literally a "liqueur" or a "cordial" to be "poured into" the Christian soul. In any case, Strier has simply misconstrued the poem's figurative movement. Herbert has not discarded a "physical" image of infused grace for a more appropriate expression of God's "favor" as a kind of looking; he has rather expanded the original and primary metaphor of the "glance" itself:

> If thy first glance so powerfull be,
> A mirth but open'd and seal'd up again;
> What wonders shall we feel, when we shall see
>   Thy full-ey'd love!
>   When thou shalt look us out of pain,
> And one aspect of thine spend in delight
> More then a thousand sunnes disburse in light,
>   In heav'n above.   (ll. 17–24)

The contrast at work here is between the experience of grace in this life – a mere "glance" from God's "sweet and gracious eye" – and the full gaze of God in eternity. Strier cites Revelation 21:4 as the subtext of the stanza: "And God shall wipe away all the tears from their eyes . . . neither shall there be any more pain"; but he could as well have cited 1 Corinthians 13:12: "For now we see through a glass darkly; but then face to face; now I know in part; but then shall I know even as I am known"; or 1 John 3:2: "for we shall see him as he is." From the passage in the first Epistle of John as well as Revelation 21:23, St. Thomas develops the notion of the "beatific vision" of God through sanctifying grace as a figure for eternal life.[84] There is, therefore, no basis for seeing "The Glance" as a rebuke to the Thomist conception of grace, once that conception is correctly understood.

The metaphors of *looking* and of *smelling* or *tasting* are complementary, not

---

Aquinas had been universally understood in the Catholic Church, and if all parties had used the same terms with the same meanings."

[83] *Love Known*, pp. 139–40.

[84] *Summa Theologiae* I.12. 5: "Et hoc augmentum virtutis intellectivae illuminationem intellectus vocamus; sicut et ipsum intelligibile vocatur lumen vel lux. Et istud est lumen de quo dicitur Apoc. 21,23, quod *claritas Dei illuminabit eam*, scilicet societatem beatorum Deum videntium. Et secundum hoc lumen efficiuntur deiformes, idest Deo similes; secundum illud I Io. 3, 2: *cum apparuerit, similes ei erimus, et videbimus eum sicuti est.*"

contrasting. A "glance" is as physical as a "cordial," and both figurative complexes deploy physical actions and experiences as analogies for spiritual actions and experiences. These metaphors do not depict grace *merely* as a relationship that in no way transforms the soul. The whole purpose of the metaphor of the "gracious eye" of God – the reason it confers "a sugred strange delight" – is that it *changes* the life of the *regenerate* Christian. Indeed, it confers life where before was only death, anticipating the end of the pain of our earthly human condition prophesied by the Book of Revelation. The verse following the one quoted by Strier proclaims, "Behold, I make all things new" (21.5). The image of the Savior's restorative "glance" does not necessarily imply a Calvinist or Lutheran view of grace; it is prominent in the fifth stanza of the *Cántico espiritual* of San Juan de la Cruz:

> Mil gracias derramando
> pasó por estos sotos con presura
> y, yéndolos mirando,
> con sola su figura
> vestidos los dejó de hermosura.   (*Vida y obras*, p. 627)

> [Spreading a thousand graces he passed hastily through these groves and, looking at them while going, with only his countenance, he left them clothed in beauty.]

In his own prose commentary on this stanza, San Juan remarks that Christ "not only communicates to [creatures] their natural being and graces by looking at them," but also "supernatural" being, "when He made himself man, raising him in the beauty of God and, as a result, all creatures in Him, by having united himself with the nature of them all in man."[85]

There are important connections here. San Juan indicates the necessary relationship between grace and the Incarnation (perhaps there is a physical aspect to grace after all), while Strier rightly insists upon the importance of the Incarnation in Herbert's poetry. Strier derives this emphasis from Luther's preoccupation with "the personal character of the Bible," as expressed in "the second advent of Christ (the first is the Incarnation; the third, His coming in glory; the second advent is the entry of Christ into the individual believer's life)."[86] To illustrate this Lutheran motif in Herbert, Strier quotes "Christmas":

---

[85] *Vida y obras*, p. 644: "Y no solamente les comunicó el ser y gracias naturales mirándolas . . . mas también . . . comunicándolas el ser sobrenatural; lo cual fue cuando se hizo hombre ensalzándole en hermosura de Dios y, por consiguiente, a todas las criaturas en Él, por haberse unido con la naturaleza de todas ellas en el hombre."

[86] *Love Known*, p. 154. See also Strier, "Ironic Humanism in *The Temple*," in "*Too Rich to Clothe the Sunne*": *Essays on George Herbert*, ed. Claude J. Summers and Ted-Larry Pebworth (Pittsburgh: University of Pittsburgh Press, 1980), p. 39.

> O Thou, whose glorious, yet contracted light,
>   Wrapt in nights mantle, stole into a manger;
> Since my dark soul and brutish is thy right,
>   To Man of all beasts be not thou a stranger:
>   Furnish & deck my soul, that thou mayst have
>   A better lodging then a rack or grave.   (9–14)

Here again, a metaphorical complex is regarded as specifically Protestant in its implications because Catholic sources have been insufficiently investigated. In a communion poem in the *Heráclito cristiano*, Francisco de Quevedo deploys almost identical tropes for the coming of Christ into the heart of the penitent in a manner analogous to his coming into the flesh in his birth in a stable:

> Pues hoy pretendo ser tu monumento,
> porque me resucites del pecado,
> habítame de gracia, renovado
> el hombre antiguo en ciego perdimiento.
>   Si no, retratarás tu nacimiento
> en la nieve de un ánimo obstinado
> y en corazón pesebre, acompañado
> de brutos apetitos que en mí siento.
>   Hoy te entierras en mí, siervo villano,
> sepulcro, a tanto güesped, vil y estrecho,
> indigno de tu Cuerpo soberano.
>   Tierra te cubre en mí, de tierra hecho;
> la conciencia me sirve de gusano;
> mármor para cubrirte da mi pecho.[87]

[Since today I undertake to be your monument, in order that you might revive me from sin, dress me in grace, having renewed the old man in blind perdition. If not, you will return to your birth in the snow of an obstinate spirit and in a manger heart, accompanied by brutish appetites that I feel within me. Today you bury yourself in me, rude servant, a sepulchre to such a guest, vile and narrow, unworthy of your sovereign body. Earth covers you in me, made out of earth; conscience serves me as a worm; my breast gives marble to cover you.]

The resemblance between the metaphors of these two poems is striking, and although it is not likely to be the result of direct influence,[88] it is certainly not attributable to mere coincidence. Both poets realize that in order for the

[87] Salmo XXII, *Obras completas* I. 35.
[88] The dedication of the work to Quevedo's aunt is dated 1613, but most of his poems were not published until after his death in 1645. It is worth recalling, however, as James V. Mirollo, *The Poet of the Marvelous: Giambattista Marino* (New York: Columbia University Press, 1963), pp. 252–54, has noted, that Herbert's elder brother Edward knew and imitated Spanish poetry. There is also George Herbert's own interest in Valdés (Valdesso) and in Spanish proverbs.

new relationship of grace to flower, their souls must be transformed or sanctified by grace. Just as Quevedo feels within himself "brutish appetites" and begs That Christ "dress" him "in grace," so Herbert prays that Christ "furnish & deck" his "dark" and "brutish" soul. Grace certainly is divine "favor" and involves a new relationship between God and man, but it also changes the latter from within. As both poets suggest, if a man is not changed by grace, then Christ enters him only as a grave – a stone sepulchre indicative of the deathliness of sin, of the sinner's obstinacy and hardness of heart. Indeed, both poets favorably contrast natural stone with the hardness of man's heart. In "The Sepulchre" Herbert writes,

> Where our hard hearts have took up stones to brain thee,
> And missing this, most falsly did arraigne thee;
> Onely these stones in quiet entertain thee,
>   And order.   (13–16)

In a poem called "On the Death of Christ, Against the Hardness of Man's Heart," Quevedo writes that man's heart must be of stone or diamond, but then corrects himself:

> Mas no es de piedra, no; que si lo fuera,
> de lástima de ver a Dios amante,
> entre las otras piedras se rompiera.[89]

> [But it is not stone; for if it were, from the pity of seeing God as lover, among the other stones it would have broken.]

This is, of course, a development of the breast of marble from the manger poem quoted above.

Such parallels help to establish a context for the interpretation of grace in Herbert's poems. If, as critics such as Lewalski and Strier assert, *The Temple* is informed by an extreme Reformation view of grace in which it is *merely* God's arbitrary favor, and effects no actual sanctification in the penitent, then it is difficult to understand Herbert's continual recourse to the same experience of inner transformation as Catholic poets like Quevedo. If the Calvinist view – that the grace of regeneration amounts to no more than the sheer imputation of righteousness to a human soul, which remains essentially corrupt – is Herbert's view, then interpretations of *The Temple* must inevitably arrive at the perspective of Stanley Fish and Barbara Harman. Indeed, the antihumanism of post-structuralist theory seems an apt secular counterpart to the antihumanism that Strier finds at the heart of the Protestant Reformation.[90]

---

[89] *Obras completas* I. 158. On the ironic use of the stone motif in Quevedo's poetry, see Elizabeth B. Davis, "Quevedo and the Rending of the Rocks," *Scripta Humanistica* 18 (1986) 58–72.

[90] See Strier, *Love Known*, pp. 1–4, 21, as well as "Ironic Humanism in *The Temple*," passim. See the quotation from Luther's *Commentary on Galatians*, above n. 34; and Calvin, *Institutes* III.

In both the current ideological and the older theological schemes, the "fiction" of a coherent self, of personal human identity, is swept away. According to Harman, the speech of the poems of *The Temple* (like Donne's Holy Sonnets) marks an assertion by the speaker of self-manifestation since speech insists upon the presence of the speaker; however, the effort is repeatedly frustrated: "Though the speaker of 'The Holdfast' is aggressive about self-assertion, he is blocked three times by an interlocutor who is clearly less interested in rejecting the speaker's admittedly flawed positions than in rejecting, and finally pre-empting, speech itself."[91] Ironically, Richard Strier likewise sees "The Holdfast" as "a quintessential Herbert poem" in its dramatization of "the Reformation doctrine of grace" and "the strangeness and wonder of faith alone."[92] But while both Harman and Strier see the poem as a denial of any human complacency or self-sufficiency, for the former it is a matter of desperation, for the latter of praise and celebration.

Neither reading, however, attends sufficiently to the exact text of the poem or to its broader Christian context. As the poem opens, the speaker is gently rebuked in his proud resolve first to be strictly obedient to God's laws, second to trust absolutely in God, and finally even to confess his trust:

> Then I confess that he my succour is:
> But to have nought is ours, not to confess
>   That we have nought. I stood amaz'd at this,
>   Much troubled, till I heard a friend expresse,
> That all things were more ours by being his.
>   What Adam had, and forfeited for all,
>   Christ keepeth now, who cannot fail or fall. (8–14)

The key line is 12: "That all things were *more ours* by being his." Strier maintains that "more ours" means "*more secure*,"[93] but there is no warrant for the words not meaning what they say. Because we are children of Adam by nature, we inherit his sin; that is, his loss, his nothingness, for evil in the Christian view of it has no substantial being. "Therefore if things are deprived of all good," St. Augustine remarks, "they are altogether nonexistent:

xi. 23 (II. 58) "This is equivalent to saying that man is not just in himself but that the righteousness of Christ is communicated to him by imputation, while he is strictly deserving of punishment. Thus vanishes the absurd dogma, that man is justified by faith, inasmuch as it brings him under the influence of the Spirit of God, by whom he is rendered righteous." Ilona Bell, "Revision and Revelation in Herbert's 'Affliction (I)'," *JDJ* 3 (1984) 73–96, expressly sets out to "suggest some similarities between Reformation Protestantism and modern literary theory which help to explain why Herbert's poetry has suddenly become so alluring" (74). Context makes it clear that she means *post*modern theory.

[91] *Costly Monuments*, pp. 41, 43, 51. See Jacques Derrida, *Speech and Phenomena and Other Essays on Husserl's Theory of Signs*, trans. David B. Allison (Evanston, IL: Northwestern University Press, 1973), pp. 48–59, for the dismantling of self-presence in speech.

[92] *Love Known*, pp. 67, 73.

[93] *Love Known*, p. 72.

therefore so long as they exist, they are good: Therefore whatever things are, are good. And that evil whose origin I was seeking is not a substance; because if it were a substance, it would be good."[94] It is not man's nature as such that is evil, but the loss of that nature and the defacement of the divine image in which it was made. Adam lost the purity of original being, and man has no source of being in himself: "all things" can only be *at all* by being His. Only the participation by grace in the Incarnation – in God made man – restores human identity and makes a "coherent self" possible as anything but a fiction.

Harman is, then, perfectly correct in saying that "Affliction (I)" is the "story" of a man who has come to learn that he is "utterly without means," that in the world of his own self "there *never were* either means or possibilities – only the illusion of them." She is surely wrong, however, to say that God "cross-biases" the speaker "not because he has specific plans which counter the plans one has for oneself," but rather His whole purpose lies in "countering every attempt by the self to have plans, to determine who he is, to define the terms of existence."[95] God's plan for man is, to the contrary, quite specific, and it is intended to enable him "to determine who he is, to define the terms of existence," in the only way possible: "Thou shalt love the Lord, thy God, with all thy heart, and with all thy soul, and with all thy mind" (Matthew 22: 37). Despite his sinfulness, St. Augustine explains, man is still part of God's creation and is moved to praise: "You made us for yourself, and our hearts are restless until we rest in you."[96]

"Affliction (I)" is a poem about a restless heart that desires to praise, but is "cross-biased" not by God but by its own sinful nature. The speaker is not sinful because he wishes to define a coherent self; it is the incoherence and inconstancy of his selfish complaining that is the most notable manifestation of his sinfulness. As in "The Collar," the speaker cannot decide whether he is a retiring scholar or an ambitious worldling, a servant of God or a servant of self:

> What pleasures could I want, whose King I served,
>   Where joyes my fellows were?
> Thus argu'd into hopes, my thoughts reserved
>   No place for grief or fear.   (13–16)
>
> .   .   .   .
>
> Whereas my birth and spirit rather took
>   The way that takes the town;
> Thou didst betray me to a lingring book
>   And wrap me in a gown.   (37–40)

---

[94] *Confessiones* VII. xii.18, *Patrologia Latina* 32. 743: "Ergo si omni bono privabuntur, omnino nulla erunt: ergo quamdiu sunt, bona sunt: ergo quaecumque sunt, bona sunt. Malumque illud quod quaerebam unde esset, non est substantia; quia si substantia esset, bonum esset."

[95] *Costly Monuments*, pp. 90, 95. Cf. Bell, "Revision and Revelation," p. 86.

[96] *Confessiones* I. i. 1, *Patrologia* 32. 661: "et tamen laudare te vult homo, aliqua portio creaturae tuae. Tu excitas, ut laudare te delectet; quia fecisti nos ad te, et inquietum est cor nostrum, donec requiescat in te." Veith, *Reformation Spirituality* p. 45, says that Reformation

The speaker's desire to be a tree, so that at least he might be useful (57–60), shows the impulse to praise inherent in man as "a part of God's creation." But his restless discontent reveals the effect of sin – the inability to settle into a rôle or coherent identity: "Well, I will change the service, and go seek / Some other master out" (63–64). It is only God's grace – His love for man – that enables the speaker to fulfill his nature and create a true, consistent self out of the chaos of sin. Once again the *Confessions* provides a pertinent gloss on the paradoxical closing couplet of "Affliction (I)": "What am I to you," Augustine writes, "that you command me to love you, and grow angry with me unless I do so, and threaten great miseries? Is it a small misery itself, if I do not love you?"[97] Likewise Herbert suggests that, for man, not to love God is worse than completely forgetting himself or being forgotten by God; not to love God is not fully to exist, but only God can give this capacity to love: "Ah my deare God! though I am clean forgot, / Let me not love thee, if I love thee not" (65–66).

Nothing is worse than not loving God because it is the love of God that fulfills human nature and makes possible the only complete self available to a human being: "our hearts are restless until we rest in you." All the other miseries and "afflictions" mentioned in this and other poems of complaint are insignificant by comparison. In refusing to grant sufficient weight to the Christian experience of grace, the new-historicist or cultural poetics paradigm inevitably trivializes the poetry of Herbert and his contemporaries. For this reason, Michael C. Schoenfeldt's effort to assimilate "Affliction (I)" to "the intense frustration bred by the perpetual experience of submission and prostration at the Jacobean court" is defective. Although the closing line is not "morally optimistic," it is not true that "the poem confronts the chilling possibility of a malevolent deity."[98] As attractive as such Byronic defiance might be to a postmodern sensibility, it is incompatible with the Christian

---

theologians, unlike Aquinas, deny that man truly desires God. On this point, as on so many, Augustine has more in common with St. Thomas than with the supposedly "Augustinian" Reformation.

[97] *Confessiones* I. v. 5, *Patrologia* 32. 663: "Quid tibi sum ipse, ut amari te jubeas a me, et nisi faciam irascaris mihi, et mineris ingentes miserias? Parvane ipsa est, si non amem te?" The many parallels between the *Confessions* and *The Temple* would make an interesting study. For the general similarity between Herbert and Augustine, see Mark Taylor, *The Soul in Paraphrase: George Herbert's Poetics* (The Hague: Mouton Press, 1974), pp. 1–8. Fine critical work along these lines has been done by William H. Pahlka, *Saint Augustine's Meter and George Herbert's Will* (Kent, Ohio and London: Kent State University Press, 1987); by M. Thomas Hester, "Altering the Text of the Self: The Shapes of 'The Altar'," in *A Fine Tuning: Studies of the Religious Poetry of Herbert and Milton* (Binghamton, NY: Medieval & Renaissance Texts & Studies, 1989), pp. 95–116; and by Chauncey Wood, "An Augustinian Reading of George Herbert's 'The Pulley'," also in *A Fine Tuning*, pp. 145–59. See also the comments of James Boyd White, *"This Book of Stars": Learning to Read George Herbert* (Ann Arbor: University of Michigan Press, 1994), pp. 31–32, 34, 35.

[98] *Prayer and Power: George Herbert and Renaissance Courtship* (Chicago: University of Chicago Press, 1991), pp. 76, 78.

realization – dramatized here by Herbert – of both the infinite distance between the earthly court of King James and the heavenly "court," and the way that unfathomable abyss is bridged by God's love.[99] Grace, therefore, is the enabling of this love by and for God within the soul.

Perhaps the poem that best exemplifies the life of grace in Herbert's poetry is "The Flower." This poem, too, has been seized on by a number of critics as exemplary of a strictly Protestant paradigm of grace;[100] but, as Anthony Low observes, "In it, Herbert describes events in his interior life that resemble mystical experience," and the garden imagery (as in "Grace") is reminiscent of the interior garden of Santa Teresa's *Vida*.[101] What is more, the emblematic image informing the poem seems to have been almost inevitable to poets of widely differing religious commitment. Marcantonio Flaminio (1498–1550), a reform-minded Italian Catholic, makes the trope explicit in a brief Latin epigram:

> *Comparat animum suum flori.*
> Ut flos tenellus in sinu
> Telluris almae lucidam
> Formosus explicat comam,
> Si ros et imber educat
> Illum; tenella mens mea
> Sic floret, almi Spiritus
> Dum rore dulci pascitur.
> Hoc illa si caret, statim
> Languescit; ut flos arida
> Tellure natus, eum nisi
> Et ros et imber educat.[102]

> [*He compares his soul to a flower.* As a delicate flower in the bosom of the nourishing earth unfolds in beauty its shining petals if the dew and the rain draw it forth, just so my delicate soul flowers when it feeds on the sweet dew of the nourishing spirit; if she lack it, forthwith she languishes as a flower born in dry earth, unless dew and rain nourish it.]

---

[99] See Marion White Singleton, *God's Courtier: Configuring a Different Grace in George Herbert's* Temple (Cambridge: Cambridge University Press, 1987), pp. 15ff, for how "The courtier in *The Temple* confronts his tradition by rewriting it."

[100] For example, Lewalski, *Protestant Poetics*, pp. 23, 171, 199, 287, 309; Strier, *Love Known*, pp. 248–52; Veith, *Reformation Spirituality*, p. 48.

[101] *Love's Architecture*, p. 110. See also Low, *The Georgic Revolution* (Princeton: Princeton University Press, 1985), p. 91.

[102] Marci Antonii, Joannis et Gabrielis Flaminiorum, *Carmina* (Prati: Typis Raynerii Guasti, 1831), pp. 256–57. Although Flaminio was interested in Luther and attracted to the concept of justification by faith, he was associated with the reforming circle of Cardinal Pole and could by no means be regarded as a crypto-Protestant. See Carol Maddison, *Marcantonio Flaminio: Poet, Humanist and Reformer* (Chapel Hill University of North Carolina Press, 1965), pp. 107–18, 119–153, and esp. 158–59.

Even reduced to this simple form, the metaphor makes the main point: man is a "plant" whose spiritual flourishing, like his physical existence, depends upon nurture descending from "above" as dew or rain. The Dutch Protestant poet, Jan Luyken (1649–1712), presents a version of the flower trope closer to Herbert's in its elaboration:

> *De Ziele in aandacht over de nieuwe Kreatuur.*
> Toen 't zaadje sturf in 's aardryks schoot,
> En scheen vergeeten en verlooren,
> Toen groenden 't Bloempjus door dien dood,
> En kwam gelyk een nieuw gebooren,
> Uit duistere aarde in 't schoone licht,
> Om reuk en verwen voor te draagen.
> Begroet van 's hemels aangezicht,
> Met dauw en zooneschyn in 't dagen;
> Zo wast de nieuwe kreatuur,
> Als eigen wil gaat in 't verderven,
> In dood en graf, al smaakt het zuur,
> Daar groent een leven door dat sterven;
> Een bloem in 't Paradys zo schoon,
> Al zien 't geen werelds blind gebooren,
> Hy staat voor God en zynen Zoon,
> En ruikt door aller Eng'len kooren.
> Ô JEZUS lief! ô eeuwig Goed!
> Hoe vuurig lust het my te worden
> Een Bloempje aan uw Roozenhoed,
> Daar nooit een lovertje verdorden!
> Ô Heere JEZUS voert my aan,
> Om altyd in den dood te gaan![103]

[*The Soul in Devotion About the New Creature.* When seedling died in earth's womb and seemed forgotten and abandoned, then the little blossom grew green by its death and came like a newborn out of the dark earth into lovely light spreading fragrance and color around, greeted by the face of heaven with dew and sunshine falling on it. So the new creature grows: When it goes into destruction of its own will, into death and the grave, though the taste is sour, there a life grows green through that dying, a blossom in paradise so lovely, though none of the world's blind race see it: it stands before God and his Son and gives a fragrance through the choirs of angels. Oh dear Jesus! Oh eternal Good! How fiercely I desire to become a blossom on your rosy hood, where foliage never withers! Oh Lord Jesus, command me to enter always into that death!]

The similarities between this poem and "The Flower" are remarkable, especially its closing prayer for eternal life through worldly death, which is

---

[103] Joanne Luiken, *Jezus en de Ziel* (Amsteldam: Korbelis vander Sys, 1722), p. 72.

also reminiscent of Richard Crashaw's repeated invocations of mystical death. Although Luyken was a Protestant, his poem provides no evidence that Herbert's "Flower" is a strictly indigenous growth of Reformation soil. There was no consensus about grace based on Luther and Calvin. Luyken came from an Anabaptist background and was influenced in later life by the mysticism of Jacob Boehme.[104] The Dutch Anabaptists (or Mennonites) had views on grace, predestination, and free will very similar to those of Arminius,[105] and Boehme, who could be accused of semi-Pelagianism, came into conflict with the Lutheran authorities of his day.[106] The use of the same flower metaphor as an image of the effect of grace by the Italian Catholic, the Dutch Anabaptist, and Herbert is a further indication of the complexity and elusiveness of the theme throughout the poetry of the sixteenth and seventeenth centuries.

Herbert's development of the flower conceit is far more subtle than Flaminio's or Luyken's – he weaves back and forth between the flower and the soul, rather than clearly demarcating the tenor and vehicle of the metaphor. In this way Herbert is able to evoke a more immediate sense of the changing moods of experience than Flaminio and Luyken, and the quality of this experience is crucial for interpretation of the poem. According to Stanley Fish, "The Flower" is characteristic of Herbert's demand that we "experience the full force of this admission in all its humiliating implications":[107]

> We say amisse,
> This or that is:
> Thy word is all, if we could spell.   (19–21)

Fish, however, has mistaken humility for humiliation. "There is nothing easy about the 'letting go' this poetry requires of us," he continues. "We are, after all, being asked to acquiesce in the discarding of those very habits of thought and mind that preserve our dignity by implying our independence."[108] But this complaint misses the point of the poem: there is no humiliation in

---

[104] Frank Warnke, ed. and trans., *European Metaphysical Poetry* (New Haven: Yale University Press, 1961), p. 68, points out that Luyken was an Anabaptist and comments on the stylistic similarities among religious poets of diverse "ideological" commitments. Warnke prints a text and translation of this Luyken poem, pp. 250–51.

[105] Carl Bangs, *Arminius: A Study in the Dutch Reformation*, 2nd ed. (Grand Rapids, MI: Zondervan, 1985), pp. 169–70.

[106] Peter Erb, "Introduction," in Jacob Boehme, *The Way to Christ*, trans. Erb (New York: Paulist Press, 1978), pp. 7–8, 15.

[107] *Self-Consuming Artifacts*, p. 156.

[108] Ibid., p. 157. Cf. Robert B. Shaw, *The Call of God: The Theme of Vocation in the Poetry of Donne and Herbert* (Cambridge, MA: Cowley Publications, 1981), p. 104: "Fish's reading of the poems makes them into barren exercises in dialectic. Seeing the poems as 'self-consuming', he would have us experience a sense of void upon coming to the end of one. It would be truer to Herbert's thought, as I understand it, if we experienced instead a sense of the divine plenitude." See also Terry G. Sherwood, *Herbert's Prayerful Art* (Toronto: University of Toronto Press, 1989), pp. 146–49.

"discarding" what are merely illusions, given man's ontological status as a contingent creature. Moreover, although he has no dignity or independence apart from God, dignity and independence are precisely the gifts of God's grace: *The Temple*, Herbert says, is "a picture of the many spiritual conflicts that have passed betwixt God and my Soul, before I could subject mine to the will of Jesus *My Master*: in whose service I have now found Perfect freedom."[109] In whose *service* I have now found perfect *freedom*! The poem makes good the paradox, and the feat of style by which Herbert evokes the sense of *grace*, with all its resonance, is one of the great achievements of the English lyric:

> And now in age I bud again,
> After so many deaths I live and write;
>   I once more smell the dew and rain,
> And relish versing: O my onely light,
>   It cannot be
>   That I am he
> On whom thy tempests fell all night.   (36–42)

Above all, Fish has mistaken the tone. As Anthony Low observes, "'The Flower' devotes proportionately more time to winter and change than to spring ... Yet critics rightly read the poem as a brilliant expression of joy."[110] The reason this apparent disproportion is so effective is that it is faithful to the reality of the human situation, which, in its fallen state, is wholly lacking in the "dignity" of independence. From one viewpoint, it seems that we are tossed incomprehensibly by the "power" of an arbitrary master:

> These are thy wonders, Lord of love,
> To make us see we are but flowers that glide:
>   Which when we once can finde and prove,
> Thou has a garden for us, where to hide.
>   Who would be more,
>   Swelling through store,
> Forfeit their Paradise by their pride.   (43–49)

In both this stanza and its predecessor, the possibility of damnation is raised, but this reference, far from dampening the joyousness of the poem, heightens it. The sense of release is intensified by the reminders of the grim reality of unregenerate human nature – sin and its consequences – from which we are

---

[109] Izaak Walton, *Lives*, intro. George Saintsbury (London: Oxford University Press, 1927), p. 314.
[110] *Love's Architecture*, p. 112. Some of Strier's best pages (243–50) in *Love Known* are devoted to reading "The Flower" as an intense examination of experience, but he too is bemused by the supposed "grimness" at its close. A similar viewpoint is found in Vendler, pp. 48–54, who is supported by Richard Todd, *The Opacity of Signs: Acts of Interpretation in George Herbert's* The Temple (Columbia: University of Missouri Press, 1986), pp. 58–59.

delivered by God's grace. Moreover, it is not a matter of the obliteration of human personality or will; it is only a matter of "letting go" of illusions. It is the "Lord of love" who *makes us see*, but *we* must still "finde and prove." Far from diminishing individual identity, grace enhances and fulfills it, enabling us to see ourselves and God truly – to see things as they really are. That is why Herbert found "perfect freedom" in the "service" of Christ. As Rosalie Colie remarks, "The indefinable 'something' of *logos* once understood, all things become clear – the last shall be first, the small great, the least thing sufficient for total content."[111] Herbert's perspective is, therefore, quite compatible with a famous utterance of St. Thomas Aquinas: "For since grace does not take away nature, but perfects it, it is proper that natural reason serve faith just as the natural inclination of the will is subject to charity."[112]

Of course both Herbert and St. Thomas were acquainted with the recalcitrance of human nature; both knew that while grace could finally perfect nature, nature could never adequately express or manifest grace. But although natural responses to grace all are defective and must be finally relinquished, they are not, for all that, meaningless or contemptible. "The Forerunners" is not, therefore, a poem of Puritan iconoclasm, as Strier maintains.[113] One does not write a *poem* regretfully taking leave of poetry, if poetry is no better than a trivial diversion. The worst that Herbert says about poetry is that, like any created art, it falls infinitely short of the absoluteness of Godhead:

> Yet if you go, I passe not; take your way:
> For, *Thou art still my God,* is all that ye
> Perhaps with more embellishment can say. (31–33)

Herbert's is a rather mild renunciation compared with St. Thomas' notorious leavetaking from theology: "All that I have written seems to me nothing but straw – compared with what I have seen and what has been revealed to me." The key word here is "compared," since it suggests, as Joseph Pieper points out, that "the fragmentary character of the *Summa Theologiae* is an inherent part of its statement."[114] The incompleteness of *The Temple*, its reiterated intimations that the poetry is quite inadequate to cope with its subject, is likewise an inherent part of its statement.

Thus Herbert, like St. Thomas, has anticipated (one might even say "preempted") critics such as Fish. The latter is right to point out "that both as a

[111] *Paradoxica Epidemica: The Renaissance Tradition of Paradox* (1966; rpt. Hamden, CT: Shoestring Press, 1976), pp. 214–15.
[112] *Summa Theologiae* I. 1. 8: "Cum enim gratia non tollat naturam, sed perficiat, oportet quod naturalis ratio subserviat fidei; sicut et naturalis inclinatio voluntatis obsequitur caritati."
[113] *Love Known*, p. 217. Cf. the more balanced view of William H. Pahlka, *Saint Augustine's Meter and George Herbert's Will* (Kent, OH: Kent State University Press, 1987), p. 143.
[114] *Guide to Thomas Aquinas*, trans. Richard and Clara Winston (1962; rpt. New York: Mentor-Omega, 1964), p. 139.

poem and as an experience, *The Temple* is unfinished,"[115] insofar as it is the work of Herbert alone, but it does not follow that "The Forefunners" is a "powerful comment on the difficulty, if not the impossibility, of the self-consuming enterprise of Herbert's art."[116] It is not as if Herbert has grimly surrendered an otherwise complete human poetic achievement to the whims of a ferocious Calvinist God. It is in surrendering the poems to God that they are completed and *The Temple's* purpose attained:

> *Lord, my first fruits present themselves to thee:*
> *Yet not mine neither: for from thee they came.*
> *And must return.* ("The Dedication," 1–3)

If grace, understood as a reciprocity between God and man enabling and fulfilling fragmentary human nature, is drained out of Herbert's poems, then we are left not even with Fish's readings of "The Forerunners" and "Love (III)" as episodes of devastating mortification; we are left, finally with Jonathan Goldberg's reading of "The Bag":

> The death of Jesus, in which this story – and all utterance – occurs, is the movement of words that do not arrive at final signification, and that (by telling three stories at once) derive from an origin in repetition that must, perforce, deoriginate all utterance and replace/displace it within the already written. In this "strange storie" the very notions of fullness, origin, presence, and Being (of all that supposedly inheres in voice) are replaced by spacing (literally, the making of space), repetitive motion, tracing, dissolution, undoing: death. The "being" of writing.[117]

This particular critical "utterance" comes close to gibberish, but it is an appropriate comment from Goldberg's death-obsessed postmodernist perspective: if there is no divine grace, no sacramental quality transforming our lives and works, then *The Temple* ("and all utterance") is nothing but "the movement of words that do not arrive at final signification." There is no reason to suppose that Herbert would be surprised by such an attitude; he was, after all, the author of "Vanity (I)" and knew well the human propensity for becoming entangled in a labyrinth of excessive subtlety:

> What hath not man sought out and found,
> But his deare God? who yet his glorious law
> Embosomes in us, mellowing the ground
>   With showres and frosts, with love & aw,
> So that we need not say, Where's this command?
>   Poore man, thou searchest round
> To finde out *death*, but missest *life* at hand. (21–28)

---

[115] *The Living Temple*, p. 157.
[116] *Self-Consuming Artifacts*, p. 223.
[117] *Voice Terminal Echo*, p. 121.

"The Church Militant" likewise manifests little confidence in "the late reformation" and the condition of the Church in the coming years:

> Nay, it shall ev'ry yeare decrease and fade;
> Till such a darknesse do the world invade
> At Christs last coming, as his first did finde.   (226, 229–31)

This was a troubling poem when it was first submitted for publication,[118] and it is probable that Herbert was not altogether sanguine about the future of the Christian faith in his own time. Whatever anxieties the poet endured over the specific historical situation, however, become in his poem a manifestation of the perennial tension between the temporal order and the order of grace. He knew that the Word could only be heard by men within the history of the world, but that it could never be comprehended or contained within the historical process. He would undoubtedly reject the absolute claims made for revolution in our day as he rejected similar claims made for "reformation" in his own. Neither the one nor the other is a means to grace or salvation. After Herbert's death, *The Temple* inspired a somewhat improbable disciple in Henry Vaughan: amid the dislocations of the mid-century, he peered deeply into the abyss of history, seeking the ineffable gleams of grace.

iii

Because of the circumstances in which his most memorable poetry was written, Henry Vaughan furnishes an especially poignant vision of the life of grace. These same troubled circumstances also highlight the extravagance of the claim that Vaughan was an adherent of militant, ideological Calvinism. Although he is not notably a proponent of Protestant poetics, even Christopher Hill, who treats Vaughan as a hopeless reactionary characterized by "fierce despair" in politics and "escapism" in religion, nevertheless sees him as the poet most taken with the dynamic of Calvin's theology:

> He is one of the few poets who feels Calvinist predestinarianism on his pulses. He has a powerful sense of the total vileness and corruption of the mass of mankind. A few only are vicariously redeemed by God's inscrutable Providence. Even Vaughan's tears are sent by God: "for I till drawn came not to thee" ["The Agreement," 61, 68]. In poem after poem Vaughan returns to and harps on his sinfulness."[119]

---

[118] According to seventeenth-century sources, the printing license for *The Temple* was delayed on account of uneasiness over ll. 235–36: "Religion stands on tiptoe in our land, / Readie to passe to the *American* strand." See Hutchinson's commentary, p. 547.

[119] *The Collected Essays of Christopher Hill* (Amherst: University of Massachusetts Press, 1985), I, 211, 219. Halewood, pp. 125–39; and Lewalski, *Protestant Poetics*, pp. 317–51, are the principal advocates of an exclusively and aggressively Protestant interpretation of Vaughan's poetry, and their work has evidently been influential. Before about 1970

The trouble here is that none of the features of Vaughan's poetry mentioned by Hill is peculiar to Calvinism. St. Thomas Aquinas, as well as St. Augustine, affirms predestination as a part of divine providence and maintains that it is wholly gratuitous: "But there is no reason why He has chosen these for glory and rejected those except the divine will."[120] Even in the face of the radical version of predestination developed by Luther and Calvin, the Council of Trent merely warns against the "rash presumption of election."[121]

There is nothing either in Vaughan's poetry or prose to suggest that his conception of grace and predestination is incompatible with that of St. Thomas. In "The Agreement," the poem cited by Hill, the speaker prays that his election be assured by penitential tears:

> Wherefore with tears (tears by thee sent)
> I beg, my faith may never fail![122]   (61–62)

Vaughan's critics rarely mentioned Calvin, and his influence on the poet, if acknowledged, was seen as moderate. For example, Ross Garner, *Henry Vaughan: Experience and the Tradition* (Chicago: University of Chicago Press, 1959), p. 26, remarks that while the Augustinian temper of Vaughan and Anglicanism generally was "not uninfluenced by Calvin," still "the official stand of the Anglican church . . . was Thomistic." Similarly, James D. Simmonds, *Masques of God: Form and Theme in the Poetry of Henry Vaughan* (Pittsburgh: University of Pittsburgh Press, 1972), p. 35, maintains that the poet's concept of faith "participates in a central movement of the Reformation and the Counter Reformation." Simmonds suggests, pp. 85–116, that anti-Puritan satire is a crucial element in Vaughan's entire canon. The exception among earlier critics is James Roy King, *Studies in Six 17th Century Writers* (Athens: Ohio University Press, 1966), pp. 121–57, who sees Vaughan's as a "toned down or smoothed out" Calvinism (p. 133). In the most prominent and widely praised book on Vaughan since the advent of Protestant poetics, Jonathan F. S. Post, *Henry Vaughan: The Unfolding Vision* (Princeton: Princeton University Press, 1982), p. 160n, sets out to show "how Vaughan, as a poet, was certainly responsive in his verse to the auditory imagination, a sensitivity with inevitable theological overtones that places him in a line with Protestant Reformers, like Luther and Calvin, who valued the 'inner voice' over visual ceremony."

[120] *Summa Theologia* I. 23. 5 ad 3: "Sed quare hos elegit in gloriam, et illos reprobavit, non habit rationem nisi divinam voluntatem." Question 23 of Part I of the *Summa* is devoted entirely to the issue of predestination, which is also treated in Question 6 of *De Veritate, Quaestiones disputatae* XI. St. Thomas differs from Calvin (and Luther) in denying the arbitrariness of God's judgments and the incompatibility of the grace of predestination and free will. Those who say that God predestines to grace those whom He knows will use grace well "seem to have distinguished between what results from grace, and what results from free will, as if the same thing could not result from both" (*Summa Theologiae* I. 23. 5: "Sed isti videntur distinxisse inter id quod est ex gratia, et id quod est ex libero arbitrio, quasi non possit esse idem ex utroque").

[121] *Decretum de iustificatione*, Cap. 12: "Praedestinationis temerarium praesumptionem cavendam esse," Denzinger, No. 805. See also the Bellarmine quotations supra nn. 13, 14.

[122] Vaughan is quoted throughout from *The Works of Henry Vaughan*, ed. L. C. Martin, 2nd ed. (Oxford: Clarendon Press, 1957).

But the plea for tears, tears that are the gift of God, far from being a distinctive mark of Calvinism, is a commonplace in Counter-Reformation devotional literature. Richard Crashaw, for example, attributes the tears of Mary Magdalene in "The Weeper" to the action of the love of God:

> Twas his well-pointed dart
> That digg'd these wells, and drest this Vine;
> And taught the wounded HEART
> The way into these weeping Eyn.[123]   (stz. xviii)

Similarly, Lope de Vega prays for the grace of penitential tears in his "Soliloquia III":

> dadme licencia, Señor,
> para que, desecho en llanto,
> pueda en vuestro rostro santo
> llorar lágrimas de amor.
>
> .   .   .   .   .
>
> dejadme llorar de amor,
> como otras veces de pena.[124]

[Give me leave, Lord, in order that, dissolved in a flood of weeping, I might be able to cry tears of love before your holy face . . . allow me to weep from love as other times from pain.]

By the same token, there is nothing especially Calvinist about Vaughan's mention of prevenient grace, which Hill seems to find decisive:

> So thou, who didst the work begin
> (For *I till drawn came not to thee*)
> Wilt finish it, and by no sin
> Will thy free mercies hindred be.   (67–70)

We have already taken note of the affirmations of the necessity of prevenient grace in St. Thomas and the Council of Trent's *Decree on Justification*; Vaughan's near contemporary, Pedro Espinosa (1578–1650), puts the same conceptions into devotional verse:

---

[123] Crashaw is quoted throughout from *The Complete Poetry of Richard Crashaw*, ed. George Walton Williams (New York: New York University Press, 1972).

[124] *Obras escogidas*, ed. Federico Carlos Sainz de Robles, 4th ed. (Madrid: Aguilar, 1964), II. 98. See also William Alabaster's "Penitential Sonnets," 14, in which all tears are said to derive from God's "treasure" above, in *The Sonnets of William Alabaster*, ed. G. M. Story and Helen Gardner (London: Oxford University Press, 1959), p. 9. Although he died in the Church of England, Alabaster was a Jesuit when he wrote his poetry.

¿Quién busca a Dios, si Dios no lo convida?
¿Dasme el buscarte? Dame el merecerte;
y, pues tu muerte es precio de mi vida,
sea mi vida precio de tu muerte.

        .   .   .   .   .   .

¿Querrásme desmayado, y no animoso,
o que piense medroso
que para culpas tales
el mar de tus piedades se ha agotado,
o que tu gracia es cosa merecida,
o no eres ya resurrección y vida?
No hay tal: porque no hubiera
santo en la impírea esfera
si sin misericordia lo juzgaras.[125]

[Who seeks God, if God does not invite him? Do you allow me to seek you? Allow me to merit you; and since your death is the price of my life, let my life be the price of your death. . . . Do you want me despondent, and not spirited, or, fearful, should I think that for such faults the sea of your mercy has dried up, or that your grace is something merited, or that you are not resurrection and life? It cannot be: for there would not be a saint in the heavenly sphere if you judged without mercy.]

It cannot be supposed that Espinosa "feels Calvinist predestinarianism on his pulses," but it would be very difficult to distinguish the theological orientation of these lines from what can be inferred from Vaughan's "The Agreement." We must begin by recognizing that, as with Donne and Herbert, something is at stake in Vaughan's poetry besides Reformation polemics, and that his spiritual imagination was not formed in a manner excluding Catholic sources.

When his activities as a translator are taken into account, it becomes obvious that Vaughan was steeped in contemporary Catholic literature from the continent as well as medieval and Patristic writings. Towards the end of *Olor Iscanus*, first published in 1651 but dated 1647, Vaughan gives translations of thirteen of the "meters" of Boethius and seven of the Latin odes of the Polish Jesuit Casimir Sarbiewski (1595–1640). Some of his prose publications of the period when the two versions of *Silex Scintillans* were being written and published (1650, 1655) are especially interesting in this connection. In 1651 Vaughan published a translation of *The Praise and Happiness of the Country Life* by the sixteenth-century Spanish bishop, Antonio de Guevara, and *The Mount of Olives, or Solitary Devotions* (1652) closes with a translation of a work on the state of blessedness by the eleventh-century Archbishop of Canterbury, St. Anselm. *Flores Solitudinis* (1654) comprises translations of two works by the Spanish Jesuit Juan

---

[125] "Salmo de penitencia para alcanzar perdón de los pecados," ll. 23–26, 185–93, *Poesías completas*, ed. Francisco López Estrada (Madrid: Espasa Calpe, 1975), pp. 98, 104.

Eusebio Nieremberg (1595–1658), a translation of a work by the fifth-century bishop of Lyons, St. Eucherius, and a mainly translated *Life of Paulinus of Nola* (354?–431). This list of publications would not enhance the *curriculum vitae* of a man anxious to appear a staunch Protestant in the England of the 1650s.

In addition, it is clear that Vaughan was not oblivious to the tenor of these works. In a preface "To the Reader" he refers favorably to "*Prince* Lewes, *the oldest Son of* Charles *King of* Naples," who gave up all his prospects, including marriage to "*The youthfull Princesse of* Majorica," in order to "*put on the rough and severe* habit *of the* Franciscans." Then he closes the preface to *Flores* with a very thinly veiled attack on the Commonwealth Parliament's Act for the Propagation of the Gospel in Wales (1649/50), which cost both his brother Thomas and his friend Thomas Powell their ecclesiastical livings:

> *All that may bee objected is, that I write*
> *unto thee out of a land of darkenesse, out*
> *of that unfortunate region, where the Inhabitants*
> *sit in the shadow of death: where destruction*
> *passeth for propagation, and a thick black night*
> *for the glorious day-spring.* (*Works*, pp. 216–17)

These works in prose clearly went into forming the mind of the poet, and the Nieremberg texts are of particular interest. As a Spaniard and a Jesuit, he would have been especially obnoxious to English Protestant hostility, and yet Vaughan obviously read him attentively and even imitates specific figures of speech. Barbara Lewalski rightly associates the emblem that opens the 1650 edition of *Silex Scintillans* with "Herbert's synecdoche of the stony heart,"[126] but the language of Vaughan's Latin epigram, as well as the engraving of the heart-shaped flint giving off sparks from the blows of the divine hand, also recalls the Nieremberg text rendered by Vaughan as *Of Temperance and Patience*. In his discussion of the virtue of patience, Nieremberg explains how "It turnes all that is *Evill* into *Good*," making a benefit of afflictions: "Certaine Divine Raies break out of the Soul in adversity, like sparks of fire out of the afflicted *flint*" (*Works*, pp. 248, 249).[127] This passage, plainly echoed in Vaughan's emblem, suggests that the "force" (*vis*) that God uses on the heart of the poet is personal suffering rather than specifically irresistible grace:

---

[126] *Protestant Poetics*, p. 318.

[127] In his commentary on *Authoris (de se) Emblema*, Martin gives the original Latin from Nieremberg, *De Arte Voluntatis* (1639), p. 139: "Subsiliunt è plagis quaedam animo diuinae luces, velut scintillae è silice afflicto." See also M. M. Mahood, *Poetry and Humanism* (London: Jonathan Cape, 1950), p. 266.

Surdus eram, mutusq; Silex: Tus (quanta tuorum
  Cura tibi est!) aliâ das renovare viâ,
Permutas Curam; Jamq; irritatus Amorem
  Posse negas, & vim, Vi, superare paras,
Accedis propior, molemq; & Saxea rumpis
  Pectora, fitq; Caro, Quod fuit ante Lapis.
En lacerum! Coelosq; tuos ardentia tandem
  Fragmenta, & liquidas ex Adamante genas. (5–12)

[I was deaf and dumb, a flint: You (how great is your care for your own!), agree to renewal by another way; you change the cure: and now, angered, you deny that love can do it, and you prepare to conquer force with force; you draw nearer, and you smash the boulder of my rocky breast, and what before was stone becomes flesh. See it shattered! and the fragments at last flashing towards your heavens, my cheeks flowing out of adamant.]

Thus, from the outset, Vaughan sets forth a theme pervasive not only in both parts of *Silex Scintillans*, but also throughout continental ascetic literature exemplified by the work of Nieremberg: that God's mysterious providence brings good out of evil, that suffering is the way of redemption.

The poetry therefore seems consistent with the life: apparently Vaughan's conversion from the vanities of a misspent youth was prompted by tragedy: the untimely death of his brother William in 1648, compounded by the desolation of the Church of England with the triumph of the Puritans in the Civil War. Unlike Milton, Vaughan was the kind of peculiarly Anglican Protestant for whom the Reformation was properly over; he valued much in the Catholic heritage and saw the real threat to religion not in Rome, but in the iconoclasm of the Puritan dissent from the established church. Hence *Silex Scintillans* is in many ways compatible with Catholic devotional traditions; moreover, it flaunts a fair proportion of anti-Puritan assertiveness for a work of piety. Christopher Hill is not unjust in his assessment of Vaughan's grim view of "the vileness and corruption of the mass of mankind"; however, human depravity is exemplified in *Silex Scintillans* not by Rome but by Commonwealth sectarianism:

But here Commission'd by a black self-wil
  The sons the father kil,
The Children Chase the mother, and would heal
  The wounds they give, by crying, zeale.
                    ("The Constellation," 37–40)

I skill not your fine tinsel, and false hair,
                    Your Sorcery
And smooth seducements: I'le not stuff my story
  With your Commonwealth and glory.   ("The Proffer," 33–36)

Vaughan's disapproval of the Puritans is not simply a matter of politics, ecclesiastical organization, or even liturgy: in "White Sunday" he bitterly attacks their conception of grace; their complacent assurance of election; their confidence in the immediate presence of the Holy Spirit; and their presumptuous personal interpretation of Scripture. Vaughan pointedly contrasts the Apostles at the descent of the Spirit on Pentecost with his Puritan contemporaries:

> Can these new lights be like to those,
> These lights of Serpents like the Dove?
> Thou hadst no *gall*, ev'n for thy foes,
> And thy two wings were *Grief* and *Love*.
>
> Though then some boast that fire each day,
> And on Christs coat pin all their shreds;
> Not sparing openly to say,
> His candle shines upon their heads.   (9–16)

Against the sectarian pretense of personal revelation, Vaughan opposes "thy Book" – probably, as Alan Rudrum maintains, the Bible rather than the "book" of nature:[128]

> Yet while some rays of that great light
> Shine here below within thy Book,
> They never shall so blinde my sight
> But I will know which way to look.   (17–20)

Recourse to the Bible is conventional Protestantism, but Vaughan's language suggests certain reservations about the Calvinist heritage of scriptural interpretation. Calvin maintains "that those who are inwardly taught by the Holy Spirit acquiesce implicitly in Scripture; that Scripture, carrying its own evidence along with it, deigns not to submit to proofs and arguments, but owes the full conviction with which we ought to receive it to the testimony of the Spirit." He adds, "Then only, therefore, does Scripture suffice to give a saving knowledge of God when its certainty is founded on the inward persuasion of the Holy Spirit."[129] When Vaughan's "White Sunday" is set against such passages from the *Institutes*, the crisis of the Reformation in seventeenth-century England is adumbrated. Calvin might well have disapproved of much that occurred in "the world turned upside down" of the Civil War; as Christopher Hill shrewdly remarks, "No Calvinist could logically have confidence in democracy: his religion was for the elect, by definition a minority."[130] Nevertheless, Calvin's method of interpreting the Bible by the inner light of the Spirit leads directly to the "new lights" deplored

---

128 Alan Rudrum, ed., *Henry Vaughan: The Complete Poems* (New Haven: Yale University Press, 1976), p. 593.

129 *Institutes* I. vii. 5, i. viii. 13, trans. Beveridge, I. 72, 83.

130 *The World Turned Upside Down: Radical Ideas During the English Revolution* (New York: Viking Press, 1972), p. 128.

by Vaughan, who firmly rejects the concept of unmediated grace and personal assurance on which it is based:

> For though thou doest that great light lock,
> And by this lesser commerce keep:
> Yet by these glances of the flock
> I can discern Wolves from the Sheep.   (21–24)

The Bible is not the plain, self-authenticating book stipulated by Luther and Calvin; it can only be read in "glances of the flock" – a phrase that suggests something like "glimpses of truth afforded the Church." There is, then, contrary to Georgia B. Christopher, a significant incompatibility between Vaughan's conception of "the transforming work of the Spirit" and that of "the dissenters whom he contemns."[131]

The Protestant doctrinal consensus, which forms the basis of Protestant poetics, was never more than an idea – perhaps a goal to be worked toward. In England the unity of the Reformation depended on a fierce nationalism that, during Elizabeth's reign, Philip II allowed to coalesce around fear and loathing of Spain. The Civil War marked the unraveling of that very delicate fabric of unity, and Vaughan is undoubtedly the most intense singer and prophet of the disillusionment. In Vaughan's world, it is as if none of the current conceptions of the Church is satisfactory, a situation recalling the perplexity of the speaker of Donne's Satyre III. The concept of the Church of England as a *via media* between Rome and Geneva, evidently agreeable to Donne and Herbert, was overwhelmed by the mid-century conflict, and, in Vaughan's view, the congregation of elect saints had proven to be a mob of squabbling hypocrites: "Who Saint themselves, they are no *Saints*" ("St. Mary Magdalen," 72). In Louis Martz's poignant phrasing, "It is as though the earthly church had vanished, and man were left to work alone with God."[132] Although this sense of the solitude of the believer is certainly bound up with the spiritual life of the Reformation period, it is not, therefore, an exclusively Protestant phenomenon: it occurs, for example, in the Spanish devotional poets as well as English, and seems as much a result of a general disillusion-ment with the confident zeal of the reformers of the previous century – humanist and Protestant alike – as of a specific theological position. Opposed as their programs finally turned out to be, Luther and Erasmus (for instance)

---

[131] "In Arcadia, Calvin . . .: A Study of Nature in Henry Vaughan," in *Essential Articles for the Study of Henry Vaughan*, ed. Alan Rudrum (Hamden, CT: Shoestring Press, 1987), p. 177.

[132] *The Paradise Within* (New Haven: Yale University Press, 1964), p. 13. See also Thomas O. Calhoun, *Henry Vaughan: The Achievement of Silex Scintillans* (Newark: University of Delaware Press, 1981), esp. pp. 37–57, on the psychological trauma suffered by Vaughan during the Interregnum. Simmonds, p. 98, points out that in "St. Mary Magdalen" Vaughan "hits Calvinism at its crucial center, the doctrine of election." See M. Thomas Hester, "'Ask thy father': ReReading Donne's *Satire III*," *Ben Jonson Journal* 1 (1994) 201–18, for the perplexed anguish of Donne's persona in assessing the fate of the Church.

both entertained, at least some of the time, great expectations for the renewal of social and religious institutions on the basis of a moral and spiritual re-education of individuals, especially of the laity.

In England the devotional poets display a progressive curtailment of expectation, a retreat from the larger social and religious institutions. Donne becomes Dean of St. Paul's Cathedral, one of the most famous preachers in the realm; but Herbert accepts the tiny rural parish of Bemerton, while his friend, Nicholas Ferrar, withdraws into the quasi-monastic community at Little Gidding – an "Arminian Nunnery" in the eyes of hostile Puritans.[133] By Vaughan's time, even the remnant seems scattered, and there is nothing left but to abandon the world and await the Apocalypse. Surveying the ruins in "The Brittish Church," with her "ravish'd looks / Slain flock, and pillag'd fleeces" (16–17), Vaughan retreats to the inward recesses of the soul to nourish "The Seed growing secretly":

> Glory, the Crouds cheap tinsel still
> To what most takes them, is a drudge;
> And they too oft take good for ill,
> And thriving vice for virtue judge.   (37–40)
>
> .   .   .   .
>
> Then bless thy secret growth, nor catch
> At noise, but thrive unseen and dumb;
> Keep clean, bear fruit, earn life and watch
> Till the white winged Reapers come!   (45–48)

The Spanish poet Quevedo evinces the same disillusion with worldly glories:

> Miré los muros de la patria mía,
> si un tiempo fuertes, ya desmoronados,
> de la carrera de la edad cansados,
> por quien caduca ya su valentía.[134]
>
> [I saw the walls of my fatherland, if once strong, now fallen in decay, weary from the race of time, which now enfeebles their gallantry.]

---

[133] Stewart, *George Herbert*, p. 26.

[134] *Heráclito cristiano* XVII, 1–4, *Obras completas* I, 31. *Soledad* (solitude) and *desengaño* (disillusion) are topoi in the Spanish literature of the Renaissance. On the former see Karl Vossler, *Poesie der Einsamkeit in Spanien*, 2nd ed. (München: C. H. Beck'sche Verlagsbuch-handlung, 1950); on the latter see (among others) Otis H. Green, *Spain and the Western Tradition* (Madison: University of Wisconsin Press, 1966), IV, 43–76. In French poetry of the period, the theme of disillusionment with the world and the power of mortality is forcefully expressed in the devotional sonnets of Jean-Baptiste Chassignet (1578?–1635?), and the sense of disillusion and the attraction of solitude is a pervasive theme in secular terms in the poetry of Théopile de Viau (1590–1626) and Antoine-Girard de Saint-Amant (1594–1661). Perhaps the best evidence for the importance of the theme of alienation and withdrawal from a hostile world in the seventeenth century is the continuing popularity

Coming amid the penitential verse of the *Heráclito cristiano,* these lines intimate a socio-political context for Quevedo's sense of personal sin.

With a similar sense of disillusionment, Vaughan rejects the false joy of this world for the "solitary years":

> As leafs in Bowers
> Whisper their hours,
> And Hermit-wells
> Drop in their Cells.   ("Joy," 23–26)

Here Vaughan recalls Pedro Espinosa, who for a time actually took up the life of a hermit.[135] Both poets seek the grace of God as a new relationship with Him, entailing a radical transformation of their lives. Vaughan's "Love-sick" is a spirited manifestation of the paradox of grace, the sense of utter human desolation and worthlessness that earnestly demand, nonetheless, God's love:

> O come and rend,
> Or bow the heavens! Lord bow them and descend,
> And at thy presence make these mountains flow,
> These mountains of cold Ice in me! Thou art
> Refining fire, o then refine my heart,
> My foul, foul heart! Thou art immortal heat,
> Heat motion gives; Then warm it, till it beat,
> So beat for thee, till thou in mercy hear,
> So hear that thou must open: open to
> A sinfull wretch, A wretch that caused thy woe,
> Thy woe, who caus'd his weal; so far his weal
> That thou forgott'st thine own, for thou didst seal
> Mine with thy blood, thy blood which makes thee mine,
> Mine ever, ever; And me ever thine.   (9–22)

To William Halewood this passage is "radically Augustinian," and it is, providing "Augustinian" does not signify "Protestant."[136] The urgency of the plea, the excited thirst for the divine presence, is no discovery of the Reformation. In a "Psalm asking for the coming of God to the Soul of the poet," Pedro Espinosa prays with the same fervor as Vaughan and in similar metaphors:

---

throughout the period of *De constantia libri duo* (1584) by the Flemish humanist, Justus Lipsius (1547–1606), with its interlude of garden solitude at the beginning of Book II. Post, *Henry Vaughan,* pp. 25–44, discusses "the Disenchanted Muse" of *Olor Iscanus,* but does not apply the concept to *Silex Scintillans.*

[135] Francisco López Estrada, "Prólogo," *Poesías completas,* p. xiv.

[136] *The Poetry of Grace,* p. 138. For Halewood's association between Augustine and the Reformation, see pp. 16–17, 36–37.

him to be *made* again "one selfsame spirit" with divinity (*contigo un mismo espíritu*). So he asks to be "inundated" and "hidden" in the flames of God's love (*anégame y escóndeme en tus llamas*). The human sinner, his life slipping through his hands as he is distracted by worldly and fleshly temptations, can only find identity and purpose in the presence of God's being. He must learn, with Herbert in "The Holdfast" (12), "That all things were more ours by being his."

There is no more moving account of the experience of grace in *Silex Scintillans* than "The Night." Halewood sees in the "silence" of this poem an "almost compulsively repeated image of reconciliation between God and man," and Lewalski regards it as characteristic of the Protestant poet's identification with "certain New Testament types of his Christian pilgrimage" (here Nicodemus).[139] But there is no poem by Vaughan that shares more with the devotional and mystical poetry of Counter-Reformation Spain.[140] For Vaughan, as for the Spaniards, the night is a symbol for the dark recesses of the soul, where the beloved Spouse is sought in secret:

> O who will tell me, where
> He found thee at that dead and silent hour!
> What hallow'd solitary ground did bear
>   So rare a flower,
>   Within whose sacred leafs did lie
> The fulness of the Deity.   (13–18)
>
>   .   .   .   .   .   .
>
>   Dear night! this worlds defeat;
> The stop to busie fools; cares check and curb;
> The day of Spirits; my souls calm retreat
>   Which none disturb!
> *Christs* progress, and his prayer time;
> The hours to which high Heaven doth chime.   (25–30)
>
>   .   .   .   .   .   .
>
>   There is in God (some say)
> A deep, but dazling darkness; As men here
> Say it is late and dusky, because they
>   See not all clear;
>   O for that night! where I in him
> Might live invisible and dim.   (49–54)

[139] *The Poetry of Grace*, p. 126; *Protestant Poetics*, p. 330.

[140] Ross Garner, *Henry Vaughan*, pp. 55–59, 143, 159–60, draws comparisons between Vaughan's poems, including "The Night," and the mystical theology of San Juan de la Cruz, but he does not consider the saint's poetry. Rudrum's commentary on "The Night," *Complete Poems*, p. 628, questions efforts to align the poem with Calvinism by observing that, since the Anglican service of his beloved "Brittish Church" was illegal when the poem was published, the disparagement of worship in buildings of "carv'd stone" was in all likelihood an attack on the Puritans, who had all the buildings, rather than on Anglican ritual.

The obvious and ultimate source for the doctrine of this poem – especially the last stanza – is the negative theology of Dionysius the Areopagite, an author quoted respectfully almost 1700 times by St. Thomas Aquinas, but dismissed by Luther as "pernicious" and "more of a Platonist than a Christian."[141] The poetic feeling of the passage, however, and the evocation of a secret, enchanted nocturnal landscape of the spirit, is strikingly reminiscent of the "dark night of the soul" depicted by San Juan de la Cruz:

> 1. En una noche escura,
> con ansias, en amores inflamada,
> ¡oh dichosa ventura!,
> salí sin ser notada,
> estando ya mi casa sosegada;
> 2. a escuras y segura
> por la secreta escala, disfrazada,
> ¡oh dichosa ventura!,
> a escuras y en celada,
> estando ya mi casa sosegada;
> 3. en la noche dichosa,
> en secreto, que nadie me veía
> ni yo miraba cosa,
> sin otra luz y guía
> sino la que en el corazón ardía.
> 4. Aquésta me guiaba
> más cierto que la luz de mediodía
> a donde me esperaba
> quien yo bien me sabía,
> en parte donde nadie parecía.
> 5. ¡Oh noche que guiaste!,
> ¡oh noche amable más que el alborada,
> ¡oh noche que juntaste
> Amado con amada,
> amada en el amado transformada![142]

[1. On a dark night, anxious, inflamed with love, – oh joyful venture! – I went out unnoticed, my house now being hushed; 2. in darkness and secure by the secret staircase, disguised, – oh joyful venture! – in darkness and concealed, my house now being hushed; 3. in the joyful night, in secret, so that no one saw me and I saw not a thing, without any other light and guide save what was burning in my heart. 4. That guided me more surely than the light of noon to where he was awaiting me whom well I know, in a place where no one appeared. 5. Oh night that guided! oh night dearer than the dawn! oh night that joined the Lover with beloved, beloved in the Lover transformed!]

---

[141] Pieper, *Guide to St. Thomas Aquinas*, p. 45; *Pagan Servitude of the Church*, Dillenberger, p. 343.
[142] "Canciones del alma," *Vida y obras*, p. 539.

Vaughan's night, like San Juan's, is silent and secret – the dark, hidden place where God awaits those who seek Him. Vaughan's "deep, but dazling darkness" is the counterpart to San Juan's light burning in the heart, which is a surer guide than the light of noon and dearer than the dawn. Like San Juan, whom the night "joined" (*juntaste*) to God in mystical marriage, Vaughan longs for "that night" where he "might live invisible and dim" in God – even as San Juan is "disguised" (*disfrazada*) and "concealed" (*celada*). Above all, there is in the work of both poets the creation of a mysterious spiritual setting in which the inward work of grace is intimated.

Clearly, Jonathan Post oversimplifies the poem by calling it "a response to the invading darkness rather than an exercise in mystical ascent"; it is the inner darkness of mystical night that provides refuge from the apocalyptic darkness of the Interregnum. Post himself furnishes a fine explanation of how Vaughan is able "to create a still point in the center of the poem" and evoke "the timeless rediscovery of Christ in the present life." Hence Vaughan's "reluctance to dissolve into rapture" in no way diminishes the mystical resonance of his "timeless vision."[143] Mysticism's definitive characteristic is not ecstatic passion, but rather the apprehension through grace of God's timeless presence.

Such depictions of the experience of grace as an obscure gleam in the stillness of the night are antithetical to a conception of grace as irresistible, and they are necessary to balance images of God's love as violent, consuming fire. It is necessary that the images of grace seem to contradict one another in order to suggest that none of them is definitive. What the poems finally suggest is an experience of grace that is concrete and undeniable, but inaccessible to a finished conceptual formulation. Somehow there is space within the gratuitous gift of salvation for choice, or, as St. Thomas puts it, an act can be the result both of grace and free will. For Vaughan, it is man's need to listen to "His still, soft call" during "loud, evil days":

> God's silent, searching flight:
> When my Lords head is fill'd with dew, and all
> His locks are wet with the clear drops of night;
>   His still, soft call;
>   His knocking time; The souls dumb watch,
> When Spirits their fair kinred catch.
>
>   Were all my loud, evil days
> Calm and unhaunted as is thy dark Tent,
> Whose peace but by some *Angels* wing or voice
>   Is seldom rent;
>   Then I in Heaven all the long year
> Would keep, and never wander here. (31–42)

---

[143] Post, *Henry Vaughan*, pp. 201, 206, 207.

A sonnet by Lope de Vega adapts the same image of the calling, knocking Bridegroom from Canticles 5: 2 to represent the mysterious relationship between grace and free will:

> ¿Qué tengo yo, que mi amistad procuras?
> ¿Qué interés se te sigue, Jesús mío,
> que a mi puerta cubierto de rocío
> pasas las noches del invierno escuras?
>
> ¡Oh cuánto fueron mis entrañas duras,
> pues no te abrí. ¡Qué extraño desvarío
> si de mi ingratitud el hielo frío
> secó las llagas de tus plantas puras!
>
> ¡Cuántas veces el Ángel me decía:
> "Alma, asómate agora a la ventana,
> verás con cuánto amor llamar porfía"!
>
> ¡Y cuántas, hermosura soberana,
> "Mañana le abriremos," respondía,
> para lo mismo responder mañana![144]

> [What do I have, that you attempt my friendship? What benefit follows for you, my Jesus, that at my door covered with dew you pass the dark winter nights? Oh how hard were my bowels, since I did not open to you! What strange delirium, if with my ingratitude the cold frost dried the wounds in your pure soles! How many times the angel said to me, "Soul, lean out the window now, and you will see with what love he persists in calling!" And how often, sovereign beauty, I answered, "Tomorrow I shall open to him," only to answer the same tomorrow!]

In an ironic fashion Lope's perverse persona affords an unexpected insight into the deepest mystery of grace. The redemption is analogous to the creation: in the latter, God the Creator, whose name is I AM (Exod. 3: 14), who is being itself, communicates that being to nothingness and yet affords his creatures an existence and identity of their own. In the redemption of guilty human beings, God freely confers his goodness and integrity where before was only the moral and spiritual disorder of sin, and yet this work of regeneration renews that individual person: precisely by the infusion of the human mind with grace, that mind becomes free and lives as a complete person. The personae of Vaughan's "The Night" and of Lope de Vega's sonnet, listening to the call of Christ out of the quiet dark, are confronted by the challenge of awakening, of *opening*, to the fearful freedom of *more* being, not less. In order to understand devotional poetry, it is necessary to reflect upon the notion of the *salvation of the soul*. The soul is the identity of the rational self; to *save* it can only mean the restoration of its rationality, that is,

---

[144] *Rimas sacras* XVIII, in *Lope de Vega: Obras poéticas*, ed. José Manuel Blecua (Barcelona: Editorial Planeta, 1969), I. 324–25.

of its power of choice and its existence within the being and goodness bestowed by God, yet distinct from Him. The paradoxical operation of grace is not merely a central issue of the Reformation, it is among the deepest perennial spiritual concerns. The complexities of this paradox are reflected in both versions of what is probably Richard Crashaw's last poem, and especially in the tension between the two versions.

iv

Crashaw is not ordinarily credited with either great force of character or of intellect: even the decisive event of his life, his conversion to Catholicism, is not infrequently attributed to a combination of sentiment and historical circumstance: "Had the Civil War not rudely terminated an epoch," Austin Warren opines, "Crashaw would probably have died an Anglican."[145] *A Letter to the Countess of Denbigh*, however, which provides a kind of negative evidence for Warren by its neglect of polemical apologetics, obliquely suggests that Crashaw had thought a good deal about his choice. Given the importance of the theme of grace among the devotional poets of the seventeenth century, it cannot be supposed that Crashaw was unaware of the theological context of his verse epistle. What is more, the treatment of the theme in this poem shows that he realized fully the human consequences of a world devoid of grace – of a world stripped of meaning and purpose, subjected to the blind forces of history.

The poem is a late one, first appearing posthumously in *Carmen Deo Nostro* (Paris, 1652) and subsequently in a pamphlet by itself (London, probably 1653).[146] In both versions the poem is an appeal to Crashaw's patroness, Susan Villiers, Countess of Denbigh, to save her soul by following him into the Catholic Church – advice that she took only in 1651, two years after the poet's death and but one before her own.[147] Unlike most of Crashaw's poems which are devotional in character, *A Letter* is an argument rather than a celebration. Although the poet does not expound Catholic dogma to the Countess, the way in which he alters his expostulation in the second version reveals that Crashaw possessed a clear understanding of the

---

[145] *Richard Crashaw: A Study in Baroque Sensibility* (1939; rpt. Ann Arbor: University of Michigan Press, 1957), p. 50. See also Itrat-Husain, *The Mystical Elements in the Metaphysical Poets* (Edinburgh: Oliver & Boyd, 1948), p. 162; and Thomas F. Healy, *Richard Crashaw* (Leiden: E. J. Brill, 1986), pp. 2ff, 155–57, passim.

[146] The actual date of the pamphlet is not absolutely certain, since the date "1653" is only handwritten on the title page of the unique copy in the British Library. See L. C. Martin, ed., *The Poems English, Latin and Greek of Richard Crashaw*, 2nd ed. (Oxford: Clarendon Press, 1957), p. xlix.

[147] Sister of the assassinated Duke of Buckingham, the Countess of Denbigh followed Queen Henrietta Maria to Paris during the Civil War, where Crashaw was probably presented to her. See Warren, *Richard Crashaw*, pp. 54–55.

69

fundamental theological issue dividing the Lutheran/Calvinist reformers from Rome, namely, the relation between human free will and divine grace. The nature of Crashaw's revision suggests that the purpose of the second version was to render a more cogent metaphorical realization of the Catholic faith proffered to the Countess.[148] Arno Esch remarks that the revision of *A Letter to the Countess of Denbigh* reduces the erotic imagery and personal focus of the first version and clarifies the argument.[149] It is this alteration in the metaphorical structure and tone of the poem that discloses the dynamic of grace.

The first twenty-six lines of the two versions contain virtually the same material; apart from some slight, though not wholly insignificant verbal alterations,[150] the only difference lies in the order of the lines. A comparison of the following passages (7–20) shows that a series of alternating questions and exclamations in the *Carmen Deo Nostro* rendition of the poem, which suggest a mood of puzzled anxiety in the speaker, give way to a stern and more confident tone in the pamphlet:

> **1652 version** (*Carmen Deo Nostro*)
>
> Say, lingering fair! why comes the birth
> Of your brave soul so slowly forth?
> Plead your pretences (o you strong
> In weaknes) why you choose so long
> In labor of your selfe to ly,
> Nor daring quite to live nor dy?
> Ah linger not, lov'd soul! a slow
> And late consent was a long no,
> Who grants at last, long time tryd
> And did his best to have deny'd.
> What magick bolts, what mystick Barres
> Maintain the will in these strange warres!
> What fatall, yet fantastick, bands
> Keep The free Heart from it's own hands!

---

[148] Richard Strier, "Crashaw's Other Voice," *SEL* 9 (1969) 144, terms *A Letter* "thoroughly anti-Calvinist"; but he does not see that the second version is *more* "thoroughly anti-Calvinist" (and more intelligently so) and dismisses it as "more characteristic" and "inferior and far less interesting" (p. 136, n. 3). Paul A. Parrish, *Richard Crashaw*, Twayne's English Authors Series No. 299 (Boston: G. K. Hall, 1980), pp. 108–09, also prefers the first version, but he thinks *it* "more typical."

[149] *Englische Religiöse Lyrik des 17. Jahrhunderts* (Tübingen, 1955), p. 134.

[150] For example, "intreated" becomes "Beseiged" (1), emphasizing the paradox of a heart that is outside the "Gate of Blisse" (2) yet subject to siege.

1653 revision

Ah! linger not, lov'd Soul; A slow
And late Consent was a long No.
Who grants at last, a great while try'de
And did his best to have Deny'de.
What Magick-Bolts, what mystick Barrs
Maintain the Will in these strange Warrs?
What Fatall, yet fantastick, Bands
Keep the free Heart from his own Hands?
Say, lingring Fair, why comes the Birth
Of your brave Soul so slowly forth?
Plead your Pretences, (O you strong
In weaknesse) why you chuse so long
In Labour of your self to ly,
Not daring quite to Live nor Die.

In the second version Crashaw moves the general religious principle ("A slow / And late Consent"), which begins in line thirteen of the 1652 version, up to line seven. All the questions in the rearranged passage are thus bunched together as an interrogation, directed almost accusingly at the Countess in the light of the general command ("linger not"), whose force is strengthened by its more prominent position at the beginning of the passage. Then there is a crucial shift, not only in arrangement, but also in punctuation; lines nine through to twelve in the early form of the poem are changed from a diffident question to a firm imperative. Coming at the end of a series of three questions in the 1653 version, these lines (17–20) now imply that the Countess has no answer for the questions; she can *only* "Plead . . . pretences."

The rearrangement of lines seven through to twenty radically alters the tone of the striking simile of the frozen waters that follows (21–26, 1652 and 1653). In the first version the image creates a mood of bewildered melancholy for the nymphs' (and the Countess') "sad self-captivity." The only significant verbal alteration, the change of "sad" to "cold," makes the passage more concrete and more precise, since it identifies the ice with the state of the Countess' religious affections rather than with the speaker's feelings about them. Moreover, "sad" could be a term of approval in the seventeenth century, meaning "steady," "firm," or "constant," – an understanding that Crashaw would not wish to encourage. Instead of an expression of uncertainty, the simile becomes an explanation, and the regret is tinged with disapproval. Whatever "pretences" the Countess may "plead," the "Magick-Bolts" and "mystick Barrs" that keep her outside the "Gate of Blisse" – the Catholic Church – are lodged in the coldness of her own heart:

> So when the Year takes cold we see
> Poor Waters their own Prisoners be:
> Fetter'd and lock'd up fast they lie
> In a cold self-captivity.
> Th'astonish'd Nymphs their Floud's strange Fate deplore,
> To find themselves their own severer Shoar. (1653, 21–26)

The effect of the changes in the first twenty-six lines of *A Letter* is to strengthen the emphasis of the poem on the problem of the Countess' will, to clarify the theme that the decision to accept or reject grace is finally hers. These modifications at the beginning of the poem may seem somewhat subtle, even obscure, but those that follow are quite drastic. In *Carmen Deo Nostro* Crashaw abruptly turns away from the Countess in line twenty-seven and directly addresses Our Savior (as "All mighty LOVE"):

> Thou that alone canst thaw this cold,
> And fetch the heart from it's strong Hold;
> Allmighty LOVE! end this long warr,
> And of a meteor make a starr.
> O fix this fair INDEFINITE.
> And 'mongst thy shafts of soveraign light
> Choose out that sure decisive dart
> Which has the Key of this close heart,
> Knowes all the corners of't, and can controul
> The self-shutt cabinet of an unsearcht soul. (1652, 27–36)

Thus, in the 1652 version, Christ Himself is called upon to solve the problem, *to make the decision for* the "irresolute" noblewoman. When, in the middle of a sentence, Crashaw again addresses the Countess, he resorts to the imagery of wounds and darts that has served him in his poetic celebrations of the mystical raptures of Santa Teresa:

> Unfold at length, unfold fair flowre
> And use the season of love's showre,
> Meet his well-meaning Wounds, wise heart!
> And hast to drink the wholesome dart.
> That healing shaft, which heavn till now
> Hath in love's quiver hid for you. (1652, 43–48)

A deep compulsion must have been required to induce Crashaw to drop these lines from the later version of the poem. Not only is their beauty impressive, but they also seem an appropriate culmination to a conventional development of imagery in seventeenth-century devotional poetry. The hard, cold, resisting heart is a familiar motif in Herbert and Vaughan as well as various Spanish contemporaries, and the prayer that this cold heart be melted in the fire of divine love seems parallel to Vaughan's "Love-sick." Donne's Holy Sonnet 10 ("Batter my heart") would, likewise, seem to provide the perfect brief model for the prayer that the divine lover end the siege of the reluctant heart with a surge of divine passion. Santa Teresa's vision, recounted in the twenty-ninth chapter of her autobiography, in which a seraph pierces her heart with a fiery spear,[151] obviously made a deep and lasting impression on Crashaw, and he adapted it to good effect in his poems honoring her. In *A Letter*, however, Crashaw seems to have fallen into the imagery of mysticism almost out of habit. He must have sensed that, in revising the poem, distinctions had to be made. He was not praying for himself, or even for the Countess, but rather persuading her: a radically different rhetorical situation. It was hardly appropriate for him to urge the raptures of mystical union on a woman who had not even entered the Church. There would have been, moreover, a growing recognition of levels of sanctity, foregrounded by his new Catholic perspective: after years of prayer and mortification, the experience of Santa Teresa might aptly be described in terms of divinely erotic passion, but the Countess was yet to give the minimum affirmative response to the courtship of Christ.

Crashaw's revision suggests a studied (although very irenic) critique of the language and perceptions of his fellow poets, as well as of his own original version. Granted that our salvation comes by grace, the poet seems to say, it must still be we ourselves who are saved; that is, the integrity of the rational soul must be poised beside the predestination folded within divine providence. It therefore follows that there must be a confrontation between two entities, or rather between Being and a being. In facing this question Crashaw raises an issue that engages the attention of current critical theory. It is just this breakthrough, this sure recognition of the presence of God (of anything, really), that is in principle denied by postmodernism. "There never was any perception," Jacques Derrida curtly avers, and he condemns us all to epistemological blindness: "And contrary to what phenomenology – which is always the phenomenology of perception – has tried to make us believe, contrary to what our desire cannot fail to be tempted into believing, the thing itself always escapes."[152] Crashaw and most of his contemporaries (Descartes and his followers might be an exception) would agree in rejecting any absolutizing of human consciousness. But for Crashaw, the slipperiness of the thing itself is an important facet of what is disclosed by its hiddenness within phenomena, as both the presence and absence of a subatomic particle are disclosed by the trace of light in a cloud chamber. Derrida's suspicion can be countered by von Balthasar's faith:

> Along with the seen surface of the manifestation there is perceived the non-manifested depth; it is only this which lends the phenomenon of the beautiful its enrapturing and overwhelming character, just as it is only this that insures the truth and goodness of the existent.[153]

[151] *Obras completas*, p. 131.   [152] *Speech and Phenomena*, pp. 103, 104.
[153] *The Glory of the Lord*, I. 442.

The reality of grace can only be glimpsed in the space among contrary patterns of imagery. Hence Crashaw, like Wallace Stevens, writes "Two Versions of the Same Poem," each a striving to track "the difficult images of possible shapes" between the lines of verse:

> The human ocean beats against this rock
> Of earth, rises against it, tide by tide,
> Continually.[154]

In the London pamphlet, Crashaw turns to an alternate strain of imagery from the poetry of grace. Instead of apostrophizing "allmighty LOVE," the poet insistently addresses the hesitant lady, pointing out that love that shaped the universe is everywhere manifest in it[155] and has provided ample means of salvation if she will but see and accept it. "Perception" is both moved *by* and is the acknowledgment *of* grace:

> Love, that lends haste to heaviest things,
> In you alone hath lost his wings.
> Look round and read the World's wide face,
> The field of Nature or of Grace;
> Where can you fix, to find Excuse
> Or Pattern for the Pace you use?   (1653, 27–32)

Indispensable to these lines is the assumption that "Nature" and "Grace" act in harmony to issue the same message concerning God who is Love; that is, if we "reade" with care the book of Creation ("the World's wide face"), the Scriptural revelation is reiterated. The Countess is called upon to perceive or "reade" the contrast between the *natural* behavior of the lower creatures and her own *unnatural* lack of gratitude (or graciousness). The image of the frozen river of the Countess' heart is recalled with additional force in the subsequent evocation of flowing waters:

> Both Winds and Waters urge their way,
> And murmure if they meet a stay,
> Mark how the curl'd Waves work and wind,
> All hating to be left behind.
> Each bigge with businesse thrusts the other,
> And seems to say, Make haste, my Brother.   (1653, 39–44)

---

[154] *The Collected Poems of Wallace Stevens* (New York: Alfred Knopf, 1954), p. 334. See Harold Bloom, *Wallace Stevens: The Poems of Our Climate* (Ithaca, NY: Cornell University Press, 1977), p. 343, for the rock "made equal to, but not the same as, the Christian emblem of truth."

[155] Cf. the last line of Dante Alighieri, *Divina Commedia*, ed. C. H. Grandgent, rev. Charles S. Singleton (Cambridge: Harvard University Press, 1972), p. 930: "l'amor che move il sole e l'altre stelle."

The experience of grace – the perception of God's redemptive presence – is possible not in any one set of signifiers but in the interstitial space of a network of signifiers.

For the invocation of Love in the 1652 version, Crashaw substitutes an account of Love's action in the World, in nature (27–56). But for fallen man it is impossible to follow the universal pattern; man lacks the capacity to save himself in his own corrupt nature without the addition of God's grace – on this point Calvin and Luther are in agreement with the Tridentine decree on justification. Following the latter, Crashaw introduces a complicating factor: while other creatures are "Suitours" to God, "Man alone is wo'ed, / Tediously wo'ed, and hardly wone" (58–59). The very figure of wooing implies a final assent lying within the human will: some freedom of will is precisely what grace restores. Therefore, instead of an invitation to irresistible rapture, as in the earlier text, Crashaw shames the Countess by contrasting her own hesitancy with the eager, persistent love of Christ, as well as the harmonious movement of other creatures. To be sure, erotic metaphors for the relationship between the soul and Christ are not wholly abandoned; however, in the 1653 *Letter*, Christ is no longer depicted as a Cupid with unerring darts – a virtual ravisher – but as a humble, oft-rejected suitor:

> When love of Us call'd Him to see
> If wee'd vouchsafe his company,
> He left his Father's Court, and came
> Lightly as a Lambent Flame,
> Leaping upon the Hills, to be
> The Humble King of You and Me.
> Nor can the cares of his whole Crown
> (When one poor Sigh sends for him down)
> Detain him, but he leaves behind
> The late wings of the lazy Wind,
> Spurns the tame Laws of Time and Place,
> And breaks through all ten Heav'ns to our embrace.
>
> (1653, 67–78)

Crashaw develops an extraordinarily complex metaphorical pattern in this poem: in sacramental fashion natural analogies are evoked that signify the perfection of nature by grace, the presence of the Savior in the world. But also acknowledged is the final inadequacy of any particular form of signification, the defectiveness of any analogy to define the redemptive presence that "Spurns the tame Laws of Time and Place." Crashaw seems to have known – always already – what the deconstructionists would tell us: signification can only be generated by differences, and signifiers necessarily indicate the absence of what they signify. Yet Crashaw would maintain, contrary to Derrida, that it is only the divine presence, the fullness of Being, that makes difference possible in the first place: only the presence of the

Creator – even if deferred or displaced – gives creatures a ground on which to enact their differences.[156]

Now the paradoxical relation between grace and nature, especially when analogy moves into sacrament, suffers resistance in a strictly Calvinist or Lutheran theology, as A. S. P. Woodhouse maintains.[157] Nevertheless, the delicate balance emerges frequently in English Protestant devotional poetry. Vaughan constantly refers to the book of nature as well as Scripture to depict the movement of grace, and the figure of Christ as patient wooer appears in his "The Night" as well as in Crashaw and Lope de Vega. Herbert likewise portrays the effects of original sin in man's alienation from nature and deploys images of natural order as analogies for the operation of grace. When he writes, "I am no link of thy great chain," in "Employment (I)" (21), Herbert laments the estrangement of sin in terms that would be acknowledged by Christian poets of every era, and he closes with a plea for restoration: "Lord place me in thy consort; give one strain / To my poore reed" (23–24). Given the context, Halewood's assertion that Herbert here affirms a Calvinist view in which (human) nature and grace are divided by an impassible gulf is rather simplistic: "the great chain concept is explicitly rejected for man in Herbert's poem; humans are omitted from the ordered associations of creation."[158] The "great chain" is not "rejected for man"; it is man who, by sin original and actual, has rejected his place in the chain.

For this reason Herbert uses recovery of a right understanding of, and harmony with, nature as a symbol of grace. There is no better example than "Mattens," which also yields an enchanting picture of Christ as a patient, long-suffering wooer offering grace that pleads rather than compels:

---

[156] Cf. Derrida, "Differance," in *Speech and Phenomena*, pp. 134–35: "Not only is differance irreducible to every ontological or theological – onto-theological – reappropriation, but it opens up the very space in which onto-theology – philosophy – produces its system and its history. It thus encompasses and irrevocably surpasses onto-theology or philosophy." Cf., however, von Balthasar, *The Glory of the Lord* I. 448: "Nothing is more incomprehensible than this dissection of the one into individual and generic unity: it is precisely in this not-being-one of both that true unity reveals and conceals itself. Above all, it is the not-being-one which separates beings and human existence that, as the most extreme enigma of Being itself, points beyond itself to identity."

[157] "Nature and Grace in *The Faerie Queene*," in *Elizabethan Poetry: Modern Essays in Criticism*, ed. Paul Alpers (New York: Oxford University Press, 1967), p. 364.

[158] *The Poetry of Grace*, pp. 108–09. Strier, *Love Known*, pp. 166–73, explicitly endorses the sentence quoted from Halewood and develops the thesis at great length.

> My God, what is a heart,
>   That thou shouldst it so eye, and wooe,
> Powring upon it all thy art,
>   As if that thou hadst nothing els to do?
>   Indeed mans whole estate
>   Amounts (and richly) to serve thee:
>   He did not heav'n and earth create,
> Yet studies them, not him by whom they be.   (9–16)

This is Crashaw's Christ, "Leaping upon the Hills, to be / The Humble King of You and Me"; it is Vaughan's and Lope de Vega's Christ, "His locks wet with dew, calling softly out of the darkness." The poem closes appropriately with the speaker beseeching God to grant him the grace to respond fittingly to the grace of divine love – to let the fresh light of dawn, when he says his morning prayers, lead him to the divine Light:

> Teach me thy love to know;
>   That this new light, which now I see,
>   May both the work and workman show:
> Then by a sunne-beam I will climbe to thee.   (17–20)

Implicit in "Mattens" is Herbert's confidence that the *vestigia Dei* in the creation, the order and beauty of the natural world, can lead man to God if he will but regard the "workman" as well as the "work." This is, of course, a recurrent theme in *The Temple*, as evidenced by many other poems such as "Providence" and "The Flower."

The significance of Herbert's affirmation of the religious significance of the creatures can be gauged by contrast with such a poem as "Contemplations" by the American Puritan, Anne Bradstreet. Ostensibly a meditation on the loveliness and design of the universe, this poem in effect repudiates the meaningfulness of the realm of creatures in man's spiritual life and affirms the gulf between nature and grace in Calvin's teaching. The poet begins by musing on the beauty of an autumn evening: "If so much excellence abide below, / How excellent is he that dwells on high?" (9–10). But as her thoughts continue to wander, she recalls that the Garden of Eden was far more lovely than earth is now, but that Adam, nevertheless, there yielded to temptation and became "a naked thral" (74). She then begins to reflect upon the lack of correspondence between man and the rest of creation:

> When I behold the heavens as in their prime,
> And then the earth (though old) still clad in green,
> The stones and trees, insensible of time,
> Nor age nor wrinkle on their front are seen;
> If winter come, and greenness then do fade,
> A Spring returns, and they more youthful made;
> But man grows old, lies down, remains where once he's laid.   (120–26)

This pagan, almost Catullan, reflection on the oblivion of mortality is not the final word. Bradstreet questions whether to "praise the heavens, the trees, the earth" (134), since they are all fated to ultimate destruction while man "was made for endless immortality" (140). The poem concludes with the thought that the world and all man's worldly works are subject to "Time the fatal wrack of mortal things, / . . . But he whose name is grav'd in the white stone / Shall last and shine when all of these are gone" (225, 231–32).[159] The difference is subtle, mostly a matter of tone, but not therefore insignificant: while Herbert suggests that the sunbeam "May both the work and workman show," to lead him to God, Bradstreet implies a complete irrelevance of the natural creatures, and man's own nature, to his supernatural end. Bradstreet, not Herbert, gives us Protestant poetics with a vengeance: "In vain for us, therefore, does Creation exhibit so many bright lamps lighted up to show forth the glory of its Author," Calvin asserts, and even Scripture will only "suffice to give a saving knowledge of God when its certainty is founded on the inward persuasion of the Holy Spirit."[160] The only meaningful reality in this vision of the human condition is within: the subjective transaction of unmediated, irresistible grace. External nature is a meaningless blank, which in two centuries will become the horrible whiteness of the whale, the impenetrable mask,[161] and in another century the chaotic dance of signifiers:

> The so-called "thing itself" is always already a *representamen* shielded from the simplicity of intuitive evidence. The *representamen* functions only by giving rise to an *interpretant* that itself becomes a sign and so on to infinity. The self-identity of the signified conceals itself unceasingly and is always on the move.[162]

If the larger natural creation and the restoration of fallen human nature are irrelevant to the operation of grace, if nature is in fact displaced rather than perfected by grace, then the freedom of the human will is finally meaningless because the terms it has to work with are meaningless.

The entire devotional tradition of Christendom is based upon the validity of the "intuitive evidence," which Calvin, four centuries before Derrida, rejects. Devotional poetry is, then, Thomist insofar as Thomism is, in Chesterton's memorable phrase, "the philosophy of common sense," the philosophy of a man who "immediately recognized a real quality in things; and afterwards resisted all the disintegrating doubts arising from the nature of those things."[163] It is within this sense of reality that Crashaw can close his

---

[159] *The Complete Works of Anne Bradstreet*, ed. Joseph R. McElrath, Jr., and Allan P. Robb (Boston: G. K. Hall, 1981), pp. 167–74.

[160] *Institutes* I. v. 14; I. viii. 13 (I. 62, 83).

[161] See *Moby-Dick*, Chapter 42, "The Whiteness of the Whale."

[162] Jacques Derrida, *Of Grammatology*, trans. Gayatri Chakravorty Spivak (Baltimore: Johns Hopkins University Press, 1976), p. 49.

[163] *Saint Thomas Aquinas: "The Dumb Ox"* (1933; rpt. New York: Doubleday Image, 1956), pp. 145, 177–78.

Letter to the Countess of Denbigh with an emphasis on the freedom of the will. The parallels with Donne's "Batter my heart" are striking since both poems compare the soul to a walled city under siege and both develop an erotic analogy of the soul's relation to God. In this particular poem, however, Donne expresses a comparatively Calvinist intonation, less in the plea for Christ to use force than in the call that the soul be "divorced" from Satan – as if man's fallen state amounted to a proper "marriage" with the Enemy, a state in which corruption itself had become natural. Crashaw insists on the paradox that to surrender to Christ is victory, to serve Him freedom. As Richard Strier points out, "Crashaw's God only knocks, breathes and shines, does not ravish but waits for 'the awful daring of a moment's surrender' to bestow the ultimate gift."[164] The strength and merit are Christ's, but the decision lies with the Countess:

> Yield to his Siege, wise Soul, and see
> Your Triumph in his Victory.
> Disband dull Feares, give Faith the day:
> To save your Life, kill your Delay.
> 'Tis Cowardise that keeps this Field;
> And want of Courage not to Yield.
> Yield then, O yield, that Love may win
> The Fort at last, and let Life in.
> Yield quickly, lest perhaps you prove
> Death's Prey, before the Prize of Love.
> This Fort of your Fair Self if't be not wone,
> He is repuls'd indeed, but You'r undone.   (79–90)

Yielding implies subjection – loss of freedom – but yielding is itself possible only if one has freedom to yield; and grace is that which restores sufficient freedom to an individual to enable him to surrender it to Christ. It is Christ himself, of course, who puts the sharpest edge on the paradox: "Though he was in the form of God, he did not deem equality with God something to be grasped at. Rather, he emptied himself and took the form of a slave, being born in the likeness of man" (Phil. 2.6–7). Lope de Vega takes up this paradox of grace and freedom in the fifteenth sonnet of the *Rimas sacras*:

> pero si, fugitivos de su dueño,
> hierran, cuando los hallan, los esclavos,
> hoy que vuelvo con lágrimas a veros,
> clavadme vos a vos en vuestro leño,
> y tendréisme seguro con tres clavos.[165]

---

[164] "Crashaw's Other Voice," p. 148.
[165] *Obras poéticas* I. 323.

[but if slaves who have fled their masters, when found, are placed in irons, today as I return tearfully to see you, nail me to you on your cross, and you will hold me secure with three nails.]

Christ on the cross is the absolute sacrifice of infinite freedom: the penitent who accepts Christ's nails as "irons," the slave who joins his master in servitude, gains the ultimate freedom willingly to sacrifice self-destructive willfulness. It is necessary that the act be voluntary since Christ voluntarily laid down His life for mankind; hence the man who would participate in this action must also do so willingly – he must have a will to be able to sacrifice it.

Part II

MEDITATION AND SACRAMENT IN
SEVENTEENTH-CENTURY POETRY

... but the *Via Media*, viewed as an integral system has scarcely had existence except on paper, it has never been reduced to practice but by piecemeal; it is known, not positively but negatively, in its differences from rival creeds, not in its own properties; and can only be described as a third system, neither the one nor the other, partly both, cutting between them, and, as if with a critical fastidiousness, trifling with them both, and boasting to be nearer Antiquity than either ...   John Henry Newman[1]

IF grace is the gift of divine life by which a man is spiritually transformed and enters into a new relationship with his Creator and Redeemer, then worship is the means by which this new life with God is expressed; it is a concrete manifestation, within this world, of the Christian's otherworldly destiny. Traditionally, Christian worship has been practised both privately, as a manifestation of the individual's personal bond with Christ, and publicly in the communal liturgies of the Church – the Body and Bride of Christ. Poetry that seeks to incarnate Christian devotion in a literary representation can be influenced by, or participate in, both the public and private aspects of worship. Although devotional poetry is ordinarily associated with individual devotional experience, the use of St. Thomas Aquinas's hymns as a part of the liturgy for the feast of Corpus Christi and the adaptation of some of Herbert's poems for congregational singing in various Protestant hymnals indicate the close connection between private devotion and public worship.[2]

Both the Protestant Reformation and the Catholic reform movement, with varying degrees of inspiration from Christian humanism, resulted in an increased focus on the individual practice of piety; and this development is

---

[1] *Lectures on the Prophetical Office of the Church* (1837), quoted by J. M. Cameron, ed., "Introduction" to J. H. Newman, *An Essay on the Development of Christian Doctrine* (Harmondsworth: Penguin Books, 1974), p. 17.

[2] See Walter J. Ong, S.J., "Wit and Mystery: A Revaluation in Medieval Latin Hymnody," *Speculum* 22 (1947) 310–41; and F. E. Hutchinson, ed., "Introduction" to *The Works of George Herbert* (Oxford: Clarendon Press, 1941), pp. xlvi–xlvii. See also Martha Winburn, "The First Wesley Hymnbook," *BNYPL* 68 (1964) 225–38; and, from the same volume, John Sparrow, "George Herbert and John Donne Among the Moravians," pp. 625–53.

reflected in the vigorous production of books of meditation and asceticism and their wide diffusion, especially among laymen, during the period. It is apparent that the intensity and broad extent of the cultivation of personal piety, something of a novelty outside the cloister, exercised a powerful influence on the flowering of devotional poetry during the latter part of the sixteenth century and throughout the seventeenth century. As the classic study of this development makes clear, "the poetry of meditation" is less important as a particular *kind* of literature than as a literature that reflects the overall effect of meditative practice on the mind of the poet. For example, the effects of the structural principles of meditation can be seen not only in Donne's Holy Sonnets and *Anniversaries,* but also in his *Songs and Sonets* and even his Satyres.[3]

Meditation and sacrament are closely associated because, insofar as it seeks to evoke in the Christian an awareness of Christ's presence, meditation is an individual reinforcement, or even representation or imitation, of the enactment of the sacraments by the Church. Moreover, along with the issue of grace and free will, the number and form of the sacraments, especially the nature and effects of the Eucharist, were the most important points of contention during the Reformation. Since the sacraments were traditionally regarded as channels of grace, the quarrel about the sacraments grows directly out of the quarrel about grace; and indeed the specific issue of the Eucharist becomes increasingly contentious as the seventeenth century wears on, and nowhere more than in England.

In a generally neglected book, Malcolm MacKenzie Ross maintains that the "Protestant revision of Eucharistic dogma" had enormous – and catastrophic – consequences for religious poetry in England.[4] Ross's most general thesis is provocative, but cogent: the attack upon the traditional Catholic doctrine of the Eucharist (*transubstantiation* in the language of St. Thomas) played a major, if inadvertent, rôle in the secularization of Western culture, and in England this shift in the spiritual consciousness of Christians can be charted in the growth and eventual decline of devotional poetry during the seventeenth century. Ross, however, seems blinded by the elegance of his own thesis in his assessment of the accomplishments of individual poets.

---

[3] Louis L. Martz, *The Poetry of Meditation,* 2nd ed. (New Haven: Yale University Press, 1962), pp. 13–22, 43–56, 107–12, 212–48. The objection of Barbara Lewalski, *Protestant Poetics and the Seventeenth-Century Religious Lyric* (Princeton, NJ: Princeton University Press, 1979), p. 147, that Martz overstates the influence of meditation at the expense of "other genres" is without force, since Martz does not treat meditation as a poetic genre. The complex point is discussed succinctly but effectively by Anthony Low, *Love's Architecture: Devotional Modes in Seventeenth-Century English Poetry* (New York: New York University Press, 1978), pp. 1–9. On the meditative aspects of the Satyres, see M. Thomas Hester, *Kinde Pitty and Brave Scorn: John Donne's Satyres* (Durham, NC: Duke University Press, 1982), pp. 58–72, 75–95.

[4] *Poetry and Dogma: The Transfiguration of Eucharistic Symbols in Seventeenth Century English Poetry* (1954; rpt. New York: Octagon Books, 1969), p. vii.

Donne, Herbert, Crashaw, and Vaughan are surely among the glories of English religious poetry, not hapless victims of an ineluctable dialectic in the history of dogma. Indeed, it is precisely an awareness of the threatened loss of the sacraments' power to make grace present in the world that gives such tremendous tension and poignancy to their sacred poetry. Hence Martz finds the flourishing of the poetry of meditation during the same period that Ross sees the disintegration of "the analogical mode of the poetic symbol," which had been "nourished" by "the dogmatic symbolism of the traditional Eucharistic rite."[5] The devotional poetry of Donne and Herbert is permeated with explicitly liturgical and sacramental symbolism, and this of course is *a fortiori* true of Crashaw, who converted because he believed that his personal spiritual fulfillment depended on the corporate sacramental life of the Church. In contrast to Crashaw's treatment of these themes there is a certain ambiguity about the relation between the individual and the Church in Donne's poetry, though not in Herbert's. Paradoxically, it is in Vaughan's poetry that the sacramental crisis is most manifest: the haunting sense of loss, pervasive in *Silex Scintillans*, the groping after a tangible sign, the peering into the darkness for a glimmer of the Bridegroom's presence – these are the marks of a man urgently seeking after what seems departed. Unlike Crashaw, however, Vaughan is unprepared to find solace in Rome.

Vaughan's poetic response to personal and political crisis highlights a recurrent theme in the devotional literature of his age, as well as of the critical theory of our own: *absent presence.* If the grace of God is the presence of His life in the human soul, then the Catholic doctrine of the transubstantiation of the elements of bread and wine into the Body and Blood of Christ in the sacrifice of the Mass is an assurance that God is objectively and factually (*ex opere operato*) present to the communicant. Any tampering with this teaching, established in the mind of Christendom for centuries, would necessarily put in question the meaning and purpose of the Eucharist, and indeed of all the sacraments, and raise doubts about the accessibility of God's grace. Now the formulations of eucharistic doctrine among the Protestant Reformers of the Continent – from the memorialism of Zwingli, to the receptionism of Calvin, to the ubiquitarianism of Luther – all do away with the objective reality of Christ's presence in what the medieval Church called the Sacrament of the Altar. In Zwingli's teaching, as the term "memorialism" announces, there is no *real presence* at all, merely a "memorial" of the Last Supper and the sacrifice on Calvary. In Calvin's view, the Body and Blood of Christ are really present *in the faith of the elect communicant;* hence communion is a sign that one already has grace rather than a means of obtaining it. Even Luther's notion of consubstantiation, by which Christ is truly present in the elements of bread and wine because He is already present everywhere in the universe, can be turned around to say that He is *no more*

---

[5] Ibid.

present in the Sacrament than He is everywhere else.[6] Ross tartly dismisses Luther's formulation: "Such an argument defends the Real Presence by abolishing it."[7] For those English Christians who, while separated from Rome, were not absolutely convinced that God's grace was always unmediated, the search for an alternative understanding of the Eucharist as a channel of grace generated enormous spiritual energy. Although the doctrinal eclecticism of the Church of England could cause anxiety, it also provided fruitful ground for devotional poetry.

Since the mode of Christ's presence in the Eucharist was such a sharply contested issue during the Reformation – among the Reformers themselves as well as in their conflicts with Rome – it is not surprising that the eucharistic Presence is latent in the background of so much devotional poetry of the age where it is not an explicit theme. A principal purpose of such poetry, like formal meditation itself, is to evoke a sense of the divine presence in the soul, analogous to the sacramental presence invoked by the liturgy. This goal is proposed by Protestant and Catholic alike. According to the Anglican bishop Joseph Hall, meditation delivers us from the narrow confines of this world into God's presence:

> By this we grow to be (as we are) strangers upon earth, and out of a right estimation of all earthly things into a sweet fruition of invisible comforts. By this we see our Saviour with Steven [Acts 7.35], we talk with God as Moses [Exod. 24.12], and by this we are ravished with blessed Paul into Paradise [2 Cor. 12.2–4] and see that heaven which we are loath to leave, which we cannot utter.[8]

Hall's Jesuit contemporary, Edward Dawson, in a brief digest of Ignatian devotional method, similarly emphasizes meditation as a means of seeing

---

[6] See Edward Peters, "Introduction" to Ulrich Zwingli, *Selected Works*, ed. Samuel Macauley Jackson (1901; rpt. Philadelphia: University of Pennsylvania Press, 1972), pp. xxvi–xxvii; and *The First Zurich Disputation* in *Selected Works*, p. 112; and *The accompt and rekenyng and confession of the faith Huldrik Zwinglius*, trans. Thomas Cotsford (Geneva, 1555; fac. rpt. Amsterdam: Theatrum Orbis Terrarum, Ltd., 1979), pp. 35–50. For Calvin see "Short Treatise on the Holy Supper of Our Lord Jesus Christ," in *Calvin: Theological Treatises*, ed. J. K. S. Reid (Philadelphia: Westminster Press, 1954), pp. 142–66; and *Institutes of the Christian Religion* IV. xvii, trans. Henry Beveridge (Grand Rapids, MI: W.B. Eerdmans, 1954), II.555–605. For Luther see "Sermons on the Catechism – The Lord's Supper," in *Martin Luther: Selections from his Works*, ed. John Dillenberger (Garden City, NY: Doubleday, 1961), p. 236; and the various texts in *Luther's Works*, gen. ed. Helmut T. Lehman, vol. 38, *Word and Sacrament*, IV, ed. Martin E. Lehman (Philadelphia: Fortress Press, 1971), esp. the controversy with Zwingli and his followers recorded in "The Marburg Colloquy and The Marburg Articles, 1529," pp. 1529. See also Roland H. Bainton, *Here I Stand* (1950; rpt. New York: New American Library, 1950), p. 108.

[7] *Poetry and Dogma*, p. 48.

[8] *The Art of Divine Meditation* (1606), in Frank L. Huntley, *Bishop Joseph Hall and Protestant Meditation in Seventeenth-Century England* (Binghamton, NY: Medieval and Renaissance Texts and Studies, 1981), p. 71.

beyond appearances and recognizing our true condition as strangers on earth surrounded by intimations of our divine home:

> The presence of God is best framed of our Understanding, by making an act of faith, wherby we beleeve Almighty God to be so present there, that he compasseth us round on every side, as the water compasseth the fish, and yet is also within us, and the things before us (as he is in all things) somwhat like the water which is entred into a sponge, and this by his divine essence, presence, and power, which penetrate the nature of every creature, and give them needfull helpe for their operations.[9]

Herbert deals with the same evocation of the divine presence in his poems on prayer, which is "Gods breath in man returning to his birth" ("Prayer [I]," 2). Our words are instantly in His presence and call Him to us:

> Of what an easie quick accesse,
> My blessed Lord, art thou! how suddenly
> May our requests thine eare invade!   ("Prayer [II]," 1–3)

Given this conformity of interests, it is difficult to agree with recent scholarship that maintains that Protestant devotional literature owes very little to the influence of continental Catholic meditative practices. In the same way, the measures of the Catholic or Counter-Reformation were – to some extent – shaped by the challenge of the Protestant Reformation, and there was reciprocal influence throughout the sixteenth and seventeenth centuries. Still the argument is made that the meditative features of the Anglican devotional poetry of the seventeenth century are derived from an exclusively Protestant approach to meditation, based on theological assumptions radically different from those of the Catholic tradition. Hence Barbara Lewalski criticizes Louis Martz's account of the influence of Catholic meditation in England because it gives little consideration to "this developing indigenous Protestant tradition."[10]

When this "indigenous Protestant tradition" is considered in any detail, however, it begins to blur around the edges. Lewalski places its "remote roots in the biblical focus and devotional practices of the pre-Reformation *devotio moderna* movement with its links to Thomas à Kempis, Erasmus, and Luther."[11] Remove the name Luther and one is hard put to find anything Protestant about such origins. In his introduction to two meditative works by

[9] "The Practical Methode of Meditation," in Louis L. Martz, ed., *The AnchorAnthology of Seventeenth Century Verse*, vol. I (Garden City, NY: Doubleday & Co., 1969), p. 501. See also Walter R. Davis, "Meditation, Typology, and the Structure of John Donne's Sermons," in *The Eagle and the Dove: Reassessing John Donne*, ed. Claude Summers and Ted-Larry Pebworth (Columbia: University of Missouri Press, 1986), p. 174, for the rôle of Dawson's short treatise on blending liturgical and private elements in meditation.

[10] *Protestant Poetics*, p. 147.

[11] Ibid., p. 148.

Joseph Hall, F. L. Huntley distinguishes Hall from the Ignatian spirituality of the Catholic Reformation by aligning his view with Origen and St. Augustine and various medieval figures like St. Bernard of Clairvaux, Hugh of St. Victor, and Jean Gerson. Huntley's handling of Gerson is especially revealing:

> Gerson has been hailed as an early "Protestant," and as a "practical" Christian rather than Merely a logician. "It was a just answer, that John Gerson reports, given by a Frenchman," Hall wrote, "who, being asked by one of his neighbors if the Sermon were done; 'No', saith he, 'it is said, but it is not done, neither will be, I fear, in haste"' (Wynter, 6: 531). Within the *Art* Gerson appears several times. Although in Chapter VII, Hall deplored the part the Chancellor had taken at the Council of Constance in condemning the doctrines of Wycliffe and Huss, he admired Gerson's appeal to the average mind, not to the unusually subtle or militarily disciplined. He depends upon Gerson as an early "Protestant" and uses him as an authority "because our adversaries [meaning the Jesuits] disclaim him for theirs" (Chapter VIII).[12]

Apparently the establishment of a Protestant meditative tradition requires that anyone not a Scholastic logician or a Jesuit be regarded as a Protestant. It is difficult to imagine what Gerson could have done to have avoided being so labeled by Joseph Hall and his twentieth-century expounder, Frank Huntley.

Subsequent developments do little to clarify the distinctive identity of Protestant meditation. "By the final decades of the sixteenth century," Lewalski writes, "a self-consciously Protestant concept of meditation was taking shape, as writers such as Thomas Rogers and Edmund Bunny produced bowdlerized versions of some famous Catholic treatises (*The Imitation of Christ*, the pseudo-Augustinian *Soliloquia animae ad Deum*, and Robert Parson's [sic] *Christian Directory*), deleting all reference to suspect Roman doctrine and adding a heavy overlay of biblical language and citations."[13] Parsons' complaints that the Protestantizing of his own work shows the poverty of Protestant devotional writing should "be greeted with some skepticism," Lewalski insists, as "polemical assertions."[14] While this assessment of Parsons is certainly correct, it is difficult to see that Rogers and Bunny were any less "polemical"; and, in any case, a massive rewriting of Catholic devotional texts to Reformation specifications and a scramble to produce new, distinctively Protestant works of this kind suggest nothing so much as a powerful Catholic influence on an emergent Protestant scheme of worship. This pressure is the only explanation for Joseph Hall's incessant

---

[12] *Bishop Joseph Hall*, pp. 26–27. See Heiko Oberman, *The Harvest of Medieval Theology: Gabriel Biel and Late Medieval Nominalism* (Cambridge, MA: Harvard University Press, 1963), esp. pp. 4–6, 385–91, for Gerson's central place in fifteenth-century Catholicism.

[13] *Protestant Poetics*, p. 148.

[14] Ibid., p. 457, n. 6.

denials of the evident affinity between his own *Art of Divine Meditation* and the work of St. Ignatius, and for his rather comical effort to turn Gerson and St. Bernard into Protestants.

The alleged characteristics of specifically Protestant meditation evaporate upon inspection. Huntley lists five: "philosophically it is Platonic, not Aristotelian; in psychology it is Augustinian, not Thomistic; its theology is Pauline Calvinist; though starting with the individual it finally becomes more public than private, and bears greater similarity to the sermon than to penitential prayer; and it finds a greater variety in subject matter in God's 'three books'."[15] The oversimplification of the first two posited criteria is breathtaking: does anyone seriously believe that Catholics were uniformly "Aristotelian" in philosophy and "Thomistic" in psychology? That no Catholics during the Middle Ages and the Counter-Reformation manifest the influence of Plato and St. Augustine? Not only would Huntley have us count Saints Bernard and Bonaventure (among others) as part of the Protestant tradition, he would also have us ignore such notable Counter-Reformation figures as Fray Luis de León, the Spanish Augustinian friar whose prose and poetry alike evince clear marks of the influence of Plato and Augustine.

The claims made for the distinctiveness of "Pauline-Calvinist" theology have been examined in Part I, and what is an insufficient basis for a poetics is equally insufficient for meditation. The close relationship between Protestant meditation and sermon has become a critical commonplace: Lewalski also raises this point, but she emphasizes the private "application to the self" where Huntley stresses the public nature of meditation. In either case the vagueness of the notion disqualifies it as a distinguishing feature of specific-ally Protestant meditation. After all, Dawson's *Practical Method* was intended for English recusants deprived of frequent recourse to Catholic sacraments and sermons; hence meditation could be regarded as a provisional substitute for a sermon. Moreover, there is no doubt that recusant writers saw their devotional works as tools in the evangelization and reconversion of Protestant England.[16] Here again private meditation is aligned with the sermon in a Catholic context. Huntley's last characteristic supposes that Protestant meditation has more variety than Ignatian meditation because it makes use of the "three books" of God's revelation: nature, Scripture, and self. But the idea of meditating on the book of nature is at least as old as St. Augustine and was certainly not forgotten by Catholics during the Counter-Reformation. Fray Luis de León again provides a handy example: his *On the Names of Christ* (1583), as Félix García observes, effects a constant "parallelism between the

---

[15] *Bishop Joseph Hall*, pp. 4–5.

[16] See John R. Roberts, ed., *A Critical Anthology of EnglishRecusant Devotional Prose, 1558–1603* (Pittsburgh: Duquesne University Press, 1966), p. 3; and M. Thomas Hester, *KindePitty and Brave Scorn*, p. 154, n. 40.

spiritual world and the sensible world";[17] and, as a treatment of the various names and titles of our Lord found in the Bible, it is, likewise, an example of Scriptural meditation. As for the "book" of the self, this is finally equated by Huntley with the Christian conscience, the significance of which Protestants found in St. Paul, St. Augustine, and Calvin.[18] But Catholics were quite as capable of learning from Paul and Augustine – without the mediation of Calvin – and the transformation of the self in Christ was virtually the entire enterprise of Spain's Counter-Reformation mystics, as it is of mystics generally.

For Barbara Lewalski, "Two elements especially characterize Protestant meditation, whatever the subject or the formal structure: a focus upon the Bible, the Word, as guiding the interpretation of the subject and providing meditative models; and a particular kind of application to the self, analogous to the 'application' so prominent in Protestant sermons of the period."[19] The trouble here is that it is difficult to imagine any scheme of Christian meditation that would not use the Bible as a model and a guide (though obviously there are differences in degree, and other influences could be combined), and that would not involve some kind of "application" of meditative themes to the spiritual life of the individual. Catholic works of devotion, both in prose and verse, are often based on scriptural motifs and liberally seasoned with scriptural allusions; and in following the Church in the interpretation of Scripture, Catholics believed themselves to be in touch with the authentic Word of God. Likewise, Catholics meditated for the same reasons as Protestants: to increase their personal contact with Christ and to realize their own individual rôles as members of His Body. What is regrettable about the devotional schema of Protestant poetics is that it fails to do justice to either Protestant or Catholic, forcing both parties into narrow ideological categories and neglecting the variety of theology and worship that flourished within the Catholic Church, as well as in the extraordinary diversity of form and expression in the many manifestations of the Reformation throughout Europe and the New World. Moreover, the affinities and repugnances within the devotional literature of the seventeenth century do not reliably accord with strict confessional boundaries.

Whatever differences in detail might obtain between Catholic and Protestant approaches to meditation, then, they shared an overriding common motivation: the longing for the divine presence. Paradoxically, the most withdrawn and intimate of *private* devotions involves the urge to escape the self; solitude is only the means to a profounder communion. The relationship between meditation and the sacrament of the Eucharist is thus illuminated in

[17] *Obras completas castellanas*, ed. Félix García, O.S.A. (Madrid: Biblioteca de autores cristianos, 1957), I. 387.
[18] *Bishop Joseph Hall*, pp. 9–10.
[19] *Protestant Poetics*, p. 148.

analogical terms, because the sacrament is a celebration not only of the Christian's communion with his Redeemer, but also with his fellow Christians. As St. Augustine puts it, citing 1 Corinthians 12: 27, "If therefore you are the body and members of Christ, it is your mystery placed on the Lord's table: you receive your mystery."[20] Meditation and sacrament (especially the Eucharist) are in different ways bound up with the mystery of individual identity in its relation both to God and fellow men; and the manner in which a devotional poet handles meditative themes can reflect his response to the sacramental crisis of the Reformation era. The quarrels between Catholics and Protestants over the nature and effects of the sacraments would eventually encourage a vision of reality in which the very notion of a sacrament became problematic. The intense fervor of the devotional poets of the seventeenth century can be seen as an anxious anticipation of this development.

i

The need to find one's personal identity within the communal worship of the Body of Christ explains the liturgical focus of so much of the religious verse of that most self-conscious and idiosyncratic of poets, John Donne. There is no question that what is generally regarded as his earliest piece of devotional poetry, "La Corona," is deeply rooted in Catholic traditions of worship, especially a particular variation on the rosary and certain readings from the Roman Breviary.[21] Lewalski concedes the "obvious debts" to the rosary tradition, though she proposes the "biblical analogues" of "La Corona" as a Protestant qualification.[22] Patrick F. O'Connell argues for a general revaluation of "La Corona," which, he says, should not be dismissed as "a series of rather unremarkable meditations on the life of Christ, a rather bloodless experiment not particularly congenial to Donne's temperament." To the contrary, O'Connell maintains, the sequence is not "simply a detached, objective presentation of Christian mysteries, but the vehicle for a careful investigation of the meaning of human activity, and in particular of

---

[20] Sermo CCIXXII, *Ad Infantes, de Sacramento*, PL 38–39.1247: "Si ergo vos estis corpus Christi et membra, mysterium vestrum in mensa Dominica positum est: mysterium vestrum accipitis."

[21] The links to rosary meditation are definitively established by Martz, *Poetry of Meditation,* pp. 107–12; and by Helen Gardner, ed., "Introduction" to *John Donne: The Divine Poems,* 2nd ed. (Oxford: Clarendon Press, 1978), p. xxiii and in the commentary on the individual sonnets, pp. 57–64. See also Low, *Love's Architecture,* pp. 42–51; and Maureen Sabine, *Feminine Engendered Faith: The Poetry of John Donne and Richard Crashaw* (London: MacMillan, 1992), pp. 43–58, esp. 56–57, for the strong Marian emphasis in the sequence.

[22] *Protestant Poetics,* p. 257. It is not much of a qualification since the rosary itself is, except perhaps for the last two mysteries, a series of biblical meditations. Low, *Love's Architecture,* p. 43, points out that "La Corona" represents a specifically Anglican adaptation of a Catholic tradition, wholly scorned by Puritans.

the vocation of the Christian artist, in the light of these mysteries."[23] The essential point of the argument is that the poet finds an identity in relation to Christ and the Church by "losing" the anxious, self-absorbed ego in liturgical mysteries. For example, "The cross is in the end the source of reconciliation of self with self, as well as with God and with other people"; and, likewise, "The resurrections he speaks of are not something other than the resurrection of Christ, but the speaker's participation in the Easter mystery . . . Man's true vocation is thus to realize in his own space and time the once-for-all saving event of Christ."[24]

In Sonnet 2, "Annunciation," Donne takes the Virgin Mary as a model for human "participation" in the mystery of salvation:

> *Salvation to all that will is nigh,*
> That All, which alwayes is All every where,
> Which cannot sinne, and yet all sinnes must beare,
> Which cannot die, yet cannot chuse but die,
> Loe, faithfull Virgin, yeelds himselfe to lye
> In prison, in thy wombe; and though he there
> Can take no sinne, nor thou give, yet he'will weare
> Taken from thence, flesh, which deaths force may trie.   (1–8)

The seventh line is striking because it treads delicately along a perilous doctrinal precipice. Sixteenth- and seventeenth-century Christians – Catholic and Protestant alike – were in general agreement that each and every human being came into the world tainted with the original sin of Adam as propagated from generation to generation by each set of parents.[25] Christ of course was the obvious exception, hence "though he there / Can take no sinne" (6–7); but there was a longstanding Catholic tradition that Mary, too, had been conceived without sin – the doctrine of the Immaculate Conception – which could be implied by Donne's next phrase, "nor thou give"; that is, Mary herself had no sin to give Jesus.[26] It is improbable, however, that the poet's

---

[23] "'La Corona': Donne's *Ars Poetica Sacra*," in *The Eagle and the Dove*, p. 119.

[24] Ibid., p. 127.

[25] Calvin, *Institutes of the Christian Religion* II. i. 7, trans. Henry Beveridge (Grand Rapids, MI: Eerdmans, 1957), I, 216: "The children being vitiated in their parent, conveyed the taint to the grandchildren; in other words, corruption commencing in Adam, is, by perpetual descent, conveyed from those preceding to those coming after them." See also the Council of Trent's *Decretum super peccato originale* in *Enchiridion Symbolorum, Definitionum et Declarationum de Rebus Fidei et Morum*, ed. Henr. Denzinger and Clem. Bannwart, S.J. (7th ed., Friburgi Brigoviae: Herder & Co., 1927), #790: "hoc Adae peccatum, quod origine unum est et propagatione, non imitatione transfusum omnibus."

[26] Although the dogma was not formally defined until 1854, the Tridentine decree explicitly excludes Mary from the general account of original sin: "Declarat tamen haec ipsa sancta Synodus, non esse suae intentionis, comprehendere in hoc decreto, ubi de peccato originale agitur, beatam et immaculatam Virginem Mariam Dei genetricem" (Denzinger #792). The Immaculate Conception was also the somewhat improbable subject of numerous seventeenth-century Spanish paintings by artists like Velàzquez and Murillo.

intentions are at all dogmatic – dogmas are what he wishes to avoid.[27] Virginity itself, which could seem mere negation, becomes the source of the (literally) infinite power of the Incarnation:

> Ere by the spheares time was created, thou
> Wast in his minde, who is thy Sonne, and Brother,
> Whom thou conceiv'st, conceiv'd; yea thou art now
> Thy Makers maker, and thy Fathers mother,
> Thou'hast light in darke; and shutst in little roome,
> *Immensity cloysterd in thy deare wombe.*   (9–14)

There is more here than just a pun on "conceiv'st, conceiv'd": because the unstated antecedent of "his," "who," and "Whom" is the "Word" or Λόλος (with its sense of "discourse" or the power of rational thought), there is a properly analogical relationship between the Mother of God and the Father. She incarnates the spiritual reality of the divine presence; her physical conception of the Son anticipates His invocation by the faithful in prayer and sacrament. In the body of the Virgin, individual devotion and corporate worship are united, and she is thus exemplary for the meditative poet. Donne thus finds a way to assimilate a mystery of the Rosary – scorned by Puritans – to the worship of the Church of England.

The analogical relationship between the Word and our words becomes explicit in the medial fourth sonnet, "Temple," which radiates an Augustinian "rhetoric of silence" throughout the sequence:[28]

> *With his kinde mother who partakes thy woe,*
> *Joseph* turne back; see where your child doth sit
> Blowing, yea blowing out those sparks of wit,
> Which himselfe on those Doctors did bestow;
> The Word but lately could not speake, and loe
> It suddenly speakes wonders, whence comes it,
> That all which was, and all which should be writ,
> A shallow seeming child, should deeply know?   (1–8)

The paradox of any human approach to the divine is that our efforts are both needless and inadequate, yet necessary (for us) and inspired. The boy Jesus

---

[27] See *The Sermons of John Donne*, ed. Evelyn M. Simpson and George R. Potter (Berkeley, Los Angeles, London: University of California Press, 1962), X, 115, where Donne maintains that "the *Romane* Church" does not hold "That the blessed *Virgin Mary* was conceived without originall sin," although it is the "common opinion." Donne correctly states the ambiguous dogmatic status of the Immaculate Conception at the time he wrote. We may surmise that a notion attractive to him as poetry he deprecated as doctrine.

[28] On the "axial" position of Sonnet 4 in "La Corona," see John Nania and P. J. Klemp, "John Donne's *La Corona*: A Second Structure," *Renaissance and Reformation* n.s. 2 (1978) 49–54. I also refer to the seminal essay by Joseph A. Mazzeo, "St. Augustine's Rhetoric of Silence: Truth vs. Eloquence and Things vs. Signs," in *Renaissance and Seventeenth-Century Studies* (New York: Columbia University Press, 1964), pp. 1–28.

"blows" on the coals of human intellect, fanning the "sparks" of intellect in the Temple rabbis, and he also blows them out by His mysterious superiority. Near the center of this central poem of "La Corona" is the ultimate paradox of the Incarnation, articulated in Augustinian terms: "The Word but lately could not speak."

The speechless Word was a popular motif in the seventeenth century: it turns up in a Nativity sermon of Lancelot Andrewes and in a sacred pastoral novel by Lope de Vega.[29] Although Gardner's commentary cites a reference in one of Donne's own sermons to St. Bernard for "the famous quibble 'Verbum infans'," the entire interlocking set of paradoxes can probably be traced back to a sermon by St. Augustine:

> What praises can we say of God's charity, what thanks can we give? He so loved us, that for our sake he by whom time itself was made came into time; and he who was younger in the world than many of his own servants, in that very world was more ancient than eternity; he who made man became a man; he was created out of a mother whom he created, carried by hands that he formed, suckled at breasts that he filled, wailed in mute infancy in a crib – the Word without which human eloquence is mute.[30]

Augustine is not merely "quibbling," and neither is Donne. Like the Bishop of Hippo preaching, the poet of "La Corona" is in much the same position as "those Doctors" in the Temple: all human words are both inspired and baffled by the Word itself. The very source of human eloquence is the ultimate indication of the inadequacy of that eloquence.

But this Augustinian view does not, as Stanley Fish argues, render all human meaning meaningless, flatten all distinctions, and level all hierarchies. According to Fish, Augustine's "sacramental view" of reality exerts necessary consequences on the Augustinian sermon and Christian rhetoric in general: "Since the vision it would persuade us to is of a universe in which all things ('and words are also things') are signs of God and therefore are finally not (separate things), its language could not function conventionally. The simplest syntactical string – subject-object-verb – assumes distinctions a sacramental view of the world denies, and one cannot write a sentence without placing the objects to which its words refer in relationships of

---

[29] Lancelot Andrewes, "Sermon 12, Of the Nativitie: Christmas 1618," in *Sermons*, ed. G. M. Story (Oxford: Clarendon Press, 1967), p. 85. Lope de Vega, *Pastores de Belén* III, in *Obras escogidas*, ed. Federico Carlos Sainz de Robles, 4th ed. (Madrid: Aguilar, 1964) II, 1277. Cf. R. V. Young, *Richard Crashaw and the Spanish Golden Age* (New Haven: Yale University Press, 1982), p. 58.

[30] Sermo CLXXXVIII, *In Natali Domini*, v.2, *PL* 38–39.1004: "Quas itaque laudes charitati Dei dicamus, quas gratias agamus? Qui nos ita dilexit, ut propter nos fieret in tempore, per quem facta sunt tempora; et multis servis suis in mundo minor esset aetate, ipso mundo antiquior aeternitate; homo fieret qui hominem fecit, crearetur ex matre quam creavit, portaretur manibus quas formavit, sugeret ubera quae implevit, in praesepi muta vagiret infantia Verbum, sine quo muta est humana eloquentia."

subordination and dependence."[31] But in order for a "thing" to be a "sign" it must be "separate" from the (other) thing which it signifies: in more than one sense do "differences carry signification."[32] It is, moreover, the sacramental view of reality (rather than the postmodernist) that affirms the distinctive historical actuality of things that are also signs: among the books of the Platonists, Augustine reports, I read "that in the beginning was the Word, and the Word was with God, and God was the Word . . . But that the Word was made flesh, and dwelt among us (John 1.1–14), I did not read there."[33]

Although Fish's way of placing Augustine in the Platonic tradition is engagingly original, he has still neglected to make an accurate account of the decisive Christian influence in the thought of the saint, which supersedes, by transforming, Platonism: "Verbum caro factum." As the faith of the incarnation of the Word, Christianity has a special stake in the actuality of things and of occurrences in time; and in the sacraments, the pre-eminent signs of Christianity, it is only by virtue of their reality and distinctiveness that things are able to mediate meaning by being what they are:

> Was not Christ sacrificed once and for all in himself, and yet is he not sacrificed in the sacrament not only during all the Easter feasts, but everyday for the people, and in any case he is not lying who, when questioned, would reply that he is sacrificed? For if the sacraments had no resemblance to the things of which they are sacraments, they would not be sacraments at all.[34]

Although things have their true and ultimate meaning only within the economy of salvation, the God of St. Augustine has not, therefore, despised the things of the world but rather has elevated them. An objective response to individual realities is a duty of the good man: "He lives in justice and

---

[31] *Self-Consuming Artifacts: The Experience of Seventeenth-Century Literature* (Berkeley: University of California Press, 1972), p. 41.

[32] Ferdinand de Saussure, *Course in General Linguistics*, trans. Wade Baskin (1959; rpt. New York: McGraw-Hill, 1966), p. 118. See also Jacques Derrida, "Difference" in *Speech and Phenomena*, trans. David B. Allison (Evanston, IL: Northwestern University Press, 1973), pp. 139–41.

[33] *Confessions* VII.ix.13–14, *PL* 32. 740, 741: "procurasti mihi . . .quosdam Platonicorum libros . . . et ibi legi, non quidem his verbis, sed hoc idem omnino multis et multiplicibus suaderi rationibus, quod in principio erat Verbum, et Verbum erat apud Deum, et Deus erat Verbum . . . Sed quia Verbum caro factum est, et habitavit in nobis (*Joan.* 1,1–14); non ibi legi." I am in debt to the work of Jaroslav Pelikan, *The Mystery of Continuity: Time and History, Memory and Eternity in the Thought of St. Augustine* (Charlottesville: University Press of Virginia, 1986), pp. 123–39, for drawing my attention to the importance of this and following passage from Augustine on sign and sacrament.

[34] St. Augustine, *Epistolarum* 98.9, *PL* 33. 363–64: "Nonne semel immolatus est Christus in seipso, et tamen in sacramento non solum per omnes Paschae solemnitates, sed omni die populis immolatur, nec utique mentitur qui interrogatus eum responderit immolari? Si enim sacramenta quamdam similitudinem earum rerum quarum sacramenta sunt, non haberent, omnino sacramenta non essent."

holiness," Augustine writes in his study *On Christian Doctrine*, "who is an unbiased judge of things."[35]

This sense of the pervasive presence of the Word within the visible things of the world – not to their obliteration, but to their enhancement and transfiguration – informs the better part of Donne's meditative poetry. A respect for the special signifying power of particular creatures accounts for his attention to the unique rôle of the Virgin Mary in the "Annunciation" sonnet of "La Corona," and it is manifest again in "Goodfriday, 1613. Riding Westward." After explaining why he is "almost . . . glad" that he is turned away from the sight of Christ's Passion, "That spectacle of too much weight for mee" (15–16), the poet adds that Mary's experience of the Crucifixion is as dreadful to consider as the Crucifixion itself:

> If on these things I durst not looke, durst I
> Upon his miserable mother cast mine eye,
> Who was Gods partner here, and furnish'd thus
> Halfe of that Sacrifice, which ransom'd us? (29–32)

Donne risks this kind of attention to the Virgin, which was suspect among many Protestants, because the body and its redemption remain very important to the love poet of *The Songs and Sonets*.[36] Such near indiscretions are not merely residual marks of Donne's Catholic upbringing: they are testimony to his abiding awareness of the saving presence of Christ in particular creatures, among them the Mother of Jesus being most notable and exemplary. In Donne's "Goodfriday," as in the *Stabat Mater*, the Mother of Christ is a model whose devotion and suffering the poet would emulate.

Of course the poem that expresses the wish is precisely the means by which the poet does emulate the Virgin before the Crucifixion, centuries after the event. A. B. Chambers points out that the poet's reluctance to view the events of the Passion is itself a way of meditating upon its meaning for him: "The self-questioning must take the form it does because only thus can Donne simultaneously affirm the impossibility and the inevitability of seeing what he cannot and yet must see."[37] According to his own measure, he shares the experience of the Crucifixion exemplified by Mary:

---

[35] *De Doctrina Christiana* I.xxvii.28, *PL* 34. 29: "Ille autem juste et sancte vivit, qui rerum integer aestimator est."

[36] The Incarnation, St. Thomas says, manifests "certain spiritual marriage between the Son of God and human nature. And therefore by means of the Annunciation the consent of the Virgin was sought after in the place of the whole human nature" (*Summa Theologiae* 3.30.1: "Quarto, ut ostenderetur esse quoddam spirituale matrimonium inter Filium Dei et humanum naturam. Et ideo per annuntiationem expetebatur consensus Virginis loco totius humanae naturae."

[37] " 'Goodfriday. 1613. Riding Westward': The Poem and the Tradition," in *Essential Articles for the Study of John Donne's Poetry*, ed. John R. Roberts (Hamden, CT: Archon Books, 1975), p. 346.

Though these things, as I ride, be from mine eye,
They'are present yet unto my memory,
For that looks towards them; and thou look'st towards mee,
O Saviour, as thou hang'st upon the tree.   (33–36)

Even though the poet is riding away from the sacrifice on Calvary, he is, nonetheless, preoccupied with the evocation of Christ's presence; and he thus exemplifies the main purpose of meditation: to make the Savior "present yet unto memory" even when He is not present in a *real* form. A further purpose is, then, to prepare the meditator for that final, full presence of the Apocalypse:

I turne my backe to thee, but to receive
Corrections, till thy mercies bid thee leave.
O thinke mee worth thine anger, punish mee,
Burne off my rusts, and my deformity,
Restore thine Image, so much, by thy grace,
That thou may'st know mee, and I'll turne my face.   (37–42)

As in his Holy Sonnets, so in his occasional divine poems and hymns, Donne is preoccupied with the absent presence of the Deity,[38] and this concern is manifest in an apparently inescapable fascination with the Catholic teaching regarding the real presence of Christ's body and blood in the sacrament of the altar – the holy sacrifice of the mass. Ordained as a clergyman in the Church of England, Donne must officially deny the Catholic doctrine of transubstantiation and its liturgical corollaries. The twenty-eighth of the *Articles of Religion* expressly repudiates transubstantiation and the reservation and adoration of the consecrated host, while asserting, "The Body of Christ is given, taken, and eaten in the Supper, only in a heavenly, and spiritual reckoning. The means by which the Body of Christ is received and eaten in the Supper, is faith."[39] But Donne is hardly so emphatic. In his first prebend sermon, he rebukes Rome because it will "obtrude to us miraculous

---

[38] See A. B. Chambers, *Transfigured Rites in Seventeenth-Century English Poetry* (Columbia and London: University of Missouri Press, 1992), p. 200: "Donne's lines [33–35] affirm an oxymoron – away 'from' but 'present yet unto' – that, in abstract terms, conjoins absence-presence." For a rather different take on Donne's longing for the absent God, see Debora K. Shuger, *Habits of Thought in the English Renaissance: Religion, Politics, and the Dominant Culture* (Berkeley and Los Angeles: University of California Press, 1990), pp. 190–97.

[39] The *Articles* are quoted in their official Latin form of 1571 from Felix Makower, *The Constitutional History and Constitution of the Church of England* (1895, rpt. New York: Burt Franklin, 1960), pp. 481–88: "Panis et vini transubstantiatio in Eucharistia, ex sacris literis probari non potest. Sed apertis Scripturae verbis adversatur, Sacramenti naturam evertit, et multarum superstitionum dedit occasionem. Corpus Christi datur, accipitur, et manducatur in Coena, tantum coelesti, et spirituali ratione. Medium autem quo corpus Christi accipitur, et manducatur in Coena, fides est. Sacramentum Eucharistiae, ex institutione Christi non servabatur, circumferebatur, elevabatur, nec adorabatur."

doctrines of Transubstantiation, and the like, upon a possibility onely," but he does not actually deny the doctrine. In the fourth prebend sermon, while implicitly condemning the Catholic definition of transubstantiation as overly precise, he nonetheless conveys a vivid sense of the reality of Christ's presence in the physical elements of the sacrament:

> This Sacrament of the Body and Blood of our Saviour, *Luther* calls safely, *Venerabile & adorabile;* for certainly, whatsoever that is which we see, that which we receive, is to be adored; for, we receive Christ. He is *Res Sacramenti,* The forme, the Essence, the substance, the soule of the Sacrament; And *Sacramentum sine re Sacramenti, mors est,* To take the body, and not the soule, the bread, and not Christ, is death. But he that feels Christ, in the receiving of the Sacrament, and will not bend his knee, would scarce bend his knee, if he saw him. The first of that royall Family, which thinks it selfe the greatest in Christendome at this day, The House of Austrich, had the first marks of their Greatnesse, The Empire, brought into that House, for a particular reverence done to the holy and blessed Sacrament. What the bread and wine is, or what becomes of it, *Damascen* thinks impertinent to be inquired. He thinks he hath said enough; (and so may we doe) *Migrat in Substantiam animae;* There is the true Transubstantiation, that when I have received it worthily, it becomes my very soule; that is, My soule growes up into a better state, and habitude by it, and I have the more soule for it, the more sanctified, the more deified soule by that Sacrament.[40]

This is a remarkably elusive and problematic passage. In a context largely aimed at Puritan undervaluing of the Eucharist, Donne ties his reverence for the sacrament to the exemplary Reformation name of Luther, but as Janel Mueller points out in her commentary on the text, Donne manipulates Luther's words to make the latter seem more devoted to the real presence than he is: "Donne's unequivocal endorsement of adoration gives the misleading impression that Luther prescribes it, ignoring his qualifications." He then makes an allusion – "perhaps intentionally cryptic," Mueller says – "to a succession of several passages in the Third Part of the *Summa Theologica.*"[41] In Donne's words, "we receive Christ. He is *Res Sacramenti,* The forme, the Essence, the substance, the soule of the Sacrament." This emphasis on Christ himself as the *form* and *substance* of the Eucharist, seems to reflect St. Thomas's discussion of the differences between this sacrament and the others. "The forms of the other sacraments involve the use of material," St. Thomas writes, "but the form of this sacrament involves only the consecration of material, and this depends upon transubstantiation." While "the forms of the other sacraments are offered in the person of the minister . . . the form of this sacrament is offered by the person of Christ himself speaking; so

[40] *Donne's Prebend Sermons,* ed. Janel M. Mueller (Cambridge, MA: Harvard University Press, 1971), pp. 80, 154–55 (Potter & Simpson VI. 15. 300; VII. 12. 320–21).
[41] *Donne's Prebend Sermons,* pp. 296–97.

that we are given to understand that the minister does nothing in the enactment of this sacrament except that he offers the words of Christ."[42] In calling Christ the "forme" and "substance" of the sacrament, Donne is, to put it mildly, using theologically loaded language. Its force is not mitigated when he castigates those who will not kneel to receive communion and offers as a favorably contrasting example the action of the founder of a militantly Catholic royal house.

In her commentary Mueller supplies the background to Donne's cryptic reference. While hunting, Rudolph of Austria encountered a "poor Priest" ("Sacerdotum pauperum") taking viaticum through the rain to a sick man. Rudolph dismounted from his horse, knelt on the wet ground, and "reverently placed his own cloak on the shoulders of the priest carrying the holy body of Christ the Lord, lest the sacred EUCHARIST suffer any damage from the rain in the journey" ("super humeros Sacerdotis sanctum Christi Domini corpus deportantis, reverenter imposuit, ne a pluvia aliquid detrimenti sacra EUCHARISTIA in itinere pateretur").[43] This is an extraordinary exemplum for Donne to offer his congregation, given the explicit language of Article 28: "The Sacrament of the Eucharist, by Christ's institution, was not reserved, carried about, elevated or adored."[44] Moreover, as St. Thomas observes, transubstantiation provides the *only* justification for the adoration of the sacrament, "since it would be contrary to the veneration of this sacrament, if any substance were there that could not be adored with the adoration of divine worship."[45]

Given Donne's explicit disdain for Puritan irreverence toward the sacrament, the latent references to Thomist doctrine, and the oblique approval of adoration of the consecrated Host, the close of the paragraph, with its somewhat strained invocation of St. John Damascene, seems an elaborate way of avoiding a straightforward and properly Protestant condemnation of transubstantiation. The passage that follows is even more surprising:

> Now this Sacrament, which as it is ministered to us, is but a Sacrament, but as it is offered to God, is a Sacrifice too, is a fearfull, a terrible thing. If the sacrifices

---

[42] *Summa Theologiae* III. 78. 1: "formae aliorum sacramentorum important usum materiae . . . sed forma huius sacramenti importat solam consecrationem materiae, quae in transubstantiatione consistit . . . quia formae aliorum sacramentorum proferuntur ex persona ministri . . . Sed forma huius sacramenti profertur ex persona ipsius Christi loquentis: ut detur intelligi quod minister in perfectione huius sacramenti nihil agit nisi quod profert verba Christi."

[43] The account of the incident by Didamus Alvarez, *De auxiliis gratiae et humani arbitrii viribus et libertate*, is quoted in Mueller's commentary to *Donne's Prebend Sermons*, pp. 297–98.

[44] Makower, *Constitutional History*, p. 486. See above, n. 36, for the text.

[45] *Summa Theologiae* III. 75. 2: "Quia contrariaretur venerationi huius sacramenti, si aliqua substantia esset ibi quae non posset adorari adoratione latriae."

of the Law, the blood of Goats and Rammes, were so, how fearfull, how terrible, how reverentiall a thing is the blood of this immaculate Lambe, the Sonne of God?[46]

In her commentary, Mueller notes the echo of the *Agnus Dei* of the mass and remarks, "Perhaps Donne's associations here reflect the religious experience of his childhood."[47] There is, however, something beyond mere boyhood reminiscence in Donne's calling the sacrament a sacrifice, "a fearfull, a terrible thing," which is hardly language typical of Protestant doctrinal formulations. In "The Marburg Colloquy," Zwingli's most damning accusation against Luther is "of speaking as if he wanted again to re-establish the sacrifice of the mass"; but in his *Admonition Concerning the Sacrament,* Luther himself attacks the "papists" because "they made the sacrament which they should accept from God, namely the body and blood of Christ, into a sacrifice and have offered it to the selfsame God," a practice that he calls a "blasphemous sacrifice."[48] The view of Calvin is a fortiori negative: "We loudly maintain that the sacrifice of the Mass is nothing else than an impious profanation of the Lord's Supper."[49] The Protestant Dean of St. Paul's Cathedral, however, proclaims that "this Sacrament of the Body and Blood of our Saviour" is a "Sacrifice" precisely "as it is offered to God," and he does so in terms less amenable to the formulations of Luther and Calvin than, again, of St. Thomas:

> The sacrifice of the old law contained that true sacrifice of the passion of Christ only in a Figure . . . And therefore it was proper that the sacrifice of the new law instituted by Christ should hold something more: namely that it should contain him who suffered, not only in meaning or a figure, but even in the reality of the thing.[50]

Like St. Thomas, Donne emphasizes the reality of the thing itself – "how fearfull, how terrible, how reverentiall a thing is the blood of this immaculate Lambe" – and calls the Eucharist a sacrifice that supersedes the sacrifices of the Old Law. In this fourth Prebend Sermon, Donne accepts and dramatizes the Thomist conviction of a real, substantial divine presence in the sacrament in a way difficult to reconcile with any of the formulations of the major continental Reformers or even the official doctrines of the Church of England.

Yet in another sermon, delivered in 1630, Donne flatly rejects both "that

---

[46] *Donne's Prebend Sermons,* p. 155 (Potter & Simpson VII. 12. 321).
[47] Ibid., pp. 298–99.
[48] *Luther's Works* 38: 51, 117, 118.
[49] *Antidote to the Council of Trent,* in Dillenberger, *John Calvin,* p. 143.
[50] *Summa Theologiae* III. 75. 1: "Sacrificia enim veteris legis illud verum sacrificium passionis Christi continebant solum in figura . . . Et ideo oportuit ut aliquid plus haberet sacrificium novae legis a Christo institutum: ut scilicet contineret ipsum passum, non solum in significatione vel figura, sed etiam in rei veritate."

heresie of Rome, That the body of Christ may be in divers places at once, by the way of Transubstantiation," and "that dream of the Ubiquetaries [i.e., Luther and his followers], That the body of Christ must necessarily be in all places at once, by communication of the divine Nature."[51] Not only is Donne's inconsistency troubling here, but also his evasion of the actual teaching of the Thomist texts with which he was undoubtedly familiar. A principal argument for transubstantiation, St. Thomas maintains, is just that any other mode of explaining Christ's presence in the consecrated elements would require local motion entailing His movement from heaven through intervening space to simultaneously diverse destinations, all of which is impossible. The body of Christ can only be in different places at the same time by conversion of substance (i.e., transubstantiation): "Hence it is obvious that the body of Christ is in this sacrament in the way of substance, and not in the way of quantity."[52] It is evident that, in Thomas's view, the glorified body of Christ enjoys a different relation to place than that with which we are familiar.

Thomas's subtle argument is based on an analogically conceived meta-physics generally opaque to modern thought. Donne, however, plainly responds to it in the fourth Prebend Sermon, while airily dismissing it only three years later. Such tergiversation about the nature of the Eucharist is not only characteristic of Donne's unsettled religious conscience – a source of anxiety throughout his life – it is also an index of his vexed preoccupation with and longing for the divine presence, for this is a key feature of transubstantiation to which he manifests alternate hostility and sympathy. There is no doubt that Donne was firmly committed to the Church of England, but he reveals some perplexity about how much of the Catholic heritage could be retained. Ambivalence of this kind, in turn, explains why the meditative procedures of the Jesuits remained important to him throughout his life, despite his frequent expressions of antipathy toward the Society of Jesus. Here again Donne is haunted by the promise of Christ's presence offered by Ignatian meditation.

It is, therefore, unsurprising that there are no direct references to the Eucharist in the Divine Poems, which are yet rife with liturgical overtones and images obliquely hinting at the concept of blood and sacrifice.[53] In the first of the three late Holy Sonnets that are unique to the Westmoreland Manuscript ("Since she whome I lovd"), there is a sense that the early death of Donne's wife – she was, perhaps significantly, in her thirty-third

---

[51] Potter & Simpson IX. 8. 201.

[52] The first part of the explanation is condensed and paraphrased from *Summa Theologiae* III. 75. 2; the quotation is from 76.1 ad 3: "Unde patet quod corpus Christi est in hoc sacramento per modum substantiae, et non per modum quantitatis."

[53] See Theresa M. DiPasquale, "Ambivalent Mourning: Sacramentality, Idolatry, and Gender in 'Since she whome I lovd hath payd her last debt'," *JDJ* 10 (1991) 45–56; and M. Thomas Hester, "*miserrimum dictu*": Donne's Epitaph for His Wife," *JEGP* 94 (1995) 13–29.

year – represents a sacrifice for his spiritual benefit: "And her soule early into heaven ravished, / Wholy in heavenly things my mind is sett" (3–4). Thus taken up into heaven, Ann Donne is to be, like Beatrice, a stream revealing the fountainhead of love in God. The complex interchange of human and divine love then takes on the features of a private liturgical ritual:

> But though I have found thee, and thou my thirst hast fed,
> A holy thirsty dropsy melts mee yett.
> But why should I begg more love, when as thou
> Dost woe my soule, for hers offring all thine.   (7–10)

The notion of sacrifice becomes explicit in "A Hymne to Christ, at the Authors last going into Germany," where the poet's dead wife joins all his loved ones and even England itself in a great holocaust:

> I sacrifice this Iland unto thee,
> And all whom I lov'd there, and who lov'd mee;
> When I have put our seas twixt them and mee,
> Put thou thy sea betwixt my sinnes and thee.
> As the trees sap doth seeke the root below
> In winter, in my winter now I goe,
> Where none but thee, th'Eternall root of true Love I may know.   (8–14)

What is sought by this exchange is an intense, consuming, and exclusive love relationship with God:

> As thou
> Art jealous, Lord, so I am jealous now,
> Thou lov'st not, till from loving more, thou free
> My soule: Who ever gives, takes libertie:
> O, if thou car'st not whom I love alas, thou lov'st not mee.   (17–21)

This meditation on sacrifice and abandonment closes with an appeal for a "Divorce to All" (22) – a longing for death:

> To see God only, I goe out of sight:
> And to scape stormy dayes, I chuse an Everlasting night.   (26–28)

In her commentary on this poem, Gardner maintains that Donne has distorted an Augustinian motif: "The prayer to be freed from 'loving more' than Christ echoes Augustine: 'Minus te amat qui tecum aliquid amat, quod non propter te amat' (*Confessions*, x.29). But the conceit of Christ as a lover who should be jealous, since all true lovers are so, is Donne's own." In fact, the jealousy of God is scriptural: it is announced in the giving of the Law (Exodus 20: 5, 34: 14; Deuteronomy 4: 24, etc.), and surely Jesus' own words provide some basis for Donne's hyperbole: "If any man come to me, and hate not his father, and mother, and wife, and children, and brethren, and sisters, yea, and his own life also, he cannot be my disciple" (Luke 14: 26). Still, Gardner feels that there is an "uncharacteristic" morbidity in this hymn and in the sonnet on his wife's death, and she ascribes it to his grief and sees a resurgence of mood after his return from the German journey.[54] Other commentators have been less charitable. For Aers and Kress, the "Hymne" marks Donne out as "a Moloch-worshipper" who sacrifices others in the interests of his own ambitions and desires.[55] This bit of simplistic literalism would not require notice, except that it does touch an important facet of this troubled poem that has been remarked with more subtlety by John Carey. The sonnet, he observes, is a testimony, "outstandingly honest, and poignant in its honesty" to Donne's consuming sense that he is insufficiently loved, and that God's love is not enough. What is more, this divine love exerts a terrible pressure: God is "jealous" not only of Donne's wife but also of the Catholic Church, "where 'saints and angels' were worshipped (so Protestants said)."[56] Carey finds the same sense of disappointment in the "Hymne" along with a reminiscence of Donne's "martyred kinsman Sir Thomas More," whose *Utopia* anticipated Donne in recommending dark churches. In the end the poem discloses "both the majestic finality of pagan suicide and the Christian martyr's thirst for union with God."[57]

Carey is a shrewd critic, but he sees Donne's *Angst* only from the outside and underestimates its depth. The tensions between pagan pride and Christian humility, between worldly ambition and personal renunciation, are the common themes of Christian spiritual struggle. Donne, however, bears the marks of a soul lost in a theological wilderness: the invocation of "Everlasting night" at the close of the "Hymne" represents a Kierkegaardian leap of "faith alone" by a man who has begun to doubt in some measure the concrete and efficacious symbols of his boyhood religion without rejecting it altogether. Likewise, the uncontrolled talk of sacrifice in the poem's second stanza evinces a preoccupation with Catholic theological language without its substance and gives at least a shadow of plausibility to the extravagant claims of Aers and Kress: if the body of the Son is not on the altar as a sacrifice to the Father, then *what is* to be offered, and to whom? Malcolm Ross claims that "Donne has a Thomist feeling for society as an organism," which is not sustained by a corresponding faith in the Communion of the Saints as a present reality, because the indispensable foundation for the unity of Christ's mystical body is the reality of his sacramental body in the

---

[54] *Divine Poems*, p. 107.
[55] "A Reading of Donne's Poetry," in David Aers, Bob Hodge, & Gunther Kress, *Literature, Language and Society in England 1580–1680* (Totowa, NJ: Barnes & Noble Books, 1981), p. 71.
[56] *John Donne: Life, Mind and Art*, p. 59.
[57] Ibid., pp. 218–19.

Eucharist.[58] Although the assurance apparent in many of *The Divine Poems* certainly qualifies this assertion, the poetry reflects the same uncertainty about the precise nature and rôle of the sacraments that emerges here and there in the sermons.

Lacking an exact sense of the mode of God's presence in the sacraments of the Church of England, Donne turns to the practice of meditation and draws unhesitatingly from the Jesuit influence of his earliest education. The clearest manifestion of this influence in his poetry comes in the "Hymne to God my God, in my sicknesse," the fruit of another crisis in the poet's life, his nearly fatal illness of 1623.[59] Lewalski discovers in this poem marks of a specifically Protestant meditative tradition and religious genre theory, but her analysis does not exhaust the poem's possibilities. It is not a hymn, she says, but a preparation for the speaker's entry into the hymning of the heavenly choirs: "Therefore he does not sing now: he proposes instead to 'tune the Instrument here at the dore' and this tuning involves not song but thought, meditation."[60] As it turns out, a virtually identical trope is deployed in Luis de Granada's *Doctrina espiritual repartida en seis tratados* (Lisbon, 1587), as translated by the Jesuit Richard Gibbons (Louvain, 1599): "For first, before we enter into meditation, it is requisite that we prepare our hart vnto this holie exercise, which is as to tune a viall, before we plaie vppon it."[61] Of course one cannot be sure that Donne took the figure from Gibbons, but there is decisive evidence for Jesuit influence in Louis Martz's crisp analysis of the "Hymne to God my God" as a meditative poem with an Ignatian structure – especially as mediated by Edward Dawson – in which the process of meditation is itself foremost in the mind of the poetic persona.[62]

Martz's analysis will not be repeated here except to note the parallel he draws between the opening stanza of the poem and the preparation of a meditation "in which the speaker placed himself securely in the presence of God."[63] Since it is a realization of the divine presence in one's life that is the goal of meditation, as Ignatius conceived it, one must learn

> to behold how God dwells in creatures, in the elements giving them being, in plants giving them vegetative life, in animals giving them sensation, in men giving them understanding; and thus in me giving being, life, sensation, and understanding; likewise making a temple of me, who was created in the image and likeness of his divine majesty.[64]

---

[58] *Poetry and Dogma*, p. 167.

[59] I follow Gardner ("Appendix E," *Divine Poems*, pp. 132–35), in rejecting Walton's 1631 dating of this "Hymn" in favor of Sir Julius Caesar's date of 1623.

[60] *Protestant Poetics*, p. 281; see also p. 170.

[61] In Roberts, *Critical Anthology*, p. 217. See also p. 232, where "quieting our imagination" is likened to "tempering our instrument."

[62] "Introduction" to *The Anchor Anthology of Seventeenth Century Verse*, I, xxxiii–xxxv.

[63] Ibid., p. xxxiii.

[64] *Ejercicios espirituales*, cuarta semana, in *Obras completas de San Ignacio de Loyola*, ed. Ignacio

Meditation is, then, a focusing of one's rational faculties (memory, under-standing, will) on what is, in some sense, there already. In a letter to a Portuguese Jesuit, Padre Antonio Brandao, Ignatius reminds his correspond-ent that even scholars, who are unable to engage in long meditations by reason of their studies, "are able to exercise themselves in seeking the presence of our Lord in all things, as in conversation with someone, walking, seeing, tasting, hearing, understanding, and in all that we do, since it is true that his divine majesty is in everything by presence, power and essence. . . . and this good exercise," he adds, "will by disposing us cause grand visitations of the Lord, although only in a brief prayer."[65]

Donne's "Hymne to God my God" is a meditation on the "disposing" oneself for the presence of God by finding that very presence in affliction: mortal illness becomes a gateway, a "strait" into the Promised Land of God's unmediated presence. The need for preparation, to "tune the instrument," is crucial:

> Since I am comming to that Holy roome,
>   Where, with thy Quire of Saints for evermore,
> I shall be made thy Musique; As I come
>   I tune the Instrument here at the dore,
>   And what I must doe then, thinke here before.   (1–5)

As in St. Ignatius' view, so in Donne's "Hymne" the invocation of the divine presence requires the realization that God is *always already present*, that rather than an "absent presence" (as fallen, alienated man is tempted to believe), He is a *present absence* – present, that is, even when absent, filling every (apparent) absence. Contemporary theorists like Foucault and Derrida tend to see the inanition of language, the evacuation of the presence of the Word, occurring in the seventeenth and eighteenth centuries.[66] In fact, the abyss

Iparraguirre, S.J., 2nd ed. (Madrid: Biblioteca de Autores Cristianos, 1963), p. 244: "mirar cómo Dios habita en las criaturas, en los elementos dando ser, en las plantas vejetando, en los animales sensando, en los hombres dando entender; y así en mí dándome ser, animando, sensando, y haciéndome entender; asimismo haciendo templo de mí seyendo criado a la similitud y imagen de su divina majestad."

[65] Cartas #66, *Obras completas*, p. 763: "se pueden ejercitar en buscar la presencia de nuestro Señor en todas las cosas, como en el conversar con alguno, andar, ver, gustar, oír, entender, y en todo lo que hiciéremos, pues es verdad que está su divina Majestad por presencia, potencia y esencia en todas las cosas . . . y causará este buen ejercicio disponiéndonos grandes visitaciones del Señor, aunque sean en una breve oración."

[66] See Michel Foucault, *The Order of Things: An Archeology of the Human Sciences* (New York: Random House, 1970), esp. pp. 47–48: "*Don Quixote* is a negative of the Renaissance world; writing has ceased to be the prose of the world; resemblances and signs have dissolved their former alliance; similitudes have become deceptive and verge upon the visionary or madness; things still remain stubbornly within their ironic identity: they are no longer anything but what they are; words wander off on their own, without content, without resemblance to fill their emptiness; they are no longer the marks of things; they lie sleeping between the pages of books and covered in dust." This phantasmagoric nominalism ("magic nominalism"

gapes already at the beginning of the Reformation. In his controversy with Erasmus over freedom of the will, Luther opens up a fateful distinction: "The Diatribe [i.e., Erasmus' *Diatribe or Sermon Concerning Free Will*] is deceived by its own ignorance in that it makes no distinction between God preached and God hidden, that is, between the Word of God and God Himself . . . Thus, He does not will the death of a sinner – that is, in His Word; but He wills it by His inscrutable will."[67] In this account the Word of God is dissociated from God Himself and thus the Word is drained of full content; Luther's *Deus absconditus* is indeed an "absent presence." There is little wonder that Donne dismisses the Lutheran "Ubiquetaries" for an account of the Eucharist, since even the presence of Christ, the Word made flesh, offers no mediation between sinful man and the "inscrutable will" of "God Hidden."

Having distanced himself from the Catholic account, however, Donne is left with the form of Ignatian meditation as a means to find the hidden God. The elaborate cartographical similitude of stanzas two through four of the "Hymne to God my God" constitutes an attempt to peer beyond the "two-dimensional" version of reality furnished by the senses' "flatt Mapps" (14) in order to discover the "Easterne riches" of the "Resurrection" in the spherical realm of the divine presence. The Jesuit meditative tradition, embedded as it is in Catholic sacramental life centered in the Mass, assumes a virtual immediacy of the divine presence in the continuity of that presence with its sacramental signs: the real presence of Christ in the elements of the Eucharist is the radiant center of a universe of signs pointing toward their Creator. Now it is precisely the continuity between sign and sacramental reality – the divine presence – that is called into question by many Protestant Reformers (witness the discontinuity asserted by Luther between "God preached and God hidden"). This question of presence is the source of the poignancy in Donne's devotional poems. The "Hymne to God my God" is a prayer that God not be hidden, that His Word truly disclose His will, that the "flatt Map" not give the true picture of the human condition.

The poem's closing stanzas derive from the geographical conceit a more precise figuration of the convergence of sin and redemption, of God's apparent absence and actual (or *real*) presence:

perhaps?), a result of a complete breakdown of confidence in the analogical predication of being, finds a parallel in Jacques Derrida's discussion of Rousseau on language, *Of Grammatology*, trans. Gayatri Chakravorty Spivak (Baltimore: Johns Hopkins University Press, 1976), p. 154: "But what is no longer deferred is also absolutely deferred. The presence that is thus delivered to us in the present is a chimera. Auto-affection is a pure speculation. The sign, the image, the representation, which come to supplement the absent presence are illusions that sidetrack us."

[67] *The Bondage of the Will* IV.x, trans. J. I. Packer and O. R. Johnston (Old Tappan, NJ: Fleming H. Revel Co., 1957), p. 170.

We thinke that *Paradise* and *Calvarie*,
    Christs Crosse, and *Adams* tree, stood in one place;
Looke Lord, and finde both *Adams* met in me;
    As the first *Adams* sweat surrounds my face,
    May the last *Adams* blood my soule embrace.

So, in his purple wrapp'd receive mee Lord,
    By these his thornes give me his other Crowne;
And as to others soules I preach'd thy word,
    Be this my Text, my Sermon to mine owne,
    Therefore that he may raise the Lord throws down.   (21–30)

Joseph E. Duncan has given a convincing demonstration that the notion of the Tree of Knowledge and the Cross of Christ standing in one place has its origin in medieval and Counter-Reformation iconography.[68] Visual images turned up by Duncan – for example, Christ's Cross sprouting out of the foliage of a tree from which the naked Adam and Eve pluck fruit – further reinforces what is already suggested by Donne's verse: the coincidence is temporal as well as local. Just as Tree and Cross occupy one spot, so likewise the Fall into sin occasioned by the eating of the fruit of the forbidden tree is, from the divine perspective, simultaneous with the redemption from sin effected by Christ's becoming "fruit" of the "tree" of the Cross. This is why Donne can confidently ask that the Lord "finde both *Adams* met in me." The evident model for this temporal convergence is an understanding of the Eucharist that is not incompatible with a version of the Real Presence that reaches back through the Middle Ages to the Patristic period. In arguing that Christ is "immolated" in this sacrament, St. Thomas Aquinas quotes Augustine: "Christ was immolated once and for all in himself, and yet he is immolated daily in the sacrament." Moreover, it is "by means of this sacrament that we are made sharers of the fruit of the Lord's passion."[69] There is a parallel in the poet's asking that the old sinful Adam be displaced,

---

[68] "Donne's 'Hymne to God my God, in my sicknesse' and the Iconographic Tradition," *JDJ* 3 (1984) 157–80. Duncan provides a corrective to Gardner's Appendix F, "Paradise and Calvarie'," *Divine Poems*, pp. 133–37, which supposes more novelty in the conceit than the evidence warrants.

[69] *Summa Theologiae* III. 83. 1: "quia scilicet per hoc sacramentum participes efficimur fructus Dominicae passionis." See above n. 39 for Augustine's words. In accepting this broad vision of the Eucharist as sacrifice, Donne was part of – indeed helped to create – a developing "high church" or "Anglo-Catholic" *via media*. Although it became an important element in the Anglican tradition, it jars uneasily against the explicit language of the Thirty-First of the Articles of Religion of the Church of England, which denies that Christ's sacrifice is in any way re-enacted in the eucharist: "Oblatio Christi semel facta, perfecta est redemptio, propitiatio, et satisfactio pro omnibus peccatis totius mundi, tam originalibus, quam actualibus. Neque praeter illam unicam, est ulla alia pro peccatis expiatio, unde missarum sacrificia, quibus, vulgo dicebatur, sacerdotem offerre Christum, in remissionem poenae, aut culpae, pro vivis et defunctis, blasphema figmenta sunt, et perniciosae imposturae" (Makower, p. 486).

that he share in the "fruit" of the Cross, wrapped in the "purple" garment of the blood of Christ's sacrifice. The Cross, redemption and life thus displace the Tree, sin and death in a mode analogous to the displacement of the accidents of bread and wine by the substance of Christ's body and blood. The "flatt Map" is really a two-dimensional image of the global reality of grace.

Augustine, Thomas, Ignatius, and Donne would all, ironically, agree with Derrida: "Only infinite being can reduce the difference in presence. In that sense, the name of God, at least as it is pronounced within classical rationalism, is the name of indifference itself."[70] It is, in the Christian view, precisely the "infinite being" of God that transcends the "difference" of the spatiotemporal. This transcendence occurs pre-eminently in the sacrament of the Eucharist, and most uncompromisingly when explained as transubstantiation, in which the words of the consecration enact the transformation of the elements of bread and wine into the actual body and blood of Christ and thus *present* what they *represent*. The drama of Donne's divine poems arises partly from his simultaneous discomfort and fascination with this conception of sacramental presence. As he stands on the brink of the abyss, the threshold leading out of the analogical realm of traditional Christianity toward the rationalistic world of modern secularism, the devotional poet affirms the reality of God's being in the world.

ii

George Herbert occupies a different position respecting the meditative and sacramental traditions of Christendom from Donne, and in some ways he engages the Catholic heritage more sympathetically than his older contemporary. Unlike Donne, Herbert was born into a Protestant family, and his mother, Magdalene Herbert Danvers, came to be celebrated by Donne as model of the personal piety of the Anglican *via media*.[71] This very freedom from the burden of a Recusant past probably made it easier for Herbert to appropriate elements of Catholic worship. Coming of age a generation later than Donne, with the established church more firmly established, Herbert

---

[70] *Of Grammatology*, p. 71.

[71] See Donne's memorial sermon for Herbert's mother, Potter & Simpson VIII. 2. 90–91: "For, as the *rule* of all her *civill Actions*, was *Religion*, so, the *rule* of her *Religion*, was the *Scripture*; And, her *rule*, for her particular understanding of the *Scripture*, was the *Church*. Shee never diverted towards the *Papist*, in undervaluing the *Scripture*; nor towards the *Separatist*, in undervaluing the *Church*. But in the *doctrine*, and *discipline* of that *Church*, in which, *God* seal'd her, to himselfe, in *Baptisme*, shee brought up her children, she assisted her family, she dedicated her soule to *God* in her life, and surrendered it to him in her death; And, in that forme of *Common Prayer*, which is ordain'd by that *Church*, and to which she had accustom'd her selfe, with her family, twice every day, she joyn'd with that company, which was about her *death-bed*, in answering to every part thereof, which the Congregation is directed to answer to, with a *cleere understanding*, with a *constant memory*, with a *distinct voyce*, not two houres before she died."

could assess the ecclesiastical and spiritual situation of his time less self-consciously. Even without the emotional ties of Donne's boyhood Catholicism, Herbert was clearly drawn to a good deal of its liturgical and devotional tradition. "The Church Militant" is only one indication of the poet's distress about the future of religion in England (see above p. 54). A consideration of his poetry in terms of devotion, as inspired both by private meditation and corporate worship, gives an even clearer indication of his sensitivity to the drying up of the channels of grace during his lifetime and of his earnest commitment to the recovery of the precious awareness of the divine presence in human life.

For this reason the effort to read Herbert's poetry as the product of an exclusively and militantly Protestant mode of meditation results in particularly forced interpretations and distorts his place in literary and spiritual history. The problems with this approach are apparent in one of the earliest and most widely cited applications of the schema of Protestant poetics to Herbert. Ilona Bell argues that *The Temple* manifests a development in Herbert's religious consciousness insofar as it deliberately departs from the Counter-Reformation devotional modes of the earlier Latin poetry. "'The Church'," she writes, "rejects the Catholic tradition of *Passio Discerpta* and begins to search for a poetry of personal experience suited to Herbert's maturing Protestant faith."[72] To argue this view requires not only a distortion of Catholic devotional practice (which evidently cannot inspire "a poetry of personal devotion"), but also a tendentious, strained explication of many of Herbert's poems.

The two poems that open "The Church," the brief shaped lyric, "The Altar," and the long monologue of Christ from the cross, "The Sacrifice," suggest by their titles alone the medieval Catholic roots of Herbert's piety. In her classic study of his sources, Rosemond Tuve demonstrates with a wealth of detail, focusing especially upon "The Sacrifice," how Herbert draws upon medieval devotional and liturgical traditions. "The Sacrifice," for example, which opens with a direct quotation of the *O vos omnes* of Lamentations 1:12, is shaped by the *Improperia* or "Reproaches" sequences of the Good Friday liturgy:[73]

> *OH all ye, who passe by*, whose eyes and minde
> To worldly things are sharp, but to me blinde;
> To me, who took eyes that I might you finde:
>   Was ever grief like mine? (1–4)

---

[72] "'Setting Foot into Divinity': George Herbert and the English Reformation," in *Essential Articles for the Study of George Herbert's Poetry*, ed. John R. Roberts (Hamden, CT: Archon Books, 1979), p. 79.

[73] *A Reading of George Herbert* (Chicago: University of Chicago Press, 1952), pp. 24ff.

The poem proceeds thus in ritual fashion through 62 such quatrains, each with the same half-line refrain, except for a slightly altered refrain in stanza 54 and its conclusion in a sixty-third stanza:

> But now I die; now all is finished.
> My wo, mans weal: and now I bow my head.
> Only let others say, when I am dead,
>   Never was grief like mine.   (249–52)

Herbert was an English Protestant, but, as Tuve argues, he was steeped in the piety of the Middle Ages, and one would be hard-pressed to find anything in "The Sacrifice" incompatible with the faith and devotion of Catholics of any period. To the contrary, the litany-like refrain of the poem, with its resemblance to "high-church" liturgical form, could be taken as a deliberate affront to Puritan objections to set prayers used in the official worship of the Church of England.[74]

Ilona Bell would have us see here, however, a subtle critique of Catholic meditative traditions. Bell concedes that the refrain, "Was ever grief like mine?", was common in Medieval Catholic poetry. "Nevertheless," she argues, "Herbert's unusual, drilling repetition calls attention to Christ's unusual grief and causes us to wonder whether Herbert intended to question the traditional participation in Christ's grief taught by Catholic meditation." She adduces one of the middle stanzas of the poem as "an overt prohibition":[75]

> Weep not, deare friends, since I for both have wept
> When all my tears were bloud, the while you slept:
> Your tears for your own fortunes should be kept:
>   Was ever grief like mine?   (149–52)

In conjunction with this stanza, Bell sees a peculiar equivocation in the last two lines of "The Sacrifice" – "Only let others say, when I am dead, / Never was grief like mine." She concedes that "The phrasing encourages us to read the conclusion twice" so that our own suffering "echoes and imitates Christ's pain, just as Catholic meditation says we should"; but she finds such an approach unsatisfactory:

---

[74] See Stanley Stewart, *George Herbert* , pp. 39, 72, for the controversy over the form of public prayer and the attitude of Herbert on the issue.

[75] " 'Setting Foot into Divinity'," p. 69. The "repetition" of the refrain is of course not at all "unusual," as anyone who has ever participated in a litany knows. Tuve, *A Reading*, pp. 24–25, makes the further point that Herbert would, in all probability, have been familiar with the *Improperia* in polyphonic settings, such as those of Palestrina and Victoria, which make moving music out of the repetition of such phrases as *sicut dolor meus*. Why such repetition in "The Sacrifice" should be "drilling" rather than gravely solemn and ceremonial is a question Bell does not address.

This reading creates problems, however, since the imitation depends upon allowing Christ to say the words first, and his words preclude any imitation. Such contrariety does not produce an illuminating Christian paradox, as the conclusion of Donne's Holy Sonnets so often do; but there is a simple solution: even as we say, "Never was grief like mine," we are insisting upon the uniqueness of our own experience and confirming our separation from Christ's Passion. Thus if we try to read "The Sacrifice" as a model of mental communion, and if we truly understand the meaning of Christ's command, we will be forced to undergo a complicated process of reassessment: ultimately "The Sacrifice" undermines the traditional meditative goal of communal suffering.[76]

Bell's reading requires attention because it has been widely admired among proponents of the theory of Protestant poetics,[77] and because it reveals important parallels between the radical implications of the Reformation and postmodern theory. The ingenious, but tendentious, argument expends inordinate care in depriving "The Sacrifice" of all interest, religious or poetic. Surely it is a lesser poem if Christ's utterance is taken as a literal injunction: "Weep not, deare friends, . . .Your tears for your own fortunes should be kept." Surely we are meant to read this as a bitterly ironic summons for us to weep, despite the hardness of our hearts. After all, frail human beings are all too willing to save their tears for their own affairs, but it was hardly Christ's purpose to encourage such selfishness. Likewise, when Bell flattens out the ambiguous paradox in the last stanza, she again reduces both the poetic and spiritual power of the poem. It is the merely obvious meaning that she favors: of course no grief can ever be comparable to that of Christ, the Man of Sorrows. It is precisely the equivocal possibilities in the interpretation of the line, however, that give the poem's closing both wit and devotional resonance: Christ is also saying that *others* must make an impossible claim, that *their* grief is like *His* (that is, unique), which is possible – since all things are possible with God (Matthew 19: 26) – by entering through grace into the sacrifice of Christ. This paradox is the point not only of the poem, but of Christianity itself.

Bell's reading of "The Sacrifice" is further vitiated by the assumption that in the midst of a deeply moving sacred poem Herbert is busy with an ecclesiastical polemic founded on a grotesque caricature of Catholic meditative modes. By insisting that Herbert is emphasizing the uniqueness of Christ's suffering in "The Sacrifice," a suffering that no human being can duplicate, Bell implies that Catholics thought that they *were* duplicating Christ's suffering through participation in Ignatian meditation or in the

---

[76] " 'Setting Foot into Divinity'," p. 70.
[77] Lewalski, *Protestant Poetics*, p. 171, heartily endorses Bell's essay and paraphrases it as part of her own argument. See also Strier, *Love Known*, p. xvii, n. 17; p. 12, n. 22; p. 49, n. 47; Veith, pp. 39, 181, and 256nn. 16,22; and Hodgkins, p. 173.

Mass. This notion distorts what Catholic spiritual writers have in mind, which is, by the imaginative power of meditation, in the words of Edward Dawson, "to imitate our Savior so neere as we can," but always "reprehending our selves, as slothful, undevout, harde, ungratefull, and that after so many illuminations and incitations to goodness."[78] It is evident that the same viewpoint obtains in "The Sacrifice," that the injunction to save our tears for ourselves is an ironic reproach; for elsewhere in the poem Christ plainly instructs His followers to *attempt* to imitate Him, to bear His cross:

> My crosse I bear my self untill I faint:
> Then Simon bears it for me by constraint,
> The decreed burden of each mortall Saint. (197–99)

Of course it is only Christ's sacrifice that is efficacious, only His death that brings life: "Man stole the fruit, but I must climb the tree; / The tree of life to all, but onely mee" (202–03). But as Heather Asals points out, "For Herbert all 'I's' become one 'I' in 'The Church' as each individual speaker contributes his identity to membership in Christ's Body, or 'The Church'." Herbert can make this identification on the model of St. Augustine's *Commentary on the Psalms* which reads "the Davidic prophecy of Christ's sufferings on the Cross as *in his own person and in ours*" (emphasis in original).[79] Herbert is thus following ancient Catholic tradition: not attempted duplication of, but participation in, Christ's suffering.

Bell and other proponents of Protestant poetics have touched upon a genuine tendency in Reformation theology, which Bell makes explicit in her later essay by comparing it with contemporary theory.[80] The utterly "hidden" God of Luther who is not revealed in Christ, and the Christ of Calvin who does not render the sinner truly righteous by His grace, are indeed not present to the believer: this theology opens up a forbidding aporia in the face of any effort toward *imitatio Christi*.[81] If Herbert is a complete follower of Luther and Calvin, then the interpretation of "The Sacrifice" offered by Bell and Lewalski must be right. As the latter puts it, "In fact Herbert's speaker is forced, painfully, to recognize and admit that he cannot in any meaningful way either apprehend Christ's sufferings or imitate his sacrifice – and that his attempt to do so is near-blasphemous folly."[82] If this interpretation is correct, however, then we must assume that not only "The Sacrifice" but most of the poems in *The Temple* are bitterly and satirically ironic, and we must further assume that

---

[78] "Practical Methode," *Anchor Anthology*, pp. 506–07.

[79] Heather A. R. Asals, *Equivocal Predication: George Herbert's Way to God* (Toronto: University of Toronto Press, 1981), pp. 42–43.

[80] "Revision and Revelation in Herbert's 'Affliction (I)'," *JDJ* 3 (1984): 73–96. See also the other material cited above in Part I, n. 90.

[81] For Luther see *The Bondage of the Will* x, as cited above, n. 67. For Calvin see *Institutes* III. 11. 23, as quoted above above Part I, n. 90.

[82] *Protestant Poetics*, p. 171.

Herbert scorned the devotional practices established by his friend Nicholas Ferrar at Little Gidding, as well as the injunctions to imitate Christ in his own *A Priest to the Temple*.[83] Finally, we must assume that the ninth chapter of this work, "The Parson's State of Life," was written in a condition of temporary derangement; for here Herbert maintains "that virginity is a higher state then Matrimony," and that he who would live thus must *"put on the profound humility, and the exact temperance of our Lord Jesus."*[84]

Fortunately we are spared these assumptions by the paucity of evidence for the radical Lutheran/Calvinist reading of Herbert. The lines beginning "Weep not, deare friends" (149ff.), which Bell interprets as "an overt prohibition" of the *imitatio Christi*, are in fact perfectly amenable to a traditional Catholic interpretation and reflect the orientation of Catholic devotional poetry. Although the editions of neither Hutchinson nor Patrides annotate it – probably because it was not deemed obscure – the stanza alludes to Christ's address to the women of Jerusalem on His way to Calvary:

> And there followed him a great company of people, and of women, which also bewailed and lamented him.But Jesus turning unto them said, Daughters of Jerusalem, weep not for me, but weep for yourselves, and for your children. For, behold, the days are coming, in which they shall say, Blessed are the barren, and the wombs that never bare, and the paps which never gave suck. Then they shall begin to say to the mountains, fall on us; and to the hills, Cover us. For if they do these things in a green tree, what shall be done in a dry?

Within this context from the Gospel according to Luke (23: 27–31), "Weep not" in "The Sacrifice" takes on a very solemn tone, reflecting Our Lord's compassion for the sufferings of humanity in the Last Days. The meaning of the words in Herbert's poem is enhanced by the recollection that Christ's meeting with the women of Jerusalem is one of the Stations of the Cross (the eighth in current practice). As Terence Cave points out, this popular Catholic devotion was deployed as a structural principle by Spanish and French writers contemporary with Herbert for meditations on the Passion.[85] Jean de la Ceppède, for example, takes up Christ's address to the women in the fifth sonnet of the third book of his *Théorèmes*, part I:

> De peuple vn gros nombreux le Cõdamné suiuoit.
> Et cent femmes parmi, dont les pleurs, & les plaintes
> A tout autre qu'au Juif (qui sa mort poursuiuoit)
> Donnoient de cent regrets cent bourrelles estreintes.
> Les oreilles de Christ de leurs cris sont atteintes,
> Il s'esmeut, il s'arreste, il se tourne, il les void,

---

[83] *Works*, p. 224. See Stewart, *George Herbert*, p. 41 and passim.

[84] *Works*, pp. 236, 237.

[85] *Devotional Poetry in France, c. 1570–1613* (Cambridge: Cambridge University Press, 1969), pp. 33, 50.

Et de sa bouche esclot ces paroles espreintes
De son coeur que l'amour vers elles esmouuoit.
O Filles de Solyme, à quoy toutes ses larmes?
Ne pleurez point pour moy. Seruez vous de ses armes
Pauurettes pour vous mesmes, & pour vous enfantins,
Les iours viendront ausquels la peuplade future
Marquera de bon-heur celles dont les tetins,
Et l'amarry brehengne ont dementi nature.[86]

[A great number of people followed the One Condemned. And among them 100 women whose tears and cries give 100 strained torments of 100 regrets to everyone except the Jew (who sought his death). The ears of Christ are attentive to their cries, he is moved, he stops, he turns, he sees them, and his mouth brings forth these words wrung from his heart moved by love toward them. Oh daughters of Sion, why all these tears? Weep not at all for me. Save those weapons for yourselves and your babes. The days are coming when future generations will mark out as happy women whose breasts and barren womb have deceived nature.]

La Ceppède interprets Christ's words not as a literal command that His followers should not share His tears, but as an expression of love and sorrow for the trials of the faithful. This is certainly the most natural understanding of His words, and there is no evidence that Herbert's use of the motif should be interpreted in a contrary sense except, of course, the general thesis of Protestant poetics that the stanza is adduced to prove.

Bell seeks to buttress her case by asserting that "The Reprisall" also "openly rejects the attempt to reenact Christ's suffering":

I Have consider'd it, and finde
There is no dealing with thy mighty passion:
For though I die for thee, I am behind;
    My sinnes deserve the condemnation.   (1–4)

Bell and her successors treat this poem as an explicitly Protestant answer to the devotional problem raised somewhat ambiguously in "The Sacrifice": "the speaker . . . announces unequivocally that he cannot participate in Christ's Passion."[87] To make this interpretation stand up, however, one must show that such awestruck humility in the face of Christ's sufferings is an exclusively Protestant phenomenon. However, the same sense of self-effacing unworthiness is a familiar stance among Catholic poets contemporary with Herbert. There is no reason to suppose that Herbert despised the human

---

[86] *Les Théorèmes sur le sacré mystère de notre Rédemption* I. iii. 5, Reproduction de l'édition de Toulouse de 1613–1622, Préface de Jean Rousset, Travaux d'Humanisme et Renaissance #LXXX (Genève: Librairie Droz, 1966) I. 359–60.

[87] " 'Setting Foot into Divinity'," p. 78. See the comparable treatments by Lewalski, *Protestant Poetics*, p. 293; and Strier, *Love Known*, pp. 50, 53–54.

shortcomings of which he was so vividly aware; rather than suggesting that even the *effort* to participate in some small measure in Christ's sufferings is blasphemous, he is instead reminding unworthy mankind just how necessary such an effort is. It is only by such an effort that one understands how futile unaided human action is, and the acknowledgment prepares the way for mankind to share in Christ's victory over sin and death by grace, as the last stanza of "The Reprisall" suggests:

> Yet by confession will I come
> Into thy conquest: though I can do nought
> Against thee, in thee I will overcome
> The man, who once against thee fought.   (13–16)

The same longing for an escape from the toils of sinful selfhood emerges in Lope de Vega's "Soliloquios amorosos de un alma a Dios":

> ¡Oh piedad desconocida
> de mi loco desconcierto,
> que a donde Vos estáis muerto
> esté segura mi Vida!
>
>   .   .   .   .
>
>   ¿Para qué puedo importaros,
> si soy . . .lo que Vos sabéis?
> ¿Qué necesidad tenéis?
> ¿Qué cielo tengo que daros?
>
>   .   .   .   .
>
>   Pero ¿quién puede igualar
> a vuestro divino amor?
> Como Vos amáis, Señor,
> ¿qué serafín puede amar?
>   Yo os amo, Dios soberano,
> no como Vos merecéis;
> pero cuanto Vos sabéis
> que cabe en sentido humano.

[Oh mercy unacknowledged by my insane disorder, for where You are dead my life might be secure! . . . How can I matter to You, if I am – what You know? What need have You? What heaven have I to give You? . . . But, who can equal your divine love? What seraph can love as You love, Lord? I love You, sovereign God, not as You deserve, but so much as, You know, human sense is capable.]

In addition to the sense that man can never worthily return the love displayed by Christ in His Passion, Lope touches on another familiar theme in Herbert – man's inability to be properly grateful. The same "Soliloquy" begins,

Manso Cordero ofendido,
puesto en una cruz por mí,
que mil veces os vendí
después que fuistes vendido.[88]

[Gentle injured Lamb, put on a cross for me, I who have sold you a thousand times after you were sold.]

Obviously Lope's poem anticipates the mood of Herbert's "Ungratefulness" and, especially, "Unkindnesse":

Yet can a friend what thou hast done fulfill?
O write in brasse, *My God upon a tree*
His bloud did spill
Onely to purchase my good-will.
Yet use I not my foes, as I use Thee.   (21–25)

It is, therefore, implausible to suggest, with Richard Strier, that Herbert's disgust with his own ingratitude in these poems (as well as Shakespeare's throughout his plays) reflects "the main outlines of Reformation, especially Lutheran ethics."[89] A hatred of ingratitude was a common feature of Medieval and Renaissance moral sentiment without the influence of Luther.

Ilona Bell further insists that Herbert rejects any sense of Christ's sacrificial presence in the Eucharist. Discussing the poem "Home," she writes, "the meditation is a failure – the speaker does not feel Christ's presence . . . The sacrifice has ended, and Christ has ascended to heaven."[90] The problem with this interpretation is that "Home" is not a poem specifically about the Eucharist or the Crucifixion, despite one reference to "the pace / The bloud did make, which thou didst waste? / When I behold it trickling down thy face" (7–9); it is rather a poem about the longing for heaven, which, to Protestants and Catholics alike, is man's *true home*. Bell's example, therefore, is not an adequate basis for denying Catholic influence on the eucharistic poetry of *The Temple*. When Herbert does turn to meditate upon the sacramental meaning of the Eucharist, as in "The Priesthood," he is filled with reverence and awe:

But th'holy men of God such vessels are,
As serve him up, who all the world commands:
When God vouchsafeth to become our fare,
Their hands convey him, who conveys their hands.
O what pure things, most pure must those things be,
Who bring my God to me!

[88] *Obras escogidas*, II, 1008.
[89] *Love Known*, p. 22. Cf. Tuve, *A Reading*, p. 69, on "the great theme of ingratitude – in the tradition generally and in Herbert." Ingratitude is, of course, the main theme of the *Improperia* of the Holy Week liturgy, which figures so prominently in Tuve's book. Further, one need only consult Dante's treatment of ingratitude in the ninth circle of the *Inferno*.
[90] "'Setting Foot into Divinity'," p. 81.

> Wherefore I dare not, I, put forth my hand
> To hold the Ark, although it seem to shake
> Through th'old sinnes and new doctrines of our land.
> Onely, since God doth often vessels make
> Of lowly matter for high uses meet,
>   I throw me at his feet!   (25–36)

If Herbert's reference to "old sinnes" might suggest the abuses in the Medieval Church, which the Reformation set out to correct, then the "new doctrines" that join in to shake the "Ark" can only be an attack upon Puritanism. Thus some doubt is once again cast upon the existence of a firm Protestant consensus in seventeenth-century England, which is so much a part of the theory of Protestant poetics. More important still is the deep sense of Christ's real presence in the sacrament manifest here. As far as it goes, the poem is not incompatible with Catholic doctrine, and its tone recalls that Herbert approved of kneeling to receive communion.[91] Such features render doubtful Christopher Hodgkins' speculation that the "new doctrines" that worry Herbert are the "Arminianism and episcopal absolutism of Laud and his bishops."[92]

In fact "The Priesthood" bears a striking resemblance to a continental Catholic devotional lyric. The argument as well as the tone echoes a sonnet by Lope de Vega that likewise deals with the priest's sense of unworthiness in handling the consecrated Host:

> Cuando en mis manos, Rey eterno, os miro
> y la cándida víctima levanto,
> de mi atrevida indignidad me espanto,
> y la piedad de vuestro pecho admiro.[93]

> [When in my hands, eternal King, I look at you and
> elevate the spotless victim, I am fearful of my bold
> unworthiness, and I marvel at the mercy in your breast.]

While Herbert is obviously not expressing, as his Spanish contemporary does, the teaching of the Eucharist as sacrifice, he nonetheless intimates a sense of awe in the presence of the sacrament that is appropriate only to a belief in the real presence in some substantial mode.

Richard Strier, however, maintains that "Herbert's eucharistic theology (like that of Cranmer and the English Renaissance Church as a whole) is closer to Calvin's than Luther's";[94] that is, that Herbert has no belief in the

---

[91] "The Parson in Sacraments," *A Priest to the Temple*, chap. XXII, *Works*, p. 259: "The Feast indeed requires sitting, because it is a Feast; but man's unpreparednesse asks kneeling."

[92] *Authority, Church, and Society in George Herbert: Return to the Middle Way* (Columbia: University of Missouri Press, 1993), p. 136.

[93] *Obras escogidas* II. 183.

[94] *Love Known*, p. xiv.

real presence of Christ's body and blood in the sacrament. Strier is certainly correct about the official belief of the Tudor church. John Jewel's authoritative *An Apology for the Church of England* (1562), for example, only allows that "Christ himself" is "presently given unto us as that *by faith* we verily receive his body and blood" (emphasis added). It is denied that "the very nature of bread is changed," and this view corresponds very well with the twenty-eighth of the Articles of Religion.[95]

In order to argue that Herbert's poetry evinces no movement away from this receptionist position associated with Calvin, Strier must deprecate the eucharistic significance of the poet's language: "Herbert frequently uses Eucharistic-sounding language – language of blood, wine, and tasting – metaphorically." Strier does not bother to explain why a poet of firm Calvinist sympathies would, in a time of religious controversy, use such ambiguous figures that would lay him open to Catholic interpretation. He insists that neither "The Agonie" nor "Divinitie" is to be read as "specifically Eucharistic." Such a reading, Strier urges, would involve a misinterpretation of line 21 of the latter: "To do this, however, is to read 'he doth bid us take his bloud for wine' backwards. Coleridge saw this. His commentary on the line was, 'Nay, the contrary: take the wine to be blood'."[96]

Strier's remark is very odd. In the first place he omits some rather significant further comments by Coleridge: "Nay, the contrary; take the wine to be blood, and *the* blood of a man who died 1800 years ago. This is the faith which even the church of *England* demands; for the Consubstantiation only *adds* a mystery to that of Transubstantiation, which it implies" (emphasis in original).[97] To be sure, Coleridge gives an inaccurate assessment of the belief of the Tudor church regarding the Eucharist, apparently thinking that it accepted consubstantiation and interpreting that in a way that "implies" the Catholic doctrine. He is apparently surprised that Herbert, who is assumed to accept this doctrine, has gotten the phrasing "wrong." Hence Coleridge is really not a good witness for Strier's view; even though both have read the crucial line without seeing its actual intention, Coleridge has a keen sense of Herbert's traditional sacramental orientation.

Here, then, is the stanza from "Divinitie":

> But he doth bid us take his bloud for wine.
>   Bid what he please; yet I am sure,
> To take and taste what he doth there designe,
>   Is all that saves, and not obscure. (21–24)

---

[95] *An Apology of the Church of England*, ed. J. E. Booty (Ithaca, NY: Cornell University Press, 1963), p. 33. On Cranmer's disbelief in the real presence, see Jasper Ridley, *Thomas Cranmer* (Oxford: Clarendon Press, 1962), pp. 279–80. Article 28 is quoted above, Part II, n. 39.

[96] *Love Known*, pp. 46–47, n. 41.

[97] *Coleridge on the Seventeenth Century*, ed. Roberta Florence Brinkley, intro. Louis I. Bredvold (1955; rpt. New York: Greenwood Press, 1968), p. 536.

In quoting this stanza Strier omits the second half of line 22, "yet I am sure," and then complains of the stanza's obscurity.[98] Now the omitted half line suggests a typically Anglican attitude of the Stuart era, that what matters in receiving the sacrament of the Eucharist is belief in the fact of the real presence without worrying about *how* it might be accomplished. This vagueness is beginning to obtain by the end of the Elizabethan period. The treatment by Richard Hooker typifies the wish to have it both ways: "The bread and the cup are the body and blood because they are causes instrumental upon the receipt whereof the *participation* of this body and blood ensueth." But, "The real presence of Christ's most blessed body and blood is not therefore to be sought for in the sacrament, but in the worthy receiver of the sacrament." Yet Hooker does not remain content with this plain Calvinist or "receptionist" formulation: " 'This is my body', and 'this is my blood', being words of promise, sith we all agree that by the sacrament Christ doth really and truly perform his promise, why do we vainly trouble ourselves with so fierce contentions whether by consubstantiation, or else by transubstantiation the sacrament itself be first possessed with Christ or no?"[99] Malcolm Ross rightly observes that Hooker's view is not reconcilable with Catholic teaching, but he does not consider why men like Hooker refrain from an unambiguously Protestant statement that would have stilled Puritan suspicions, or why Andrewes, whose influence on Herbert is great, is even less explicitly "Protestant."[100]

Line 21 of "Divinitie" seems to assert that what is received is "bloud" that we "take for" i.e. apprehend through our senses as wine. Thus understood, Herbert's line is perfectly compatible with the eucharistic theology of St. Thomas and also with his "Hymn for Corpus Christi Day" ("Pange lingua gloriosa"):

> Verbum caro panem verum
> verbo carnem efficit;
> fitque sanguis Christi merum
> et si sensus deficit,
> ad firmandum cor sincerum
> sola fides sufficit.
>   Tantum ergo sacramentum
> veneremur cernui,
> et antiquum documentum
> novo cedat ritui.
> praestat fides supplementum
> sensuum defectui.[101]   (19–30)

---

[98] *Love Known*, p. 46.
[99] *Of the Laws of Ecclesiastical Polity* V. 67. 5–6, intro. Christopher Morris (London: J. M. Dent, 1907) II. 322–23.
[100] *Poetry and Dogma*, p. 61.
[101] *Devoutly I Adore Thee: The Prayers and Hymns of St. Thomas Aquinas*, ed. and trans. Robert

[The Word-made-flesh by his word makes true bread into flesh, and wine becomes the blood of Christ and, if sense fails, faith alone suffices to assure a sincere heart. Bowed down let us venerate so great a sacrament, and let the old model give way before the new rite. Let faith supply the defect of the senses.]

St. Thomas thus suggests that our senses "take" the sacramentally present flesh and blood of Christ "for" bread and wine, but "faith alone" (*sola fides*) is sure of the real presence. Herbert's line could quite reasonably be interpreted in this way, or perhaps it could mean take this blood *in place of* or *instead of* wine.[102]

Now either of these interpretations would be appropriate because of the generally eucharistic context. While denying the relevance of this context, Strier argues that this poem and "The Agonie" are closely associated in urging the claims of faith as opposed to reason;[103] but there is no reason to regard this emphasis on faith as a sign of Herbert's Lutheranism, especially if the sacramental overtones are acknowledged. As the lines from *Pange lingua* quoted above show, St. Thomas was quite emphatic about the primacy of *faith alone* in the acceptance of Christian mysteries. The eucharistic resonance of "Divinitie" is enhanced by its ninth line, "Could not that Wisdome, which first broacht the wine"; and this resonance is unmistakable in the closing stanza of "The Agonie":

> Who knows not Love, let him assay
> And taste that juice, which on the crosse a pike
> Did set again abroach; then let him say
>   If ever he did taste the like.
> Love is that liquor sweet and most divine,
> Which my God feels as bloud; but I, as wine.   (13–18)

The closing couplet implies strongly that what is to human sensation wine is, in the divine economy, the blood of Christ: what "God feels" is surely more reliable than what the poetic persona tastes. Moreover, the sense of eucharistic Real Presence in these lines is embodied in language highly reminiscent of Catholic meditations on the Sacrament of the Altar.[104]

One recent approach to Herbert's diffidence about spelling out eucharistic doctrine is to erect this reluctance into the distinctive principle of the Church

Anderson and Johann Moser (Manchester, NH: Sophia Institute Press, 1993), pp. 88, 90. See also the sequence for Corpus Christi Day, "Lauda Sion Salvatorem," esp. 31–36, and "Adoro te devote latens Deitas," esp. 1–8, Ibid., pp. 102, 104, 68.

[102] See *OED* s.v. "take," def. 48; s.v. "for," def. 5.

[103] *Love Known*, p. 41.

[104] Martz, *Poetry of Meditation*, pp. 84–85, 292. John T. Shawcross and R. D. Emma, ed., *Seventeenth Century Poetry* (Philadelphia: J. B. Lippincott, 1969), p. 208n, gloss ll. 17–18 of "The Agonie" as referring to transubstantiation.

of England. While Strier and the other proponents of Protestant poetics interpret Herbert in terms of the radical Protestantism of the mature Cranmer and the early Tudor church, an alternative is to read Herbert's irenic ambiguities back into the instabilities of the mid-sixteenth century. Thus Cranmer's doctrinal tergiversations are seen not as a result of the politic discretion of a man attempting to please a series of disagreeing (and disagreeable) masters, but rather of a doctrinal aporia – an anticipation of deconstructive theology. In this vein John N. Wall writes, "At the heart of the Church of England is not intellectual assent to a specific doctrinal position but the entering in to something *done.*" "Essential to Cranmer's reformed church," Wall continues, "is thus not assent to a statement of belief but participation in worship enabled by the Book of Common Prayer, which brings the biblical text and the sacramental enactment of the central event of Christian history into relationship with the present moment of celebration." This view supposes, then, that "Cranmer and his followers would have found difficult to accept" such things as "the categories of thought at work in an abstracted system" that could "affirm for language an ability to be descriptive and truth speaking."[105] From such a perspective Wall subsequently asserts, "The speaker [of "Divinitie"] addresses one of the central matters of Reformation controversy – whether and in what way Christ is present in the bread and wine of Holy Communion – and asserts that human speculation, again, is a diversion rather than a furthering of the way."[106]

This study is not an appropriate occasion to debate whether such an eliding of doctrine is compatible with traditional, orthodox Christianity of any persuasion. It is sufficient to point out here that the theory of discourse on which it rests was simply unavailable either to Cranmer or Herbert. In the very passage from Cranmer's writings adduced by Wall to demonstrate that "assent to a specific doctrinal position" is not central to Anglicanism, Cranmer insists that "wheresoever the word of God is *truly* preached, without addition of man's doctrines and traditions, and the sacraments duly administered according to Christ's institution, there is the *true* church" (emphases added).[107] Cranmer is here making rigorous doctrinal discriminations and claiming truth for his assertions. The importance of written formulations, of "verbal codes," to Cranmer's mind and heart is further attested by his conduct at his execution for heresy under Queen Mary in 1556. Having hoped to save his life by recanting his Protestant beliefs, at the time of his death Cranmer recanted that recantation and first thrust into the fire his right hand, because that hand was guilty of "setting abroad of a writing contrary to the *Truth,*" and because with that hand he had "written many

---

[105] *Transformations of the Word: Spenser, Herbert, Vaughan* (Athens: University of Georgia Press, 1988), pp. 11, 12, 13.

[106] Ibid., p. 221.

[107] Quoted ibid., pp. 11–12.

things *untrue*" (emphases added).[108] It is difficult to imagine such remorse from a man who doubted the capacity of "human language" for "truth speaking," and still more difficult to fancy him holding his hand unflinchingly in the fire for anything less than what he took to be *the Truth*.

By the same token, although Herbert deprecated doctrinal controversy, it is clear from his poetry that he would not have been happy with the rite for administering communion in the 1552 Book of Common Prayer (the last that Cranmer had a hand in), which pointedly refrains from calling the consecrated elements the Body and Blood of Christ, and which included the "Black Rubric" that denied "any real and essential presence there being of Christ's natural flesh and blood." It was the addition in 1599 and subsequent versions of the Prayer Book of "The body of our Lord Jesu Christ" and "The blood of our Lord Jesu Christ" that gave Herbert a warrant for his evocation of the Real Presence in his poetry.[109]

So intense was Herbert's eucharistic devotion that in "The Agonie" he seems to have imitated, whether consciously or not, a particular Catholic poem. Louis Martz mentions how Robert Southwell's Gethsemane meditations anticipate, in a general way, the devotional lyrics of Donne and Herbert; and Ira Clark points out specific parallels between "The burning Babe" and "Love Unknown."[110] Surely, then, Herbert was not unaware of these stanzas from "Sinnes heavie loade":

> O LORD my sinne doth over-charge thy brest,
>   The poyse thereof doth force thy knees to bow;
> Yea flat thou fallest with my faults opprest,
>   And bloody sweat runs trickling from thy brow:
> But had they not to earth thus pressed thee,
> Much more they would in hell have pestred mee.   (1–6)
>
> O sinne, how huge and heavie is thy waight,
>   Thou wayest more then all the world beside,
> Of which when Christ had taken in his fraight
>   The poyse thereof his flesh could not abide;
> Alas, if God himselfe sinke under sinne,
> What will become of man that dies therein?[111]   (13–18)

[108] Quoted by F. E. Hutchinson, *Cranmer and the English Reformation* (New York: Collier-MacMillan, 1962), p. 107. See also Jasper Ridley, *Thomas Cranmer*, pp. 402–03.

[109] The differing passages from the Prayer Book are quoted in J. S. Millward, ed., *Portraits and Documents: The Sixteenth Century*, 2nd ed. (London: Hutchinson Educational Ltd., 1968), p. 88.

[110] *Poetry of Meditation*, p. 43. Ira Clark, *Christ Revealed: The History of the Neotypological Lyric in the English Renaissance* (Gainesville: University Presses of Florida, 1982), p. 89.

[111] *The Poems of Robert Southwell, S.J.*, ed. James H. McDonald and Nancy Pollard Brown (Oxford: Clarendon Press, 1967). The poem was available in a printed edition in 1602; "Christs bloody sweat," ll. 1–12, and was printed in *Moeoniae* in 1595.

The middle stanza of "The Agonie" is a brilliant compression of this conceit, which Southwell, awkwardly if movingly, develops through three stanzas:

> Who would know Sinne, let him repair
> Unto Mount Olivet; there shall he see
> A man so wrung with pains, that all his hair,
> His skinne, his garments bloudie be.
> Sinne is that presse and vice, which forceth pain
> To hunt his cruell food through ev'ry vein.   (7–12)

These lines, as F. E. Hutchinson points out in the commentary of his edition, make an unmistakable allusion to the winepress of Isaiah 63: 1–6, with its traditional eucharistic overtones.[112] The same allusion is made by Southwell in "Christs bloody sweat":

> FAT soile, full spring, sweete olive, grape of blisse,
> That yeelds, that streams, that pours, that dost distil,
> Untild, undrawne, unstampt, untouch of presse,
> Deare fruit, cleare brookes, faire oile, sweete wine at will:
> Thus Christ unforst prevents in shedding blood
> The whips, the thornes, the nailes, the speare, and roode.   (1–6)

Given this element of intertextuality, it is unlikely that the traditional eucharistic language of "Divinitie" and "The Agonie" is merely metaphorical as Richard Strier maintains. For Herbert, as for Southwell, Christ's sufferings and the shedding of His Blood are intimately associated with the Eucharist, in which He is in some way present under the form of "sweet wine."

For anyone who rejects the conception of Herbert as an exemplar of a severe Protestant poetics, the difficulty of defining his Anglicanism remains. The work of Heather Asals on predication in Herbert is, therefore, quite important because she sets out to establish a philosophical context for the poet's sacramental orientation. Although I think her argument incorrect that Herbert deliberately substitutes an equivocal predication of God for Thomist analogical predication, her discussion succeeds in opening up a problematic area in the notion of the Anglican *via media*. Seventeenth-century Anglicans like Herbert longed to retain the spiritual consolations and *ambiance* of the Catholic sacramental system under Protestant auspices. They desired to reverence the real presence in the Eucharist without acceding to the validity of the doctrine of transubstantiation; hence, on the model of Donne, it became their conscious virtue *not* to specify the mode of this presence.

---

[112] *Works*, p. 488. Hutchinson refers to what he calls "a kind of inversion of the doctrine of transubstantiation" not only in l. 18 of "The Agonie," but also in "Divinitie," l. 21, and "The Invitation," ll. 11–12. As we have already observed, these lines can be read, without forcing, as not incompatible with the doctrine of transubstantiation. For the eucharistic associations of the winepress of Isaiah 63, see Tuve, *A Reading*, pp. 59–72.

However, their desire to respond sacramentally to the natural universe as an image of the divine wisdom and a medium of divine grace entailed an acceptance, whether conscious or not, of the metaphysics of Thomist realism that gives this view of nature its coherence.

The Anglican dilemma that Herbert represents furnishes, for obvious reasons, fertile ground for various kinds of historicist ploughing. Much recent scholarship concentrates on analyzing the import of *The Temple* by determining the author's social, political, and religious orientation. By placing his poems in a particular milieu or ideological context, scholars seek to define Herbert as Calvinist or Arminian; and they speculate whether, had he lived to see the Civil War, he would have favored Parliament and the Puritans or the Stuart court and Laudian church. Critics of new-historicist inclination try to explain devotional and doctrinal motifs in *The Temple* in terms of the socio-political imperatives of Jacobean and Caroline culture. It is self-evident that knowledge of the historical background will furnish valuable insights for the interpretation of Herbert's poetry; however, unless the poetry is, at some point, considered in its own right as poetry, then there is, finally, no point in studying it at all. A look at what might be called the logic of Herbert's figurative language provides a general perspective on *The Temple* as discourse and still links it to the intellectual developments of the poet's era. Herbert's deployment of analogy, in particular, discloses an affinity with the Scholastic vision of reality that is not ordinarily attributed to him and suggests that he was resistant to the dominant intellectual inclinations of the seventeenth century.

By considering the analogical properties of Herbert's poetry, one can avoid the reductive tendencies of historicisms, old and new, which generally result in delivering the poet into the camp of the Puritans, who despised formal liturgy. This is effected by splitting apart the tenors and vehicles of metaphors – the contemporary equivalent of Puritan iconoclasm. Christopher Hodgkins, for example, concedes that "*The Temple* as a whole is permeated with ecclesiastical and liturgical language." "However," he continues, "these ecclesiastical references are, from the beginning, clearly metaphorical or otherwise internalized, representing spiritual realities that come to exist fundamentally *within* the believer."[113] Michael C. Schoenfeldt sets out "to foreground the social and political presuppositions of theological doctrine" in *The Temple* and virtually reduces Herbert's devotional poetry to a calculating ploy for heavenly preferment.[114] Apart from the specific issues involved in such judgments, the methodical dismembering of metaphors seems a heavy-handed way of dealing with poetry as witty as Herbert's. He was not a literalist, and he was not bound to any of the particular party

---

[113] *Authority, Church, and Society*, p. 169.
[114] *Prayer and Power: George Herbert and Renaissance Courtship* (Chicago: University of Chicago Press, 1991), p. 12.

platforms current in his day: such, I think, was the essential meaning of his withdrawal from the court to a rural parsonage at Bemerton. One of his strengths as a poet is the capacity to see simultaneously converging planes of reality, as manifest in the density, the resonance and the wit of his language. It is just this poetic vitality that is threatened by efforts to tie the meaning of Herbert's poetry to an a priori historical construct. The effect is to strip the interior of *The Temple* as bare as the interior of a Puritan meeting hall.

Heather Asals strives to defend the wholeness of Herbert's vision by establishing its philosophical basis through a consideration of his poetry in terms of predication. She thus covers the same ground as Malcolm M. Ross in his chapter on "The Anglican Dilemma" in *Poetry and Dogma*; that is, the crisis faced by those members of the Church of England who wished to reconcile Reformation doctrine with certain aspects of Catholic liturgical and devotional practice. Asals attempts to refute Ross in order to preserve a distinctive and substantial "Anglican" way by arguing that Herbert deliberately substitutes an equivocal predication of God for Thomist analogical predication. "Ross is wrong," she maintains, "in his assumption that analogy alone can create ontological relevance: this is not what Herbert's contemporaries, or Herbert, assumed."[115] Although neither Ross nor Asals devotes substantial discussion to the meaning of "analogy" per se, or ever actually defines the term, both appear to accept implicitly the view formulated at the beginning of the sixteenth century by Thomas de Vio Cardinal Cajetan that, for St. Thomas Aquinas, analogy is a metaphysical category referring to the nature of being itself. For Cajetan, analogy is the key to understanding the relation between Creator and creation: "And by this every concept of a creature is a concept of God: just as every creature is a certain likeness of God."[116] If this interpretation is accepted, then Asals must be arguing that Herbert is substituting a logical mode of predication for a metaphysical doctrine – a procedure in itself problematic. Ralph McInerny argues, however, that St. Thomas, contrary to Cajetan's explanation, regards analogy not as a metaphysical reality, but as a logical intention, indeed as a special kind of equivocation.[117] If either understanding of the term is accepted, then Asals' dichotomy between analogy and equivocation is put in question, and the dichotomy breaks down altogether upon consideration of the close

---

[115] Ross, *Poetry and Dogma*, pp. 55–87; Asals, *Equivocal Predication*, p. 6.

[116] *De conceptu entis* #3, in *De nominum analagia et De conceptu entis*, ed. P. N. Zammit, O.P. (Rome: Institutum Angelicum, 1934), p. 98: "Ac per hoc omnis conceptus creaturae, est conceptus Dei: sicut omnis creaturae aliqua est similitudo Dei." See also *De nominum analogia* #1, p. 3: "Est siquidem eius notitia necessaria adeo, ut sine illa non possit metaphysicam quispiam discere, et multi in aliis scientiis ex eius ignorantia errores procedant." For a thorough modern exposition of Cajetan's view, see James F. Anderson, *The Bond of Being: An Essay on Analogy and Existence* (1949; rpt. New York: Greenwood Press, 1969).

[117] *The Logic of Analogy: An Interpretation of St. Thomas* (The Hague: Martinus Nijhoff, 1961).

resemblance between what she calls "equivocation" in Herbert's poems and what St. Thomas calls "analogy."

In the first place, the evidence that Herbert consciously constructed a specifically Anglican devotional poetics based on equivocal predication is exceedingly slender. The word "equivocation" only appears twice in his extant works, both times in prose works and both times dyslogistically.[118] Moreover, there is nothing distinctively English or Protestant about the features of Herbert's poetry that Asals associates with equivocation. It will hardly serve to ascribe Herbert's use of the pun and other aspects of "metaphysical wit" to a peculiarly Anglican rebellion against the Scholastic use of analogy. Walter Ong has long since demonstrated that medieval Scholasticism itself created a highly effective "metaphysical poetry" in the hymns of St. Thomas Aquinas and Adam of St. Victor.[119] In the seventeenth century a preoccupation with conceit, paradox and pun was common in poetry throughout Europe, and it received more elaborate theoretical treatment in areas untouched by Anglican theology than in England.[120] Spain, in particular, could boast such notable metaphysical poets as Lope de Vega, Góngora, and Quevedo and, in Baltasar Gracián, perhaps the most distinguished of the baroque theorists. Gracián, a Jesuit, makes a number of approving references to St. Thomas Aquinas and even cites an "epithet" from Thomas' Corpus Christi antiphon, *O sacrum convivium*, as an example of a witty figure.[121] Hence there is no need to call upon Anglican theology to explain why "seventeenth-century poetry tends to pun."[122] Finally, the books that Asals adduces to illustrate the Anglican theology of equivocation, said to

---

See also McInerny, *Studies in Analogy* (The Hague: Martinus Nijhoff, 1968).

[118] *A Concordance to the Complete Writings of George Herbert*, ed. Mario A. di Cesare and Rigo Mignani (Ithaca: Cornell University Press, 1977), s.v. "equivocation." The references occur in the tenth chapter of *A Priest to the Temple*, *Works*, p. 240: "He suffers not a ly or equivocation by any means in his house, but counts it the art, and secret of governing to preserve a directnesse, and open plainnesse in all things; so that all his house knowes, that there is no help for a fault done, but confession"; and in *Briefe Notes on Valdesso's Considerations*, *Works*, p. 316: "Wherefore as *David's* Adultery cannot be excused, so need not *Abraham's* Equivocation, nor *Paul's* neither."

[119] "Wit and Mystery: A Revaluation in Medieval Latin Hymnody," *Speculum* 22 (1947) 310–41. Tuve, *A Reading*, p. 55, comments on the resemblance of "Metaphysical wit" to "medieval habits of mind."

[120] See Joseph A. Mazzeo, "A Seventeenth-Century Theory of Metaphysical Poetry," in *Renaissance and Seventeenth-Century Studies* (New York: Columbia University Press, 1964), pp. 29–43; and "Metaphysical Poetry and the Poetic of Correspondence," ibid., pp. 44–59; and "Modern Theories of Metaphysical Poetry," *Modern Philology* 50 (1952) 88–69. See also Frank Warnke, *Versions of Baroque: European Literature in the Seventeenth Century* (New Haven & London: Yale University Press, 1972), pp. 1–19; and Lowry Nelson, Jr., *Baroque Lyric Poetry* (New Haven and London: Yale University Press, 1960), pp. 3–17.

[121] *Agudeza y arte de ingenio*, discurso XV, in *Baltasar Gracián: Obras completas*, ed. Arturo del Hoyo (Madrid, Aguilar, 1967), p. 307. St. Ignatius enjoined upon his Company a particular reverence for Scholastic theology. See *Ejercicios*, cuarta semana, 11 regla, *Obras*, p. 272.

[122] Asals, *Equivocal Predication*, p. xii.

provide the basis for Herbert's equivocal poetics, were all published after his death. What is more, the two chief authors, Richard Baxter and James Ussher, provide dubious support for a "high-Anglican" reading of Herbert, since Baxter was a Presbyterian and Ussher a Calvinist prelate.[123]

It is certainly true that a theology of equivocation was available during Herbert's era, but such a theology could not sustain the sacramental view of reality that pervades *The Temple* and affirms the creation's capacity to bespeak its Creator. The theology that confines itself to a purely equivocal predication of God finds its most unblushing proponent in Thomas Hobbes:

> And therefore, men that by their own meditation, arrive to the acknow-ledgement of one Infinite, Omnipotent, and Eternall God, choose rather to confesse he is Incomprehensible, and above their understanding; than to define his Nature by *Spirit Incorporeall*, and then confesse their definition to be unintelligible: or if they give him such a title, it is not *Dogmatically*, with intention to make the Divine Nature understood; but *Piously*, to honour him with attributes, of significations, as remote as they can from the grossenesse of Bodies Visible.[124]

Hobbes was of course a scandal to the English clergy of the later seventeenth century, but his formulation is the genuine logical consequence of insisting that only equivocal predication of God is possible. "Things are equivocally named, when they have the name only in common, the definition (or statement of essence) corresponding with the name being different," writes Aristotle.[125] Hence Hobbes maintains that what we say of God is purely arbitrary with regard to the actual nature of godhead and merely reflects our piety. Hobbes's specific theological view grows naturally out of his rejection of metaphysics in general. For him, philosophy is the knowledge of "bodies" and their relations only; there can be no knowledge of "separated essences," much less of Being itself.[126] Given a strict interpretation of "equivocation"

---

[123] Ibid., pp. 9–14. In n. 43 (p. 117) Asals argues that the late dates of Ussher's and Baxter's works are unimportant because she is "not arguing for source" and because "both Ussher and Baxter . . . argue by the logic books that were commonly read in that day, and they, thus, give us a picture of the way in which theologians were absorbing the material in those books." In nn. 45 and 46 (p. 117) she maintains that Ussher was not such a "low" churchman as is usually supposed because he was reacting against his Irish Catholic surroundings, and that Baxter was a moderate Puritan "committed to the idea of a 'Catholic' Church." Now the fact is that Ussher and Baxter adhered to a decidedly Calvinist view of the Eucharist, whatever their fondness for *a* "Catholic" church; and Asals offers no evidence that they represent the way in which *Herbert* was "absorbing the material in those [logic] books."

[124] *Leviathan* I. 12, ed. C. B. Macpherson (Harmondsworth: Penguin Books, 1968), p. 171.

[125] *Categories* I (1a), trans. Harold P. Cook (Cambridge, MA: Harvard University Press, 1938), p. 13.

[126] *Leviathan* IV. 46, pp. 682–95.

that excludes the Thomist analogical variant, it is difficult to agree with Asals that equivocal predication can "create ontological relevance."

St. Thomas Aquinas was not unaware of this problem of metaphysical predication: "It is impossible," he writes, "for anything to be predicated univocally of a creature and God; for in all univocals, the rationale of the name is common to both things of which the name is predicated." But things that share the reason or rationale of a name (*ratio nominis* – its intelligible meaning) are to that extent equals in terms of rational essence, and a creature cannot share God's essence. "Whatever there is in God," Thomas further observes, "this is his own proper existence; for just as essence in him is the same as existence, so his knowledge is the same in him as actual knowing. Hence, since the existence proper to one thing cannot be transferred to another, it is impossible for a creature to attain the same rational essence in possessing what God possesses, just as it is impossible for it to reach the same existence."

St. Thomas introduces analogy to explain how it is possible for man to know anything at all about God and hence to say anything about Him with a certain propriety:

> And yet it cannot be said that whatever is predicated of God and creatures is altogether equivocal, since if there were no real likenesses of creatures to God, then his essence would not be a resemblance of creatures, and he would then not know the creatures in knowing his own essence. Likewise we would be unable to arrive at any knowledge of God from created things; and of the names befitting creatures, one could no more be said of him than another, since among equivocal names it does not matter whichever one is applied, because there is no likeness to the thing.[127]

---

[127] *De Veritate* II. 11, *Quaestiones Disputatae* XI, 5th ed. (Turin: Marietti, 1927), III. 58–59: "Impossibile est aliquid univoce praedicari de creatura et Deo; in omnibus enim univocis communis est ratio nominis utrique eorum de quibus nomen univoce praedicatur; et sic quantum ad illius nominis rationem univoca in aliquo aequalia sunt, quamvis secundum esse unum altero possit esse prius vel posterius, sicut in ratione numeri omnes numeri sunt aequales, quamvis secundum nomen rei unus altero prior sit. Creatura autem quantum-cumque imitetur Deum, non potest pertingere ad hoc ut eadem ratione aliquid sibi conveniat et Deo; illa enim quae secundum eamdem rationem sunt in diversis, sunt eis communia secundum rationem substantiae sive quidditatis, sed sunt distincta secundum esse. Quidquid autem est in Deo, hoc est suum proprium esse; sicut enim essentia in eo est idem quod esse, ita scientia idem est quod scientem esse in eo; unde, cum esse quod est proprium unius rei non possit alteri communicari, impossibile est quod creatura pertingat ad eamdem rationem habendi aliquid quod habet Deus, sicut impossibile est quod ad idem esse perveniat. Similiter etiam in nobis esset: si enim in Petro non differret homo et hominum esse, impossibile esset quod homo univoce diceretur de Petro et Paulo, quibus est esse diversum; nec tamen potest dici quod omnino aequivoce praedicetur quidquid de Deo et creatura dicitur, quia si non esset aliqua convenientia creaturae ad Deum secundum rem, sua essentia non esset creaturarum similitudo; et ita cognoscendo essentiam suam non cognosceret creaturas. Similiter etiam nec nos ex rebus creatis in cognitionem Dei pervenire possemus; nec nominum quae creaturis aptantur, unum magis de eo dicendum esset quam aliud; quia ex aequivocis non differt quodcumque nomen imponatur, ex quo nulla rei convenientia attenditur."

Thomas's remark that "whatever is predicated of God and creatures is not altogether equivocal" suggests a degree of equivocity in analogy. Hence, although Asals proposes Herbert's "The Sonne" as a paradigm case of the poetics of equivocation, neither the poem nor her commentary seems to violate St. Thomas' explanation of analogy:

> How neatly doe we give one onely name
> To parents issue and the sunnes bright starre!
> A sonne is light and fruit; a fruitfull flame
> Chasing the fathers dimnesse, carri'd farre
> From the first man in th'East, to fresh and new
> Western discov'ries of posteritie.
> So in one word our Lords humilitie
> We turn upon him in a sense most true:
> For what Christ once in humbleness began,
> We him in glorie call, *The Sonne of Man*.   (5–14)

"This," Asals writes, "is what I consider to be Herbert's formal 'apology' for equivocation; homonymous language turns to a 'sense most true'."[128] However, if a pun is to have a "sense most true," it cannot be, as St. Thomas would say, "altogether equivocal" (*omnino aeqivoce*). The point of this sonnet in praise of the English language is to disclose how its hidden network of correspondences mirrors the hidden correspondences of reality. The poet is at pains to show that the homophone *sun/son* (in modern spelling) is not a mere equivocation, but conceals a "real likeness." If the poem is equivocal, then it is equivocal in what St. Thomas calls a "large sense" that "includes in itself analogy," that acknowledges varying degrees of likeness within the structure of reality.[129] The literary significance of these degrees is intimated by C. S. Lewis's shrewd observation that "the *Romance of the Rose* could not, without loss, be rewritten as the *Romance of the Onion*."[130] To see how far Herbert's poem is from pure equivocation, one need only consider a literary application of sheer equivocity (also employing religious language) in an exchange between James Joyce's washerwomen: "Lord help you, Maria, full of grease, the load is with me! Your prayers."[131] The *Lord/load* and *grace/grease* puns (probably far more homophonic in the speech of Joyce's working-class Irish women than in that of most scholars) are not intended to enhance our sense of the

---

[128] *Equivocal Predication*, p. 9.

[129] *Summa Theologiae* I. xiii. 10 ad. 4: "Philosophus largo modo accipit aequivoca, secundum quod includunt in se analoga." For the sense of degrees of likeness, see the body of this article as well as the passage from *De Veritate* quoted above n. 127.

[130] C. S. Lewis and E. M. W. Tillyard, *The Personal Heresy* (London: Oxford University Press, 1939), p. 97. See also McInerny, "Metaphor and Analogy," in *Studies in Analogy*, pp. 81–83; and "Metaphor and Fundamental Ontology," in *Studies*, pp. 92, 93–94.

[131] *Finnegans Wake* (1939; rpt. New York: Viking Press, 1959), p. 214.

providential design of creation; Joyce's love of the English language was based on different considerations.

Asals, whose instincts about the sacramental resonance of Herbert's poetry are so sure, goes astray in attempting to detach the poet from the Thomist synthesis without depriving the poetry of its metaphysical significance. She thus inadvertently aligns Herbert, in a great philosophical conflict that reached a crisis in the seventeenth century, with the side of the debate that would utterly reject the "sense most true" of "The Sonne." The passages she quotes from Ussher and Baxter oversimplify the problem of predication and misconstrue the import of analogy as St. Thomas conceives it. Ussher says, "for these over-reaching terms of thing, beeing, somewhat, nature, &c. which seem to contain the Word of God as well as all other things created by him, doe not express any materiall cause of God, neither doe they contain these words God and creature, as the generall doth his specials or kinds but are *spoken of them equivocally, so that the tearm onely, and not the definition of the tearm doth agree to them*" (Asals' emphasis). Baxter is said to argue "the case for the propriety of equivocacy even more cogently. In the 'logicks commonly read in the Schools', Baxter testifies, '*Omne Analogum est AEquivocum*': '*Scotus* maintaineth, that *inter Univoca & Aequivoca non datur medium*' (*I. Dist. 8: 2*)."[132]

But the analogical predication of being does not fall under these strictures, first, because being, like the other transcendentals, is not, St. Thomas maintains, a genus.[133] Moreover, Thomas does not suppose that a definition, which is necessarily quidditative or essential, can be predicated univocally of God and creature; and he is careful to specify the mode of analogy allowable in such a context. In *De Veritate* he distinguishes between the "conformity of proportion" (*convenientia proportionis*) and the "conformity of proportionality" (*convenientia proportionalitatis*). The first mode is exemplified by our terming both an animal and its urine "healthy," since the "urine bears a certain comparison to the health of the animal" ("ex eo quod urina habet aliquam similitudinem ad sanitatem animalis"). The "being" (*ens*) of substance and accident is also related in this way. The second mode of proper proportionality is exemplified by the analogy of physical sight (*visus corporalis*) and understanding (*intellectus*); for as sight is in the eye, so understanding is in the mind. Only the latter mode of analogy can obtain between God and creature:

---

[132] *Equivocal Predication*, p. 12. Asals quotes James Ussher, *A Body of Divinitie, or the Summe and Substance of Christian Religion* (London, 1645), p. 31; and Richard Baxter, *Certain Disputations of Right to Sacraments and the True Nature of Visible Christianity* (London, 1658), pp. 427–28.

[133] *De Natura Generis* I, in *Opuscula Philosophica*, ed. Raymundi M. Spiazzi, O.P. (Turin: Marietti, 1954), pp. 177–78: "Et ideo ens genus non est, sed est de omnibus communiter praedicabile analogice. Similiter dicendum est de aliis transcendentibus." See also Anderson, *Bond of Being*, p. 280; McInerny, *Logic of Analogy*, pp. 134–35.

Therefore, since in these things that are said analogically according to the first mode, There must be some determinate relation between the entities that share the common feature by analogy, it is impossible for anything to be analogically in this mode of God and creature; for no creature has such a relation to God by which a divine perfection can be determined. But in the other mode of analogy no determinate relation is considered between those things that share something by analogy; and therefore nothing prevents some name being said analogically of God and creature according to this mode.[134]

The crucial point argued by St. Thomas is that a creature does not share or participate in a substantial attribute of God, but that the creature merely does something – namely, it exists – in a way parallel to what God does in existing. The determinate relation, then, is between the creature's act of being (or knowing) and God's act of being (or knowing), which are in some sense proportional, but infinitely distant. The point is expounded thus by Anderson:

> In its primary and elementary sense, the phrase "analogy of being" is only shorthand for the statement that, although all things are distinct from one another in their very act of existing, they are nevertheless all brought together in a community of relations through their proportionate sharing in that act.[135]

There is a certain irony in Baxter's use of Duns Scotus to support his position on the equivocity of terms used to predicate God. Although it is true that Scotus is not satisfied with the concept of analogical predication, he in fact maintains that being can be predicated *univocally* of God and creature. Otherwise, he argues, transcendentals, like being and wisdom, would be

---

[134] *De Veritate* II. 11 (III, 59): "Quia ergo in his quae primo modo analogice dicuntur, oportet esse aliquam determinatam habitudinem inter ea quibus est aliquid per analogiam commune, impossibile est per hunc modum analogiae dici de Deo et creatura; quia nulla creatura habet talem habitudinem ad Deum per quam possit divina perfectio determinari. Sed in alio modo analogiae nulla determinata habitudo attenditur inter ea quibus est aliquid per analogiam commune; et ideo secundum illum modum nihil prohibet aliquod nomen analogice dici de Deo et creatura." In the course of this discussion, St. Thomas introduces a metaphorical analogy from mathematics to explain metaphysical analogy: God's knowledge is to God as man's wisdom is to man (x/a=b/c). As Peter Geach, "Aquinas," in G. E. M. Anscombe and Peter T. Geach, *Three Philosophers* (Ithaca, NY: Cornell University Press, 1961), p. 123, points out, this metaphor is "a thoroughly bad one." It does not, however, vitiate the validity of the concept, which Geach illustrates more efficaciously from contemporary mathematical functions. See also Gerald B. Phelan, *St. Thomas and Analogy* (Milwaukee: Marquette University Press, 1948), esp. pp. 38–39.

[135] *The Bond of Being*, p. 79. See also Etienne Gilson, *The Spirit of Medieval Philosophy*, trans. A. H. C. Downes (New York: Charles Scribner's Sons, 1940), pp. 447–48, n. 14. The strictures of McInerny, *Logic of Analogy*, esp. pp. 166–69, do not alter the fundamental metaphysical point. His insistence that the analogy of names is always a logical intention, not a mode of reality, makes the proposition that Herbert was deliberately rejecting analogical predication, if anything, less tenable.

different concepts when predicated of God and creatures, entailing disconcerting consequences:

> From any notion proper to attributes as they are in creatures nothing could be concluded about God, since there is another altogether different notion in the one and the other. Indeed it could no more be concluded that God is formally wise from the notion that we apprehend in creatures, than that he is formally a stone. For some different concept of a stone could be formed from the concept of a created stone, to which concept, as it is an idea in God, this stone bears some relation, and thus it might be formally said: *God is a stone*, according to this analogical concept, just as he is wise according to that analogical concept.[136]

In the interest of affirming that being and the other transcendentals are univocal as applied to God and creatures, Scotus reduces analogy, in this passage, to sheer equivocation. Certainly, he is aiming more at Henry of Ghent than at St. Thomas, whose concept of the analogy of being, in another context, he reduces virtually to univocity.[137] The irony (a Thomist would say) is that, by claiming to know too much about the being of God, Scotus opens the door to those who assert that we know absolutely nothing. The unbridgeable gap Scotus opens up between univocal and equivocal predication was bound to be exploited by the nominalism of Ockham and lead to the "hidden God" of Luther – and of Baxter and Ussher.

The problem of theological predication was still very a much moot issue during the Reformation (indeed it remains so today) and certainly would have been familiar to Herbert, who is known to have importuned his stepfather for money to purchase divinity books.[138] Cajetan was already worried about the philosophical status of analogy at the beginning of the

---

[136] *Quaestiones in Primum Librum Sentiarum* [*Opus oxoniense*], Dist. III, Q. 2, 10; Joannis Duns Scoti, *Opera Omnia* (Paris: Vivès, 1893), IX, 21: "Quod si dicas, non, sed alia est formalis ratio eorum quae conveniunt Deo, ex hoc sequitur inconveniens, scilicet quod ex nulla ratione propria eorum, prout sunt in creaturis, potest concludi aliquid de Deo, quia omnino alia et alia ratio est istorum et illorum, imo non magis concluderetur, quod Deus est sapiens formaliter ex ratione sapientiae quam apprehendimus ex creaturis, quam quod Deus est formaliter lapis. Potest enim conceptus aliquis alius a conceptu lapidis creati formari, ad quem conceptum lapidis, ut est idea in Deo, habet lapis iste attributionem, et ita formaliter dicetur: *Deus est lapis*, secundum illum conceptum analogicum." This nineteenth-century edition is virtually a reprint of the edition of Luke Wadding (Lyons, 1639) with its extensive commentaries and scholia by other Franciscans of Wadding's era. It seems to have sparked no little interest if one considers the references to Scotus cited by Asals from the 1640s and 1650s and Milton's casual reference in *Areopagitica*. For a slightly different (and doubtless more accurate, but not for the seventeenth century) Latin text with translation of this passage, see Duns Scotus, *Philosophical Writings*, trans. Allan Wolter, O.F.M. (Indianapolis: Hackett Publishing, 1987), p. 25. For Cajetan's answer to this passage in Scotus, see *De Analogia Nominum* X.106–13, pp. 80–85.

[137] Ibid., Dist. VIII, Q. 2, 1–3, pp. 574–75. The *Commentarius* on ¶1 (p. 574) insists that "D. Thom. et Scotus possunt conciliari."

[138] See letters III and V to Sir John Danvers, *Works*, pp. 364–65, 366–67.

sixteenth century. If "the being of a substance is univocal," he remarks, "then, since being belongs explicitly to the notion of a substance, it therefore belongs explicitly in the definition of man." This proposition is not only "inconveniens et contra Aristotelem et viam communem," as Cajetan points out; it also raises the difficulty that St. Thomas raises in *De Veritate* of how "man" can be predicated of both Peter and Paul without their *being* the same man.[139] Like St. Thomas, Cajetan is at pains to stress the difference between analogicity and both univocity and pure equivocity. Equally he stresses the difference between the analogy of determinate relation and that of proportionality: "God and a creature are analogous according to the second mode: for the distance between God and a creature is infinite."[140] Writing almost a century later in 1585, Dominico Bañes maintains that arguments impugning the Thomist concept of analogy for excessively diminishing the gulf between God and creatures are really refutations of the Scotist doctrine of univocal predication. "It is not necessary to the notion of analogy," he asserts, "that the analogical term explicitly convey the dependence or proportion of one to the other."[141] Thus though a creature – say, a man – is dependent on God, this does not entail a dependency or proportion under the formal concept of being (or wisdom or any other transcendental). Hence *being* is not predicated univocally of God and creature in the way that *animal* is predicated univocally of man and horse; but it is not absolutely or "purely" equivocal, because there is some meaningful parallel between the being of God and the "participated" being of creatures. Or in other terms, human wisdom is truly similar to divine wisdom in a sense that a stone (Scotus's example) is not similar to God.

---

[139] Thomae de Vio Caietani, *In De Ente et Essentiae D. Thomae Aquinitatis* II. 20, ed. P. M.-H. Laurent (Turin: Marietti, 1934), p. 36: "Ens est univocum substantiae et accidentis: ergo in ratione substantiae expresse cadit ens; ergo in diffinitione hominis explicite cadit ens." Thomas's observation about Peter and Paul is quoted above n. 127. Cajetan's importance during the next century and a half is indicated by the plentiful references to his work in Donne's sermons.

[140] *In De Ente et Essentiae* II. 21, p. 37: "Deus autem et creatura secundo modo: infinita enim est distantia inter Deum et creaturam." See also *De Nominum Analogia* x. 108, p. 81: "Ideo oportet, huiusmodi analogis nominibus utendo ex parte unitatis, semper modum proportionalitatis subintelligi; aliter in univocationem lapsus fieret."

[141] Dominico Bañes, *Scholastica Commentaria in Primam Partem Summae Theologicae S. Thomae Aquinitatis* Q. XIII a. 5, ed. Luis Urbano (1934; rpt. Dubuque, Iowa: William C. Brown, n.d.), p. 311: "ad rationem analogiae non est necesse, ut nomen *analogum* explicite importet dependentiam aut proportionem, quae reperitur in analogatis, sed satis fuerit, quod ratio formaliter significata per illud nomen conveniat ipsis analogatis cum dependentia aut proportione unius ad aliud." It is worth remarking that Bañes was very well known as one of Santa Teresa's spiritual directors and as a leading Dominican antagonist of the views of the Jesuit Molina on grace – a controversy of great interest to English Protestants like Donne. See, for instance, his *Essays in Divinity*, p. 50; and his *Prebend Sermons*, p. 81 (Potter and Simpson, VI. 15. 301), and Mueller's commentary on the *Prebend Sermons*, pp. 206, 236, 247.

These abstruse considerations are important for an understanding of poetic language generally, and especially for an understanding of Herbert, for he wrote at a time when the mind of Christendom was undergoing a great transformation precisely with respect to the modes of human knowledge and man's relation to God. Heather Asals is handling an important issue, and handling it correctly, when she asserts that Herbert "shared many assumptions about the nature of God with St. Thomas (his predicates), and [that] he shared with Thomas a belief in the *need* to predicate God" (emphasis in original). But still to argue that Herbert "substituted equivocal predication for analogy in his own ontological system"[142] is to place him, philosophically and ecclesiastically, in an untenable position. Purely equivocal predication allows one to make no assumptions about God at all; in fact, it would undermine the sacramental theology and liturgical practice to which Herbert was plainly inclined (and which Asals herself ascribes to him). Purely equivocal predication can only serve the anti-metaphysical urge of the radical Reformation, with its hidden God, and lead ultimately to the oft-repeated agnosticism of Hobbes: "But for Spirits, they call them Incorporeall; which is a name of more honour, and may therefore with more piety bee attributed to God himselfe; in whom wee consider not what Attribute expresseth best his Nature, which is Incomprehensible; but what best expresseth our desire to honour Him."[143] If Herbert believed that all predication of God was purely equivocal, then there is no way he could "share assumptions" (or "predicates") about the nature of God with St. Thomas; equivocal predication is not about the nature of God since it is based on no real likeness between Him and the creation. Equivocal predication of God would not reflect His nature but rather, as Hobbes maintains, merely our feelings about Him.

In contemporary terms, equivocation is the language of ideology, the hermeneutic of suspicion. An effectively "equivocal" reading of Herbert's poems with ecclesiastical and liturgical titles, would suggest that the governing images and figures are significant only as indices to "the speaker's inner state." Hence when Christopher Hodgkins insists that " 'The Windows' . . . one of Herbert's most affecting architectural poems, is not about how stained-glass windows inspire devotion, but how a preacher is a window,"[144] he simply dismisses Herbert's metaphor by a didactic, critical procedure that casts aside the vehicle like a spent cartridge once the bullet of instruction is speeding on its way. However, if there were not a prior assumption that stained-glass windows *do* inspire devotion, which Herbert's poem expects to evoke in the reader, then the metaphor would have no point. An analogical reading would interpret "The Windows" as a poem about the mutually enhancing effects of "Doctrine and life, colours and light in one"

---

[142] *Equivocal Predication*, p. 15.
[143] *Leviathan* IV. 46, pp. 689–90.
[144] *Authority, Church, and Society*, pp. 169, 172.

(11). Analogy is thus inclusive of meaning: opening *windows* on the multi-layered density of reality where the symbols that man devises, like the creatures of nature, are both manifestations of, and incitements to, his spiritual experience.

What Asals offers as an equivocal use of language generally turns out to rest upon an analogical foundation. "Anthropopathia," she writes, "is a metaphor of projection which allows the poet to discover within the 'accommodated' actions of God the spiritual condition of self. 'And should Gods eare / Which needs not man, be ty'd to those / Who heare not him, but quickly heare / His utter foes'? the speaker asks in 'The Method'."[145] If these lines from "The Method" exemplify equivocation, it is only that particular, qualified sort that St. Thomas calls analogy: the lines (25–28) assume a real likeness, a responsiveness in God that corresponds to the human faculty of hearing. Although God has no "eare" in a sense of the term univocally predicable of God and man, the trope is not purely arbitrary; it is not merely the subjective attribution of human wishes to Luther's utterly unknown God. To be sure, "Gods eare" is not strictly a proportional analogy, but a metaphor. However, the poet's confidence in the metaphor rests upon the possibility of predicating analogically of God such transcendental terms as wisdom, goodness and justice as they are understood in human experience. Hence the metaphor signifies a genuine awareness of something truly in God's nature about which man can reason with *method*:

> Then once more pray:
> Down on thy knees, up with thy voice.
> Seek pardon first, and God will say,
> *Glad heart rejoyce.* (29–32)

If "Gods eare" were purely equivocal, the speaker of this poem could have no such assurance of being *heard*.

"The Method," like "The Sonne," thus establishes an analogical style of discourse that is not merely equivocal: the poet likes "our language" because its rifts are loaded with providential ore. "An Offering," with its eucharistic overtones, is still more significant in this respect: although the *language* may seem equivocal, its ultimate import – its *predication* – is not. "Come, bring thy gift," the poem begins, with a hint of approaching to receive communion by way of an allusion to Matthew 5: 23–24: "Therefore if thou bring thy gift to the altar, and there remembrest that thy brother hath ought against thee; leave thy gift before the altar, and go thy way; first be reconciled to thy brother, and then come and offer thy gift." In the fourth stanza the eucharistic reference becomes explicit:

---

[145] *Equivocal Predication*, p. 41.

There is a balsome, or indeed a bloud,
Dropping from heav'n, which doth both cleanse and close
All sorts of wounds; of such strange force it is.   (19–21)

There is certainly a play of language here: a blood that is a balsam that
cleanses and closes wounds – an "All-heal" (22). But underlying the
paradoxical figures is the complex reality of the wine/blood of the eucharistic
species: this "balsome" is *indeed* a "bloud." It operates in the realm of human
sin and suffering, but its origin is divine ("Dropping from heav'n"). "Bloud"
is not in Herbert's poem an "altogether equivocal" predication; it is an
analogical predication because it signifies the dual reality that is the marrow
of the sacrament. Although as an English Protestant Herbert stops short of
articulating the doctrine of transubstantiation, in this context it is worth
recalling that the relation between substance and accident is analogical.[146] If
Herbert's doctrine is vague, his devotion is intense. The "bloud" in his poem
has a genuinely restorative and transforming effect; it actually conveys
sanctifying grace, a "favour" that changes the offering:

Yet thy favour
May give savour
To this poore oblation;
And it raise
To be thy praise,
And be my salvation.   (37–42)

Herbert is in fact relentless in seeking out analogical likeness within
apparent equivocation. His "Anagram of the Virgin Marie" goes beyond
coincidence of sound in a homonym and finds a correspondence of meaning
in an apparently fortuitous rearrangement of letters:

MARY
Ana-{   } *gram*
ARMY
How well her name an *Army* doth present,
In whom the *Lord of Hosts* did pitch his tent!

That these four letters are patient of such reordering would seem to be pure
equivocation, the result of sheer, irrational chance; and the word "army"
would not, at first glance, seem to offer much opportunity for pious reflection
in relation to "Mary." (One need only consider what James Joyce might do
with it.) But again the point – the *wit* – of Herbert's poem is to insist that the
anagram is not merely coincidence, not purely equivocal: it is the effect of
God's providential ordering of the realm of contingent being in harmony

---

[146] Cajetan, *In de Ente et Essentia* II. 21, p. 37: "Substantia et accidens sunt analogata primo modo sub ente."

with divine purposes. Herbert's "Anagram" thus manifests the same kind of wit that Baltasar Gracián attributes to St. Augustine:

> Augustine made the center of his wit that Lady who was the center of the infinite wisdom, and he said: the Eternal Word deigned to exchange the bosom of the Father for the sacred virginal womb of his Mother, and this Lady went from being the wife of a poor carpenter to being the wife of the Architect of Heaven.[147]

As the parallel with Gracián suggests, Herbert's poetry evinces not only a penchant for witty, analogical correspondences but also a striking and, in Protestant England, unusual devotion to the Virgin Mary. This doubtless explains the irenic manner in which the poem that follows "Anagram" in *The Temple*, "To All Angels and Saints," expounds the Protestant view of intercession. Especially tender is the poem's regard for the Mother of God:

> I would addresse
> My vows to thee most gladly, Blessed Maid,
> And Mother of my God, in my distresse.
>
> Thou art the holy mine, whence came the gold,
> The great restorative for all decay
> In young and old;
> Thou art the cabinet where the jewell lay:
> Chiefly to thee I would my soul unfold.   (8–15)

This sentiment is checked only by a Reformation scruple: "alas, I dare not" (16).

More is at stake here than merely determining to call Herbert's poetry "analogical" rather than "equivocal." The similarity between Herbert's mode of perceiving reality and Gracián's reveals how the English Protestant clergyman shared the Spanish Jesuit's sense of analogical correspondence as part of the nature of things. The poems of *The Temple* must therefore be read as representing more than one level of reality at the same time. Herbert maintains a remarkable poise between the Catholic traditions of the past and the doctrinal demands of the Reformation. His aim is to capture a sense of God's sacramental presence in forms of worship, whether private devotion or liturgical ritual. Only an analogical conception of the relationship between the eternal realm of God and the temporal created world provides the terms for an adequate metaphysical foundation.

---

[147] *Agudeza y arte de ingenio* iv, in *Baltasar Gracián: Obras completas*, ed. Arturo del Hoyo (Madrid: Aguilar, 1967), p. 248: "Hizo Augustino centro de su agudeza a aquella Señora, que lo fue de la sabiduría infinita, y dijo: Dignóse el Verbo Eterno de trocar el seno del Padre por el sagrado virginal vientre de su Madre, y pasó esta Señora, de esposa de un pobre carpintero, a serlo de Arquitecto del Cielo." Gracián quotes Augustine from a Nativity sermon of questionable authenticity, *Patrologia Latina* (Appendix) 38–39.1987: "Exsultemus in fide et ad partum Virginis, quae dum desponsaretur fabro, coeli nupsit Architecto."

No more effective illustration of this principle is available than the culminating poem of "The Church," "Love (III)." An analogical consideration gives more resonance to the sexual images and implications so assiduously exhibited by Michael Schoenfeldt. The sexuality is certainly there, as it is in many other poems in *The Temple* and in Christian devotional poetry in general. But it is misleading to suggest that "Love (III)" is permeated by scarcely concealed erotic preoccupations under a surface of conventional piety. Nothing is more conventional than for Christian devotion to be expressed in unmistakably erotic figures that point beyond themselves to what, from a Christian perspective, is the most ecstatic fulfillment of the most intense desire. Hence Schoenfeldt rightly disputes Janice Lull's assertion that "Love (III)" rejects the sexual analogy "altogether"; like all analogies it is not rejected but subsumed in something greater.[148] Sexual desire is not the same as the love of God, but God loves and is loved by creatures who are subject to the desire of the flesh. When a man says to a woman, "I love you," the usage of "love" is not, as St. Thomas might say, "altogether equivocal" with respect to the statement, "God is love" (1 John 4: 8, 16). Hence the erotic metaphors in "Love (III)" are not mere figures of speech to be dispensed with once the spiritual meaning is determined, and much less are they furtive indications that the poet's devotion to God is some kind of displaced or repressed sexuality waiting to be exposed by the daring candor of postmodern criticism. In Herbert's vision of reality, sacred and profane love are analogous. Therefore metaphors and images based on this analogy disclose the mutually illuminating and enhancing character of what, in our usually limited human perspective, appear to be discrete phases of the experience of love. In Herbert's analogical vision, nothing is ever *merely* what it is; it is always something more.

For this reason there is little purpose in trying to decide whether "Love (III)" is a poem either about receiving communion or being received into heaven, or instead is a poem mainly about its title, *love* or *agape*. Louis Martz got it right four decades ago when he pointed out that it "simultaneously represents the reception of the sacrament and the admission of the redeemed to the 'marriage supper' of Revelation."[149] The Eucharist and the beatific

---

[148] *Prayer and Power*, p. 256. Janice Lull, *The Poem in Time: Reading George Herbert's Revisions of the Church* (Newark: University of Delaware Press, 1990), p. 49. See also Chana Bloch, *Spelling the Word: George Herbert and the Bible* (Berkeley: University of California Press, 1985), p. 339.

[149] *The Poetry of Meditation*, p. 319. Joseph Summers, *George Herbert: His Religion & Art* (1954; rpt. Binghamton, NY: Center for Medieval and Early Renaissance Studies, 1981), p. 89, maintains that poem is principally concerned with heaven. Strier, *Love Known*, p. 78, concedes that it suggests both communion and heaven, but argues that love itself is "the primary subject." Marion White Singleton, *God's Courtier: Configuring a Different Grace in George Herbert's* Temple (Cambridge: Cambridge University Press, 1987), p. 195, treats "Love (III)" as a communion poem. Terry G. Sherwood, *Herbert's Prayerful Art* (Toronto:

vision are, of course, the two most wondrous manifestations of God's love, since both involve in different modes the gift of God himself – the granting of the divine presence to human beings. Harold Toliver thus misses the mark in saying of "Love (III)" that "Herbert's feast of words, his would-be service as a poet, is not exactly equivalent to a church supper or arrival at heaven's threshold."[150] Equivalence is not the issue; both the sacramental and eschatological presence can be represented simultaneously because they are, analogically, the same presence.

The poem opens by evoking an allegorical scene: a weary, dusty traveler/ sinful pilgrim Christian reluctantly seeking rest at an inn/ church/ heaven. God, as "Love" (see 1 John 4: 8), is implicitly both the host of the "inn" and the consecrated Host of the Eucharist, with the term suggested by the vendor's phrase, "What d'ye lack?" – roughly translated as the seventeenth-century equivalent of "May I help you?":[151]

> Love bade me welcome: yet my soul drew back,
>> Guiltie of dust and sinne.
> But quick-ey'd Love, observing me grow slack
>> From my first entrance in,
> Drew nearer to me, sweetly questioning,
>> If I lack'd any thing.   (1–6)

Much of the poignancy of this poem grows out of the homeliness of its atmosphere, created by the simple diction with its hints of colloquialism. The dusty traveler has come upon an "inn" that is finer than he could have imagined, far too grand for the likes of him. Similarly, sinful man can only be abashed when he reflects upon what awaits him both in the sacramental and heavenly presence of God. What is most exquisite about the poem is how, using the plainest language and the simplest allegorical figures, it evokes a sense of awesome mystery. Such is the nature of the Eucharist: an awesome mystery hidden in simple everyday elements. The nature of analogy as proportion or ratio is thus clearly displayed in "Love (III)."

Its eucharistic implications are clarified by recourse to "The H. Communion." According to the latter poem, Christ "dost now . . . convey" (4) himself "by the way of nourishment and strength" (7) with the power of

---

University of Toronto Press, 1989), pp. 49, maintains that the poem "suggests . . .the communion table and the heavenly marriage."
[150] *George Herbert's Christian Narrative* (University Park: Pennsylvania State University Press, 1993), p. 210.
[151] *OED* s.v. "lack," #3. For an example see Ben Jonson, *Bartholomew Fair* II.ii. The implied or unspoken *host/ Host* pun is noticed by Arnold Stein, *George Herbert's Lyrics* (Baltimore: Johns Hopkins University Press, 1968), p. 194: "But Love is the perfect Host and becomes the body of Christ in the Eucharist." See also Strier, *Love Known*, p. 78; Schoenfeldt, *Prayer and Power*, p. 200.

"Meeting sinnes force and art" (12); that is, He is present in the eucharistic species, which are a channel or medium of supernatural grace:

> Onely thy grace, which with these elements comes,
>> Knoweth the ready way,
>> And hath the privie key,
> Op'ning the souls most subtile rooms;
> While those to spirits refin'd, at doore attend
>> Dispatches from their friend.   (19–24)

The notion that grace "comes with" the elements of the sacrament is not typical of the Reformation. Zwingli states flatly, "Sacramentes geue not grace," and Calvin maintains, "They do not of themselves bestow any grace, but they announce and manifest it." Jewel says that the sacraments "might seal his grace in our hearts," with the Zwinglian or Calvinist implication that unmediated grace already in the soul is ratified or manifest by reception of the sacraments.[152] Article 25 of the Articles of Religion calls the sacraments "not only marks of the profession of Christians, but rather certain witnesses and efficacious signs of grace."[153] Herbert can be seen to build on this notion of efficacy. His elaboration of the intercourse between the physical ("these elements") and "the souls most subtile rooms," by which grace is conferred, could serve as a rejoinder to Zwingli's insisting, "The fleshe profiteth nothing. Namely, to eate it naturallye, but to eate it spiritually profyteth much, for it gyveith lyfe" (*The accompt*, p. 43). Herbert treats the reception of the Eucharist as itself a means of transforming grace that restores the close communion between man and God that Adam enjoyed in Paradise:

> Thou hast restor'd us to this ease
> By this thy heav'nly bloud;
> Which I can go to, when I please,
> And leave th'earth to their food.   (37–40)

It is this understanding of the Eucharist that explains the overcoming of the traveler's reluctance by the "sweetly questioning" Host of "Love (III)"; the "lack" the traveler feels in approaching the feast is supplied by the feast itself. The same Love that first "made the eyes" (12) that "cannot look on thee" (10) has furnished the means to restore them, making them capable, finally, of the beatific vision:

---

[152] Huldrik Zwinglius, *The accompt rekenyng and confession of faith*, "The seuenth Article," pp. 28–39; Calvin, *Institutes* IV. xiv. 14–17, II. 503; Jewel, *Apologie*, p. 30.

[153] Makower, p. 485: "Sacramenta a Christo instituta, non tantum sunt notae professionis Christianorum, sed certa quaedam potius testimonia, et efficatia signa gratiae, atque bonae in nos voluntatis Dei, per quae invisibiliter ipse in nos operatur, nostramque fidem in se non solum excitat, verum etiam confirmat."

> Truth Lord, but I have marr'd them: let my shame
> > Go where it doth deserve.
> And know you not, sayes Love, who bore the blame?
> > My deare, then I will serve.
> You must sit down, sayes Love, and taste my meat:
> > So I did sit and eat. (13–18)

Marion White Singleton is correct in suggesting that Herbert invokes the language of the worldly courtier in this poem largely to provide a different pattern for fashioning the self, "God's courtier."[154] By the end of the poem secular concerns have faded away in the glow of the divine Presence. In the simplest possible diction Herbert effects a remarkable convergence of the Christian mysteries: Christ's sacrificial passion and death ("who bore the blame"), the sacramental feast of the Eucharist, and the heavenly marriage feast of the Lamb. These mysteries are represented simultaneously because they *exist* simultaneously from the eternal perspective of the Deity and, by grace, are made simultaneous for the communicant: the same Christ who died on Calvary and who will receive the elect in heaven, is sacramentally present in the Eucharist. The simplicity of the language reflects the wondrous realization that the overwhelming Presence is accessible, somehow, in the most ordinary things, bread and wine, and in the most ordinary actions, "So I did sit and eat."

It ought to trouble scholars who maintain that Herbert was moving towards a Calvinist position that "The H. Communion" of the Williams Ms. (*Works*, p. 200) was *not* included in *The Temple*. To be sure, even here Herbert's ironic rehearsal of the various theories of the divine Presence in the Eucharist amounts to little more than gentle raillery and seems most intent on arguing that one could be a sound Protestant without rejecting the Catholic tradition root and branch:

> ffirst I am sure, whether bread stay
> Or whether Bread doe fly away
> > Concerneth bread, not mee. (7–9)

In his commentary on this poem, Hutchinson points out that an affirmation of real presence combined with an indifference to the mode of the presence was typical of the Andrewes and Donne wing of the Church of England. It was certainly not typical of Puritans.

There is a certain poise in the devotional mood of *The Temple* that could not long survive Herbert's death. The Laudian church, which attempted to embody the *via media* between Rome and Geneva that Herbert favored (even though it might have done so by particular means that he would not have approved), was

---

[154] *God's Courtier*, pp. 194–95, 202. For a contrasting view of courtliness in *The Temple*, see Schoenfeldt, *Prayer and Power*, pp. 199–229.

obliterated by the Puritan victory in the Civil War. The Restoration church was quite a different institution, and the brief flourishing of an English "Catholic" alternative to Roman Catholicism was hardly even a memory before the Tractarian movement. It may be that this church never really existed outside the minds of its proponents, or that it flourished chiefly in the ambiguities of Tudor ecclesiastical formularies – surely the most decisive example of "equivocal predication." The view of the Eucharistic real presence endorsed by Andrewes, Donne, and, implicitly at least, Herbert is a paradigmatic instance. While Catholic doctrine specifies a substantial change in the physical elements occurring objectively (*ex opere operato*) the Calvinist teaching, accepted by Tudor churchmen like Jewel, is wholly subjective – Christ is present only in the faith of the communicant. The difference between this view and Zwingli's frank memorialism seems mainly rhetorical. The view espoused by Andrewes can, in this context, be regarded as becomingly modest or merely evasive: "We believe no less than you in the true presence: we do not rashly define anything about the manner of the presence nor, I add, do we anxiously inquire."[155] In any case, the entire *via media* position, reflected in this view of the Eucharist, although unsatisfactory both to Catholics and Puritans, was deeply lamented by the Anglican remnant in the wake of the Civil War. The most notable poet of this remnant is, of course, Henry Vaughan.

iii

The historical crisis in which Vaughan's devotional poetry was written has been poignantly portrayed by Louis Martz:

> In the year 1649 Richard Crashaw died in exile at Loreto, a little more than six months after his master King Charles died on the scaffold at Whitehall. An era had ended for English political and religious institutions, and also for English religious poetry. With Crashaw's death the power of liturgical and eucharistic symbols died away in English poetry of the seventeenth century: the symbols earlier celebrated by Southwell, Alabaster, Donne, and Herbert.

Silex Scintillans, Martz goes on to say, despite Vaughan's loyalty to the vanquished causes of royalism and Anglicanism, "marks the emergence of the layman as a central force in religious poetry of the period"; and this characteristic he shares, ironically, with Milton.[156] Yet what was for Milton an earnestly desired goal was for Vaughan a sadly inescapable calamity, and the entire body of his devotional verse is shaped by a sense of spiritual

---

[155] *Responsio ad Apologiam Cardinalis Bellarminis* quoted by Hutchinson, p. 548: "Praesentiam credimus non minus quam vos veram: de modo praesentiae nihil temere definimus, addo, nec anxie inquirimus."

[156] *The Paradise Within: Studies in Vaughan, Traherne, and Milton* (New Haven: Yale University Press, 1964), pp. 3, 4.

dispossession as real to him as the material dispossession of clerical livings suffered by his brother and their friends.

If there was a certain estrangement from Anglican ritual in Vaughan's poetry, when compared with that of his mentor Herbert, it is certainly *not* because Vaughan's "important choice was for an inner-directed evangelical religion rather than an institutional, theological faith."[157] During the years when *Silex Scintillans* was composed, as Vaughan bitterly complains in "The Brittish Church," Anglican worship was only a memory and a hope:

> Write in thy bookes
> My ravish'd looks,
> Slain flock, and pillag'd fleeces,
> And hast thee so
> As a young Roe
> Upon the mounts of spices.   (15–20)

If the "dearest Mother" of Herbert's "The British Church" (25) has been thus "ravish'd" and abandoned, Vaughan can hardly be expected to express Herbert's contentment in her ritual, which is no longer available.

As Leah Marcus suggests, "Vaughan identified himself as the Hermetic Magus of an Anglicanism gone underground. Much of his prose is designed to provide medicine for the soul and sustain his fellow Welsh Anglicans in their time of darkness by offering them works of devotion which recapture the spirit of the vanished liturgy and piece together the broken Anglican community by forging the readership into a secret community of seers. His poetry has a similar political and religious goal but it is more cryptically expressed."[158] *A cryptic expression of the spirit of the vanished liturgy* aptly designates a fair number of the poems of *Silex Scintillans*. Even those poems with a heavy overlay of esoteric symbolism from Hermetic sources often turn out to be manifestations of Vaughan's rootedness in the larger Christian tradition. "Cock-crowing," for example, displays a number of suggestively occult Hermetic terms, but Don Cameron Allen has shown that the central symbol – the crowing rooster as the awakener of the soul asleep in sin – is ultimately scriptural and was fixed in the liturgy in the hymns of Ambrose

---

[157] James Roy King, *Studies in Six Seventeenth-Century Writers* (Athens: Ohio University Press, 1966), p. 122.

[158] Leah S. Marcus, *The Politics of Mirth: Jonson, Herrick, Milton, Marvell, and the Defense of Old Holiday Pastimes* (Chicago: University of Chicago Press, 1986), p. 226. Marcus is in some ways anticipated by James D. Simmonds, *Masques of God: Form and Theme in the Poetry of Henry Vaughan* (Pittsburgh: University of Pittsburgh Press, 1972), pp. 12–13, 39–40. See also Wall, *Transformations of the Word*, pp. 280, 332; and M. Thomas Hester, " 'broken letters scarce remembered': Herbert's *Childhood* in Vaughan," *Christianity and Literature* 40 (1991) 209–22. Perhaps the *fons et origo* in this line of inquiry is E. L. Marilla in "The Religious Conversion of Henry Vaughan," *RES* 21(1945) 15–22; "Henry Vaughan's Conversion: A Recent View," *MLN* 63(1948) 394–97; and "The Secular and Religious Poetry of Henry Vaughan," *MLQ* 9 (1948) 394–411.

and Prudentius.[159] The latter provides an especially suggestive parallel to Vaughan. As his Loeb Library editor observes, the hymns of *The Daily Round* are not really "intended for congregational singing. They are literary odes in which the mythology of the classical ode is replaced by stories from the Scriptures."[160] Yet the poems derive much of their meaning from the hours of prayer of the divine office, fixed in the breviary and the liturgy, which are intended to permeate even the daily life of Christians with an awareness of and readiness for the apocalyptic final coming of the Lord. The opening hymn of Prudentius' *Daily Round* (*Liber Cathemerinon*) celebrates the rooster as a symbol of this Christian vigilance:

> Ales diei nuntius
> lucem propinquam praecinit;
> nos excitator mentium
> iam Christus ad vitam vocat.   (1–4)
>
> [The bird that is herald of day foretells the light at hand; now Christ the awakener of minds calls us to life.]

Prudentius closes the hymn with a deprecation of vain, illusory distractions of a mortal life of sin, figured as sleep, and an invocation of Jesus to burst through night and flood the soul with light:

> sat convolutis artubus
> sensum profunda oblivio
> pressit, gravavit, obruit
> vanis vagantem somniis.
>   sunt nempe falsa et frivola
> quae mundiali gloria,
> ceu adormientes, egimus:
> vigilemus, hic est veritas. (85–92)
>
>   .   .   .
>
>   tu, Christe, somnum dissice,
> tu rumpe noctis vincula,
> tu solve peccatum vetus,
> novumque lumen ingere.   (97–100)

(Quite enough has a deep forgetfulness constricted, weighed down, and buried our sense, our limbs curled up and wandering in empty dreams. Surely false and foolish are those things we have undertaken, as if asleep, for worldly glory. Let us be vigilant – here is the truth . . . You, oh Christ, shatter our slumber, break the bonds of night, dissolve our ingrained sin, and pour in new light.)

[159] "Henry Vaughan: 'Cock-crowing'," in *Image and Meaning: Metaphoric Traditions in Renaissance Poetry*, rev. ed. (Baltimore: Johns Hopkins University Press, 1968), pp. 226–41.

[160] H. J. Thompson, ed. & trans., "Introduction" to *Prudentius* (Cambridge, MA: Harvard University Press, 1969) I, xiii. The Latin text of Prudentius is quoted from this edition.

Vaughan's poem likewise opens by reflecting upon the rooster's capacity to anticipate the coming of the light and sees in this capacity a symbol for the vigilance, the anticipation of the coming of Christ, that ought to prevail in man:

> If such a tincture, such a touch,
> So firm a longing can impowre
> Shall thy own image think it much
> To watch for thy appearing hour?   (13–16)

As in Prudentius' poem, sleep is identified with the sinful condition of mortality, and Christ is invoked to come as light into this life and to sweep away once and for all the "Veyle" (37) of fleshly existence with a flood of apocalyptic luminosity:

> To sleep without thee, is to die;
> Yea, 'tis a death partakes of hell:
> For where thou dost not close the eye
> It never opens, I can tell.
>   In such a dark Ægyptian border,
>   The shades of death dwell and disorder.   (25–30)
>   .   .   .   .   .   .
> O take it off! make no delay,
> But brush me with thy light, that I
> May shine unto a perfect day,
> And warme me at thy glorious Eye!
>   O take it off! or till it flee,
>   Though with no Lilie, stay with me!   (43–48)

Like Prudentius, Vaughan invests the constant vigilance implicit in the concept of set hours of prayer with the urgency of personal longing for the coming of Christ. The poet can thus be seen both as drawing inspiration from the liturgical forms and as reinvigorating them with the force of his devotion. Such recourse to the "daily round" of ecclesiastical prayer, with varying degrees of explicitness, recurs throughout both parts of *Silex Scintillans*. Although the traditional communal forms of ecclesiastical worship are suppressed in a Puritan regime, Vaughan keeps alive their memory and spirit in the language, especially the titles, of *Silex Scintillans*. As Herbert includes in *The Temple* "Mattens" and "Even-song," so Vaughan includes "The Morning-watch" and "The Evening-watch," with the term "watch" suggesting the heightened sense of apocalyptic anticipation created by the situation of the Church of England in Vaughan's day.

   In the first of these poems, in a manner reminiscent of Herbert's poems "Providence" and "Prayer (I)," the order of human prayer unites man with the order of nature, itself a prayer in honor of the Creator:

> The rising winds,
> And falling springs,
> Birds, beasts, all things
> Adore him in their kinds.
> Thus all is hurl'd
> In sacred *Hymnes*, and *Order*, the great *Chime*
> And *Symphony* of nature. Prayer is
> The world in tune,
> A spirit-voyce,
> And vocall joyes
> Whose *Eccho is* heav'ns blisse. (12–22)

Vaughan's predilection for corporate worship is further indicated by the untitled poem beginning "Joy of my life!", in which the Communion of the Saints is regarded as a source of spiritual guidance:

> Gods Saints are shining lights: who stays
> Here long must passe
> O're dark hills, swift streames, and steep ways
> As smooth as glasse;
> But these all night
> Like Candles, shed
> Their beams, and light
> Us into Bed. (17–24)

In "Church-Service" participation in public worship seems an occasion of grace: "O how in this thy Quire of Souls I stand / (Propt by thy hand) / A heap of sand!" (9–11). In "St. Mary Magdalen" Vaughan favorably contrasts this most cherished of Counter-Reformation saints with Puritans "who Saint themselves" (72), and "The Knot" gives a view of the Virgin Mary that shows the influence of a Catholic devotions, albeit with some of Herbert's qualifications:

> Bright Queen of Heaven! Gods Virgin Spouse!
> The glad worlds blessed maid!
> Whose beauty tyed life to thy house,
> And brought us saving ayd.
>
> Thou art the true Loves-knot; by thee
> God is made our Allie,
> And mans inferior Essence he
> With his did dignifie. (1–8)

The phrase "Queen of Heaven" is precisely the kind of Catholic tribute to Mary that John Calvin loathed:

Those who formerly read the absurdities of Catharinus would not know that the putrid carcase is still breathing, did they not read his harangues delivered in the

Council, in which the mother of Christ is called his most faithful associate, and represented as sitting on his throne to obtain grace for us! Many before him have given loose reins to their impudence, but none I believe was found, while seeking to deck the blessed Virgin with fictious titles, to call her the associate of Christ.[161]

By calling her "Queen of Heaven," Vaughan, in direct contradiction to Calvin, places the Blessed Virgin on a throne in heaven. Although he does not call her Christ's "associate," by calling her "the true Loves-knot" between God and man, he implicitly acknowledges her rôle as Mediatrix – a notion strengthened by the closing stanza:

> And such a Knot, what arm dares loose,
>> What life, what death can sever?
> Which us in him, and him in us
>> United keeps forever.   (13–16)

The Virgin Mary thus holds an eternal place in the economy of salvation. If the preceding quotations are any indication, Vaughan's poem would have filled Calvin with contemptuous rage, and he would not have recognized the poet as a "Calvinist."

It is undeniable, then, that Vaughan was deeply attached to the practise of formal devotion in public worship as well as private. The importance of this attachment can be gauged by his bitter denunciation of the Puritans' suppression of Anglican liturgical rites, and especially of the celebration of Christmas in 1644:[162]

> And shall we then no voices lift?
>> Are mercy, and salvation
> Not worth our thanks? Is life a gift
>> Of no more acceptation?
> Shal he that did come down from thence,
>> And here for us was slain,
> Shal he be now cast off? no sense
>> Of all his woes remain?
> Can neither Love, nor suff'rings bind?
>> Are we all stone, and Earth?
> Neither his bloudy passions mind,
>> Nor one day blesse his birth?
> Alas, my God! Thy birth now here
> Must not be numbred in the year.   ("Christs Nativity," II.5–18)

---

[161] *Antidote to the Council of Trent*, in Dillenberger, p. 135. See also Calvin's denial of "special privilege to the Virgin," ibid., p. 204.

[162] See "An ordinance for the better observation of the monthly fast; and more especially the next Wednesday, commonly called the Feast of the Nativity of Christ, throughout the kingdom of England and dominion of Wales, 19 December 1644," in J. P. Kenyon, ed., *The Stuart Constitution 1603–1688: Documents and Commentary* (Cambridge: Cambridge University Press, 1969), p. 266.

Vaughan's piety is not satisfied with a merely inward, individual spiritual life; worship should find expression in public liturgy, and even private devotion requires the sustenance of formal ritual. The incarnate God must be adored by incarnate means, His presence objectively manifest. Vaughan's distress at the liturgical depredations of the 1640s is not just nostalgia for the loss of familiar traditions: he implicitly accuses the Puritans of failing to grasp the significance of the Incarnation.

Such a consideration of Vaughan's devotional life raises the issue of how he regarded the Eucharist, which is usually a reliable index of liturgical orientation. "Dressing" would seem to suggest, in some lines at least, that Vaughan accepted the Calvinist view of the matter, especially as formulated in the Tudor Anglicanism of Jewel:

> Give him thy private seal,
> Earnest, and sign; Thy gifts so deal
> That these forerunners here
> May make the future cleer;
> Whatever thou dost bid, let faith make good,
> Bread for thy body, and Wine for thy blood.   (19–24)

This language seems to reflect Jewel's Calvinist terminology, who calls the sacraments "certain visible words, seals of righteousness, tokens of grace"; and who says that in the Eucharist "by faith we verily receive his body and blood."[163]

Yet even in this poem, there is a strong pull toward something more concrete and immediate than what is allowed by the Calvinist teaching that Christ's presence in the sacrament is wholly subjective – actual only in the faith of the communicant. Indeed, it is with Vaughan as with so many seventeenth-century devotional poets; the longing for Christ's presence is paramount:

> Give to thy wretched one
> Thy mysticall *Communion,*
> That, absent, he may see,
> Live, die, and rise with thee;
> Let him so follow here, that in the end
> He may take thee, as thou doest him intend.   (13–18)

As theology these lines are rather ambiguous, but the urgency for contact with Christ is unmistakable – to "see, / Live, die, and rise with thee." Moreover, the close of the poem explicitly rejects what the poet takes to be Puritan indifference to the awesome holiness of the sacramental presence:

---

[163] *An Apology for the Church of England,* pp. 31, 33.

> Give me, my God! thy grace,
>   The beams, and brightnes of thy face,
>   That never like a beast
>   I take thy sacred feast,
> Or the dread mysteries of thy blest bloud
> Use, with like Custome, as my Kitchin food.
>   Some sit to thee, and eat
>   Thy body as their Common meat,
>   O let not me do so!
>   Poor dust should ly still low,
> Then kneel my soul, and body; kneel, and bow;
> If *Saints*, and *Angels* fal down, much more thou.   (31–42)

Perhaps even more than Herbert, Vaughan apprehends the sacrament in a way that is not compatible with the Calvinist view in which the elements themselves always remain mere creatures: one cannot rightly worship or even reverence mere bread and wine. Such worship would be tantamount to idolizing one's own faith in the status of the elements as signs.

The implicit teaching in "Dressing" takes a more specific theological cast in other poems. In "The Holy Communion," for example, the Eucharist is treated as a means of conveying grace: "But grace, and blessings came with thee so rife" (3); the action of the sacrament is compared to the animation of the body by the soul and the creation of the beauty of the world out of chaos (5–8). In this poem (26–29) and also in "Easter-day" (15–16), Christ's blood is said to heal and give sight to the "inward Eys" of the mind. In "The Passion" Vaughan recalls the image that Herbert deploys in "The Agonie" to identify what to human sensation is wine with what Jesus experienced as the shedding of blood:

> Most blessed Vine!
> Whose juice so good
> I feel as Wine,
> But thy faire branches felt as bloud,
>   How wert thou prest
>   To be my feast!   (15–20)

In "The Sap" the "dew" of grace for which the "sapless Blossom" thirsts is identified with the Eucharist by means of association with "the Prince of *Salem* . . . who deals / To thee thy secret meals" (13–14).[164] The poem continues by emphasizing the actual transforming power of the Eucharist:

---

[164] For the Eucharistic associations of Melchisidek, King of Salem, see Tuve, *A Reading of George Herbert*, pp. 71–72.

> He gave his sacred bloud
> By wil our sap, and Cordial; now in this
>   Lies such a heav'n of bliss,
> That, who but truly tasts it, no decay
>   Can touch him any way,
> Such secret life, and vertue in it lies   (26–31)

One "truly tasts" by purifying the "vessel where you put it" by means of "A powerful, rare dew" that is hid within (37–43) – obviously the tears of penitence. Thus received, the sacrament conveys "a lively sense / Of grace against all sins" and "Comfort such, as even / Brings to, and comes from Heaven" (47–50).

Given his view of the sacrament, it is not surprising that Vaughan's eucharistic poetry reflects the language and style of St. Thomas Aquinas's Eucharistic hymns. L. C. Martin notes the parallel between the final couplet of Vaughan's "The Holy Communion" and a stanza in Thomas's Corpus Christi sequence, *Lauda Sion Salvatorem*:[165]

> How art thou now, thy flock to keep,
> Become both *food*, and *Shepheard* to thy sheep! (51–52)

> Bone pastor, panis vere,
> Jesu nostri miserere.
> Tu nos pasce, nos tuere,
> Tu nos bona fac videre
> In terra viventium.[166]   (#12)

> [Good shepherd, true bread, Jesus, take pity on us. Feed us, watch over us, make us see what is good in the land of the living.]

Vaughan's wording, however, suggests that he may have come upon St. Thomas's hymn by way of Richard Crashaw's rendering, which first appeared in the 1648 edition of *Steps to the Temple*:

> JESU MASTER, Just and true!
> Our FOOD, and Faithfull SHEPHARD too!
> O by thy self vouchsafe to keep,
> As with thy selfe thou feed'st thy SHEEP.   (XIII)

The text of Vaughan shares with Crashaw's translation the *food / shepherd / sheep* progression and likewise rhymes the last word with *keep*.

The relationship of Vaughan to St. Thomas and Crashaw becomes more

---

[165] In his commentary to *The Works* of Vaughan, p. 740. See also Rudrum's commentary to his edition of Vaughan's *Complete Poems*, p. 574.

[166] The Latin texts of *Lauda Sion* and, subsequently, of *Adoro Te* are quoted from *Devoutly I Adore Thee*. They are also found in George Walton Williams, ed., *The Complete Poetry of Richard Crashaw* (New York: New York University Press, 1972), where they are set on facing pages to Crashaw's translations.

compelling and significant in the culminating eucharistic poem of *Silex Scintillans* II, "The Feast," which, like Herbert's "Love (III)," effects a coalescence of earthly holy communion with the apocalyptic marriage feast of the Lamb. Crashaw's English rendering of St. Thomas's *Adoro Te* had also appeared in the 1648 *Steps to the Temple* and reminiscences of this poem, as well as of Thomas's *Pange Lingua*, another Eucharistic hymn, are apparent in "The Feast."[167] Now the constant theme of the Thomist Eucharistic hymns, faithfully reflected by Crashaw, even when his language and style depart radically from his model, is that Christ is powerfully and efficaciously present in the sacrament, though hidden from human sense, as the beginning of *Adoro Te* shows:

> Adoro te devote, latens Deitas
> Quae sub his figuris vere latitas
> Tibi se cor meum totum subicit
> Quia te contemplans totum deficit.

> [I adore thee devoutly, hidden godhead that beneath these forms lies concealed. To you my heart yields itself wholly since contemplating you it is wholly abandoned.]

The sight and the other senses, except for hearing, which alone admits belief, are useless, the poem continues. The penitent thief and Thomas the Apostle could at least see Christ's humanity, although his deity was hidden. "Nevertheless I acknowledge thee to be my God" ("Deum tamen meum te confiteor"). The poem closes with longing for the final revelation of Christ in glory. He will be the same God as is present in the sacrament, but He will be accessible to full human perception:

> Jesu quem velatum nunc adspicio
> Oro fiat illud, quod tam sitio,
> Ut te revelata cernens facie
> Visu sim beatus tuae gloriae.

> [I pray, Jesus, whom I now behold veiled: allow that for which I thirst so much, that perceiving you with face revealed I may be blessed with vision of your glory.]

Crashaw increases the affectivity of this closing by expanding the figure of thirst:

---

[167] See the commentaries in Martin, p. 751; and Rudrum, p. 637. Jonathan F. S. Post, *Henry Vaughan: The Unfolding Vision* (Princeton, NJ: Princeton University Press, 1982), p. 160, n. 4, sees in Vaughan's responsiveness to "the auditory imagination, a sensitivity with inevitable theological overtones that places him in a line with the Protestant Reformers, like Luther and Calvin, who valued the 'inner voice' over visual ceremony." As the second stanza of *Adoro Te* shows, however, St. Thomas had already made the ear, not the eye, the organ of faith: "Visus, tactus, gustus in te fallitur / Sed auditu solo tuto creditur."

Come love! Come LORD! and that long day
For which I languish, come away.
When this dry soul those eyes shall see,
And drink the unseal'd sourse of thee.
When Glory's sun faith's shades shall chase,
And for thy veil give me thy FACE.   (51–56)

Thus we see that the convergence of the reception of holy communion in time
with admission to the eternal wedding feast of the Lamb – a motif that we
have already noticed in Herbert – is operative in medieval Catholic poetry and
its baroque imitators.

Vaughan closes his poem, "The Feast," with the same identification of
sacramental and eternal supper, both founded on Christ's sacrificial shedding
of blood:

Some toil and sow,
That wealth may flow,
   And dress this earth for next years meat:
But let me heed,
Why thou didst bleed,
   And what in the next world to eat.   (73–78)

The virtual identification of the two feasts, sacramental and apocalyptic, is
possible because the sacrament of the Eucharist is that unique action by which
eternity bursts in upon time, in which earthly man in his temporal condition
is in the presence of his eternal Lord:

O drink and bread
Which strikes death dead,
   The food of mans immortal being!
Under veyls here
Thou art my chear,
   Present and sure without my seeing.   (37–42)

Not only do these lines recall the very language of veiled presence in *Adoro Te*;
in addition, Vaughan stresses, in this poem more explicitly than in others, the
effective, grace-conferring power of the sacrament:

How dost thou flye
And search and pry
   Through all my parts, and like a quick
And knowing lamp
Hunt out each damp,
   Whose shadow makes me sad or sick?

O what high joys
The Turtles voice
   And songs I hear! O quickning showers

> Of my Lords blood
> You make rocks bud
> And crown dry hils with wells & flowers!   (43–54)

In a poem that so evidently reflects the influence of *Adoro Te* in other ways, it is difficult not to recall the close of Crashaw's rendering of the Latin hymn with its image of "this dry soul those eyes shall see, / And drink the unseal'd sourse of thee." Moreover, in the next stanza, where Vaughan writes, "My soul and all, / Kneel down and fall" (58–59); there is an inevitable suggestion of Vaughan's anti-Puritan sentiments on the issue of kneeling to receive communion, an attitude he also shared with Crashaw.[168]

When Vaughan's eucharistic poems are considered as a group, it is obvious that his piety implies a larger view of the sacrament than is allowed by rigorous Calvinism. The leading expounder of Vaughan as firmly and typically Protestant attempts to dismiss these poems as merely "conventional";[169] however, Vaughan's definition of Protestantism retains a good deal of Catholic tradition. Given the intense self-consciousness of Vaughan's ferocious attack on Puritanism, and his constant recourse to Catholic devotional sources, it is improbable that he would unwittingly reproduce "conventional" meditations on the Eucharist without a full commitment of belief. In his distress over Commonwealth depredations of the Church of England, Vaughan sought a sense of Christ's presence and power in the Eucharist that went far beyond anything conceived by Tudor churchmen such as Cranmer and Jewel, and possibly even beyond what Laud would have countenanced.[170] The typically "high" Anglican attitude of an Andrewes or a Donne, that the mode of Christ's presence in the Eucharist could be safely ignored, although generously irenic, was always vulnerable in an era as fiercely contentious as the seventeenth century. By asserting that Christ is not present at all in the sacrament, that it conveys no efficacious reality, Zwingli had made the issue inescapable. In the Puritan liturgical reforms Vaughan thought that he saw the result: the utter collapse of any real relation

---

[168] For the overtones of religio-political controversy in Crashaw's "Hymn to the Name of Jesus," see Eugene R. Cunnar, "Crashaw's Hymn 'To the Name Above Every Name': Background and Meaning," in *Essays on Richard Crashaw*, ed. Robert M. Cooper (Salzburg: Institut für Anglistik und Amerikanistik, Universität Salzburg, 1979), pp. 102–28.

[169] Lewalski, *Protestant Poetics*, p. 337.

[170] Ross, *Poetry and Dogma*, p. 62, maintains that "Laud's doctrine of Eucharistic sacrifice is wholly and typically Protestant." The adverbs "wholly" and "typically" seem to me to be wanting in the subtlety that the case requires. Likewise, when he refers to Vaughan's "certainty that the glories of the hidden garden are locked forever against flesh and time" (p. 95), Ross does not adequately take into account Vaughan's historical situation and the extent to which the poet strove against this limitation of radical Reformation theology. Whether Vaughan could attain a successful resolution to his own spiritual strife without abandoning the Reformation altogether is a question beyond literary criticism as such.

between God and man. His eucharistic poetry represents his effort to restore this relation by an imaginative engagement with liturgy.

Cajetan had perceived early on, in his response to Zwingli, *Errors in a Booklet on the Lord's Supper* (1525), that a great deal hinged upon the literal interpretation of *est* and the reference of *hoc* in the words of consecration, "Hoc est corpus meum":

> Consequently referring the pronoun "this" to the bread goes against the true meaning of the words, because bread is never the body of Christ. Referring the pronoun "this" to the body of Christ goes against the effectiveness of the same words because the body of Christ is not made the body of Christ nor is it transformed into the body of Christ. Consequently the pronoun "this" must refer to that which pertains to both being and becoming, that is, that which is indicated uniquely as becoming and being the body of Christ.[171]

The issue of predication, of the relation between word and reality, is crucial. For Heather Asals sacramental presence is necessarily referred to what she calls equivocal predication: " 'This' (one thing) is *both* 'bread' *and* 'my Body' (two things)"; but Cajetan maintains that what the confection of the sacrament requires is an analogical predication of indeterminate relation between being and becoming, parallel to the indeterminate relation between God and creature.[172] The realms of time and eternity, being and becoming, converge in the words of consecration that simultaneously state and effect a truth. Hence in "The Feast" Vaughan asserts that Christ is "Under veyls here . . . Present and sure without my seeing." The "bread" is not a separate reality parallel to the reality of Christ's body; it is merely a "veyl," merely a limitation in the power of temporal, human "seeing" to perceive what is, to the eye of faith, "here . . . Present."

The simultaneity of being and becoming is central to the Thomist conception of the sacramental action of eucharistic consecration as Cajetan articulates it. "Recall . . . that these words not only express the truth, but also bring about the truth they express." Hence the language of the sacrament is not only representation but also *presentation* that unites the simultaneous present of eternity with the unfolding of temporality: "Together and in the very same instance, it is verified that this has become and is the body of Christ."[173] The same line of inquiry is fundamental to the theoretical musings of Jacques Derrida:

---

[171] *Cajetan Responds: A Reader in Reformation Controversy*, ed. & trans. Jared Wicks, S.J. (Washington, D.C.: Catholic University of America Press, 1978), p. 166.

[172] Asals, *Equivocal Predication*, p. xii; Cajetan, *In* De Ente et Essentia II. 21, p. 37: "infinita enim est distantia inter Deum et creaturam." Of course St. Thomas, following Aristotle, sees analogy as a kind of equivocation in the *Summa*. See above, n. 129.

[173] *Cajetan Responds*, pp. 165, 166.

As soon as we admit this continuity of the now and the not-now, perception and nonperception, in the zone of primordiality common to primordial impression and primordial retention, we admit the other into the self-identity of the *Augenblick*; nonpresence and nonevidence are admitted into the *blink of an instant.* There is a duration to the blink, and it closes the eye.[174]

This brandishing of radical ontological discontinuity in the face of Husserl's supposition of phenomenological continuity within subjective self-identity would seem to mark Derrida as a contemporary Zwingli. But it must be borne in mind that the Thomist version of the Eucharist expounded by Cajetan does not presuppose any univocal or determinate relation between God and creatures. In fact, the *eye* must "blink" in order to "see" the Presence hidden beneath the "veyls." By hearing alone can it be safely believed, Thomas maintains; "nonpresence" and "nonevidence" are the very realm of faith.

It is, finally, only in the paradoxes of poets that the simultaneity of analogical levels of being and reality attains even a fitting, though surely not an adequate, expression. Robert Southwell's "Of the Blessed Sacrament of the Aulter" compresses most of the enigmas of absent presence scattered through Aquinas and Vaughan into a single stanza:

> That which he gave he was, o peereless gifte,
> Both god and man he was, and both he gave,
> He in his handes him self did trewelye lifte:
> Farre off they see whome in them selves they have.
> Twelve did he feede, twelve did their feeder eate,
> He made, he dressd, he gave, he was their meate.   (7–12)

Perhaps the most notorious affront to spatio-temporal physics in these lines, "He in his handes him self did trewelye lifte," is repeated by La Ceppède: "Soit que ie vo' reçoiue en cète riche table, / Où vous mesme en vos mains vous portastes iadis"[175] (Let me receive you on this rich table, where of old you carried yourself in your hands). La Ceppède, moreover, tells us the ultimate source of the paradox in his own commentary on the sonnet, and it is the Church's most compelling prose poet of time and eternity, St. Augustine:

Who is carried in his own hands? A man can be carried in the hands of others. No one can Be carried in his own hands. We do not discover how this might be literally understood of David himself; however, in Christ we do discover it, for Christ was carried in his own hands when, offering his very own body, he said, "This is my body"; for he was carrying that body in his hands.[176]

---

[174] *Speech and Phenomena*, p. 65.

[175] *Théorèmes* II Partie, II, 50 (p. 258).

[176] Ibid., p. 259: "Quis portatur in manibus suis? (*dit-il*) Manibus aliorum potest portari homo. Manibus suis nemo portatur. Quomodo intelligatur in ipso Dauide secundum literam non

This passage indicates how deeply important to Christian devotion and liturgy a sense of the awesome presence of divinity latent within the forms and signs of the temporal world has always been. In varying degrees Donne, Herbert and Vaughan responded to what they perceived as a threat to man's sacramentally mediated access to this presence in the anti-liturgical temper of the more militant parties in the Reformation. They found ways to reconcile reform with Catholic tradition. For Crashaw, it was impossible to respond adequately, to recover a sense of Christ's sacramental presence, within the framework of Protestant doctrine. Thus doctrine, more than personal circumstances, explains his conversion to Catholicism.

iv

In some ways the life and literary career of Richard Crashaw are the obverse of Vaughan's. While the latter was, in a sense, an exile within his own country during the years of the Civil War and Commonwealth, which he long survived (although his muse did not), Crashaw became a literal exile and died young, enacting in his life, almost literally, the principle that a Christian is a stranger and pilgrim on earth. While Vaughan's devotional poetry and prose constitute an "underground" reconstruction of a mode of Anglican religious practice that was still in the process of formulation when interrupted by the Civil War, Crashaw's poetry reflects his increasing self-abandonment to what had come to seem to him the central, continuous tradition of Christian worship. The difference is indicated by the two poets' relation to St. Thomas's hymns for the feast of Corpus Christi: the Thomist marks in Vaughan's eucharistic poems lie under the surface, emerging here and there in a striking phrase or figure; Crashaw, on the other hand, provides effusive and elaborate translations. Their significance is only underscored by the evasive title given *Adoro Te* in the 1648 edition of *Steps to the Temple*, "A Hymne to Our Saviour by the Faithful Receiver of the Sacrament." The text of the hymn (Crashaw's English version as well as the Latin original) is problematic in the light of the twenty-eighth of the Articles of Religion of the Church of England, which forbids worship of the sacrament, and would certainly have offended Puritan sensibilities. The editor or publisher of the London volume apparently tried to disguise this fact from potential censors with a misleading title. Under no such compulsion, Thomas Car called the poem "*The Hymn of* St. Thomas *in Adoration of the Blessed Sacrament*" when he published it in Paris four years later in *Carmen Deo Nostro*.[177]

inuenimus, in Christo autem inuenimus, ferebatur enim Christus in manibus suis, quando commendans ipsum Corpus suum, ait, Hoc est corpus meum; ferebat enim illud corpus in manibus suis." The text is from *Enarrationes in Psalmos* XXXIII. ii. 9, found with only insignificant verbal differences in Migne 36–37. 306.

[177] See Williams' headnote, *Complete Poetry*, p. 172.

It is important to notice, however, that Crashaw's preoccupation with the blending of intense personal devotion, often of a mystical turn, and the traditional forms of liturgical practice is not the product solely of his later Catholic years. Although Crashaw's conversion was certainly the result of a considered, rational decision and not due to the pressure of external circumstances, nevertheless, he remained within the same broad tradition that Donne, Herbert, and Vaughan found persisting in the Church of England. For the purposes of the present study, Crashaw's more overt resistance to the secularizing tendencies of Reformation radicalism is important because it illuminates the continuity between the puritanism of the past and the current puritanism of postmodernism. His poetry is especially provocative in relation to deconstruction in its paradigmatic Derridean formulation. Although enthusiasm for deconstruction has waned somewhat in recent years, giving way to more insistently historicist approaches associated with the practice of Michel Foucault, deconstruction remains the indispensable analytic technique of all postmodern theory: "If early readings of Derrida mistook the notion of *différance* as antihistorical," insists David Lee Miller, "it seems clear now that it is, on the contrary, profoundly historical, perhaps the most powerful formulation in our own time of the irreducible problem of temporality."[178] Henry Louis Gates, Jr., thus pays oblique tribute to the pervasiveness of the Derridean perspective in the ongoing postmodernist project when he demands exemption from the deconstruction of "the process of exploring and reclaiming our subjectivity [as women, as blacks, etc.]," although "we readily accept, acknowledge, and partake of the critique of *this* [Western male] subject as transcendent."[179] In other words, critics and theorists who are unhappy with the implications of deconstruction for their own ideological prefer-ences, or with the unsavory Nazi associations of Paul de Man and Martin Heidegger,[180] are still content to apply its corrosive solvents to ideas of their perceived enemies. Deconstruction, however, is an equal opportunity

---

[178] *The Poem's Two Bodies: The poetics of the 1590* Faerie Queene (Princeton, NJ: Princeton University Press, 1988), p. 16.

[179] *Loose Canons: Notes on the Culture Wars* (New York: Oxford University Press, 1992), p. 35.

[180] See David Lehman, *Signs of the Times: Deconstruction and the Fall of Paul de Man* (New York: Poseidon Press, 1991); and David H. Hirsch, *The Deconstruction of Literature* (Hanover, NH, and London: Brown University Press, 1991). Hirsch says that the "hegemony of deconstruc-tion is faltering" (p. 18) because of its inherent contradictions and its political associations: "What is more difficult for even the most dedicated of deconstructionists to explain is why we should want to start rebuilding a postmodern world with two failed philosophies, one that led to the Soviet gulag, and the other that was powerless to reveal Auschwitz as an evil and in fact put itself at the service of an ideology that led to Auschwitz." But in fact Hirsch's own fervent polemic is a testimony to the persistence of the deconstructionist ideology embedded in academic assumptions, despite its inherent contradictions. Perhaps one can hardly expect an ideology that begins with an assault on the centrality of Λόγος to be much abashed by its own lapses in logic.

venture: we all go into the abyss together. Derrida puts the deconstructionist version of the human condition in its starkest terms, and the baroque ardor of Crashaw's language can be understood as a response to the postmodernist vision as it emerged three and half centuries in advance of Derrida in puritan iconoclasm.

Crashaw's earliest surviving poetry, the student work *Epigrammatum Sacrorum Liber* (1634), is based upon the New Testament readings of the Book of Common Prayer and often reveals a fascination with Christ's sacramental presence in the Eucharist. Consider, for example, the startling conceit of the epigram on Luke 11: 27:

> Et quid si biberet Jesus vel ab ubere vestro?
> Quid facit ad vestram, quòd bibit ille, sitim?
> Ubera mox sua & Hic (ô quàm non lactea!) pandet:
> E nato *Mater* tum bibet ipsa suo.

In Crashaw's own English version, the poem has drawn what his editor has called "extravagant comment":

> Suppose he had been Tabled at thy Teates,
> Thy hunger feels not what he eates:
> Hee'l have his Teat e're long (a bloody one)
> The Mother then must suck the Son.

Crashaw was certainly not unaware of the overtones of sexual perversion, incest, and cannibalism that might be evoked in this epigram by some modern critics. However, the poem, as Williams points out, is addressed not to Christ's Mother, but to the anonymous woman in the crowd who cries out, "Blessed be the paps which thou has sucked."[181] Since the eucharistic reference is unmistakable – in the Latin version the mother will "drink" her own son – it is evident that Crashaw is attempting to impart some sense of the truly shocking implications of Holy Communion. But it is truly shocking only for a man with a belief not merely in a vague "real presence," but in the actuality of Christ's Body and Blood under the outward forms of the sacrament. More than a decade before his conversion, then, Crashaw already sought to expand the boundaries of Tudor eucharistic doctrine in a way not dissimilar to Donne, Herbert, and Vaughan.

---

[181] *Complete Poetry*, p. 14. The more prurient commentaries include William Empson, *Seven Types of Ambiguity* (1930; rpt. New York: Meridian Books, 1955), p. 250; and Robert M. Adams, "Taste and Bad Taste in Metaphysical Poetry: Crashaw and Dylan Thomas," in *Seventeenth Century English* Poetry, ed. W. R. Keast (New York: Oxford University Press, 1962), p. 271. For further discussion see R. V. Young, *Richard Crashaw and the Spanish Golden Age*, pp. 23–30, 177 n. 15; and Thomas F. Healy, "Crashaw and the Sense of History," in *New Perspectives on the Life and Art of Richard Crashaw*, ed. John R. Roberts (Columbia and London: University of Missouri Press, 1990), pp. 49–65.

The distinction is not acknowledged in all quarters. Thomas F. Healy, for example, asserts that Article 28 "rejects transubstantiation but it does not really hold against Aquinas's view of the Sacrament, which like so much Eucharist doctrine is not sufficiently clear to determine what Aquinas accepted in relation to the seventeenth-century notion of transubstantiation or the Laudian idea of real presence." Under the influence of a Laudian notion of real presence, which St. Thomas may or may not have shared, "Crashaw is unable to 'Taste thee GOD', which he would have been able to do if the bread and wine had been transubstantiated, the body and blood only hidden by the appearances of bread and wine." Hence "Crashaw avoids indicating a substantial change in the elements in both poems [*Adoro Te* and *Lauda Sion*]."[182] In the first place, whatever strictures one may wish to lay upon St. Thomas, lack of clarity is not one of them; and, in the wake of the fairly recent formal definition of Christ's presence in the Eucharist in terms of transubstantiation by the fifth Lateran Council (1215), the Angelic Doctor quite explicitly sets out to defend transubstantiation as the correct explanation of the action of the Eucharist (*Summa Theologiae* III.78.1). The teaching of the Council of Trent on transubstantiation is thoroughly Thomistic, and it ought to be of some significance that Thomas's hymns were written for the feast of *Corpus Christi*. Healy has apparently failed to grasp the distinction between "substance" and "accident" in Scholastic terminology. According to the theology of transubstantiation, the whole *substance* (i.e., essential reality) of the bread and wine is converted into the Body and Blood of Christ, but the *accidents* (i.e., species or appearances) of bread and wine remain behind and are so apprehended by the taste, touch, sight and smell of the communicant. Therefore, in St. Thomas's *Adoro Te*, "Visus, tactus, gustus in te fallitur," only hearing, the organ of faith, can recognize the substantial presence of the Body and Blood beneath or behind the accidents of bread and wine. And the poetry follows directly from the theological doctrine that the substance of Christ's Body "is not visible to the corporal eye, nor is it subject to any other sense, nor to the imagination."[183]

Crashaw's determination to bring home the shocking nature of the Eucharist thus rests on a thoroughly Thomistic foundation, and it is evident in another of the Latin epigrams on John 6: 10–15, "To the guests at the miraculous dinner of the five loaves":

[182] Thomas F. Healy, *Richard Crashaw* (Leiden: E. J. Brill, 1986), pp. 123, 124. On p. 123, n. 11, Healy directs the reader to the *Summa Theologiae* III.73–77, as the passage where "Aquinas's view of the sacrament is most extensively considered," thus ignoring III.78.1, where Thomas writes, "forma huius sacramenti importat solam consecrationem materiae, quae in transubstantiatione consistit."
[183] *Summa Theologiae* III 76. 7: "Substantia autem, inquantum huiusmodi, non est visibilis oculo corporali, neque subiacet alicui sensui, neque imaginationi."

Joann. 6. *Ad hospites coenae miraculosae quinque panum.*
Vescere pane tuo: sed & (hospes) vescere Christo:
  Est panis pani scilicet ille tuo.
Tunc pane hoc CHRISTI rectè satur (hospes) abibis,
  Panem ipsum CHRISTUM si magìs esurias.

[Feed on your bread, but also, guests, feed on Christ: he is of course the bread of your bread. Then you will depart rightly filled with this bread of CHRIST, guests, if you hunger more for CHRIST himself the bread.]

The emphasis here is, again, that the faithful must see beyond the mere signs and recognize that the physical world is permeated with Christ's presence but most especially in the sacraments.

Such a convergence of intimate, even mystical experience with the traditions of public worship is the crowning achievement of Crashaw's mature hymns.[184] This bridging of the individual and the communal, this embedding of personal devotion in the continuity of theological and liturgical tradition, gives Crashaw's poetry a surprising significance amidst the continuing onslaught of current literary theory. In particular, Crashaw offers fascinating possibilities in the wake of deconstruction, shedding a good deal of light on what often seems only darkness visible. For to many scholars, deconstruction is less a method or a system than a voracious devourer of discourse, crumbling generic and disciplinary boundaries, grinding up poetry, politics, and psychiatry indifferently with its insatiable appetite for texts. The academic uproar of the last thirty years might well be given a cinematic title, "The Invasion of the Book-Snatchers," as familiar beloved authors turn glassy-eyed countenances upon the horror-struck professor, revealing that their souls have been sucked out, their papery cadavers possessed by the malignant spirits of foreign exegetes.

This may seem an oddly recherché context for Crashaw, who is regarded by one critic as the author of "a fairy-tale of childish pietism,"[185] and who is often described as a kind of poetic confectioner, specializing in rococo cake decoration. However, recent years have witnessed a resurgence of interest in Crashaw's poetry, frequently with an emphasis on just those issues that currently agitate the progressive elements in the academy. For example, Maureen Sabine has found in "Crashaw's feminine sympathies" – uncharacteristic of the poets of his age or of many critics earlier in the twentieth century – an affirmation of important elements of feminism.[186] Eugene R. Cunnar has addressed the involvement of even so apparently ethereal a poem

---

[184] For a full discussion see Young, *Richard Crashaw*, pp. 111–42.

[185] Yvor Winters, *Forms of Discovery* (Chicago: Alan Swallow, 1967), p. 92.

[186] "Crashaw and the Feminine Animus: Patterns of Self-Sacrifice in Two of His Devotional Poems," *JDJ* 4 (1985) 69–94. See the superb development of this thesis in *Feminine Engendered Faith: The Poetry of John Donne and Richard Crashaw* (London: Macmillan, 1992), pp. 111–45.

as "To the Name of Jesus" with seventeenth-century religious controversy, suggesting in Crashaw an appeal to the highly politicized mood of university scholarship in our day.[187] This same poem, "To the Name of Jesus," yields an interesting perspective on the matter of deconstruction, precisely because it represents the culmination of trends that began with the Reformation. Derrida has done less to open up new intellectual vistas than to recover ancient controversies for critical discussion. Although deconstruction purports to be a general decentering of the "ontotheology" of the Western philosophical tradition, attention is mainly directed toward modern philosophy that begins with Descartes, especially post-Enlightenment "critical" philosophies. The burden of Derrida's critique is that *all* Western philosophy, however it claims to have broken from classical metaphysics deriving from Plato and from Judaeo-Christian philosophy, remains covertly logocentric, wedded to the concept of Being as presence.[188] In this way Derrida raises a fundmental issue that literary scholars all too often have ignored: what is this *logocentricism* that the most self-consciously skeptical and anti-metaphysical systems of modern thought seem unable to elude? Derrida, perhaps inadvertently, forces the critic to take seriously the metaphysical structure of the early literature from which modern thinkers have characteristically sought to distance themselves. In the specific instance here in question, deconstruction leads us to acknowledge that seventeenth-century devotional poetry is not mere versified piousness, but involves a distinct vision of the nature of reality, conceived in response to puritan iconoclasm. By the same token, the devotional poets enable us to see exactly what is at stake in the execution of the textual strategies of various post-structuralist theories. Richard Crashaw, a poet who has been accused of being long on emotion and short on intellect,[189] turns out to be raising the same issues of presence, logos, and identity that currently preoccupy the most sophisticated literary theorists. In the light of characteristic, deconstructive rhetorical strategies, "To the Name of Jesus" discloses a paradoxical convergence of the poem, with its Christian background, and the themes of post-structuralist theory, and furnishes a fitting conclusion to our consideration of meditation and sacrament.

In the face of the postmodern project of deconstructing the Logos, the extravagant paradoxes of Crashaw's baroque conceits appear confrontational rather than decorative. But his poems were already confrontational in the seventeenth century as a challenge to the Calvinist separation of nature and grace. Deconstruction begins by seeking to dislodge what is not only the fundamental principle of Western metaphysics, but of ordinary common

---

[187] See above n. 168. See also the many of the essays in Roberts, ed., *New Perspectives*.

[188] On this point see Robert Magliola, *Derrida on the Mend* (West Lafayette, IN: Purdue University Press, 1984), p. 4.

[189] E.g. by Joan Bennett, *Five Metaphysical Poets* (Cambridge: Cambridge University Press, 1964), p. 102.

sense: it begins with a denial of the principle of identity.[190] The Reformation never went so far in any of its versions; however, in reducing the sacraments, especially the Eucharist, to mere signs, devoid of real *presence*, the more radical Reformers did anticipate the deconstruction of the sign.[191] Iconoclasm and indifference toward the sacraments bespeak a general distrust of the senses and the physical world resulting in the sense of estrangement from reality that is the peculiar predicament of modern man. The philosophical culmination of this sense of alienation is deconstruction.

Derrida takes up the fundamental proposition of Saussurian linguistics, that "differences carry signification,"[192] and uses it to unravel the apparent unity of the sign. Since the signifier exists only insofar as it *differs* from the signified, then the latter is necessarily *deferred*, spatially and temporally, by signification. The "originary" or "transcendental signified" can never be present in meaning; it can only be *re*-presented. But this is as much as to say that it cannot *be*. "The present alone is and ever will be" is Derrida's formulation of Husserl's typically "logocentric" thesis; "Being is presence or the modification of presence."[193] But presence is precisely what is forever unattainable to our knowledge and signifying. Discourse can only refer to discourse: "Speech represents itself; it *is* its representation. Even better, speech is *the* representation of itself."[194] The ultimate victim of this dismantling of the self-presence of speech is the speaker: the autonomous individual consciousness of Western humanism. This deconstruction of the intentional subject rests on Derrida's perception of the dislocation of presence in time and space. Since only what is present *is*, existence in time entails a continuous slippage of being. It is not merely time that slips through our fingers; it is our own self-identity:

> The *I am*, being experienced only as an *I am present*, itself presupposes the relationship with presence in general, with being as presence. The appearing of the *I* to itself in the *I am present* is thus originally a relation with its own possible disappearance. Therefore, *I am* originally means *I am mortal. I am immortal* is an impossible proposition. We can even go further: as a linguistic statement "I am he who am" is the admission of a mortal.[195]

---

[190] Magliola, p. 5. On St. Thomas Aquinas as the "philosopher of common sense" see G. K. Chesterton, *St. Thomas Aquinas: The Dumb Ox, Collected Works of G. K. Chesterton* (San Francisco: Ignatius Press, 198), I, 513.

[191] On the pervasive tension over the state of sacramental signs in Donne's secular poetry, see M. Thomas Hester, "'this cannot be said': A Preface to the Reader of Donne's Lyrics," *Christianity and Literature* 39 (1990) 365–85; and "'Let Me Love': Reading the Sacred 'Currant' of Donne's Profane Lyrics," in *Sacred and Profane: Secular and Devotional Interplay in Early Modern British Literature*, ed. Helen Wilcox, Richard Todd, and Alasdair MacDonald (Amsterdam: VU University Press, 1996), pp. 129–50.

[192] Saussure, *Course in General Linguistics*, p. 118.

[193] *Speech and Phenomena*, p. 53.

[194] Ibid., p. 57. Emphasis in original.

[195] Ibid., p. 54. Emphases in original.

Hence the subjective consciousness – "solitary mental life" is Husserl's phrase – seems "stricken in its very possibility by what we are calling time."[196]

Before returning to Crashaw, it is worth observing once again that this melancholy vision of the human condition is not a deconstructive novelty. St. Augustine, for instance, was equally preoccupied with the problem of time, and he too perceived the important connection with language:

> So much you gave to these things, because they are parts of a whole, which do not all exist at the same time, but all function in the universe, of which they are parts, succeeding one another and then giving way. Notice how our speech operates in the same way by means of signifying sounds. For an utterance is not complete, if one word does not give way, when its syllables have sounded, so that another can succeed it.[197]

Augustine perceives that in its very temporal progression, speech lacks complete reality, and, in this, it faithfully mirrors the incompleteness of human, indeed of all temporal, existence. There is a striking parallel here with Derrida, but of course Augustine would not accept that "I am he who am" can only be "the admission of a mortal." The discontinuity of mortal existence is not an insufficiency in being itself. The very incompleteness of being as it unfolds in time and space entails an absolute Being as its ground; the stream of our words into the abyss of oblivion – of signifiers pursuing elusive signifieds – veils the Being of the immutable Word of God:

> And what was being spoken is not ended, and something else spoken, so that everything might be said, but everything is said at the same time and eternally; otherwise there would be time and change, and no true eternity or immortality.[198]

Once a deconstructive context is established for this kind of Christian contemplation, poetry like Crashaw's assumes a different profile. "To the Name of Jesus," routinely regarded as a "sensuous" poem,[199] discloses a generally unacknowledged depth. The hymn opens with a principal motif of

---

[196] Ibid., p. 68.

[197] *Confessiones* IV. X. 15, Migne 32. 699: "Tantum dedisti eis, quia partes sunt rerum, quae non sunt omnes simul; sed decedendo ac succedendo agunt omnes universum, cujus partes sunt. Ecce sic peragitur et sermo noster per signa sonantia. Non enim erit totus sermo, si unum verbum non decedat cum sonuerit partes suas, ut succedat aliud."

[198] Ibid. XI. vii. 9, Migne 32. 812–13: "neque enim finitur quod dicebatur, et dicitur aliud ut possint dici omnia; sed simul ac sempiterne omnia. Alioquin jam tempus et mutatio, et non vera aeternitatis, nec vera immortalitas." For further discussion of this point, see R. V. Young, "Derrida or Deity? Deconstruction in the Presence of the Word,' in *Issues in the Wake of Vatican II*, Proceedings of the Eighth Convention of the Fellowship of Catholic Scholars, ed. Paul L. Williams (Scranton, PA: Northeast Books, 1985), pp. 105–20.

[199] See, for example, Paul A. Parrish, *Richard Crashaw*, Twayne's English Authors Series #299 (Boston: G.K. Hall, 1980), p. 136: "The 'Hymn to the Name of Jesus' celebrates the Holy Name and celebrates as well the sensuous way to God."

Derridean deconstruction, the deferral of the signified by the very signifier
that seeks to grasp it, make it present, in a word or name: "I Sing the NAME
which None can say." (1).[200] The text begins in contradiction: what "None
can say" "I" can, nonetheless, "Sing." As it develops, the meaning of the
distinction between *singing* and the solitary *saying* of the individual "I"
emerges: *singing* is tied to harmony; it invokes a multitude of voices – indeed
a symphony of "All Things that Are, / Or, what's the same, / Are Musicall'
(56–58).

The second line of the poem at first appears to qualify the antithesis of the
first line: "I Sing the NAME which None can say / But touch't with An
interiour RAY." But *is* the hymn's singing voice so "touch't" that it may
"say" the "NAME"? Perhaps not. Although the letters of the name, *Jesus*, are
inscribed in the title, they are not, as Anthony Raspa has observed, uttered by
the voice of the poem in all its 239 lines.[201] When the singer looks within, he
finds an insufficiency, an absence, where he sought "An interiour RAY." Here
we see a second motif anticipating Jacques Derrida, who deconstructs
Husserl's notion of the intentional consciousness thus:

> This movement of différance is not something that happens to a transcendental
> subject; it produces a subject. Auto-affection is not a modality of experience
> that characterizes a being that would already be itself (*autos*). It produces
> sameness as self-relation within self-difference; it produces sameness as the the
> nonidentical.[202]

Crashaw "deconstructs" the self, as it were, thus:

> Awake, My glory. SOUL, (if such thou be,
> And That fair WORD at all refer to Thee)
>   Awake and sing
>   And be All Wing;
> Bring hither thy whole SELF; and let me see
> What of thy Parent HEAVN yet speakes in thee.
>   O thou art Poore
>   Of noble POWRES, I see,
> And full of nothing else but empty ME,
> Narrow, and low, and infinitely lesse
> Then this GREAT mornings mighty Busynes.   (13–23)

A self looks inside itself – a "SOUL" looks at its "whole SELF" – and finds that
self "full" of emptiness, "full of nothing else but empty ME" – full of the
emptiness of the self – of "sameness as the nonidentical."

<hr/>

[200] See Derrida, *Of Grammatology*, p. 89, on the way "Metaphor shapes and undermines the
proper name."
[201] *The Emotive Image: Jesuit Poetics in the English Renaissance* (Fort Worth: Texas Christian
University Press, 1983), p. 54.
[202] *Speech and Phenomena*, p. 82.

To find the "interiour RAY" the singer of the hymn must turn outside: "Goe, SOUL, out of thy Self, and seek for More" (27). In himself the singer is insufficient to invoke the Name. He must call upon the aid of "NATURE and ART!" (69). All are called into the total harmony of "the long / And everlasting series of a deathlesse SONG" (84–85) in order that the unsayable NAME might be sung. But these forces can only be deployed by virtue of a paradox: the feeble human singer can only call upon the symphony of Creation in the name of the NAME itself. He orders his own SOUL to "beat a summons in the Same / All-soveraign Name" (35–36). "Shall we dare This, my Soul?" he cries; "we'l doe't and bring / No Other note for't, but the Name we sing" (44–45). As it turns out the singer, the "I" can sing because he expresses not himself, not "empty ME," but Love: "I have Authority in LOVE'S name to take you / And to the worke of Love this morning wake you" (53–54).[203]

At this point it should be clear that Crashaw and Derrida are traversing the same (non-identical) territory in opposite directions. Derrida has undertaken to deconstruct the entire "metaphysics of presence"; Crashaw's hymn (virtually all of his poetry) is an invocation of presence. But with this difference, the hymn invokes not the signified behind the signifier, but the *signifier itself,* the NAME of Jesus. This name does not merely re-present, the Name of Jesus is presence itself – the presence of the Word (or Λóγος). Things do not lie behind this Word, it lies behind them: "the wealth of one Rich WORD" is the source of "New Similes to Nature" (95–96). The theological background of Crashaw's doxology of the Word as presence is explained by the sixteenth-century Augustinian friar, Luis de León: Hebrew *Dabar* (*Word* or *Logos*) signifies "the *very being* and *reality* of things," and therefore Christ is rightly called by the proper name *Dabar,* "because he is the thing that most is of all things and their primary and original being, whence all their being, their substance, their life, their power flow into creatures."[204] In the divine economy, then, the ordinary sign relationships are reversed: the signifier is "originary", not an arbitrary noise.

While the Christ's proper name as divine is *Dabar* (*Word* or *Λóγος*), his proper name as human is *Jesus,* not only because it means "salvation," but because, as Fray Luis points out, its Hebrew form, *Jehosuah,* contains all the letters, in pronounceable form, of the ineffable Name of God, the

---

[203] On the promise and "the name of the other," see Jacques Derrida, *Mémoires for Paul de Man,* trans. Cecile Lindsay, Jonathan Culler, and Eduardo Cadava (New York: Columbia University Press, 1986), p. 150.

[204] Fray Luis de León, *Obras completas castellanas,* ed. Félix García, O.S.A., 4th ed. (Madrid: Biblioteca de autores cristianos, 1957), I, 774: "Y significa también, y con esto concluyo, cualquiera cosa de *ser,* y por la misma razón el *ser mismo* y la *realidad* de las cosas; y así Cristo debidamente es llamado por nombre proprio *Dabar,* porque es la cosa que más es de todas las cosas, y el ser primero y original, de donde les mana a las criaturas su ser, su substancia, su vida, su obra."

Tetragrammaton.[205] It is the Old Testament "NAME which None can say"; the name celebrated by Crashaw can be not merely said but sung. When the hymn begins with the brash assertion that the name that cannot be said can yet be sung, the identity of the two different names, the ineffable Tetragrammaton and the Name of Jesus, is implied. Crashaw thus inverts Derrida's concept of "differance," which "produces" the "transcendental subject" by way of "sameness as the nonidentical." In the hymn, "To the Name of Jesus," the two names, the ineffable Name of the Father and Jesus, the Name of the Son, are not the same name, but they name an identical nature. To highlight this identity in difference, the poem does not *say* the Name that it *sings* in cascading imagery of musical sound, sweetness and light.

In "Plato's Pharmacy," his deconstruction of the Phaedran myth of writing, Derrida unveils the radical equivocation embedded in the designation of writing as "pharmakon": is it a remedy or medicine, or is it a poison? (Consider the ambiguity attaching to the English word "drug" in current American culture.) At issue is the way writing seems to call into question the reciprocal relation between the *logos* – spoken discourse, the living voice – and the "father of logos" – the speaking subject uttering the word. The textual inscription of *logos* necessarily effaces the presence of the speaker in representation:

> The disappearance of the good-father-capital-sun is thus the precondition of discourse, taken this time as a moment and not as a principle of *generalized* writing. That writing (is) *epekeina tes ousias*. The disappearance of truth as presence, the withdrawal of the present origin of presence, is the condition of all (manifestation of) truth. Nontruth is the truth. Nonpresence is presence. Differance, the disappearance of any originary presence, is *at once* the condition of the possibility *and* the condition of the impossibility of truth.[206]

Doubtless Derrida would regard the transaction of names in Crashaw's hymn as one more repetition of the Platonic "family scene."[207] Although the economy of the Christian Trinity remains unspoken in this Derridean text, surely it lurks in the blank spaces of the margins? For Christ is the Son of the ultimate originary "Father of Logos."

The Jesus of the Gospel according to St. John precisely reverses the

---

205 Ibid., I. 774–75: "el original de este nombre *Jesús*, . . . es *Iehosuah* . . .tiene todas las letras de que se compone el nombre de Dios, que llaman de *cuatro letras*, y demás de ellas tiene otras dos. Pues, como sabéis, el nombre de Dios, de *cuatro letras*, que se encierra en este *nombre*, es nombre que no se pronunica, o porque son [*sic* – "sin"?] vocales todas . . . o por la religión . . . Mas, aunque no se pronuncia en sí, ya veis que en el nombre de *Jesús*, por razón de dos letras que se le añaden, tiene pronunciación clara y sonido formado y significación entendida." See also Raspa, p. 54.

206 *Dissemination*, trans. Barbara Johnson (Chicago: University of Chicago Press, 1981), p. 168.

207 Ibid., pp. 142–55.

Derridean formulation; He is the Logos who makes the Truth and the speaking Father present:

> I am the Way, the Trueth, and the Life;
> no man commeth vnto the Father but by mee.
> If ye had knowen mee, ye should haue knowen my
> Father also: from henceforth ye know him, and
> haue seene him.   (*John* 14: 6–7)

Fray Luis de León explains that it is the Old Testament name of God that cannot be pronounced because it is inscribed without vowels;[208] literally voiceless, it is reverentially unutterable. Nonetheless, Jesus pronounces this name within his own Name as well as in the name of the Father: "Verely, verely I say vnto you, Before Abraham was, I am" (John 8: 58).

Against the spiritual identity of names, Derrida emphasizes the materiality of writing, of the drug of textuality that disperses or "disseminates" the central presence of the logos: "the *pharmakon* always penetrates like a liquid" and it can be diversely designated as "medicine," "brew," "drink," "potion," or "poison."[209] But *Jesus* is the name of the Logos incarnate, the material presence of the Deity. Moreover, as Fray Luis de León notes, the name "Jesus" means "health" or "salvation"; hence this word, too, is a kind of *pharmakon*: "the health of Jesus is ordained the remedy for the sickness that we have."[210] In Crashaw's hymn the Name is asked to "dissipate" its "spicy Powres" in "balmy showrs" (167, 169), and it is referred to as a potion or elixir – "the spirit of Soules extracted" (166). But in this poem, a written text that claims to be the singing of a hymn, the Name attains its climactic presence and power as it is inscribed in the blood of the martyrs, literally "witnesses" to the name of Christ. They "bore" the Name on "their Bold BRESTS" and "wore" it "In Center of their inmost Soules" and "stood up" against "the teeth of Hell" to "teach" it (203–05). The Name is written in the blood of the martyrs that is also the blood of Christ:

> Each wound of Theirs was Thy new Morning;
> And reinthron'd thee in thy Rosy Nest,
> With blush of thine own Blood thy day adorning.
> It was the witt of love o'reflowd the Bounds
> Of WRATH, and made thee way through All Those WOUNDS.
> (220–24)

When Crashaw was writing, "wit" still retained its sense of "intelligence," of "discourse of reason," of λόγος. It is the "witt of love" – the Logos – that

---

[208] *Obras* I. 774–75. See above n. 205.

[209] *Dissemination*, p. 152.

[210] *Obras* I. 776: "Y si para nosotros Cristo es *Jesús* y *salud*, bien se entiende que tenemos enfermedad nosotros, para cuyo remedio se ordena la *salud* de *Jesús*."

deconstructs the rationalistic logic of torture, suffering, and death. The result is the Christian version of dissemination, in Tertullian's famous phrase, "The blood of Christians is seed" ("semen est sanguis Christianorum").[211] Although Crashaw's hymn to "the name above every name" (Phil. 2: 9) celebrates the name of the Logos as it pervades the creation, the poem finally centers on the Name as *signed* in Jesus' blood and *witnessed* in the blood of the martyrs. In worrying over the issue of "words and wounds," Geoffrey Hartman remarks, "the poets themselves depict most clearly the power of words, their balm and venom."[212] In Crashaw's hymn the wound utters the Word, *Jesus*, the Name of Salvation, the ultimate "talking cure." Derrida's "deconstruction of Western metaphysics" furnishes a productive perspective and terminology for the poem because it recalls the dismantling and *reconstruction* of metaphysics already (always already?) begun by the Christian tradition itself. The "witt of love" also overflows the boundlessness of the abyss. The principal concerns of the seventeenth-century tradition of devotional poetry converge thus in Crashaw's "Hymn to the Name of Jesus." The intimate longing of private meditation is fulfilled by the sacramental presence of Christ, collapsing the *deferrals* of time and space; Jesus graciously arrives in the spirit of the worshipper who *deferentially* articulates His saving Name.

---

[211] *Apologeticus* L. 13, ed. and trans. T. R. Glover (Cambridge, MA: Harvard University Press, 1931), pp. 226–27.
[212] *Saving the Text: Literature, Derrida, Philosophy* (Baltimore: Johns Hopkins University Press, 1981), p. 122.

Part III

BIBLICAL POETICS IN THE SEVENTEENTH CENTURY

Thus at the root of true Scriptural interpretation there lies the transition from the Old to the New Testament, which is far more than merely the fulfillment of the promise, the definitive form of what was provisional, the manifestation of what was hidden, the transition and the correspondence from type to antitype: what is involved, rather, is that radically new re-creation of all meaning through the death of God's Logos. In so far as Scripture is the "body of the Logos" and not only the unparticipating testimony to his death and resurrection, the transition in Scripture from the *littera* to the *spiritus* is a participation in the event of salvation, and without this participation the letter's becoming spirit would be unthinkable in the Christian sense.   Hans Urs von Balthasar[1]

RECENT years have witnessed a surge of interest in the Bible as a literary inspiration for the devotional poetry of the seventeenth century. Scholars have come to recognize in Sacred Scripture – especially in the Psalter and the other poetical books – a source of generic models and metaphoric textures as well as of traditional typological symbolism. This new literary interest in Scripture has been almost exclusively associated with the Reformation, and biblical poetics is often regarded exclusively as a component of Protestant poetics, with its emphasis on private interpretation and the "application" of scriptural passages to individual experience.[2] At the same time postmodernist

---

[1] *The Glory of the Lord: A Theological Aesthetics*, vol. I, *Seeing the Form*, trans. Erasmo Leiva-Merikakis (San Francisco: Ignatius Press, 1982), p. 549.

[2] The most influential account of the Bible as a source of generic, figurative, and symbolic models is in Chapters 2–4 of Barbara K. Lewalski, *Protestant Poetics and the Seventeenth-Century Religious Lyric* (Princeton, NJ: Princeton University Press, 1979). Other works that stress a uniquely Protestant interest in the Bible include William Halewood, *The Poetry of Grace: Reformation Themes and Structures in English Seventeenth-Century Poetry* (New Haven: Yale University Press, 1970), esp. 124–25; Frank L. Huntley, *Bishop Joseph Hall and Protestant Meditation in Seventeenth-Century England* (Binghamton, NY: Center for Medieval and Early Renaissance Studies, 1981), pp. 9–12; John N. King, *Reformation Literature: The Tudor Origins of the Protestant Tradition* (Princeton, NJ: Princeton University Press, 1982), pp. 6–7, 16–17 469–70; Richard A. McCabe, *Joseph Hall: A Study in Satire and Meditation* (Oxford: Clarendon Press, 1982), pp. 218–19; Martin Elsky, "The Sacramental Frame of George Herbert's 'The Church' and the Shape of Spiritual Autobiography," *JEGP* 83 (1984) 313–29;

literary theory has posed a dichotomy not only of speech and writing, but also of the book and writing; and this dichotomy threatens to dismantle the traditional identification of Scripture (viz. Writing) and the Bible (viz. the Book):

> The idea of the book is the idea of a totality, finite or infinite, of the signifier; this totality of the signifier cannot be a totality, unless a totality constituted by the signified pre-exists it, supervises its inscriptions and its signs, and is independent of it in its ideality. The idea of the book, which always refers to a natural totality, is profoundly alien to the sense of writing.

The above quote is, of course, from Jacques Derrida, who adds, subsequently, "What writing itself, in its nonphonetic moment, betrays, is life."[3]

It is helpful to remain attentive to the primary texts of deconstruction because they lay out so baldly the theological implications of postmodernism. If Derridean deconstruction has begun to seem passé, it is not, as Stanley Fish points out, because Derrida and his epigones have ceased to exercise influence, but rather because so many assumptions of deconstruction have been assimilated into academic thought and are now largely taken for granted:

> Not surprisingly, the elaboration of these notions by deconstructionists, feminists, sociologists, cultural anthropolgists, and others met with resistance, and some resisted not by engaging with the new arguments point by point but by dismissing them as obviously nonsensical and betting that in a short time they would fade away like a bad dream. It was a losing bet; if there is now no vigorous discussion of deconstruction in the academy, it is because its lessons have been absorbed and its formulations – the irreducibility of difference, the priority of the signifier over the signified, the social construction of the self – have been canonized; and if poststructuralism has given way to postmodernism as the new all-purpose term, it is because the implications of the first term are now being extended far beyond the realm of aesthetics and philosophy to the very texture of everyday life.[4]

There is an element of hyperbole here, but Fish is, regrettably, correct in suggesting that the response of traditional critics and scholars to the

---

Chana Bloch, *Spelling the Word: George Herbert and the Bible* (Berkeley: University of California Press, 1985), esp. pp. 114–15, 121–66 passim; and Richard Todd, "'So Well Attyr'd Abroad': Background to the Sidney-Pembroke Psalter and its Implication for the Seventeenth-Century Religious Lyric," *TSLL* 29 (1987) 74–93.

[3] *Of Grammatology*, trans. Gayatri Chakravorty Spivak (Baltimore: Johns Hopkins University Press, 1976), pp. 18, 25. For an example of a "theological" appropriation of deconstruction, see Mark C. Taylor, *Erring: A Deconstructive A/theology* (Chicago: University of Chicago Press, 1984). See also Terry R. Wright, "Through a *Glas* Darkly: Derrida, Literature, and the Specter of Christianity," *Christianity and Literature* 44 (1994) 73–92.

[4] *There's No Such Thing as Free Speech and It's a Good Thing, Too* (New York/Oxford: Oxford University Press, 1994), p. 57.

deconstructionist challenge has not always been edifying. Propositions that are ignored rather than refuted too easily become the unexamined clichés of academic discourse. Contemporary versions of Protestant poetics have often read back into devotional poets of the seventeenth century an "application of the Bible to the self" that looks suspiciously like the "deconstruction" of Sacred Scripture. Such a reading is unintentionally ironic because these poets were acutely aware of the temptation to expropriate the authority of the revealed text to subjective purposes. To bind the meaning of Scripture to the inner assurance of the individual is, in effect, an anticipation of the deconstructive gambit, dissemination.

Insofar as the Protestant Reformation stresses the *letter* and *text* of Scripture at the expense of its rôle as the embodiment of the Logos, giving voice to the Church in ritual and sacrament, it can be seen as the first step in the *deconstruction* of the Christian tradition rather than a restoration of its origins. Hence the relationship of seventeenth-century devotional poetry to Sacred Scripture is in need of reappraisal, for the Bible furnishes yet another context in which devotional poets confront a clash of opposing forces. While much that is currently counted as *Protestant* poetics is traceable to the medieval Catholic heritage or is part of the common development of Christian humanism, there were genuinely new approaches to the Bible during the seventeenth century, which provide some of the tinder for the blaze of secularization gleaming through the modern world. In the face of this tendency, Protestant and Catholic poets alike had recourse to a shared Christian culture centered on the personal presence of Jesus. The spiritual dynamic of biblical poetics finds in the scriptural text not the dead trace of an absent presence, but the living voice of the embodied Logos. The poet seeks to rewrite the Word of God in his own imitation or version of "scripture," thus inscribing the word – Christ's name and presence – in his own soul in the blood of the Lamb.

This growing focus on personal spirituality during the period of the Reformation inspires a new and lively interest in the literary aspects of the Bible as a source of generic models for Christian poets, but this is not a distinctive feature of Protestant poetics. There is certainly plentiful evidence that the Psalms, for example, were regarded by Protestants as a "compendium of lyric kinds," expressing a great variety of emotional states and moods. A typical instance is George Wither's *Preparation to the Psalter* (1619), in which he notes "that these holy Hymnes are not written all in one kind of *Poesie*, but the Prophet hath made use almost of all sorts."[5] Such an awareness of the various rhetorical, generic and figurative aspects of the Psalter cannot, however, be attributed to a peculiarly Protestant theology or spirituality. The Psalms, after all, have always played a dominant rôle in the development of Christian worship and devotion; for example, they lie at the heart of the

---

[5] Lewalski, *Protestant Poetics*, pp. 45–47.

opus Dei that St. Benedict made central to Catholic prayer life. "The singing of psalms and hymns often is portrayed as peculiarly Protestant," writes Anthony Low. "But their use in devotion goes back to the earliest Christian periods."[6] Hence it is not at all surprising to find Wither's literary observations anticipated by the Psalm commentary of such a distinctively Counter-Reformation figure as St. Robert Bellarmine:

> And in Psalm 1 and in almost all those that follow he encourages virtues, reproves vices, invites, attracts, warns, threatens; and he does not comprise all these things in a plain narration, but in varying kinds of poems, with poetic diction, and an abundance of admirable metaphors, and in short he thus ravishes souls in love, and in the praise of God, with a new manner of utterance, so that nothing could be sweeter, nothing more salutary to sing or hear.[7]

There is a similar parallel between Protestant and Catholic attitudes on the use of the poetical books of Scripture as a literary substitute for undesirably profane songs and ballads. The point can be demonstrated from Barbara Lewalski's citation of a comment in the Sternhold-Hopkins doggerel version of the Psalter as if it reflected a uniquely Protestant perspective: "In the tradition of Luther and Coverdale, the Sternhold-Hopkins title page presents the Psalms as a wholesome substitute for licentious secular lyric – 'Very mete to be used of all sortes of people privately for their solace and comfort: laying apart all ungodly Songes and Ballads, which tend only to the norishing of vyce, and corrupting of youth'."[8] In fact, Luther and Coverdale borrowed this tradition from the Christian humanism of Erasmus, who, in the preface to his Greek/Latin edition of the New Testament, urged that the Gospels be translated into to all languages:

[6] *Love's Architecture: Devotional Modes in Seventeenth-Century English Poetry* (New York: New York University Press, 1978), p. 13. See also Peter Brown, *Augustine of Hippo* (Berkeley: University of California Press, 1967), pp. 174–75, on how St. Augustine works the language of the Psalms into the texture of the *Confessions*, thus defining himself in scriptural terms; Christopher Dawson, *The Formation of Christendom* (New York: Sheed & Ward, 1967), p. 139, on the Psalms as the new poetry of Christian culture, "which could be applied by the individual Christian to express his own thoughts and feelings, yet it was at the same time the voice of the Church and the voice of Christ."; and Rivkah Zim, *English Metrical Psalms: Poetry as Praise and Prayer, 1535–1601* (Cambridge: Cambridge University Press, 1987), pp. 26–27, on the continued stability during the Reformation of the Christian devotional tradition: "Since the fourth century, at least, Christian commentators had regarded the Book of Psalms as applicable to all the conditions of mankind's spiritual and emotional experience."

[7] *In Omnes Psalmos Dilucida Explanatio* (Brixiae, 1611), "Praefatio," sig. a⁴r: "Denique in Psal. 1. & sequentibus fere omnibus hortatur ad virtutes, retrahit a vitijs, inuitat, allicat, minatur, terret; atque haec omnia non simplici narratione complectitur, sed vario carminum genere, phrasibus poeticis, & metaphoris plurimis, & admirabilibus, denique nouo quodam genere dicendi ita rapuit animos in amorem, & laudem Dei, vt nihil dulcius, nihil salutarius cani, audirive possit."

[8] *Protestant Poetics*, p. 50. But cf. Zim, *English Metrical Psalms*, pp. 3–6, for evidence that biblical literature was not widely or absolutely opposed to pagan, secular literature.

Would that, as a result, the farmer sing some portion of them at the plow, the weaver hum some parts of them to the movement of the shuttle, the traveller lighten the weariness of the journey with stories of this kind! Let all the conversation of every Christian be drawn from this source.[9]

Erasmus' influence was not confined to Luther and Coverdale and their followers. Marcantonio Flaminio, associated with the humanist circle around Reginald Pole in the late 1540s, justifies his own Latin rendering of a selection of the Psalms in similar terms:

> While I am first to bring
> The mystical hymns of David to the Latin muses,
> And sing pleasingly to the pious;
> Not representing, while scarcely sane, Jove's insane passions,
> Nor the drunken orgies of Bacchus,
> Nor the sports or despicable rites of Apollo
> But the praise of the almighty God.

The purpose of Flaminio's elegant Latin version is expressly didactic in the Erasmian mode, aimed at attracting particularly the young to a more wholesome kind of reading:

> Oh, if only chaste boys and girls would learn these,
> And their minds be formed
> On holier studies while young and impressionable.
> Why, oh parents, why does it help
> To pollute your children with worthless trifles
> And filthy song?[10]

An interest in the Psalms as a literature of popular edification continued among Catholic writers throughout the sixteenth century. The Spanish Augustinian, Fray Luis de León (1528–91), translated twenty-one of the Psalms into a variety of lyric meters, as well as two chapters of the Book of Job (6–7) and the last chapter of Proverbs into terza rima, and the Song of Songs into ottava rima. Fray Luis was hardly writing in "the tradition of Luther and

---

[9] "The Paraclesis," in *Christian Humanism and the Reformation*, ed. and trans. John C. Olin (New York: Harper & Row, 1965), p. 97.

[10] "Ad Alexandrum Farnesium Card. amplissimum," *Marci Antonii Joannis Antonii et Gabrielis Flaminiorum Forocorneliensium Carmina* (Prati: Typis Raynerii Guasti, 1831), pp. 239–40: "Dum primus ipse mystica /Davidis ad Latias deduco carmina Musas, / Piisque grata concino; / Non Jovis insani referens male sanus amores, / Non ebriosa Liberi / Orgia, non ludos Phoebi exsecrandave sacra, / Sed maximi laudes Dei . . . O utinam haec discant pueri castaeque puellae, / Mentesque sanctioribus / Formentur studiis, dum parva et mobilis aetas. / Quid, o parentes, quid juvat / Futilibus nugis et turpi carmine vestros / Contaminare liberos?"

Coverdale," yet his prefatory note to these translations is equally emphatic about the salutary effects of substituting sacred for lascivious secular verse:

> And no one ought to regard verse as a novelty or as foreign to Holy Scripture, because it is rather very appropriate and quite ancient, for since the beginning of the Church until today many men great in letters and holiness have made use of it ... And may it please God that this poetry alone reign in our ears, and that in the street and squares no other songs would sound by night, and that in these songs the tongue of the child would loosen, and that the secluded maiden would gladden herself with this, and the workman who labors would lighten his labor here. But perdition has carried the Christian name to such shamelessness and license, that we make music of our vices and, not content with them in secret, sing out our confusion in happy voices.[11]

Humanist scholarship, in which Erasmus is the key figure, clearly exerted an important influence on Christian poets, Catholic and Protestant alike, throughout the sixteenth and seventeenth centuries. Although the development of biblical poetics has been ascribed to "the pervasive Protestant emphasis upon the bible as a book ... requiring philological and literary analysis,"[12] Flaminio and Fray Luis exemplify the same concerns at work among Catholics. Fray Luis was both a poet and a Scripture scholar of distinction, and his keen literary and philological talents were displayed not only in his commentaries on specific books of the Bible and verse translations, but also in his massive blend of explication and meditation, *On the Names of Christ*.[13] Flamino likewise evinced a scholar's interest in the metrical form of the Hebrew Psalms in his prose preface to Cardinal Farnese, and a poet's

---

[11] *Obras completas castellanas*, ed. Félix García, O.S.A., 4th ed. (Madrid: Biblioteca de autores cristianos, 1967), II. 970: "Y nadie debe tener por nuevos o por ajenos de la Sagrada Escritura los versos, porque antes le son muy propios y tan antiguos, que desde el principio de la Iglesia hasta hoy los han usado en ella muchos hombres grandes en letras y en santidad ... Y pluguiese a Dios que reinase esta sola poesía en nuestros oídos, y que sólo este cantar nos fuese dulce, y que en las calles y en las plazas, de noche, no sonasen otros cantares, y que en éstos soltase la lengua el niño, y la doncella recogida se solazase con ésto, y el oficial que trabaja aliviase su trabajo aquí. Mas ha llegado la perdición del nombre cristiano a tanta desvergüenza y soltura, que hacemos música de nuestros vicios, y, no contentos con lo secreto de ellos, cantamos con voces alegres nuestra confusión."

[12] Lewalski, *Protestant Poetics*, p. ix.

[13] In addition to his Latin lectures and treatises – Fray Luis was Professor of Sacred Scripture at the University of Salamanca – he wrote commentaries in Spanish on Job, the Song of Songs, and several Psalms. *Of the Names of Christ* is a typological study in the form of a Platonic dialogue. Fray Luis felt that Scripture study was important for all Christians, and regretted what he regarded as necessary restrictions imposed by the Church as a result of the Reformation. See *Obras* I.403–04. For an account of sophisticated literary/philological approaches to Scripture developed by Medieval scholars, see Beryl Smalley, *The Study of the Bible in the Middle Ages* (1952; rpt. Notre Dame IN: University of Notre Dame Press, 1964), pp. 120–21, 125, 233–34, 284–85, 300–01, 367.

preoccupation with the proper methods of translation ("neque reddita / Fuere verbis verba") in his introductory verses "Ad Lectorem."[14]

Of course the ultimate test of a biblical poetics is the appearance of poetry that is shaped by the poet's meditation on the forms and textures of Sacred Scripture. Lewalski observes that Herbert's "Church" is intended as "a book of Christian Psalms." "Several poems throughout the collection," she adds, "show Herbert's speaker in quasi-typological terms, taking on the rôle of New Covenant psalmist as he appropriates and turns to his own uses the Psalmist's words and forms."[15] Such a modeling of a collection of religious poems in a variety of lyric forms on the Book of Psalms is not, however, an exclusively Protestant practice. Ira Clark, who stresses the "Reformed" context of what he calls the "neotypological" lyric, concedes that the identification of a poetic persona with a scriptural figure "involves the deepest concerns of many Anglican traditionalists and Counter-Reformers" as well as the most unequivocal Protestants, and that the "first formulators" of this "new lyric" were two Jesuits, Robert Southwell and William Alabaster.[16] A true picture of the status of biblical poetics emerges with a consideration of the devotional poetry of the continent. Jean de la Ceppède wrote a highly personal verse paraphrase of the penitential psalms, *Imitation de Pseaumes de la Pénitence* (1594, 1612), which includes Latin hymns and original devotional pieces as well as scriptural imitations. P. A. Chilton points out that la Ceppède seems to have regarded psalm paraphrases as an integral part of the "devotional exercises of the Counter Reformation," and finds in his psalm *Imitation* "a preoccupation with the problems of personal redemption and grace." Moreover, la Ceppède's more famous *Théorèmes* take as their main source the Bible, and his poetry generally "emphasizes a moral and reflective application of Scripture for spiritual rather than intellectual benefit."[17]

Francisco de Quevedo's *Heráclito cristiano* (1613), with its resemblance to Donne's Holy Sonnets, comprises twenty-eight poems in various verse patterns, each designated a *salmo*. Since Quevedo explicitly calls these poems an "imitation of David" and sets forth in them a panorama of shifting spiritual states, they would clearly seem to be what Lewalski calls Herbert's "Church," "a book of Christian Psalms."[18] Many of Pedro Espinosa's religious lyrics are also called *salmos*, and since they deploy a greater variety of themes, including praise and thanksgiving as well as penitence, his

---

[14] *Carmina*, pp. 199, 238–39.

[15] *Protestant Poetics*, pp. 300, 302. See also p. 51.

[16] *Christ Revealed: The History of the Neotypological Lyric in the English Renaissance* (Gainesville: University Presses of Florida, 1982), pp. xii, 3, see pp. 29–63.

[17] *The Poetry of Jean de la Ceppède: A Study in Text and Context* (Oxford: Oxford University Press, 1977), pp. 24, 49ff, 71, 135.

[18] Francisco de Quevedo, *Obras completas*, ed. José Manuel Blecua, 2nd ed. (Barcelona: Editorial Planeta, 1968), I.19ff. See above, Part I, pp. 13–15, for parallels with the Holy Sonnets.

collection offers an even more thorough imitation of the Psalter than Quevedo's contritely weeping Heraclitus.[19]

None of this is really surprising in view of the pervasive influence of Ignatian meditation in every culture touched by the Counter-Reformation. As Anthony Raspa observes, "In this general scriptural current, the most suggestively poetic Biblical events to the meditative mind were those that seemed to enlighten it deeply about its own self and creation."[20] The assimilation of the self to scriptural types was a common preoccupation of Catholics and Protestants during the sixteenth and seventeenth centuries, and the Bible thus became an element of personal self-realization at the beginning of the modern era that would, in our time, begin to question the very concept of personal identity. The situation during the Renaissance is well described by Rivkah Zim with specific reference to the Psalms:

> Imitation of the Psalms in life as well as in literature promoted a consciousness of self, which was expressed in lyric and dramatic forms emphasizing the emotional intensity of personal experience. This consciousness and expression of self provided an obvious paradigm for different literary kinds of introspection and devotion. Renaissance poets learnt to apply a Judaeo-Christian concept of the unique integrity of the individual's sentient self in their writing by imitating inherited themes and forms of biblical poetry.[21]

i

"Postdate the whole Bible," Donne advises his congregation, "and whatsoever thou hearest spoken of such, as thou art, before, beleeve all that to be spoken but now, and spoken to thee."[22] This counsel of the Anglican preacher about how sinners should let the Bible speak to them for the purpose of reforming their lives is plainly a practical extension of the "moral sense" mentioned by St. Thomas as part of the spiritual meaning of Scripture, in which "things done is Christ, or that signify Christ, are signs of what we ought to do."[23] Such an application of the moral sense of scriptural figures is a commonplace among religious writers of the sixteenth and seventeenth centuries. Fray Luis de León dedicates his translation of and commentary on the Book of Job to Santa Teresa's successor as Mother Superior of the

---

[19] Pedro Espinosa, *Poesías completas*, ed. Francisco López Estrada (Madrid: Espasa-Calpe, 1975), pp. 94–153.

[20] *The Emotive Image: Jesuit Poetics in the English Renaissance* (Fort Worth: Texas Christian University Press, 1983), pp. 87–88.

[21] *English Metrical Psalms*, p. 204.

[22] *The Sermons of John Donne*, ed. George R. Potter and Evelyn Simpson, 10 vols. (Berkeley: University of California Press, 1953–62), VI. 220. See also II. 55 and VII. 51.

[23] *Summa Theologiae* I. 1. 10: "secundum vero quod ea quae in Christo sunt facta, vel in his quae Christum significat, sunt signa eorum quae nos agere debemus, est sensus moralis." See also Donne, *Sermons* II. 97.

Discalced Carmelites, Ana de Jesús, "since as valiant soldiers delight in the bold deeds of those before them, so you, in this militant patience that you profess, desire to become acquainted with the excellent example of Job."[24] Similarly, Vincenzo Bruno treats the directions given Moses for building the Tabernacle, in Exodus 25, as applicable to every Christian soul: "Which words were not spoken vnto *Moises* alone: but also to euery one of vs, whom God will haue to build a spirituall Tabernacle in which him selfe desireth to dwell by grace."[25] Perhaps most notable in this regard is la Ceppède, who, in the dedicatory epistle to his paraphrase of the penitential Psalms, declares that he has taken David as his "Pilot" in sailing the "bark" of penitence through the "invincible storm" of God's wrath.[26] La Ceppède thus applies the Psalms in the way recommended by Donne in a sermon on Psalms 38: 2: "But these *Psalmes* were made, not onely to vent *Davids* present holy passion, but to serve the Church of God, to the worlds end" (II. 55).

The heuristic force of biblical models for Christian life was regarded as considerable. Fray Luis de León saw sacred Scripture as "consolation in the travails of life and a clear and faithful light in its darkness."[27] For Donne, the Bible was a mode of self-discovery or, more accurately, self-recovery. Preaching on the text of Psalms 38: 3, "A *Psalm of Remembrance*," he remarks, "The art of *salvation*, is but the art of *memory*." But this is not always an easy matter: "There may be enough in *remembering our selves*; but sometimes, that's the hardest of all; many times we are farthest off from our selves; most forgetfull of our selves" (II. 73, 74). Since saving the soul means saving the self, or personal identity, biblical figures that help us remember who we are, that put our sufferings and temptations in the context of the Communion of the Saints, play a critical rôle in the self-restoration that constitutes salvation. Hence the poetry of penitence, a poetry of self-exploration, will naturally turn to the Psalms for a pattern.

The manner in which these scriptural poems are appropriated for personal devotion is, therefore, a crucial issue, and Donne insists as adamantly as his Catholic contemporaries that the Bible be read in the context of Church teaching and interpretation. "The Scripture is thine onely *Ephod*," he remarks in an early sermon (1618), "but *Applica Ephod*, apply it to thee by his Church, and by his visible Angels, and not by thine own private interpretation" (I. 283);

---

[24] *Obras completas castellanas* II. 27: "Que como los valientes soldados gustan de conocer los hechos hazañosos de los que fueron, ansí V.R., en esta milicia de paciencia que profesa, desea reconocer este ejemplo excelente, que tal es el de Job, como por su escritura parece."

[25] *The First Part of the Meditation of the Passion, & Resurrection of Christ our Sauiour* (1599?), in John R. Roberts, ed., *A Critical Anthology of English Recusant Devotional Prose*, Duquesne Studies Philogical Series 7 (Pittsburgh: Duquesne University Press, 1966), p. 235.

[26] *Imitation de la Pénitence de David* is included, with its own pagination, in *Théorèmes sur le Sacré Mystère de Notre Rédemption*, pref. Jean Rousset (Genève: Librairie Droz, 1966), "A Madame Louyse D'Ancesune, pp. 4–5.

[27] *Obras* I. 403: "que las escribieron para que nos fuesen en los trabajos de esta vida consuelo, y en las tinieblas y errores de ella clara y fiel luz."

and in a late sermon (1629) he reproves the "Pharisee" who is "separated by following private Expositions . . . with a contempt of all Antiquity; and not only an undervaluation, but a detestation of all opinions but his owne, and his, whom he hath set up for his Idol" (IX. 168).[28] These strictures resemble the view of Cardinal Cajetan uttered a century earlier that "An interpretation of Scripture is beyond all doubt the true one if we receive it handed on as the consensus of the saints and it is then defined by an ecumenical council."[29] Donne's attack on "private Expositions" also recalls Erasmus, who maintains the authority of the Church Fathers and the Bishops in biblical interpretation against Luther's appeal to the private inspiration of individuals:

> If they say: what can a congregated synod, in which perhaps nobody is inspired by the Spirit, contribute to an understanding of Scripture? I answer: what can the private gathering of a few contribute, none of whom probably has the Spirit?[30]

Like Erasmus, Donne manifests a profound love of Scripture as an inspiration to personal devotion and holiness, and he also shares the same distrust of eccentric, individualistic, sometimes crude biblical zeal, which he saw in the Puritans of his day as Erasmus had seen in the Lutherans of his own. For Donne, as for Erasmus, the Bible is important not as a source of subjective revelations, but as a means of integrating the individual with the larger community of fellow believers, past and future as well as present. The Bible is the common text of Christians, bringing them together and ensuring Catholicity, not the secret code of a quasi-Gnostic elite.[31] Donne, therefore, maintains that Scripture speaks to the individual insofar as he is a member of the Body of Christ, of the Church, of which Scripture is the Book.

It is an oversimplification to explain the "pervasive self-dramatization" of Donne's Holy Sonnets and hymns as the result of a "characteristic Protestant and typological meditative focus upon the self."[32] When Donne sets out to exorcise the proud, alienated self in his devotional poems he is drawing on a tradition of scriptural interpretation that goes back to Patristic times. Biblical types furnish a means of restoring and confirming the *identity* of the redeemed self through *identification with* the scriptural models of God's

---

[28] See also *Sermons* I. 235; VI. 282–83.

[29] *Cajetan Responds: A Reader in Reformation Controversy*, ed. and trans. Jared Wicks, S.J. (Washington, D.C.: Catholic University of America Press, 1978), p. 126.

[30] "A Diatribe or Sermon Concerning the Free Will," in *Erasmus-Luther: Discourse on Free Will*, ed. and trans. Ernst F. Winter (New York: Frederick Unger Publishing Co., 1961), p. 17. See also Johan Huizinga, *Erasmus and the Age of Reformation* (Princeton, NJ: Princeton University Press, 1984), p. 165; and Marjorie O'Rourke Boyle, *Rhetoric and Reform: Erasmus' Civil Dispute with Luther*, Harvard Historical Monographs Vol. LXXI (Cambridge, MA: Harvard University Press, 1983), pp. 50, 107–09, 142–43, 158.

[31] See Boyle, *Rhetoric and Reform*, pp. 142–43.

[32] Lewalski, *Protestant Poetics*, p. 254.

Providence. The invocation of these types in his poems, along with pervasive allusions to biblical passages and scenes, grounds the individual experience of the persona in the corporate experience of the Church embodied in Scripture.

Donne's seventh Holy Sonnet, "Spit in my face yee Jewes," begins with a certain bravado, which quickly gives way to the speaker's rueful realization that only Christ's death, and his own, is sufficient satisfaction for the sins of any individual, not to mention the whole world. In the poem's sestet the marvel of divine love revealed in the Incarnation of the Son is framed as the antitype to the selfish, deceptive disguise of Jacob:

> Oh let mee then, his strange love still admire:
> Kings pardon, but he bore our punishment.
> And *Jacob* came cloth'd in vile harsh attire
> But to supplant, and with gainful intent:
> God cloth'd himselfe in vile mans flesh, that so
> Hee might be weake enough to suffer woe. (9–14)

It was standard practice among commentators to deflect attention from Jacob's deceit by regarding him as a figure for Christians supplanting the Jews as the chosen people of God.[33] Donne, however, with his eye on the wonder of God's love for sinful mankind, stresses the difference between type and antitype. The effect is to underscore both continuity and discontinuity: the blessing that Jacob wins by deception is the same blessing – the blessing of the same God – that the new Israel, the Church, receives; but it comes in a way at once more miraculous and more ordinary. The extraordinary event associated with the Old Testament Patriarch is *supplanted* by the ordinary but transcendent love of God in the New Dispensation.

The traditional Catholic resonance of Donne's procedure is suggested by the similar effect of Lope de Vega's deployment of typology in Sonnet LIV of his *Rimas sacras*:

> Sacó Moisés de Egipto al pueblo hebreo,
> pasó el Jordán seguro, y por memoria
> comió el cordero y celebró la gloria
> de aquel divino general trofeo.
> Instituyó la Pascua con deseo
> de eternizar aquella dulce historia,
> la libertad, el triunfo, la vitoria
> figura deste pan que adoro y creo.
> Memoria sois Cordero soberano,
> de la salida de otro Egipto fiero,
> Pascua divina del linaje humano.

---

[33] See for example, St. Augustine, *Sermones* V. 4, *PL* 38–39. 55; and St. Thomas Aquinas, *Summa Theologiae* 2–2. 110. 3 ad 3, who cites Augustine, *Contra Mendacium* 10. 23, *PL* 40. 533.

Y así, como Moisés más verdadero,
nos da la bendición de vuestra mano
Pascua, pasto, pastor, pan y cordero.[34]

[Moses took the Hebrew people out of Egypt, crossed the Jordan safely
and as a memorial ate the lamb and celebrated the glory of that divine
universal conquest. He instituted the Passover with the desire of immor-
talizing that sweet history; he represents the freedom, the exultation, the
victory of this bread that I adore and believe. You are a memorial,
sovereign Lamb, of the escape from another fierce Egypt, divine Passover
of the human lineage. And so, as a more authentic Moses, you give us
the blessing of your hand – Passover, pasture, Shepherd, bread, and
lamb.]

In Lope's poem, as in Donne's, a moment of intense personal devotion –
Donne's for the suffering Christ, Lope's for His Presence in the Sacrament – is
apprehended in terms of an Old Testament type. The type is invoked,
however, for the purpose of being dismissed. Our Lord "cloth'd . . . in vile
man's flesh" *supplants* Jacob the "supplanter" by means of His "strange
love." Christ in the Sacrament is "a more authentic Moses" – shepherd,
sheep, and pasture; sacrificing priest and sacrificial lamb – who leads all
humanity ("the human lineage") out of the "fierce Egypt" of sin, original and
actual.

Donne himself explicates very plainly, in *Essays in Divinity*, the "other
fierce Egypt" in a way that could serve as a gloss on Lope's sonnet:

Thou hast delivered me, O God, from the Egypt of confidence and presumption, by interrupting my fortunes, and intercepting my hopes; And from the
Egypt of despair by contemplation of thine abundant treasures, and my portion
therein; from the Egypt of lust, by confining my affections; and from the
monstrous and unnaturall Egypt of painfull and wearisome idleness, by the
necessities of domestick and familiar cares and duties.[35]

Donne and Lope are alike in illuminating personal spiritual experience in the
light of universal salvation history. The Old Testament type, in each case,
defines the antitype by means of opposition; yet, although its significance
depends on the superseding of its imperfection in the fulfillment of Christ, the
"shadowy type" maintains a shadowy presence. While the historical Moses of
the Old Covenant is displaced by a "more authentic Moses," and while Jacob
who came "But to supplant, and with gainfull intent" is unfavorably
contrasted with the love of God incarnate; still, both types are integral in
their defectiveness to the expression of such perfection as mortal man can

---

[34] *Obras poéticas*, ed. José Manuel Blecua (Barcelona: Editorial Planeta, 1969), I. 343–44.
[35] *Essays in Divinity*, ed. Evelyn Simpson (Oxford: Clarendon Press, 1952), p. 75. Although
there is no question of influence one way or the other, it is interesting to note that Lope's
Rimas sacras and Donne's *Essays* are almost exactly contemporary.

apprehend. The use of biblical types is thus a way for the poet to express the insufficiency of his vision, of his experience, and of the very expressiveness of his poetry. The imperfect type represents the imperfection of the human condition and the defectiveness of the poet's capacity for representation.

The poet's sense of inadequacy is especially evident when he attempts to confront directly the suffering of the crucified Christ. In "Spit in lmy face, yee Jewes," Donne veers away from identification with the Passion into typological indirection; in "What if this present were the worlds last night?" he establishes, as we have observed in Part I (pp. 22–28), an equivocal relationship with the Petrarchan love sonnet. Typology extends forward into eschatology: the Crucifixion converges with the Day of Judgment, and "This beauteous forme" of the Crucified One is taken (or mistaken) as a hopeful sign that "assures a pitious mind" (14):

> Marke in my heart, O Soule, where thous dost dwell,
> The picture of Christ crucified, and tell
> Whether that countenance can thee affright,
> Teares in his eyes quench the amasing light,
> Blood fills his frownes, which from his pierc'd head fell,
> And can that tongue adjudge thee unto hell,
> Which pray'd forgiveness for his foes fierce spight?   (2–8)

The speaker of this poem reframes the stark scriptural account in terms of the Petrarchan topos of the living image of the beautiful beloved engraved in the heart of the lover. As an effort to come to terms with the overwhelming reality of the Incarnation, suffering, and death of the Second Person of the Holy Trinity, the poem functions, again, as the sign of its own inadequacy. The very frivolousness of the comparison between the Petrarchan erotic ritual and the incarnation of divine love as both Savior and Judge highlights the poet's inability to rewrite the somber biblical accounts of the Passion and Last Things.

Lope de Vega makes poetry out of the same dilemma in *Rimas sacras* LXXIII, "A Cristo en la Cruz" ("To Christ on the Cross"), which likewise attributes conventional poetic beauty to the crucified Lord:

> ¡Oh vida de mi vida, Cristo santo!
> ¿adónde voy de tu hermosura huyendo?
> ¿Cómo es posible que tu rostro ofendo,
> que me mira bañado en sangre y llanto?   (*Obras poéticas* I. 354–55)
>
> [Oh life of my life, holy Christ! Where do I go fleeing from your beauty? How is it possible that I vex your countenance that, bathed in blood and tears, beholds me?]

The insufficiency of such flattery and of the speaker's efforts generally is evident from the sense of shame and confusion that ensues:

A mí mismo me doy confuso espanto
de ver que me conozco, y no me enmiendo;
ya el Ángel de mi guarda está diciendo
que me avergüence de ofenderte tanto.

[To myself I afford a confused fear with seeing that I know myself, and do not amend myself; now my guardian Angel is saying that I might at least be ashamed of offending you.]

This failure of repentance prompts a plea that Christ take the matter into His own hands, but those hands are nailed, paradoxically doing everything possible to save mankind by the passivity of the Passion:

Detén con esas manos mis perdidos
pasos, mi dulce amor; ¿mas de qué suerte
las pide quien las clava con las suyas?
¡Ay Dios!, adónde estaban mis sentidos,
que las espaldas pude yo volverte,
mirando en una cruz por mi las tuyas?

[Restrain with those hands my lost steps, my sweet love; but in what fashion can he ask this who nails those hands with his own? Oh God! Where were my senses, that I could turn my back on you, beholding yours against the cross for me?]

The principal issue of this meditation on the Crucifixion is the inability of the speaker of the poem to look at the crucified Savior face to face. Like Donne in "Spit in my face," where the persona admits that he crucifies Christ daily (8), Lope evokes a sense of sin by accusing himself of nailing Christ's saving hands to the cross with his own sinful hands. In this sonnet by Lope de Vega and in both the Holy Sonnets by Donne, the scriptural event of the Crucifixion is reconstructed in dramatic terms, which prove in some measure inadequate. Lope, especially, shows the dubiousness of the Petrarchan trope, since it is the occasion of turning his back on the suffering Christ.

Donne elaborates this theme of man's inability to look upon the sacrifice on the cross in "Goodfriday, 1613. Riding Westward." With a characteristically witty turn at the close, he makes the act of turning his back upon the affliction of his sovereign Lord both the sin and the means of penance:

Though these things, as I ride, be from mine eye,
They'are present yet unto my memory,
For that looks towards them; and thou look'st towards mee,
O Saviour, as thou hang'st upon the tree;
I turne my backe to thee, but to receive
Corrections, till thy mercies bid thee leave.
O thinke mee worth thine anger, punish mee,
Burne off my rusts, and my deformity,
Restore thine Image, so much, by thy grace,
That thou may'st know mee, and I'll turne my face.   (33–42)

The essential common factor in these poems by Donne and Lope de Vega is the effort to reread Scripture by retelling the scriptural story in personal terms. But the retelling of the biblical material turns into a retelling of the self: in trying to accommodate the revealed account of God's providential acts to his own individual longings and circumstances, the individual discovers his own shortcomings.[36] The effort to write a penitential meditation on Christ's Passion discloses that the penitent cannot or will not look upon the cross: thus the intense effort to repent mainly reveals how deep the need is. Only Christ's grace can arrest Lope's steps toward perdition; Donne's rider is so far from facing the reality of the Crucifixion that only the sign of indifference, his back turned away, can be bared for "Corrections." Similarly, the invocation of Old Testament types, a Jacob or a Moses, with whom a Christian penitent might identify, yields the realization that these, like the penitent himself, are shadowy figures, whose flawed natures gain resonance only as indices of what they are not – the fulfillment of Christ's Incarnation.

Biblical poetics, then, more than a systematic allusiveness to Scripture or generic imitation, involves the attempt of the poet to write his way into the sacred text, to move through the written book of revelation into the secret book of life. The biblical poet's success thus becomes his failure: undertaking to retell – to elaborate – the revealed account of the suffering and death of Our Lord, the poet learns that he cannot even *face* the cross. The distance between the poet and his scriptural theme is, however, the space of grace, the opening into the ineffable mystery, inscribed less in the characters of the text than in the inscrutable countenance of Christ, where "Blood fills his frownes" ("What if this present," 6).

Donne's Holy Sonnets are not, therefore, representations of unmitigated despair, contrary to Barbara Lewalski's interpretation of "O might those sighes and teares returne againe" as a poem "about the condition of fruitless grief." The speaker of this poem, she says, "is unable to distinguish essentially between his present and his past griefs, and so does not experience the effect of true sorrow described in 2 Corinthians 7: 10 – which could be almost the text for this sonnet: 'For godly sorrow worketh repentance to salvation not to be repented of, but the sorrow of the world worketh death'."[37] But in fact there is a clear distinction established in the mind of the sonnet's persona between "this holy discontent" and his erstwhile "Idolatry." Erotic ardor is misplaced love: *passion* (i.e. suffering) with the wrong motivation and goal. Even more than most sins, it is ultimately its own punishment:

[36] For a similar perception, with a different interpretation, of these incongruities, see William Kerrigan, "The Fearful Accommodations of John Donne," *ELR* 4 (1974) 337–63. More in keeping with my view are Gillian R. Evans, "John Donne and the Augustinian Paradox of Sin," *RES*, New Series, 33 (1982), No. 129: 1–22; and M. Thomas Hester, " 'let them sleepe': Donne's Personal Allusion in *Holy Sonnet IV*," *PLL* 29 (1993) 346–50.

[37] *Protestant Poetics*, p. 267.

> O MIGHT those sighes and teares returne againe
> Into my breast and eyes, which I have spent,
> That I might in this holy discontent
> Mourne with some fruit, as I have mourn'd in vaine;
> In mine Idolatry what showres of raine
> Mine eyes did waste? what griefs my heart did rent?
> That sufferance was my sinne, now I repent;
> 'Cause I did suffer I must suffer paine.   (1–8)

The very term "passion" suggests what the Petrarchan tradition exhibits, that sinful or disordered love is a form of suffering, a self-deluded pursuit of suffering for its own sake. The simple recognition of this contrast between the willful, defiant suffering of profane love and suffering with and for Christ in His Passion is an unmistakable indication that the speaker has already begun to "Mourne with some fruit."

The closing sestet adds a further distinction between the more commonplace sins of the flesh and the helpless frustration of Petrarchan love, which is literally "Idolatry" because it pays to the Lady that suffering devotion due only to God. In one way such sin is obviously worse than mere carnality, and yet at the same time it points toward the true love of God because it so insistently proclaims its own futility:

> Th'hydroptique drunkard, and night-scouting thiefe,
> The itchy Lecher, and selfe tickling proud
> Have the remembrance of past joyes, for reliefe
> Of comming ills. To (poore) me is allow'd
> No ease; for, long, yet vehement griefe hath beene
> Th'effect and cause, the punishment and sinne.   (9–14)

The sonnet thus recalls the *Confessions* of St. Augustine, and his preoccupation with the theme of disordered love – intense, erotic passion – converted to the love of God. "You arouse delight in praising you," Augustine writes, "because you made us for yourself, and our heart is restless until it rest in you." Here is Donne's "holy discontent," and Augustine likewise reveals his acquaintance with erotic "Idolatry," the fashionable affectation that often accompanies it, and the misery it brings:

> To love and be loved was sweet to me, more so if I might also enjoy the body of
> my lover. And so I defiled the stream of friendship with the filth of
> concupiscence and clouded its luster with the hell of lust; and though foul
> and disgraceful, with exceeding vanity I played the rôle of urbane dandy. I fell
> violently into the love in which I longed to be seized. My God, my mercy, how
> good you were to me in sprinkling so much gall over that sweetness! For I was
> also beloved, and I came secretly to the bond of enjoyment, and I was tangled in
> knots of wretched pleasure, so that I might be beaten with fiery iron rods of
> jealousy, and suspicion, and anxiety, and rage, and strife.[38]

---

[38] *Confessionum* 1.1 (*PL* 32. 661): "Tu excitas, ut laudare te delectet; quia fecisti nos ad te, et

All this time, Augustine goes on to remark, he was actually starving for inner food, for God himself; hence his sin punished him by deprivation as well as by the actual misery it entailed. Such is Donne's point also, and his "confession," like Augustine's, is fruitful simply because it is a *confession* in every sense – not only an admission of guilt, but also a realization and acknowledgment of his radical dependence on God's grace.

Much the same sense of misspent tears, suffering, and strife informs one of the "psalms" of Quevedo's *Heráclito cristiano*:

> Trabajos dulces, dulces penas mías;
> pasadas alegrías
> que atormentáis ahora mi memoria,
> dulce en un tiempo, sí, mas breve gloria,
> que llevaron tras sí mis breves días;
> mal derramados llantos,
> [si sois castigo de los cielos santos,]
> con vosotros me alegro y me enriquezco,
> porque sé de mí mismo que os merezco,
> y me consuelo más que me lastimo;
> mas, si regalos sois, más os estimo,
> mirando que en el suelo,
> sin merecerlo, me regala el cielo.[39]

> [Sweet travails, sweet pains of mine; departed joys that now torment my memory, sweet at one time, yes, but a brief glory, that carry away with them my brief days; poorly shed floods of tears, (if you are chastisement of the holy heavens,) I congratulate and pride myself on you, because I know that I deserve you by myself, and I am consoled more than I grieve; but, if you are providential afflictions, I esteem you more, seeing that here on the ground, without my deserving it, heaven cherishes me.]

Quevedo elaborates the paradoxical nature of profane love, the same theme treated in the Donne sonnet: it is a source of "sweet pains," a pleasure that torments. He exploits the equivocal possibilities of the Spanish word *regalo*,

---

inquietum est cor nostrum, donec requiescat in te." *Confessionum* 3.1 *PL* 32. 683): "Amare et amari dulce mihi erat, magis si et amantis corpore fruerer. Venam igitur amicitiae coinquinabam sordibus concupiscentiae, candoremque ejus obnubilabam de tartaro libidinis; et tamen foedus atque inhonestus, elegans et urbanus esse gestiebam abundanti vanitate. Rui etiam in amorem quo cupiebam capi. Deus meus, misericordia mea, quanto felle mihi suavitatem illam, et quam bonus aspersisti! quia et amatus sum, et perveni occulte ad vinculum fruendi, et colligabar laetus aerumnosis nexibus, ut caederer virgis ferreis ardentibus zeli, et suspicionum, et timorum, et irarum atque rixarum." See Donne's citation of Augustine's *Confessions* on this topic in a Lincoln's Inn sermon (*Sermons* II.107–08):"*Audiebam eos exaltantes flagitia*, sayes that tender blessed Father, I saw it was thought wit, to make Sonnets of their owne sinnes, *Et libebat facere, non libidine facti, sed libidine laudis*, I sinn'd, not for the pleasure I had in the sin, but for the pride I had to write feelingly of it." I am grateful to M. Thomas Hester for reminding me of this reference.

[39] "Salmo X," *Obras completas*, I. 25.

which means not only "pleasure," "gratification," "gift," or "luxury," but also "an affliction dispensed by Providence." In the Donne and Quevedo poems erotic love is a *regalo* in both senses: both pleasure and pain, both punishment and gift. The twist is that, because it is heaven's punishment which the lover deserves for his sinfulness, it is also a blessing which he can in no way deserve – a gracious affliction or visitation of Providence, demonstrating God's care for him in the fact of chastisement. Donne acknowledges the same "affliction" of grace when he regards the "vehement griefe" of his "Idolatry" as "Th'effect and cause, the punishment and sinne."

The final lines of the same "Psalm X" by Quevedo shed light also on the conclusion of Donne's Holy Sonnet 5 ("If poysonous minerals"). The octave of the sonnet is a complaint that man, unlike lower creatures, faces the possibility of damnation because his nature includes "intent or reason" (5); but the sestet is a sharp rejoinder with echoes of Job, Romans, and the Psalms:[40]

> But who am I, that dare dispute with thee?
> O God, Oh! of thine onely worthy blood,
> And my teares, make a heavenly Lethean flood,
> And drowne in it my sinnes black memorie.
> That thou remember them, some claime as debt,
> I thinke it mercy, if thou wilt forget.   (9–14)

To be remembered by God is to be in His favor, to be saved; but to be remembered is also to have one's sins remembered. Hence salvation means to be forgotten as well as remembered: to "drowne" in a "Lethean flood" of grace (Christ's blood) and responsive contrition (the penitent's tears).

As Donne teases the paradox out of a play on remembering and forgetting, so Quevedo creates a paradoxical convergence of loss and gain in his "Psalm":

> Perdí mi libertad, mi bien con ella;
> no dejó en todo el cielo alguna estrella
> que no solicitase,
> entre llantos, la voz de mi querella:
> ¡tanto sentí el mirar que me dejase!
> Mas ya me he consolado
> de ver mi bien, ¡oh gran Señor!, perdido,
> y, en parte, de perderle me he holgado,
> por interés de haberle conocido.   (14–22)

> [I lost my liberty, my good along with it; the voice of my complaint has not left any star in the heaven that it did not entreat between sobs: how I sorrowed for the look that left me! But now I have consoled myself for seeing my good, oh great Lord! lost, and, in part, I have been content to lose it, in the interest of having known it.]

---

[40] See Lewalski, *Protestant Poetics*, pp. 269, 481–82 nn. 47–49.

Lying behind Donne's sonnet is Psalm 25: 7: "Remember not the sinnes of my youth, nor my transgressions: according to thy mercie remember thou me, for thy goodnesse sake, O Lord." Just so, lying behind Quevedo's "Psalm" is Jesus' instruction to his disciples to take up the cross and follow Him: "For whosoever will save his life shall lose it: and whosoever will lose his life for my sake shall find it. For what is a man profited, if he shall gain the whole world and lose his own soul?" (Matthew 16: 25–26; cf. Mark 8: 35–36, Luke 9: 24–25). The Spanish word *bien* (rendered "good" above) means a gain or benefit (the plural, *bienes*, means "worldly goods"), but it also means supreme or highest good. The implication of the poem is that one must give up "goods" for the Good – and be repaid with *interest.* Sin is the loss of liberty and with that the good of looking at God and being looked at by Him (ambiguity seems purposive). But the penitent is consoled for the loss – indeed, is content with it – because only the loss has disclosed to him what it was that he lost, has enabled him to recognize his true Good as opposed to the "brief glory" over which he "poorly shed tears," as he puts it in the first part of the poem. The sobs of grief over what has departed are signs of contrition, and this is only possible in this earthly life. Just as Donne, in "At the round earths imagin'd corners," begs God, "here on this lowly ground, / Teach mee how to repent" (12–13); so Quevedo realizes that "on the ground" the only heavenly *regalos* are providential afflictions, because sinful man knows only the good he has lost. What is lost is saved "in the interest of [for the sake of] having known it."

A biblical poetics is practised in Donne's Holy Sonnets insofar as the spiritual drama of the individual is conceived in biblical terms, and in this regard his poems include features that are common among contemporaneous Catholic poets of the continent. The distinguishing marks of this approach include more than the imitation of the genres of the Bible and plentiful allusions to biblical texts, although these are important elements in such poems. At the center of biblical poetics is the development of a pervasive tension between the episodes of salvation history recounted in Sacred Scripture and the personal experience represented in the "scripture" of the poet. Old Testament types are invoked in order to identify the Christian penitent with their defectiveness in relation to the fulfillment of the Incarnation. "Truth banishes shadow," St. Thomas Aquinas writes, "light disperses night."[41] Even as the Old Testament is both superseded and fulfilled by the New, so the individual Christian reader is both included within, and defined by, opposition to the Bible message as a whole. Members of the Body of Christ, sacramental participants in the Incarnation, share in the new light; but they see this light only against the dark background of sinful human history in which they are caught up. Since man in this pilgrim state, *in via,* can

---

[41] *Lauda, Sion, Salvatorem* 23–24, in *Devoutly I Adore Thee: The Prayers and Hymns of Saint Thomas Aquinas*, trans. & ed. Robert Anderson & Johann Moser (Manchester, NH: Sophia Institute Press, 1993), p. 102: "Umbram fugat veritas, / Noctem lux eliminat."

only see the light against the darkness, the fleeing shadows are *still there*, present and operative in their very absence, known as darkness only by the influx of light, even as the light is known only by its routing of the dark. Similarly Donne, Lope de Vega, and Quevedo all face the Crucifixion by turning away from it; they participate in Christ's Passion in the very realization that they have disabled themselves with wasted tears of profane passions. This distance from God opened up by sin becomes the space in which Christ is revealed and union made possible. In what might appear to profane eyes an aporia, the soul, the self, is hopelessly lost in order that it can be saved in grace.

The Old and New Testaments thus constitute the primary binary opposition of Western history, but this dichotomy does not yield an endless flux of fruitless dissemination. The seed is not all withered in stony ground, devoured by birds of prey along the footpath of history, or choked in the tangled briars of theory: some of it falls on good soil ("this lowly ground"). The devotional poetry of the seventeenth century offers some of the best fruits of the scriptural seeding process. Even as there could be no New Testament without an Old Testament, and no single Christian Bible without the opposition of the two (even as there could be no nuptial union without the opposition of man and woman), so there can be no biblical poetry without the poet's recognition that his poem is *different from* the Bible with which it aspires to continuity. But, as the doctrine of the Trinity shows, in Christianity opposition is also complementarity: within the pure simplicity of the God-head there is a distinction of Persons.[42]

ii

It is a commonplace of Herbert criticism to observe that a fruitful method of reading his poems is indicated by the country parson's "third means" of reading the Bible, "a diligent Collation of Scripture with Scripture. For all Truth being consonant to it self, and all being penn'd by one and the self-same Spirit, it cannot be, but that an industrious, and judicious comparing of place with place must be a singular help for the right understanding of the Scriptures" (*Works*, p. 229). This advice, given in *A Priest to the Temple*, is lyrically reiterated in "The H. Scriptures (II)": "This verse marks that, and both do make a motion / Unto a third, that ten leaves off doth lie" (5–6).[43] Yet

---

[42] See Robert Magliola, *Derrida on the Mend* (West Lafayette, IN: Purdue University Press, 1984), pp. 135ff. for an effort to reconcile the deconstructionist notion of *différance* with the Christian dogma of the Trinity.

[43] See, for example, Martz, *The Poetry of Meditation*, rev. ed. (New Haven and London: Yale University Press, 1962), p. 296; Joseph Summers, *George Herbert: His Religion and Art* (1954; rpt. Binghamton, NY: Center for Medieval and Early Renaissance Studies, 1981), p. 80; Lewalski, *Protestant Poetics*, p. 105; Chana Bloch, *Spelling the Word: George Herbert and the Bible* (Berkeley: University of California Press, 1985), pp. 10–12; and Richard Todd, *The*

there is more here than just a means of reading the Bible; Herbert also offers a mode of reading the self:

> Then as dispersed herbs do watch a potion,
> These three make up some Christians destinie:
> Such are thy secrets, which my life makes good,
> And comments on thee: for in ev'ry thing
> Thy words do finde me out, & parallels bring,
> And in another make me understood.   (7–12)

"The constellations of the storie" (4) of Sacred Scripture are the patterns of identity in the human soul. Although postmodernist and "Protestant" readings of Herbert both insist that his poetry diminishes the self, he in fact realizes the meaning and identity of the self in God's Word, manifest in Scripture and sacrament.

In this understanding of the place of the Bible in Christian life, Herbert is part of an ancient Christian tradition. The crisis of St. Augustine's conversion experience comes in the sound of a childlike voice chanting, *Tolle, lege; tolle, lege* – "Take, read." Recognizing that the chant is part of no children's game, Augustine determines that the voice can only be interpreted as a divine command that he follow the pattern of St. Anthony and find his destiny in the first passage of Scripture to which he might open. Thus compelled in spirit, Augustine discovers in St. Paul's epistolary admonition to the Romans (13: 13–14) his own vocation to be a celibate dedicated to God: "Not in revelry and drunkenness, not in bedrooms and in lewdness, not in strife and emulation; but put on the Lord Jesus Christ and make no provision for the flesh in its lusts." For the saint this passage is not just a record of Paul's teaching three centuries before or a series of general precepts; without ceasing to be both an historical document and a statement of doctrine, the text of Scripture is also a direct communication to the individual, uniquely framed to his special situation. "I wished to read no further," Augustine continues; "there was no need. At once indeed with the end of that saying, as if my heart were bathed in the light of certainty, all the shadows of doubt were scattered" (*Confessions* VIII. 12).[44]

Twelve hundred years later Santa Teresa of Ávila recounts how a woman of her acquaintance "became a nun only by reading what the Gospel says, 'Many are called but few are chosen' [Matthew 20: 16]."[45] The saint herself is best

---

Opacity of Signs: An Interpretation of George Herbert's The Temple (Columbia: University of Missouri Press, 1986), p. 122. See also the fine comments on this poem by William H. Pahlka, *Saint Augustine's Meter and George Herbert's Will* (Kent, OH, and London: Kent State University Press, 1987), pp. 118–19; and James Boyd White, *"This Booke of Starres": Learning to Read George Herbert* (Ann Arbor: University of Michigan Press, 1994), pp. 165–66.

[44] PL 32. 762: "Nec ultra volui legere; nec opus erat. Statim quippe cum fine hujusce sententiae quasi luce securitatis infusa cordi meo, omnes dubitationes tenebrae diffugerunt."

[45] *Obras completas de Santa Teresa de Jesús*, ed. Éfren de la Madre de Dios, O.C.D. and Otger

able to explain her experience of ineffable and "elevated graces" that "remain well inscribed in the very interior of the soul" by comparing her experience to that of Old Testament Patriarchs:

> Well then if the faculties hold no images and do not understand these graces, how can they be remembered? I do not understand either; but I do understand that certain truths regarding God's grandeur remain so fixed in the soul that, when she had no faith he tells her who he is, and that she is bound to believe him as God, from that point on she adored him as much even as Jacob did when he saw the ladder, for with that he must have understood other secrets, that he knew not how to utter; for with only the sight of a ladder that angels ascended and descended, if there had been no more interior light, he would not have understood such great mysteries. (6 *Moradas* 4. 6)[46]

Jacob's vision at Bethel (Gen. 28: 12) furnishes "parallels" for Teresa's mystical rapture and makes her "understood," just as Herbert proposes in "The H. Scriptures (II)." The Old Testament theophany thus becomes a type of "some Christians destinie," and Teresa does not hesitate to invoke even the definitive divine self-disclosure of the Old Covenant (Exod. 3: 2) as an analogue for her own religious experience:

> And neither did Moses know how to say all that he saw in the bramble, except what God wished that he might say; but if God had not shown his soul secrets with certainty in order that he would see and believe that he was God, he would not have brought forth so many and such great labors; but he must have understood such great matters within the thorns of that bramble bush, that they gave him spirit in order to do what he did for the people of Israel.
>
> (Moradas 4. 7)[47]

For Santa Teresa, as for St. Augustine more than a millennium earlier, the meaning of Scripture is not just what it *says* literally in the text about its subject, but also what it reveals to the individual Christian in the depths of the

---

Steggink, O.Carm., 2nd ed. (Madrid: Biblioteca de Autores Cristianos, 1957), p. 32: "Comenzóme a contar cómo ella había venido a ser monja por sólo leer lo que dice el Evangelio: 'Muchas son los llamados y pocos los escogidos'."

[46] Ibid., p. 414: "Pues si no tienen imagen ni las entienden las potencias, ¿cómo se pueden acordar? Tampoco entiendo eso; mas entiendo que quedan unas verdades en esta alma tan fijas de la grandeza de Dios, que cuando no tuviera fe que le dice quién es y que está obligada a creerle por Dios, le adorara desde aquel punto por tal, como hizo Jacob cuando vio la escala, que con ella devía de entender otros secretos, que no los supo decir; que sólo ver una escala que bajavan y supían ángeles, si no huviera más luz interior, no entendiera tan grandes misterios."

[47] Ibid., "Ni tampoco Moysén supo decir todo lo que vio en la zarza, sino lo que quiso Dios que dijese; mas si no mostrara Dios a su alma secretos con certidumbre para que viese y creyese que era Dios, no se pusiera en tantos y tan grandes trabajos; mas devía entender tan grandes cosas dentro de los espinos de aquella zarza, que le dieron ánimo para hacer lo que hizo por el pueblo de Israel."

soul about his "destinie." Both Teresa and Augustine "find themselves" in "the constellations of the storie."

Herbert's concept of the personal elaboration of typology in "The H. Scriptures (II)" is, therefore, traditional. The concept is exemplified in "The Bunch of Grapes." The long sojourn of the Israelites in the wilderness between the Red Sea and the Promised Land is treated as a figure for the uncertain pilgrimage both of the Church and of the individual Christian:

> I did towards Canaan draw; but now I am
> Brought back to the Red sea, the sea of shame.
>
> For as the Jews of old by Gods command
>   Travell'd, and saw no town;
> So now each Christian hath his journeys spann'd:
>   Their storie pennes and sets us down.   (6–11)

The parallel is so compelling that Herbert's persona ventures to demand that the type be fulfilled with a complete symmetry in each detail. If his personal sinning and suffering is enfolded within the providential design of sacred history, then he must likewise enjoy the same foretaste of promised fruition as the Israelites before him:

> But where's the cluster? where's the taste
> Of mine inheritance? Lord, if I must borrow,
> Let me as well take up their joy, as sorrow.   (19–21)

The answer to his complaint is suggested by the method of "The H. Scriptures (II)": "This verse marks that, and both do make a motion / Unto a third, that ten leaves off doth lie" (5–6); that is, the figurative meaning that any particular passage in Scripture holds for a particular Christian can only be inferred by juxtaposing it to other texts. The ultimate import of the bunch of grapes brought back by the Israelite scouts from Canaan (Numbers 13: 25) is thus revealed in the winepress of Isaiah 63: 3 and Christ's identification of himself with the "true vine" (Jn. 15: 1):

> But can he want the grape, who hath the wine?
>   I have their fruit and more.
> Blessed be God, who prosper'd *Noahs* vine,
>   And made it bring forth grapes good store.
>   But much more him I must adore,
> Who of the Laws sowre juice sweet wine did make,
> Ev'n God himself being pressed for my sake.   (22–28)

The promise is fulfilled, then, not in a place or an object, but in a person: the cluster brought back from the Valley of Eschol is a type of the incarnate Word – palpable in the sacrament, accessible in the Body of the Church, intelligible in the preaching of the Gospel – the sweet wine of salvation.

189

Herbert's typological procedure in this poem is grounded in an approach
to the Bible well illustrated by Cornelius à Lapide's allegorical commentary on
the verse that Herbert takes from Numbers. "The cluster hanging on the
pole," Lapide says, "is Christ hanging on the cross"; and even more
significantly, "The two bearers are the two testaments: the Jews go in front;
the Christians follow; the latter (the Christian) bears salvation before his gaze;
the former (the Jew) behind his back; the latter shows deference, the former
contempt."[48] Herbert makes essentially the same invidious comparison in
"The Bunch of Grapes." The Christian speaker is holding on to the same pole
bearing salvation as the Jews who went before him, but, as the poem closes, he
realizes that he has a better view of the nature of the "promised land."

The conjunction of the grape cluster of Numbers with Isaiah's wine press
may have been suggested to Herbert by St. Augustine's explanation of the
heading of Psalm 8 as it appears in the Vulgate: *In finem pro torcularibus,
Psalmus ipsi David* ("Unto the end for the wine presses, a Psalm for David
himself"). The wine presses, Augustine remarks, do not appear in the actual
text of the psalm, so they must be taken as a figure for the Church, like the
threshing floor (Luke 3: 17); for even as the husks are separated from the grain
on the latter, so in the wine press the grapes are separated from their skins,
indicating in each figure the separation of the elect from the lost among
whom they dwell on earth. There is, however, another way of understanding
the wine press not incompatible with ecclesial symbolism:

> For the divine Word can also be understood as the grape: for it is said that the
> Lord is also the grape cluster, hung from the pole, which those who were sent
> ahead by the people of Israel bore out of the land of the promise just like the
> crucified one (Numbers 13: 24). And accordingly the divine Word, when in the
> necessity of utterance, makes use of the sound of a voice, by which it is
> conveyed into the ears of listeners, the meaning is contained within that sound
> as wine is contained within a grape skin: and thus that "grape" comes into the
> ears as into the treadmills of the wine presses. For there it is separated, insofar as
> the sound has an effect in the ears; the significance is, moreover, drawn out of
> the memory of the hearers as out of a kind of vat and passes thence into moral
> discipline and intellectual habit, as out of the vat into the cellars, in which, if it
> does not turn sour through negligence, it is matured by the aging process.
> (*Enarrationes in Psalmos* VIII. 2)[49]

---

[48] Cornelius à Lapide, S.J., *Commentaria in Scripturam Sacram* (Paris: Ludovicus Vivès, 1868)
II.259: "hic uva pendens in vecte, est Christus pendens in cruce . . . Duo bajuli sunt duo
testamenta: praeunt Judaei, sequuntur Christiani; salutem hic (Christianus) ante conspectum
suum gerit, ille (Judaeus) post dorsum: hic obsequium praefert, ille contemptum."

[49] *PL* 36–37. 109–110: "Nam et Verbum divinum potest uva intelligi: dictus est enim et
Dominus botrus uvae, quem ligno suspensum, de terra promissionis, qui praemissi erant a
populo Israel, tanquam crucifixum attulerunt (*Num.* XIII. 24). Verbum itaque divinum, cum
enuntiationis necessitate usurpat vocis sonum, quo in aures pervehatur audientium, eodem
sono vocis tanquam vinaciis, intellectus tanquam vinum includitur: et sic uva ista in aures

Herbert describes essentially the same process: the Word conveyed in Scripture, even as the grape cluster is borne by the Israelite scouts from the Promised Land on a pole, after being well aged in the cellars of tradition, it becomes the wine of significance when it is heard by the ears and comprehended by the minds of the faithful. Christ the Word, by means of biblical words, enters into the life of the Christian in his moral conduct and mental attitude. "The bunch of Grapes" thus illustrates the Christian use of the Bible even as it expounds that use.

A similar process is at work in Sonnet C of Lope de Vega's *Rimas sacras*:

> ¿Cuándo en tu alcázar de Sión y en Beth
> de tu santo David seré Abisac?
> ¿Cuándo Rebeca de tu humilde Isaac?
> ¿Cuándo de tu Josef limpia Aseneth?
>
> De las aguas salí como Jafet,
> de llama voraz como Sidrac,
> y de las maldiciones de Balac
> por la que fue bendita en Nazareth.
>
> Viva en Jerusalén como otro Hasub,
> y no me quede en la ciudad de Lot,
> sabiduría eterna, inmenso Alef.
>
> Que tú, que pisas el mayor querub,
> y la cerviz enlazas de Behemoth,
> sacarás de la cárcel a Josef.[50]

[When in your castle of Sion and in Beth shall I be the Abishag of your holy David? When the Rebecca of your humble Isaac? When the pure Asenath of your Joseph? I came out of the waters like Japhet, out of the devouring flame like Shadrac, and out of the curses of Balak by her who was blessed in Nazareth. May I live in Jerusalem like another Hashub, and let me not remain in the city of Lot, oh wisdom eternal, oh immense Aleph. For you, who tread upon the greatest Cherub, and lasso the neck of Behemoth, you took Joseph out of jail.]

Like Herbert, Lope derives a Christian's spiritual "storie" from the typological adventures of various Old Testament figures, whose experience is transfigured in foreshadowing Christ. It is only because David, Isaac, and Joseph are in various ways figural anticipations of the Messiah that Lope de Vega, virile to a fault, can offer himself in the rôle of their brides. Further, even as the stories of these Old Testament exemplars only realize their fulfilling significance in the Incarnation, so the experience of the Christian persona is provisional and incomplete: having escaped the flood, the fire, and

---

venit, quasi in calcatoria torculariorum. Ibi enim discernitur, ut sonus usque ad aures valeat: intellectus autem memoria eorum qui audiunt, velut quodam lacu excipiatur, inde transeat in morum disciplinam et habitum mentis, tanquam de lacu in cellas in quibus, si negligentia non acuerit, vetustate firmabitur.

[50] *Obras poéticas* I. 370–71.

the curse of sin, it still remains for the Savior to bring him out of the prison of sin, out of Sodom, the doomed earthly city, into the final security of the heavenly Jerusalem.

When Lope's sonnet is set alongside "The Bunch of Grapes," it is clear that Herbert and his Spanish contemporary are reflecting on the same spiritual problem and resolving it similarly. What is more, the comparison serves to illuminate the profound spiritual implications shared by the two poems. Both are concerned with the persistence of struggle and insecurity in earthly life, even for the Christian, and both place this lack of certainty and peace in an Augustinian typological context. In Herbert's poem the journey of each individual through the wilderness of this life re-enacts the generation-long journey of the children of Israel through the waste places of the Sinai desert. The poet looks for – and finds – something greater than the promise afforded the Israelites by the grapes brought back from Canaan; in the "wine" of word and sacrament the Christian both enjoys and awaits the presence of Christ, who is both revealed and concealed by the mediating signs. The Word is paradoxically in and out of the words; the signified presence of Christ both realized and deferred by the sacramental signifiers that re-present Him. Hence the Christian journeys toward a land of promise where he *always already* dwells. Lope de Vega identifies the graces vouchsafed the Christian with a series of miraculous escapes and nuptial consummations brought about by divine intervention for Old Testament figures. But the poem closes with a reminder that although he has already been delivered by Christ and espoused to Him, the Christian does not yet dwell in Jerusalem in the eternal bliss of the Lamb's spousal embrace; for he is not yet free of his own personal Sodom. Thus both poems evoke a sense of the contingency of temporal life, of the unfinished character of earthly human existence, despite the assurance of Christ's triumph over sin and death.

The provisional nature of the Christian life is further stressed and elaborated in Herbert's poems that develop out of New Testament passages. "Coloss. 3.3 *Our life is hid with Christ in God*" expounds the "double motion" of temporal life in a figure that recalls Donne's "Goodfriday. 1613." The life of grace is hidden in the same way as the movement of the sun that appears daily to the eye of the casual terrestrial observer conceals an oblique, annual movement compelled by the *primum mobile*:

> *My* words & thoughts do both express this notion,
> That *Life* hath with the sun a double motion.
> The first *Is* straight, and our diurnal friend,
> The other *Hid* and doth obliquely bend. (1–4)

The life of grace is likewise hidden to the casual worldly beholder and to the usual means of human knowledge and perception, because the source of its energy is in the risen Christ. If mankind as a whole is divided into citizens of the City of Man and of the City of God – not easily distinguishable in a temporal perspective – even so the individual Christian simultaneously leads two lives opposed to each other:

> One life is wrapt *In* flesh, and tends to earth:
> The other winds towards *Him*, whose happie birth
> Taught me to live here so, *That* still one eye
> Should aim and shoot at that which *Is* on high:
> Quitting with daily labour all *My* pleasure,
> To gain at harvest an eternall *Treasure.*   (5–10)

This poem thus provides a further explanation of how the Christian of "The Bunch of Grapes" is both journeying through the wilderness and living in the Promised Land at the same time. He leads in effect two lives: one open and one hidden, one earthly and one heavenly, a "double motion" that poses a mystery for those who do not acknowledge this grace.

In his sense of the hidden mystery of the life of grace, Herbert shares in a scriptural vision that crosses confessional lines. Cornelius à Lapide, commenting on the same verse from Colossians, remarks, "The world does not see your divine life of grace, which you have; and the life of glory, which you await: just as it does not see the glorious life to which Christ rose, and in which he now lives." Most important, Cornelius continues, the life of glory that the saints expect,

> now is hidden, which is to say, your life is like the winter, in which the sun, that is, Christ, is hidden; you are like trees dried up on the outside, without a leaf, that is, without adornment, dignity, and beauty; but on the inside you have a live root, namely charity in God, as if fastened and living in the vital earth. Summer will come, namely the revelation and glory of Christ, when you will burst out into greenness again, and you will be given live fruit and foliage, namely the gifts of blessedness in body as in soul.[51]

Even Cornelius's seasonal metaphor closely resembles Herbert's figure of the hidden life of grace awaiting the eternal harvest of glory.

As Chana Bloch points out, "Coloss. 3.3" is characteristic of Herbert's poems in which (contrary to Stanley Fish) "the self is not effaced but

---

[51] *Commentarii in Scripturam Sacram* IX. 664–65: "Mundus non videt vestram divinam vitam gratiae, quam habetis; et gloriae, quam expectabis: sicut non videt vitam gloriosam, ad quam resurrexit, quaque vivit jam Christus in Deo, id est, apud Deo . . . vita gloriae, quam Sancti expectant, jam est abscondita, q.d. Vita vestra est quasi hiems, in qua sol, id est Christus, occultatur; vos estis quasi arbores exterius aridae, sine fronde, id est, sine decore, specie et pulchritudine; sed interius habetis radicem vivam, scilicet charitatem in Deo, quasi in terra vitali defixam et viventem. Veniet aestas, scilicet Christi revelatio et gloria, cum revirescetis resurgendo, ac vitales dabitis frondes et fructus, scilicet dotes beatitudinis, tam in anima, quam in corpore.

improved."[52] The apparent "loss of self" in the Christian's earthly life is deceptive: although there is a "double motion," as Herbert puts it, the ultimate movement is toward an "eternall *Treasure*," even as the hidden life of Cornelius' tree in winter is the same life that flourishes in the rejuvenation of the summer of glory. Likewise, Herbert's poem has two messages that are the same: the poem as a whole and the "hidden" sentence that runs diagonally from line to line in italics: "*My Life Is Hid In Him, That Is My Treasure.*" Scripture must be read in the same way as Herbert's poem: the message buried in the text no more contradicts the larger discourse than the hidden life of grace diminishes human life in time. Just as the italicized sentence crystallizes the meaning of Herbert's poem as a whole, so the interior life of grace fulfills the meaning of temporal life, ultimately revealing it in glory.[53]

Chana Bloch recognizes that typical contemporary readings of Herbert often fail to acknowledge the Christian fullness of the poet's vision, leaning toward an excessively secular humanism (as exemplified by Helen Vendler) or a postmodernist anti-humanism (as exemplified by Stanley Fish. But Bloch herself is ready to accept a radically Protestant view of *The Temple*, derived from critics such as Lewalski and Strier, without noticing that it is compromised in a similar way. In the first place, Bloch's own emphasis on the Incarnation as *the* unique event that defines Herbert's conception of "what it means to be a Christian"[54] is incompatible with Lewalski's attempt to make Calvinism normative for *The Temple* and the seventeenth-century religious lyric generally:

> Yet, partly because of their doctrine of the sacraments as signs rather than conduits of special grace, Protestants saw the spiritual situation of Christians to be notably advantaged by the New Covenant but not different in essence from that of the Old Testament people, since both alike depend on signs which will be fulfilled in Christ at the end of time. The Old Testament is still *figura*, but in the sense of a real historical time of preparation for and expectation of the future. And the Christ of the *eschaton* rather than the incarnate Christ of the Gospel is the ultimate antitype for all the types.[55]

As we have seen, however, the climactic turn of "The Bunch of Grapes" is precisely to establish an *essential difference* between the condition of mankind under the Old Covenant and the New. As Bloch acknowledges: "The Christian reader learns that just as he transcends the fate of the ancient Israelites, so he can free himself from the old groove of faults, the nagging dissatisfactions of his own life. He is not doomed to go on repeating himself

---

[52] *Spelling the Word*, p. 31. See also pp. 35–36.
[53] See Todd, *Opacity of Signs*, p. 172, for an enlightening comment on this poem. For a slightly different take, see Pahlka, p. 115.
[54] *Spelling the Word*, pp. 114–15.
[55] *Protestant Poetics*, pp. 125–26.

forever, but can move out of bondage to the past into an eternally present fulfillment."[56]

Thus Bloch demonstrates that in Herbert's poetry the "situation" of Christians differs "in essence from that of the Old Testament people." She does not seem to take the next step, however, and recognize that what provides the Christian opportunity of "an eternally present fulfillment" in Herbert's poetry is his understanding of the sacraments not as mere "signs" but as "conduits of special grace." This view is evident in "The Bunch of Grapes" and quite explicit in "The H. Communion." The importance of the Eucharist as a channel of grace is apparent in Bloch's own linking of "The H. Communion" with "Decay," which ends on a despairing note over the contrast between the ready access to God enjoyed by the Old Testament Patriarchs ("One might have sought and found thee presently / At some fair oak, or bush, or cave, or well"; 6–7) and His confinement "In some one corner of a feeble heart" as "the world decays" (12, 16). "It required a steadfast truthfulness on Herbert's part," Bloch writes, "to include a poem that contradicts his own most firmly held beliefs."[57] She compares the Patriarchs of "Decay" to the unfallen Adam of "The H. Communion," who "might to heav'n from Paradise go, / As from one room t'another" (35–36). "The H. Communion" asserts unequivocally, however, that what is lost in the "decay" of the world is restored in the Eucharist:

> Onely thy grace, which with these elements comes,
> > Knoweth the ready way,
> > And hath the privie key,
> > Op'ning the souls most subtile rooms;
> While those to spirits refin'd, at doore attend
> > Dispatches from their friend.   (19–24)

If this poem, like "Sion" and "Aaron," may truly be said to "contain an implicit criticism of the Roman Catholic church with its sacrificial liturgy of the Mass, its splendid churches and elaborate vestments,"[58] it also contains an *explicit* rejection of the view that the sacraments are not channels of actual grace. While Herbert is a reformer who differs with the Catholic Church over the externals of worship and discipline, he parts company with Calvinist Puritanism over the essential meaning of the sacraments. For "The H. Communion" marks out the Eucharist as the means by which mankind has been brought back into God's presence on a footing equal to Adam before the Fall:

---

[56] *Spelling the Word*, p. 146.

[57] Ibid., p. 140. Bloch does not here remark that Herbert is plainly referring to the notion – shared by Donne, Godfrey Goodman, and Sir Thomas Browne among others – that the world was in a state of decrepitude as nature grew aged and decayed.

[58] Ibid., p. 134.

> Thou hast restor'd us to this ease
>   By this thy heav'nly bloud;
> Which I can go to, when I please,
>   And leave th'earth to their food.   (37–40)

Though God be departed from "oak, or bush, or cave, or well" as "the world grows old" and lapses into "Decay," still the "feeble heart" is renewed by the power of grace in the sacrament. As in "The Bunch of Grapes," the "eternally present fulfillment" comes by way of the Eucharist, which decisively distinguishes the situation of the Christian from his Old Testament types.

Perhaps what is most striking about the reflections upon Scripture in "The Church" is the poet's confident apprehension of the text's universal significance in specifically personal terms. "The Pearl. Matth. 13.45" is a meditation on the import of the pearl of great price – a similitude for the Kingdom of Heaven – as it applies individually to the Christian courtier who speaks the poem. Arnold Stein observes that the "basic plot" of the poem is "rejecting the ways of the world, the flesh, and the devil, each in a stanza," with the usual order altered so that the devil (intellectual pride in learning) is rejected in the first stanza with the world ("the wayes of Honour") and the flesh ("the wayes of Pleasure") rejected in the second and third. "The plot is basic and the formula for human temptation is the standard one," Stein says, "but Herbert's conception and performance are markedly fresh and individual."[59] The most distinctive feature in Herbert's handling of this traditional theme is the jaunty, almost racy, sophistication he musters for the deprecation of temptations that are all worldly and sophisticated in some measure:

> I know the wayes of Honour, what maintains
> The quick returns of courtesie and wit:
> In vies of favours whether partie gains,
> When glorie swells the heart, and moldeth it
> To all expressions both of hand and eye,
> Which on the world a true-love-knot may tie,
> And bear the bundle, wheresoe're it goes:
> How many drammes of spirit there must be
> To sell my life unto my friends or foes:
>   Yet I love thee.   (11–20)

The tension generated by the speaker's obvious emotional entanglement with, even relish in, the maze of the world as it strains against his assertion of fidelity to Christ, "Yet I love thee," endows the poem with subtle power. The third stanza, dealing with pleasure, adds to the sophisticated complexity by means of figures displaying an urbane knowledge of musical terminology.[60]

---

[59] *George Herbert's Lyrics* (Baltimore: the Johns Hopkins University Press, 1968), p. 33.
[60] See Stein, pp. 34–35. On the musical tropes see Joseph Summers, *George Herbert*, pp. 158–59; and Pahlka, p. 132.

The assertive self-effacement of the speaker becomes more intense in the concluding stanza as he insists that he knows exactly what he is doing and is fully in control of his act of renunciation:

> I know all these, and have them in my hand:
> Therefore not sealed, but with open eyes
> I flie to thee, and fully understand
> Both the main sale, and the commodities;
> And at what rate and price I have thy love;
> With all the circumstances that may move: (31–36)

The self-assurance and self-possession of this tone are obviously at odds with the theme of the Gospel text, with its implication that the merchant has, in worldly terms, taken a great risk in selling *everything* in order to purchase the "pearl of great price." Hence we are not surprised when the speaker's tone alters abruptly from knowing self-confidence to humility in the final four lines:

> Yet through these labyrinths, not my groveling wit,
> But thy silk twist let down from heav'n to me,
> Did both conduct and teach me, how by it
>   To climbe to thee. (37–40)

In his commentary on this text from Matthew, Cornelius à Lapide offers a whole series of diverse but compatible symbolic meanings for the pearl, but he insists that one meaning is pre-eminent: "The first and most precious pearl, from which all virtues, and all the saints like pearls are brought forth, and have their fitness and value, is Christ himself."[61] This interpretation certainly works well enough with Herbert's poem since Christ is, throughout, the object of his address and of his vigorous protestation of love. Christ therefore is the "pearl" that the courtier-poet professes to love amidst the snares of courtly temptation.

But in the closing lines there is the realization that such self-confident certitude is inappropriate, and the refrain is altered from an assertion of the speaker's love to a recognition that he still must "climbe." Cornelius also identifies the pearl of Matthew 13: 45 with humility and cites Thomas à Kempis from *The Imitation of Christ* (I. 2): "If you wish usefully to know something, and to learn, love to be unknown, and to be regarded as nothing. This is the highest and most useful knowledge, a true recognition and contempt of oneself."[62] It is difficult to imagine a more pointed and effective

---

[61] *Commentaria in Scripturam Sacram* VIII. 287: "Porro prima et pretiosissima margarita, à qua omnes virtutes, omnesque sancti quasi margaritae progignuntur, suumque habent decorum et pretium, est ipse Christus."

[62] Ibid., "Talis quoque est humilitas, nimirum ut docet nos Thomas θεοδίδακτοσ de imitat. Christi lib. 1. cap. 2. Si vis utiliter aliquid scire, et discere, ama nesciri, et pro nihilo reputari. Haec est altissima et utilissima scientia, sui ipsius vera cognitio, et despectio."

reminder to Herbert's pious courtier, so self-consciously proud of his knowing rejection of worldly sophistication, so concerned lest Christ mistake him for a naif, unaware of what is being surrendered. Louis Martz has pointed out how much Herbert shares in the spirit of Thomas à Kempis,[63] and the *Imitation* (I. 5) furnishes a fine account of the the poet's approach to the Bible:

> Almighty God speaketh to us in His Scripture in divers manners without accepting of persons: but our curiosity oft hindereth us in reading of Scripture, when we will reason and argue things that we should meekly and simply pass over. If thou wilt profit by reading of Scripture, read meekly, simply, and faithfully, and never desire to have thereby the name of cunning. Ask gladly and hear meekly the sayings of Saints, and mislike not the parables of ancient Fathers, for they were not spoken without great cause.[64]

In *A Priest to the Temple*, Herbert remarks, *"Curiosity in prying into high speculative and unprofitable questions, is another great stumbling block to the holinesse of Scholars"* (*Works*, p. 238), almost as if he were thinking of *The Imitation*. "The Pearl" unfolds one of the "divers manners" in which "Almighty God speaketh to us in His Scriptures" and closes on a note of meekness and simplicity. The courtier persona, who begins each stanza with "I know," comes finally to realize that what he must *know* is the limit of his own knowledge; that is, the humility of self-knowledge.

"The Odour. 2.Cor.2.15" is another striking example of Herbert's reimagining of a passage of Scripture in singularly personal terms. The text stresses the effect of the preacher of the Word, of the bearer of the Gospel: "For we are unto God a sweet savour of Christ, in them that are saved, and in them that perish: to the one we are the savour of death unto death; and to the other the savour of life unto life. And who is sufficient for these things?" (2 Cor. 2: 15–16). Commentators – Catholic and Protestant alike – are principally interested in the diverse effect of the evangelist's fragrance upon the damned and the saved. "Note what calamities ensue when the Word of God is despised and contemned," writes Zwingli. "And note too that failure to believe the Word of God is a sure sign that the wrath of God will soon overtake us. The Word of God and the messenger of the Word are a sweet smell or savour (II Cor. 2); but a savour of life to some, and of death to others."[65] Similarly, Calvin cites this passage by way of encouraging frustrated preachers in his commentary on John 12: 40: "Let them be satisfied to know that God approves of their labor; that although the savor of their doctrine does men no good, and that the wicked turn it into a source of death to

---

[63] *Poetry of Meditation*, pp. 285–87.

[64] *The Imitation of Christ*, trans. Richard Whitford (1530, rpt. New York: Pocket Books, 1953), p. 13.

[65] *On the Clarity and Certainty or Power of the Word of God*, in *Zwingli and Bullinger*, ed. G. W. Bromily (Philadelphia: Westminster Press, 1953), pp. 74–75.

themselves, it is as Paul testifies, good and pleasing before God."[66] Cornelius à
Lapide is likewise concerned to vindicate the work of the evangelist in the face
of the intransigence of the wicked: "For the fragrance and fame of the life,
preaching, and conversion of the Apostles breathed life upon the good, death
upon the wicked: because the wicked, not bearing such a splendor of holiness,
rather confirmed themselves in their wickedness, envy, or hatred."[67]

Herbert, however, is preoccupied with the end of verse 16: "And who is
sufficient for these things?" To participate in the "sweet savour" or "odour"
of Christ (in using "odour" rather than "savour" Herbert echoes the Vulgate
or Douay-Rheims rather than the Geneva or Authorized version),[68] to take
Christ as "*My Master*," that is, would indeed leave "a sweet content, / An
orientall fragrancie" (4–5); but as Cornelius, citing St. Ambrose, remarks,
"How few are such suitable ministers, who would everywhere be the good
odor of Christ?"[69] Herbert worries about the fitness of the servant to attain to
this "good odor":

> *My Master*, shall I speak? O that to thee
>   *My servant* were a little so,
>   As flesh may be;
>   That these two words might creep & grow
> To some degree of spicinesse to thee! (11–15)

The servant is compared to a pomander, a scent ball, in a silver container
hung at the girdle or on a chain around the neck, which gives off its fragrance
when warmed or squeezed or rubbed. The implication is that the servant
needs the action of God upon him if he is to be more than a "speaking sweet":

> Then should the Pomander, which was before
>   A speaking sweet, mend by reflection,
>   And tell me more:
>   For pardon of my imperfection
> Would warm and work it sweeter then before. (16–20)

Since the fragrance of the pomander is released by friction, there is a parallel
in the conceit to a further remark of Cornelius à Lapide on the "bonus odor
Christi": "Just as aromatics breathe more fragrance the more they are ground

---

[66] *Calvin: Commentaries*, ed. Joseph Haroutounian (Philadelphia: Westminster Press, 1958),
p. 278.
[67] *Commentaria* IX.361: "Fragrantia enim et fama vitae, praedicationis et conversionis
Apostolorum, bonis aspirabat vitam, improbis mortem: quia tantum sanctitatis fulgorem
improbi non ferentes, in sua improbitate, invidia, odiove sese magis obfirmabant."
[68] Matthias Bauer, "'A Title Strange, Yet True': Toward an Explanation of Herbert's Titles," in
George Herbert: Sacred and Profane, ed. Helen Wilcox and Richard Todd (Amsterdam: VU
University Press, 1995), p. 111, has also noted that Herbert has echoed the Vulgate here.
[69] *Commentaria* IX.361: "Quam pauci tam idonei ministri, qui ubique sint bonus odor
Christi?"

up, even so Christ, the Apostles, Martyrs, and all the Saints, the more they have been afflicted and as it were ground up by persecutions and tribulations, the sweeter the fragrance they have dispersed in their virtues."[70] What engages Herbert's attention is less affliction and persecution as such than the grinding up or crushing – the *contrition* – of whatever separates a man from Christ. The lordship of Christ is sweet in Herbert's soul, and he wishes to return that sweetness; that is, he wishes to enter into a reciprocal relation with Christ – "*My Master*, which alone is sweet" – so that the poet's own "unworthiness" (21–22) will be transfigured by his life in the Lord:

> This breathing would with gains by sweetning me
> (As sweet things traffick when they meet)
>   Return to thee.
> And so this new commerce and sweet
> Should all my life employ and busie me.   (26–30)

What emerges from this closing stanza, then, is an explicit formulation of the theme that pervades *The Temple*: the meditative poet enters into Scripture in order that Christ might be as present to him as he to Christ.

Herbert's biblical poetics is thus consistent with his theology of grace and sacrament and his general devotional orientation. Even as grace is the power of transformation in Christ, and meditation and sacrament the channels of His gracious presence, so the Bible is His living Word. It is not a bare text or an endless weave of signifiers floating over an abyss of meaninglessness – it is the voice of Christ speaking through His Bride, the Church, and sounding in the hearts and minds of the faithful. "Let my heart / Suck ev'ry letter" (1–2), Herbert writes in "The H. Scriptures. I"; "Thou art joyes handsell," he continues: "heav'n lies flat in thee, / Subject to ev'ry mounters bended knee" (13–14). Scripture is effectual in prayer, "subject to" the "bended knee." As a "handsell" it is like a sacrament, which in Latin means literally a "pledge," not heaven itself but an assurance of it, heaven "flattened" out to accommodate our two-dimensional world and lead us out of it like Donne's "flatt Mapp" in his "Hymne to God my God, in my sicknesse." As a message the Gospel is a sign, different from what it signifies; but it is precisely this difference that guarantees the prior existence of that from which it differs: it is the flatness of the text that signifies the fullness of its signified.

iii

Richard Crashaw is not usually thought of as a biblical poet, but he, too, like Donne and Herbert, was preoccupied with the assimilation of the self to

---

[70] Ibid., "Sicut aromata quo magis conteruntur, eo majorem spirant fragrantiam: ita Christus, Apostoli, Martyres, omnesque Sancti, quo magis persecutionibus et tribulationibus pressi et quasi contriti fuerunt, eo suaviorem virtutibus suae sparserunt odorem."

scriptural types. Within this context the biblical elements of Crashaw's hymns begin to emerge. It is important to recall that Christian liturgical hymns are scriptural in inspiration and draw their form from the *Psalms* and canticles of the Bible. Crashaw's feastday hymns are all attempts to combine an imitation of liturgical celebration with private meditation, and in that sense they have a basis in Scripture.[71] His English translation of the *Stabat Mater* is a revealing example of how he reorients a public hymn, by means of an "application to the self," toward private meditation without losing its liturgical overtones. It is generally overlooked that the cult of the Blessed Virgin constitutes an identification on the part of the faithful with a figure from Scripture: in the *Stabat Mater* Mary thus becomes a "type" of the faithful Christian at the foot of the Cross. In Crashaw's version this sense of re-experiencing in one's own life a New Testament event is paramount:

> By all those stings
> Of love, sweet bitter things,
> Which these torn hands transcrib'd on thy true heart
> O teach mine too the art
> To study him so, till we mix
> Wounds; and become one crucifix. (stz. X)

Crashaw's entire ten-line stanza (of which the last six lines are here quoted) is woven from a single line of the Latin original: "Fac me plagis vulnerari" ("Make me be wounded with the blows"). Throughout the piece Crashaw's method is to adapt the inner life of Mary, developed from hints in Scripture and the Latin hymn, to the spiritual situation of his own time.

In the Gospel According to Luke (2: 35), Mary is told by Simeon that a sword will pierce her soul, and in John (19: 35) she is placed at the site of the Crucifixion. The original hymn is, of course, a meditation on the latter verse, and the former is mentioned in the first stanza. Crashaw elaborates the scriptural passages into a "scripture" of blood and wounds written in the soul. Scripture is "applied" to the self as the Passion of Christ is "written", not only in the words of the Gospels but in the heart of His Mother. In stanza III "His Nailes write swords in her," and as the poem draws to a close His very

---

[71] On the association between hymns and psalms and scriptural song, see Low, *Love's Architecture*, pp. 12–35. On Crashaw's combination of liturgy and meditation in his hymns, see ibid., pp. 118–24; A.B. Chambers, "Christmas: The Liturgy of the Church and English Verse of the Renaissance," in *Literary Monographs*, ed. Eric Rothstein and Joseph Anthony Wittreich, Jr. (Madison and London: University of Wisconsin Press, 1975), 6. 109–53; A. R. Cirillo, "Crashaw's 'Epiphany Hymn': The Dawn of Christian Time," *SP* 67 (1970) 67–88; Walter R. Davis, "The Meditative Hymnody of Richard Crashaw," *ELH* 50 (1983) 107–29; Elizabeth Hageman, "Calendrical symbolism and the Unity of Crashaw's *Carmen Deo Nostro*," *SP* 77 (1980) 161–79; Paul G. Stanwood, "Time and Liturgy in Donne, Crashaw, and T. S. Eliot," *Mosaic* 12, No. 2 (1979) 91–105; and R. V. Young, *Richard Crashaw and the Spanish Golden Age* (New Haven and London: Yale University Press, 1982), pp. 113–42.

wounds have "transcrib'd" His sufferings in her heart.[72] It is this experience that the poet would share in order to "mix / Wounds" with the Crucified Christ and become "one crucifix" with Him. In Crashaw's vision Jesus, the Word of God, is by the wounds of His Passion *written* – "transcrib'd" – in the heart of the Blessed Virgin, who thereby becomes the model for all Christians. In this way biblical narrative and image are rewritten in the soul of the believer, and the Bible becomes the book in which the salvation of the individual is inscribed even as he is joined with the Communion of the Saints by means of the sacraments.

In much the same way, Crashaw's meditation on the Gospel narrative of the finding of the Christ Child by the Wise Men (Matthew 2: 1–12) becomes an account of the mystical discovery of Christ in the soul of the individual believer. Despite its elaborate format of alternating voices of the "Three Kings" and the "Chorus," the "Hymn in the Glorious Epiphanie" is as much a personal reflection on the meaning of the individual's search for Christ as T. S. Eliot's "The Journey of the Magi." It is also a poem deeply involved with the text of Scripture, interpreting one passage by juxtaposing it with another. The significance of the coming of the Kings is suggested by their prophecies, first of the eclipse of the sun during the Crucifixion of Christ (Matthew 27: 45, Mark 15: 33, Luke 23: 44) and then of the conversion of Dionysius the Areopagite (Acts 17: 34), traditionally as a result of this miraculous eclipse. Once again scriptural passages become the occasion – the pretext – for a reinscription of the Bible in the heart and soul of the believer. For those who once worshipped the sun of this world, the "elaborate love-eclipse" (152) at the time of the Crucifixion makes it their duty

> To'injoy his Blott; and as a large black letter
> Use it to spell Thy beautyes better;
> And make the night it self their torch to thee.   (186–88)

"The right-ey'd Areopagite" (191), in Crashaw's day still generally identified with the author of the sixth-century *Mystical Theology*, will interpret this mysterious writing:

> And teach obscure MANKIND a more close way
> By the frugall negative light
> Of a most wise and well-abused Night
> To read more legible thine originall Ray   (208–11)

As in the translation of the *Stabat Mater* here in the Epiphany meditation, a poem in the form of a liturgical hymn deploys a set of scriptural passages in order to explore the most intimate relations of Christ and the individual soul. The collocation of biblical verses is interpretive: the discovery of the Savior of

---

[72] See the useful comments of George Walton Williams, *Image and Symbol in the Sacred Poetry of Richard Crashaw* (Columbia: University of South Carolina Press, 1963), p. 118.

Israel by the heathen Magi, the enlightening darkness of the eclipse at the hour of Christ's death, and the conversion of Dionysius are arranged as a pattern of significance for the reader of the Bible, just as Herbert explains in "The H. Scriptures. II": "This verse marks that, and both do make a motion / Unto a third that ten leaves off doth lie" (5–6). The reader must re-enact this pattern in his own spiritual life, according to Herbert's perception that the verses "make up some Christians destinie" ("The H. Scriptures. II" 8). Crashaw, like Herbert and like the Areopagite, seeks to make the written Word more "legible," to help the individual to "read" the "Ray" of God's grace in the dark recesses of his own soul.

In addition to his paraphrase of Psalms 23 and 137, Crashaw also uses implicit allusions to psalm verses in poems that treat explicitly New Testament themes. The continuity of the two testaments is thus affirmed, and their interrelationship establishes a means of reciprocal interpretation. The device is fairly obvious in "Charitas Nimia," in which, as George Williams points out, the opening stanza echoes the Prayer Book version of Psalm 144: 3–4:[73]

> Lord, what is man? why should he coste thee
> So dear? what had his ruin lost thee?
> Lord what is man? that thou hast overbought
> So much a thing of nought? (1–4)

The purpose of Crashaw's poem is to create a New Testament context for this psalm motif, and his approach is similar to Cardinal Bellarmine's. In the commentary of the latter, the Psalmist's wondering exclamation about the mercies of God serves as provocation to even greater admiration and gratitude among us who have benefited from the Incarnation:

> And if David says these things, and says them with such a feeling of piety, what would be suitable for us to do, to feel, to say, whom God has not only noticed, but for whom he took the form of a servant and humbled himself in that form, made obedient even to death, even death on the cross.[74]

Crashaw uses the same phrases of wonder from the psalm to make the same point about the enormity of Christ's sacrificial passion and death recorded in the Gospels. In "Charitas Nimia," as in Crashaw's version of the *Stabat Mater*, the wounds of the slain Christ become implements of writing. The wounds are literally inscribed in Christ's hands and feet; however, by a metaphorical reversal, they become instruments of power. In "The Flaming Heart" there

---

[73] *Complete Poetry*, p. 48n. See also Williams' remarks in *Image and Symbol*, pp. 31–32, where additional echoes of Psalms 8: 4 and Job 7: 17 are noted.

[74] *In Omnes Psalmos*, p. 871: "Et si haec Dauid dicit, & tanto sensu pietatis dicit, quid nos facere, sentire, & dicere par esset, quibus Deus non solum innotuit, sed formam serui accepit, & in ea forma humiliauit semetipsum factus obediens vsque ad mortem, mortem autem crucis."

"was never found / A nobler weapon than a WOUND," and "The wounded is the wounding heart" (71–72, 74). Just so, in "Charitas Nimia" the ink in which man's sin is inscribed is the blood of the Lamb, pouring out of His wounds:

> If my base lust
> Bargain'd with Death and well-beseeming dust,
>   Why should the white
>   Lamb's bosom write
>   The purple name
>   Of my sin's shame?   (55–60)

Sin is thus dissipated in discourse; the incarnate Word takes sin upon Himself by setting it down in His own blood. Old and New Testament expression converge in this "writing" of Christ, read in the soul of the redeemed Christian.

Like "Charitas Nimia," "To the Name of Jesus" is a biblical poem tying together specific texts from Old and New Testament, but the procedure here is more oblique and sophisticated. There is, further, an intriguing parallel with Henry Vaughan's poem beginning, "And do they so?" – generally accepted as a Protestant exemplar of biblical poetics.[75] In place of a title, the heading of this piece is a quotation of Romans 8: 19, in Beza's Latin version. Here is the verse in the King James version, along with verses 21–23:

> For the earnest expectation of the creature,
> waiteth for the manifestation of the sonnes of
> God . . . Because the creature itselfe also shall
> be delivered from the bondage of corruption, into
> the glorious libertie of the children of God.
> For wee know that the whole creation groaneth,
> and travaileth in paine together untill now. And
> not only they, but our selves also, which have the
> first fruites of the spirit, even we our selves
> groane within our selves, waiting for the adoption,
> to wit, the redemption of our body.

Vaughan's reflection on this passage leads him to consider his own unworthy attitude toward divine grandeur. The scriptural image of the entire creation longing for Christ is an expression of His glory, which inspires the poet to love God with the constancy of the lesser creatures:

> O let me not do lesse! shall they
>   Watch, while I sleep, or play?
> Shall I thy mercies still abuse
>   With fancies, friends or newes?   (31–34)

---

[75] Lewalski, *Protestant Poetics*, p. 343, calls this "a classic Protestant kind." See also pp. 345, 297.

Even as Vaughan's poem is a direct meditative response to the eighth chapter of Romans, so Crashaw's "To the Name of Jesus" is similarly a meditation on the text of Philippians 2: 9–10: "Wherefore, God also hath highly exalted him and given him a name which is above every name, That at the name of Jesus every knee should bow, of *Things* in heaven, and *things* in earth, and *things* under the earth." In its form the hymn resembles a number of the poems by Pedro Espinosa called *salmos*, which, like Crashaw's poem, are written in an irregular alternation of long and short lines with plentiful rhymes but no fixed rhyme scheme.[76] Espinosa's "Psalm calling for the coming of God to the soul of the poet" seems especially close to Crashaw's poem in form and conception. It begins with an allusion to Psalm 129 (KJV 130) and includes further references to Psalm 148 (KJV 149) and Canticles. Like Crashaw's hymn, Espinosa's "Psalm" involves a meditation on the creatures and many personal invocations of God and the angelic powers. The following passage conveys some sense of Espinosa's lush imagery and exalted rhetoric:

> Levanta entre gemidos, alma mía,
> el grito afectuoso,
> pidiendo amor, pues Dios te lo ha mandado.
> ¡Oh mi esperanza, oh gloria, oh mi alegría,
> oh mi Esposo gentil, oh dulce Esposo,
> querido mío, amante regalado,
> más florido que el prado!
> Ven, ven, no tardes; ven, sabroso fuego;
> no tardes: luego, luego,
> tu rayo me deshaga.[77]

[Lift up among groans, soul of mine, the impassioned cry, seeking love, since God has commanded it of you. Oh my hope, oh glory, oh my joy, oh my gentle Spouse, oh sweet Spouse, oh my desired one, delicate lover, more flowered than the meadow! Come, come, do not delay; come delicious flame; do not delay: then, then, may your ray melt me.]

Espinosa's verses, like Crashaw's, are psalm-like in their free, chanting quality and in the use of impassioned address to the Deity, and both poets weave into their own poetic texture the actual language of the scriptural psalms as well as other books of the Bible. Both poems are biblical in theme, mood, and style.

There are also similarities of detail between Crashaw's "To the Name of Jesus" and Vaughan's poem, "And do they so?" Like Vaughan, Crashaw dwells upon the parallel longing of man and of nature for the coming of Christ. The third of the seven sections of the hymn on the Holy Name is "An address to other creatures, asking their help," and it is only after he has dealt

[76] A form called by the Spanish the *silva*. For a discussion of a possible influence of the metrics of Góngora and Espinosa on Crashaw, see Young, *Richard Crashaw*, pp. 143–69.
[77] "Salmo pidiendo la venida de Dios al alma del poeta," 1–10, *Poesías completas*, pp. 116–17.

with the natural creatures as a means to God that the poet effects a "Return to self-address, with greater confidence," preparatory to the "Invocation" and "Celebration of the Name."[78] As the choirmaster of the earthly creation the poet dares to join the heavenly hosts in the celestial harmony of praise to the Name of Jesus:

> May it be no wrong
> Blest Heavens, to you, and your Superior song,
> That we, dark Sons of Dust and Sorrow,
> A while Dare borrow
> The Name of Your Delights and our Desires,
> And fitt it to so farr inferior LYRES. (97–102)

"To the Name of Jesus," is an example of biblical poetics at work in two senses: it is a hymn both of praise and personal reflection, in the manner of the psalms; and it is a meditation on the personal implications for the poet of a scriptural text. Just as Vaughan asks in his poem, "What does this passage of the Epistle to the Romans mean to me?" so Crashaw shows how individual Christians might respond to the Pauline injunction that every knee must bow at the name of Jesus.

Further, he shows himself to be a biblical poet in his use of allusion to the Bible and of biblical language in his own text. At the very center of his poem, as the Name itself is invoked, he recalls the passage from Romans that inspired Vaughan:

> Lo how the thirsty Lands
> Gasp for thy Golden Showres! with long stretch't Hands
> Lo how the laboring EARTH
> That hopes to be
> All Heaven by THEE,
> Leapes at thy Birth. (129–34)

George Williams points out the echo of Psalm 143: 6 (in the Prayer Book version) in the phrase "thirsty Lands / Gasp"; in addition, the phrase "laboring EARTH" suggests that the entire passage is inspired by the "creature" in travail of Romans 8: 22. Crashaw intimates that the "creature," the earth, will be delivered of its travail only when the Name, Jesus, is born into glory. The pregnancy and womb imagery in this poem is linked to the Messianic Psalm 109 (KJV 110): "The people shall be willing in the day of power; in the beauties of holiness from the womb of morning, thou hast the dew of thy youth." Crashaw plainly echoes this verse in his hymn: "WELCOME to our dark world, Thou / Womb of Day! / Unfold thy fair Conceptions; And display / The Birth of our Bright Joyes" (161–64). The

---

[78] See Martz, *Poetry of Meditation*, pp. 331–52, for this structural analysis of Crashaw's "Hymn to the Name of Jesus."

ultimate scriptural source of this hymn is, of course, the account of the bestowal of the name Jesus at the time of Our Lord's Circumcision (Luke 2: 21), but the allusions to Romans and Psalm 109 embedded within the poem have the force of prophecy. The implicit juxtapositioning of these diverse scriptural passages conveys an expectation of the final apocalypse, which will redeem the entire creation from its labor:[79]

> O see, so many WORLDS of barren yeares
> Melted and measur'd out in Seas of TEARES.
> O see, the WEARY liddes of wakeful Hope
> (LOVE'S Eastern Windowes) All wide ope
>   With Curtains drawn,
> To catch The Day-break of Thy DAWN.   (143–48)

This apocalyptic element explains how the apparent digression on the martyrs (197–224) fits into the structure of the poem as a whole, and it prepares for the vision of Judgment Day that is the poem's conclusion.[80] In addition, the passage on the martyrs suggests how man redeemed by Christ can imitate Him by writing out the Word in his own bloody script. A "martyr" is literally a "witness," and what the martyrs witness to is Christ; He is what they *reveal* in their wounds: "What did their Weapons but sett wide the Doores / For Thee: Fair, purple Doores, of love's devising" (216–17). Just as Christ's wounds are "written" in the heart of His Mother and of all the faithful, so His Name is inscribed in the blood of the martyrs. They are thus a "book" of Scripture: in revealing Christ through their wounds, the martyrs anticipate the final Revelation – another term for "Apocalypse." The key to it all is love: the "Doores" are "Of love's devising." This theme has been already established by the allusion to the eighth chapter of Romans. In explicating the typological "name of Christ" from Isaiah 5: 1, "well-beloved" (*amado*), Fray Luis de León adduces the same verses from Romans that are cited explicitly by Vaughan, implicitly by Crashaw. "All things, guided by a secret motion," writes the Spanish friar, "loving their own good, also love Him and pant with their desire and moan for his coming in the manner the Apostle writes of it . . . This is nothing at all except an appetite and a desire for Jesus Christ, who is the author of this liberty, as St. Paul says, and for whom all clamor."[81]

---

[79] See the Messianic explanation of Psalm 109 by Fray Luis de León in *Of the Names of Christ, Obras I*, 780–82, along with the comments by Young, *Richard Crashaw*, pp. 137–38.

[80] For further discussion of the martyrs' passage, see Young, *Richard Crashaw*, pp. 139–42. Of course this hymn involves important references to contemporaneous political and religious controversy. See Eugene R. Cunnar, "Crashaw's Hymn 'To the Name Above Every Name': Background and Meaning," in *Essays on Richard Crashaw*, ed. Robert M. Cooper (Salzburg: Institut für Anglistik und Amerikanistik, Universität Salzburg, 1979), pp. 102–28.

[81] *Obras I*, 753: "Porque todas las cosas, guiadas de un movimiento secreto, amando su mismo bien, le aman tambien a Él y suspiran con su deseo y gimen por su venida en la manera que el Apóstol escribe . . . Lo cual no es otra cosa sino un apetito y un deseo de Jesucristo, que es el autor de esta libertad, que San Pablo dice, y por quien todo vocea."

The allusions to Scripture in Crashaw's hymn "To the Name of Jesus" are not, therefore, merely adventitious or decorative; they are central to the development of its complex structure of meaning. In meditating upon the mysterious grandeur of the Holy Name, as set forth in the Epistle to the Philippians (and suggested in Luke), Crashaw makes use of the Messianic prophecy of Psalm 109 and the enigmatic intimations of a text from Romans. This cross-referencing of Scripture requires a profound sense of the typological unity of the Bible, recalling Herbert's advice to the country parson to practise "a diligent Collation of Scripture with Scripture" (*Works*, p. 229). "To the Name of Jesus" is, then, biblical in its psalm-like form, in its meaning, and in its metaphoric texture.

iv

The similarities between Crashaw's "To the Name of Jesus" and Vaughan's "And do they so?" are not merely adventitious. Both poems reflect a vision of reality in which the Bible is a means of interpreting human experience, and thus both poets share a portion of the common Christian heritage that survived the dislocations and conflicts of the Reformation. Despite his rancor over Puritan depredations of the Church of England, Vaughan – like Donne, Herbert, and Crashaw in their diverse ways – retains a scriptural orientation that emphasizes the strife between the sacred and the secular rather than narrowly sectarian conflicts. If the immediate embodiment of the Antichrist in the apocalyptic moments of *Silex Scintillans* is the Puritan regime, the ultimate source of Vaughan's anxiety is his sense that the divine presence is departing from an increasingly cold, rationalistic world. The Bible is the guidebook, the ancient map, that leads to the recovery of the lost treasure of grace.

This point is explicit in "The hidden Treasure," which meditates on Matthew 13: 44 as a precept for the attitude that a Christian should nurture towards the world: "Againe, the kingdome of heauen is like vnto a treasure hid in a field: the which when a man hath found, hee hideth, and for ioy thereof goeth and selleth all that hee hath, and buyeth that field." Like Herbert in "The Pearl," which meditates on the very next verse (Matthew 13: 45), Vaughan asserts that he, too, is not unacquainted with worldly knowledge and its attractions, but he sees that, pursued for its own sake, it brings man to an abyss:

> The worlds lov'd wisdom (for the worlds friends think
> There is none else) did not the dreadful brink
> And precipice it leads to, bid me flie
> None could with more advantage use, then I.   (15–18)

Mere wordly wisdom consists of "False stars and fire-drakes, the deceits of night / Set forth to fool and foil thee" (4–5); however, the individualism of personal inspiration is equally misleading: "And private Tapers will but help to stray / Ev'n those, who *by them* would finde out the day" (27–28).

The Bible steers the Christian between the vulgar fashion of the knowing world and private eccentricity:

> I'le seal my eyes up, and to thy commands
> Submit my wilde heart, and restrain my hands;
> I will do nothing, nothing know, nor see
> But what thou bidst, and shew'st, and teachest me.   (29–32)

As the name of Jesus is written in the wounds of Crashaw's martyrs, so Vaughan longs to have the Bible inscribed in his heart even as the Ten Commandments were incised in stone. In "H. Scriptures," which recalls the title of his own volume, *Silex Scintillans,* and its opening Latin emblem, as well as Herbert's "Judgement," Vaughan seeks to internalize the Scriptures that proclaim the benefit of Christ's death:

> O that I had deep Cut in my hard heart
>   Each line in thee! Then would I plead in groans
> Of my Lords penning, and by sweetest Art
> Return upon himself the *Law,* and *Stones.*
>   Read here, my faults are thine. This Book, and I
>   Will tell thee so; *Sweet Saviour thou didst dye!*   (9–14)

The metaphor of inscription is a way of suggesting that the Holy Scriptures must be indelibly impressed into the mind and imagination. Vaughan's devotion to the Bible takes a practical form in *Silex Scintillans* in the numerous poems beginning or ending with scriptural citations that provide their origin and spiritual substance. It is as if Vaughan has undertaken a Christianized version of Horace's advice in the *Ars Poetica:* "scribendi recte sapere est et principium et fons / rem tibi Socraticae poterunt ostendere chartae" (309–10).[82] Only Vaughan substitutes "biblicae chartae" for "Socraticae chartae."

"The Ass," with the subtitle "St. Matt. 21," provides an example of how the most improbable aspect of a scriptural incident can become a trope for the Christian life. The ass that bears Christ into Jerusalem embodies the humility, obedience, and faith that characterize the true follower of the Lord:

---

[82] Q. Horati Flacci *Opera*, ed. Edward C. Wickham, 2nd ed. H. W. Garrod (Oxford: Clarendon Press, 1912): "The origin and basis of writing correctly is wisdom: / The Socratic pages will be able to furnish you with subject matter."

Teach both mine eyes and feet to move
Within those bounds set by thy love;
Grant I may soft and lowly be,
And minde those things I cannot see;
Tye me to faith, though above reason,
Who question power, they speak treason:
Let me thy Ass be onely wise
To carry, not search mysteries;
Who carries thee, is by thee lead,
Who argues, follows his own head.   (15–24)

As numerous commentators point out,[83] the donkey that Jesus rides into Jerusalem is here compared to the familiar figure of the "Ass Bearing mysteries." The Christian must imitate the lowly wisdom of this beast that knows how "To carry, not search mysteries." Like his mentor Herbert, Vaughan is suspicious of religious controversy, which for him is inevitably associated with the disputatious Puritans. The patient, docile ass accepts the burden of mysterious doctrine without attempting to solve all its riddles. Equally adverse to the example of the ass is any skeptical rationalism that demands an explanation for everything.

As Jonathan Post observes, the poetic persona of *Silex Scintillans* frequently identifies himself with Job;[84] Towards the close of "The Ass," the tame beast of burden in the Gospel is juxtaposed to his wild cousin, who appears in Job 39: 5–8:

When thus thy milde, instructing hand
Findes thy poor *foal* at thy command,
When he from wilde is become wise,
And slights that most, which men most prize;
When all things here to thistles turn
Pricking his lips, till he doth mourn
And hang the head, sighing for those
Pastures of life, where the Lamb goes:
O then, just then! break or untye
These bonds, this sad captivity,
This leaden state, which men miscal
Being and life, but is dead thrall.
And when (O God!) the Ass is free,
In a state known to none but thee;
O let him by his *Lord* be led,
To living springs, and there be fed

---

[83] See the notes to the poem in the editions of Martin, Fogle, and Rudrum.

[84] Jonathan F. S. Post, *Henry Vaughan: The Unfolding Vision* (Princeton, NJ: Princeton University Press, 1982), pp. 172–73.

Where light, joy health and perfect peace
Shut out all pain and each disease;
Where death and frailty are forgotten,
And bones rejoyce, which once were broken!   (45–64)

"Who hath sent out the wild asse free? or who hath loosed the bands of the wild asse?" the Lord asks Job (39: 5). "Those who moralize this scripture," writes Fray Luis de León in his *Exposición del Libro de Job*, "understand by the wild ass men who are detached from the world and who distance themselves from it in soul and body as much as possible." Such a man is a "hermit at heart" and is regarded by "lovers of the world" as an ass because he "despises what they adore, and flees what they love, and embraces what they detest." It is God alone, however, who "hath sent the wild asse free"; for it is "without doubt a marvelous work, and very worthy of God, to make an angel of a man" and generally to free from the desire of comfort, praise, pleasure, and prestige a creature naturally inclined to them. "For nature is the very greatest attachment, and necessity a powerful knot, and custom and common fashion a chain of iron, bonds and prisons truly greater than the powers of man."[85]

Vaughan also "moralizes" the scriptural text, but in a way that deepens the paradox set forth by Fray Luis. The "wild asse" that God sets free is identified with the tame ass that Jesus rides into Jerusalem. It is precisely the man whom Jesus "Findes . . . at thy command," who is "soft and lowly," who is "onely wise / To carry, not search mysteries" who will come into the ultimate freedom, the "state" known only to God. Vaughan thus combines the serviceable ass of Matthew with the wild ass of Job to set forth a biblical illustration of Herbert's *sententia* that the service of God is perfect freedom. Moreover, he achieves this end by deploying Herbert's understanding of how Holy Scripture should be read: "This verse marks that, and both do make a motion / Unto a third, that ten leaves off doth lie" ("The H. Scriptures. II. 5–6). The "moralizing" of the ass from two different scriptural passages shows how "in ev'ry thing / Thy words do finde me out, & parallels bring" (10–11), since our scorn for the ass all too aptly defines human nature.

Francisco Quevedo presents another famous scriptural donkey, Balaam's ass from Numbers 22, as a similar emblem of the clash between human pride and humility. "And the Asse saw the Angel of the Lord standing in the way, and his sword drawn in his hand: and the asse turned aside out of the way,

---

[85] *Obras* II. 644–45: "Los que moralizan esta escritura, por el *asno salvaje* entienden a los hombres desasidos del mundo, y que con el alma y cuerpo se alejan dél cuanto pueden . . . Es, pues, el ermitaño de corazón el *asno salvaje*. Asno, porque ansí lo juzgan los amadores del mundo, estimando por locura y menos saber el despreciar lo que ellos adoran, y el huir lo que aman, y el abrazar lo que abominan . . . Porque es sin duda maravillosa obra, y muy digna de Dios, hacer del hombre ángel . . . Que la naturaleza es atadura grandísima, y la necesidad ñudo fuerte, y la costumbre ye el estilo común cadena de hierro, ataduras y prisiones verdaderamente mayores que las fuerzas del hombre."

and went into the field: and Balaam smote the asse, to turne her into the way"
(Numbers 22: 23). Until the Lord opens his eyes, Balaam, blinded by pride
and his will to curse the chosen people, is unable to see what his lowly beast
has seen. Like Vaughan, Quevedo stresses the headstrong violence of human
nature opposed to the graciousness of humility represented by the ass:

PONDERA CON EL SUCESO DE BALÁN CUÁNTO ANTES ES DIOS
OBEDECIDO DE UNA MALA BESTIA QUE DE UN MAL MINISTRO
A maldecir el pueblo, en un jumento,
parte Balán profeta, acelerado;
que a maldecir cualquiera va alentado:
tal es el natural nuestro violento.
Dios, que mira del pueblo el detrimento,
rey en guardar su pueblo desvelado,
clemente, opone a su camino, armado
de su milicia, espléndido portento.
Obedece el jumento, no el profeta;
y cuando mereció premio y regalo,
más obstinado a caminar le aprieta.
Teme la asnilla al ángel, sufre el palo:
y halló el cielo obediencia más perfeta
en mala bestia que en ministro malo.[86]

[IN VIEW OF THE AFFAIR OF BALAAM HE REFLECTS HOW MUCH
MORE READILY GOD IS OBEYED BY A STUBBORN BEAST THAN BY
A STUBBORN SERVANT
To curse the people the prophet Balaam departed in haste on a mule;
for anyone goes with wings to curse: such is the violence of our nature.
God, who looks upon harm to the people, a clement king vigilant in
guarding his people, places in his path a splendid armed portent from his
soldiery. The mule obeys, not the prophet; and when the one deserves
favor and reward, the other more determined to proceed urges him on.
The little ass fears the angel and endures the stick: and heaven finds more
perfect obedience in a stubborn beast than a stubborn servant.]

The irony of the poem arises from the contradictory associations of the
donkey as a symbol both of humility and intractable stubbornness. Quevedo
highlights the element of humility by showing how fallen human nature is
more stubborn than any ass.

An additional feature that Vaughan's biblical poetry shares with that of
continental contemporaries is the invocation of Old Testament personages
and events in a way that suffuses their standard typological significance with
personal overtones. Such a procedure could be viewed as a distinctively
Protestant "application to the self" of the abstract types of Medieval figural
exegesis; but the implicit individualism of this interpretive gambit, like so

---

[86] *Obras completas* I. 164.

many other aspects of seventeenth-century devotional poetry, appears on both sides of the confessional divide. What is at work everywhere in the spiritual life of the age is a determination not just to appropriate scriptural models for the intimate personal development of the individual, but even to inhabit the written text as a spiritual home.

Both Vaughan and Lope de Vega, for example, take episodes involving Isaac and Jacob from the Book of Genesis – which receives its classic typological treatment in St. Augustine's *City of God* – and explore the individual human implications of the texts in relation to seventeenth-century moral and spiritual concerns. In the *City of God* Augustine is largely interested in Isaac's marriage to Rebecca as a prophecy of the Incarnation. Augustine quotes Genesis 24: 2–3, where Abraham makes his servant place his hand under his master's thigh and swear not to take a wife for Isaac from among the Canaanites: "What else does this show," Augustine asks, "except that the Lord God of heaven and the Lord of earth was to come in flesh descended from that thigh?"[87] In other contexts he calls Rebecca a type of the Church,[88] and Isidor of Seville finds a moral quality in Rebecca by deriving her name from "patience, or she who will have endured much."[89]

In "Isaacs Marriage," however, Vaughan focuses on the spiritual and moral response of the young Patriarch to a personal situation. The poem's epigraph is Genesis 24: 63, in which Isaac is described as going forth into the fields to meditate or pray as he awaits news of his father's servant, who has been sent to fetch him a bride. Isaac's solemn religious attitude toward marriage stands in contrast to the shallow sophistication that Vaughan sees as characteristic of the society of his own time:

> But being for a bride, prayer was such
> A decryed course, sure it prevail'd not much.
> Had'st ne'er an oath, nor Complement? thou wert
> An odde dull sutor; Hadst thou but the art
> Of these our dayes, thou couldst have coyn'd thee twenty
> New sev'ral oathes, and Complements (too) plenty;
> O sad, and wilde excesse! and happy those
> White dayes, that durst no impious mirth expose!   (11–18)

[87] *De civitate Dei* XVI. 33; *PL* 41. 512: "quid aliud demonstratum est, cum eidem servo dixit Abraham, *Pone manum tuam sub femore meo, et adjurabo te per Dominum Deum coeli et Dominum terrae, ut non sumas filio meo Isaac uxorem de filiabus Chananoerum* (*Gen.* xxiv,2,3), nisi Dominum Deum coeli et dominum terrae in carne, quae ex illo femore trahebatur, fuisse venturum?"

[88] See *Sermones ad Populum* I. xi; *PL* 38–39. 39; and *Enarrationes in Psalmos* CXXVI.8; *PL* 36–37. 1673.

[89] *Etymologiarum sive Originum Libri XX*, ed. W. M. Lindsay, 2 vols. (Oxford: Clarendon Press, 1911), VII. vi, 35: "Rebecca patientia, sive quae multum acceperit."

The poem takes off with Isaac's soul, which, at the prospect of the marriage, rises on the wings of contemplation. Although Vaughan, as a Protestant, does not call marriage a sacrament, it embodies a mysterious significance with apparently sacramental implications for the individual, as well as typological implications for the Church:

> This brought thee forth, where now thou didst undress
> Thy soul, and with new pinions refresh
> Her wearied wings, which so restor'd did flye
> Above the stars, a track unknown, and high,
> And in her piercing flight perfum'd the ayer
> Scatt'ring the *Myrrhe*, and incense of thy pray'r.   (47–52)

Isaac is, then, both a model for the individual Christian of any era and a link in the typological chain of Old Testament patriarchs:

> Thus soar'd thy soul, who (though young,) didst inherit
> Together with his bloud, thy fathers spirit,
> Whose active zeal, and tried faith were to thee
> Familiar ever since thy Infancie. (63–66)

> .   .   .   .
> Then, who would truly limne thee out, must paint
> First, a *young Patriarch*, then a *marri'd Saint.*   (71–72)

As "Patriarch" and "Saint" Isaac combines Old and New Testament roles in conventional typological fashion, but, by exploring the scriptural figure's interior consciousness, Vaughan makes him a personally sympathetic character for his own time.

   Lope de Vega's sonnet, "De Isaac y Rebeca," takes the same incident, alluding specifically to Genesis 24: 65, where Rebecca covers herself with her cloak upon seeing Isaac, and makes a similar point about the spiritual life of the individual by interpreting the personal gesture of a typological figure:

> Isaac adelantándose al camino
> viole la honesta virgen, y del manto
> hizo rebozo al rostro peregrino.
> Ejemplo para el alma, esposo santo,
> que cuando vos venís en pan divino,
> se cubra de humildad a favor tanto.[90]

> [Isaac saw the chaste maiden approaching on the way, and with her cloak she veiled her pilgrim face. An exemplum for the soul, a holy spouse, for when you come upon the divine bread, let yourself be covered with humility at such favor.]

---

[90] *Obras poéticas*, I. 368.

"Married saint" and *esposo santo* are about as close a parallel between English and Spanish as one could ask, but this verbal echo is important principally for what it shows about the similarity of the two poets' methods. Like Vaughan, Lope takes the distant, solemn figures of Isaac and Rebecca, types of Christ and the Church, and endows them with individual human qualities, which serve as models for the conduct of contemporaneous Christians. Through the medium of Scripture, the poet enters into the lives of the Old Testament types, which become, in turn, portals into the life of Christ and the Church. The biblical poem is a means by which the Christian poet and his readers go back into the lives of the Patriarchs to discover their Christian identity in the present.

In "De Raquel y Jacob," Lope paints an even more intimate portrait of an ancient Patriarch and his bride. His sonnet evokes an erotic longing on the part of Jacob that, while it has typological implications, stresses the intensely human:

> Bajaba con sus cándidas ovejas
> por el valle de Aram Raquel hermosa,
> el oro puro y la purpúrea rosa
> mezclando las mejillas y guedejas,
> ellas lamiendo a la canal las tejas,
> y ella mirando el pozo cuidadosa,
> anticipóse a levantar la losa
> el que fue mayorazgo por lentejas.
> Bebió el ganado caluroso, y luego
> diola beso de paz, y por despojos
> lágrimas que lloró perdido y ciego.
> Muy tierno sois, Jacob. ¿Tan presto enojos?
> Sí, que en llegando al corazón el fuego,
> lo que tiene de humor sale a los ojos.[91]

[Lovely Rachel with her shining white sheep descended through the valley of Haran, her cheeks and locks mixing pure gold with the purple rose. With the sheep licking the tiles of the trough and she, anxious, gazing at the well, he who was firstborn by pottage goes ahead and lifts the covering stone. The over-heated herd drank, and immediately he gave her a kiss of peace, and for spoils tears that he wept lost and blind. You are tender, Jacob. Do vexations come so soon? Yes, for when fire comes into the heart, whatever fluid it has comes out at the eyes.]

Lope's sonnet is a dramatization of Genesis 29: 9–11 that recounts the scriptural incident exactly. What interests the poet, however, is the emotional experience of Jacob, which is scanted in both the Bible and theology.

St. Augustine's account in the *City of God* lays stress upon the Patriarch's innocence: although he sired twelve sons and a daughter by four different

---

[91] Ibid., p. 366.

women, Jacob never sought but one wife, Augustine says. Since he was deceived into marriage with Leah, and since "at that time when for the sake of multiplying offspring, no law forbade having several wives, he also took her to whom alone he had already made a promise of marriage." As for the children by the handmaids Bilhah and Zilpah, that was the doing of his wives, "who held lawful power over the body of their husband."[92] But while Augustine is concerned to exonerate Jacob from his apparent sexual excess, Lope, whose own intense passions were well known, is interested in the feelings of the man who moves the stone from the well on his own initiative when he sees Rachel; who weeps when he kisses her; who cries, when deceived with Leah, "What is this thou hast done vnto mee? did not I serue with thee for Rachel?" (Genesis 29: 25); who agrees to serve another seven years for the younger sister. By ascribing the tears that follow Jacob's kiss to the fire in his heart, Lope turns a hint in Scripture into the language of Petrarchan love poetry: "And Iacob serued seuen yeeres for Rachel: and they seemed vnto him but a few dayes, for the loue hee had to her" (Genesis 29: 20). By finding in a Patriarch, a type of the elect Christian, Jacob who became Israel – by finding in this remote scriptural figure longing and frustration – Lope makes him one of us and finds for us a place in the Bible's story of salvation.

Vaughan handles the story of Jacob with a similar motive in "Jacobs Pillow, and Pillar," insofar as Jacob becomes a figure of consolation. The poem opens with a vision, a vivid realization of the import of Jacob's theophany at Bethel:

> I see the Temple in thy Pillar rear'd,
> And that dread glory, which thy children fear'd,
> In milde, clear visions without a frown,
> Unto thy solitary self is shown. (1–4)

St. Augustine interprets this episode as a prophecy of the coming of Christ:

> This concerns prophecy; and Jacob did not pour perfume over the stone in the manner of idolatry, as if making it a god; for he did not adore that stone or sacrifice to it; but since the name of Christ is derived from *chrism*, that is, from anointing, assuredly something is figured forth here that concerns a great mystery.[93]

This typological dimension is certainly not absent from Vaughan's poem, but it is modified by a personal concern of Vaughan's. The piety of the "solitary self" is contrasted with the sectarian tendencies of the Puritan mobs of the 1640s and 1650s: " 'Tis number makes a Schism: throngs are rude, / And God

---

[92] *De civitate Dei* XVI. 38. 3; *PL* 41. 517–18.

[93] Ibid., 38. 2; *PL* 41. 517: "Hoc ad prophetiam pertinet: nec more idololatriae lapidem perfudit oleo Jacob, velut faciens illum deum; neque enim adoravit eumdem lapidem, vel ei sacrificavit: sed quoniam Christi nomen a chrismate est, id est ab unctione; profecto figuratum est hic aliquid, quod ad magnum pertineat sacramentum."

216

himself dyed by the multitude" (5–6). Much of the poem is devoted to the contrast between the impious barbarism of the crowd and the quiet devotion of the individual, or of the faithful remnant. At the close the poem circles back to Jacob and finds solace for oppressed Anglican loyalists in the figure of the persecuted Patriarch, who endured as much and remained faithful, even though he lacked the assurance of the Incarnation and the sacramental presence of the Savior:

> But blessed *Jacob*, though thy sad distress
> Was just the same with ours, and nothing less;
> For thou a brother, and blood-thirsty too
> Didst flye, whose children wrought thy children wo:
> Yet thou in all thy solitude and grief,
> On stones didst sleep and found'st but cold relief;
> Thou from the Day-star a long way didst stand
> And all that distance was Law and command.
> But we a healing Sun by day and night,
> Have our sure Guardian, and our leading light;
> What thou didst hope for and believe, we finde
> And feel a friend most ready, sure and kinde.
> Thy pillow was but type and shade at best,
> But we the substance have, and on him rest.   (41–54)

Jacob is still viewed in terms of "type and shade," but he is also, like Christians of Vaughan's day, and indeed of ours, an individual working out his salvation in fear and trembling. The poetry of *Silex Scintillans* gives voice to the anguish of the seventeenth-century Christian enduring the suffering and uncertainty of Civil War – a macrocosm of the family "war" experienced by Jacob. As a biblical poet, Vaughan places the one conflict in the context of the other. By locating the events of his own time in the text of Scripture, he shows how in God's written Word, as George Herbert says in "The Bunch of Grapes," "each Christian hath his journeys spann'd: / Their storie pennes and sets us down" (10–11).

At first glance "Jacobs Pillow, and Pillar" would seem to be a decidedly "Protestant" poem with its emphasis on the faith and devotion of the individual Christian. However, in the face of more than a century of religious conflict and intellectual dislocation that left doubt and anxiety everywhere, Catholic and Protestant alike exhibit a marked concern for individual spiritual life. Although the specific preoccupations of the Catholic Lope de Vega and the Protestant Henry Vaughan are different, they share a poetic impulse to make the remote Patriarchs, Isaac and Jacob, into something more than *types* (in the general modern sense as well as the technical theological sense). Both poets find familiar, sympathetic qualities in Old Testament figures; they give them human substance and, above all, *voice*, so that the bare

217

text of Scripture speaks again to the minds of contemporary men and women and is reinscribed in their hearts.

* * *

Writing in 1835, Rev. R. Cattermole deplored the comparative neglect of sacred poetry among his contemporaries and sought to explain it by calling attention to the prevalence of manifold inducements to materialism:

> Now, in the present age, the prodigious development of the mechanical sciences, and the impulse imparted by this and other causes to civilization, as distinguished from mental culture, have greatly enlarged the proportionate number of sensualists and worldlings, by widening, beyond all precedent, the spheres of ordinary enjoyment and gainful exertion. In these considerations, therefore, we are in some degree supplied with the means of accounting for the diminished esteem in which the noblest and most intellectual of the arts is held, in an age which puts forth peculiar claims to intelligence and philosophy; and for the measure of encouragement it continues to receive, being lavished chiefly upon the least worthy of its productions.

In addition to this general materialism, Cattermole also notes "the absorbing interest attached, in our days, to all questions that relate to political rights and the proceedings of governments. The politician – he who is such by taste and temper, not from duty and the necessity of his social position, is a worldly unimaginative being."[94] And this was more than a century before the advent of television.

Without speculating about the "proportionate number" of sensualists, worldlings, and politicians among the current members of university English departments, one may still observe that a preoccupation with the gadgetry of electronic technology (the post-industrial version of the "mechanical sciences") and with questions of politics has tended to elevate the manipulation of means over the contemplation of ends. Such an academic environment would seem to hold less promise for the serious consideration of devotional poetry than Cattermole's England of 1835, and yet the religious poetry of the seventeenth century remains a subject of considerable scholarly interest. It is the contention of this study that the devotional poets remain worthy of attention precisely because, in some measure, they anticipate and protest the cultural conditions, indicated in a somewhat curmudgeonly fashion by Cattermole, that would seem to entail their own obsolescence. Donne, Herbert, Crashaw, and Vaughan – central figures of this inquiry – wrote at the threshold of the modern age; and their poetry senses and recoils from the incipient emergence of the characteristic features of modernity: the predominance of concern for the immediate and sensory over the spiritual, of

---

[94] "Introductory Essay," *Sacred Poetry of the Seventeenth Century*, ed. R. Cattermole (1835; rpt. New York: Burt Franklin, 1969), I, viii–ix.

the political over the religious, of the temporal over the eternal. They responded to what would become the definitive attribute of the modern age, secularization, when it was but a little cloud, no larger than a man's hand.

For this reason, the two approaches to the devotional poets most widely practised over the last twenty-five years both have something wrong and something right. The advocates of the Protestant poetics interpretation of the religious lyric in England have performed a great service in forcing contemporary scholarship to take very seriously the doctrinal and theological concerns of the poets. They have, however, sometimes failed to make a sufficient distinction between poetry and versified theological polemic, with the result that comparatively minor differences between Catholic and Protestant poets have been emphasized at the expense of far more important similarities. Postmodernist criticism, assuming, as the term implies, a certain disillusionment with optimistic rationalism of the modern era as a whole, is in a position to respond sympathetically to the devotional poets' anxious questioning of human nature and mankind's worldly prospects. What the typical postmodernist critic does not acknowledge or appreciate are their affirmations. Donne looked into the same abyss as Derrida, and Herbert was as aware of the doubtful status of the nature of "man" as Foucault; but the poets believed, and embodied their belief in poetry, that man's humanity and the order of his world was guaranteed not by his own frail discourse, but by the Word of God. In the seventeenth century the religious poetry of Donne and his successors presented a challenge to moral and spiritual complacency (their own as well as their readers'); it continues to pose such a challenge in the twentieth century.

BIBLIOGRAPHY

PRIMARY SOURCES

Alabaster, William. *The Sonnets of William Alabaster.* G. M. Story and Helen Gardner. London: Oxford University Press, 1959.

Andrewes, Lancelot. *Sermons.* Ed. G. M. Story. Oxford: Clarendon Press, 1967.

Aristotle. *Categories.* Ed. and Trans. Harold P. Cook. Cambridge, MA: Harvard University Press, 1938.

Augustine of Hippo, Saint. *Opera Omnia. Patrologia Latina.* 32–47. Ed. J.-P. Migne. Paris, 1844–1855.

Bañes, Dominico. *Scholastica Commentaria in Primam Partem Summae Theologicae S. Thomae Aquinitatis.* Ed. Luis Urbano. 1934. Rpt. Dubuque, IA: William C. Brown, N.D.

Bellarmine, Saint Robert. *In Omnes Psalmos Dilucida Explanatio.*Brixiae, 1611.

———. *Opera Roberti Bellarmini Politiani, S.J.* 7 vols. Venice, 1721–28.

Bernard of Clairvaux, Saint. *Opera Omnia. Patrologia Latina.* 182–185. Ed. J.-P. Migne. Paris, 1844–1855.

Boehme, Jacob. *The Way to Christ.* Trans. Peter Erb. New York: Paulist Press, 1978.

Bradstreet, Anne. *The Complete Works of Anne Bradstreet.* Ed. Joseph R. McElrath, Jr. and Allan P. Robb. Boston: G. K. Hall, 1981.

Cajetan, Thomas de Vio, Cardinal. *Cajetan Responds: A Reader in Reformation Controversy.* Ed. and Trans. Jared Wicks. Washington, D.C.: Catholic University of America Press, 1978.

———. *De Nominum Analogia et de Conceptu Entis.* Ed. P. N. Zammit, O.P. Rome: Institutum Angelicum, 1934.

———. *In* De Ente et Essentia *D. Thomae Aquinitatis.* Ed. P. M.-H. Laurent. Turin: Marietti, 1934.

Calvin, John. *Calvin: Commentaries.* Ed. Joseph Haroutounian. Philadelphia: Westminster Press, 1958.

———. *Calvin: Theological Treatises.* Ed. J. K. S. Reid. Philadelphia: Westminster Press, 1954.

———. *Institutes of the Christian Religion.* Trans. Henry Beveridge. 2 vols. Grand Rapids, MI: W. B. Eerdmans, 1957.

———. *John Calvin: Selections From His Writings.* Ed. John Dillenberger. Garden City, NY: Doubleday & Co., 1971.

Castiglione, Baldasarre. *The Book of the Courtier.* Trans. Sir Thomas Hoby. In *Three Renaissance Classics.* Ed. Burton A. Milligan. New York: Charles Scribner's Sons, 1953.

Cattermole, R. Ed. *Sacred Poetry of the Seventeenth Century.* 2 vols., 1835. Rpt. New York: Burt Franklin, 1969.

Ceppède, Jean de la. *Les Théorèmes sur le Sacré Mystère de Notre Rédemption.* Reproduction de l'édition de Toulouse de 1613–1622. Préface de Jean Rosset. Genève: Librairie Droz, 1966.

Crashaw, Richard. *The Complete Poetry of Richard Crashaw.* Ed. George Walton Williams. New York: New York University Press, 1972.

——. *The Poems English, Latin and Greek of Richard Crashaw.* Ed. L. C. Martin. 2nd ed. Oxford: Clarendon Press, 1957.

Daniel, Samuel. *Poems and a Defence of Ryme.* Ed. Arthur Colby. Sprague. 1930. Rpt. Chicago: University of Chicago Press, 1965.

Dante Alighieri. *Divina Commedia.* Ed. C. H. Grandgent and Rev. Charles S. Singleton. Cambridge: Harvard University Press, 1972.

Dawson, Edward. *The Practical Methode of Meditation.* In Louis L. Martz, Ed. *The Anchor Anthology of Seventeenth-Century Verse.* Vol. I. Garden City, NY: Doubleday & Co., 1969.

Donne, John. *The Complete Poetry of John Donne.* Ed. John T. Shawcross. Garden City, NY: Doubleday & Co., 1967.

——. *The Divine Poems.* Ed. Helen Gardner. 2nd ed. Oxford: Clarendon Press, 1978.

——. *Donne's Prebend Sermons.* Ed. Janel Mueller. Cambridge, MA: Harvard University Press, 1971.

——. *Essays in Divinity.* Ed. Evelyn M. Simpson. Oxford: Clarendon Press, 1952.

——. *John Donne's Poetry: Authoritative Texts and Criticism.* Ed. A. L. Clements. 2nd edn. New York: W. W. Norton & Co., 1992.

——. *Letters to Several Persons of Honour,* 1651. Intro. M. Thomas Hester. Facsimile Rpt. New York: Delmar, 1977.

——. *The Sermons of John Donne.* Ed. George R. Potter and Evelyn M. Simpson. 10 vols. Berkeley: University of California Press, 1953–1962.

Enchiridion Symbolorum, Definitionum et Declarationum. Ed. Henr. Denzinger et Clem. Bannwart, S.J. 17th edn. Friburgi Brisgoviae: Herder & Co., 1928.

Erasmus, Desiderius. *Christian Humanism and the Reformation.* Ed. and Trans. John C. Olin. New York: Harper & Row, 1965.

——. *Erasmus-Luther: Discourse on Free Will.* Ed. and Trans. Ernst F. Winter. New York: Frederick Unger, 1961.

Espinosa, Pedro. *Poesías completas.* Ed. Francisco López Estrada. Madrid: Espasa Calpe, 1975.

Flaminio, Marcantonio. *Marci Antonii, Joannis Antonii et Gabrielis Flaminiorum Forocorneliensium Carmina.* Prati: Typis Raynerii Guasti, 1831.

Gaselee, Stephen, Ed. *The Oxford Book of Medieval Latin Verse.* Oxford: Clarendon Press, 1928.

Gracián, Baltasar. *Obras completas.* Ed. Arturo del Hoyo. Madrid: Aguilar, 1967.

Herbert, George. *The Latin Poetry of George Herbert: A Bilingual Edition.* Trans. Mark McCloskey and Paul R. Murphy. Athens: University of Ohio Press, 1965.

——. *The Works of George Herbert.* Ed. F. E. Hutchinson. 2nd ed. Oxford: Clarendon Press, 1945.

Hobbes, Thomas. *Leviathan.* Ed. C. B. MacPherson. Harmondsworth: Penguin Books, 1968.

Hooker, Richard. *Of the Laws of Ecclesiastical Polity.* Ed. Christopher Morris. 2 vols. London: J. M. Dent, 1907.

Horace. *Q. Horati Flacci Opera.* Ed. Edward C. Wickham. 2nd ed. H. W. Garrod. Oxford: Clarendon Press, 1912.

Ignacio de Loyola, San. *Obras completas de San Ignacio de Loyola.* Ed. Ignacio Iparraguirre, S.J. Madrid: Biblioteca de Autores Cristianos, 1963.

Isidor of Seville, Saint. *Etymologiarum sive Originum Libiri XX.* Ed. W. M. Lindsay. 2 vols. Oxford: Clarendon Press, 1911.

Jewel, John. *An Apology of the Church of England.* Ed. John E. Booty. Ithaca, NY: Cornell University Press, 1963.

Joyce, James. *Finnegans Wake.* 1939. Rpt. New York: Viking, 1959.

Juan de la Cruz, San. *Vida y obras de San Juan de la Cruz.* Ed. Crisógono de Jesús, O.C.D., Matías del Niño Jesús, O.C.D. and Lucinio del SS. Sacramento, O.C.D., 5th ed. Madrid: Biblioteca de Autores Cristianos, 1964.

The Judgement of the Synode Holden at Dort. London, 1619. Facsimile Rpt.: Amsterdam, 1974.

Kenyon, J. P., Ed. *The Stuart Constitution, 1603–1688: Documents and Commentary.* Cambridge: Cambridge University Press, 1969.

Lapide, S. J., Cornelius à. *Commentaria in Scripturam Sacram.* 20 vols. Paris: Ludovicus Vivès, 1868.

Luiken, Joanne. *Jezus en de Ziel.* Amsteldam: Korbelis vander Sys, 1722.

Luis de León, Fray. *Obras completas castellanas.* Ed. Félix García, O.S.A. 2 vols. 4th ed. Madrid: Biblioteca de Autores Cristianos, 1957.

Luther, Martin. *The Bondage of the Will.* Trans. J. I. Packer and O. R. Johnson. Old Tappan, NJ: Fleming H. Revel, 1957.

——. *Luther's Works.* Gen. Ed. Helmut T. Lehman. Vol. 38: *Word and Sacrament* IV. Ed. Martin E. Lehman. Philadelphia: Fortress Press, 1971.

——. *Martin Luther: Selections from his Writings.* Ed. John Dillenberger. Garden City, NY: Doubleday & Co., 1961.

Makower, Felix. *The Constitutional History and Constitution of the Church of England.* 1895. Rpt. New York: Burt Franklin, 1960.

Martz, Louis L., Ed. *The Anchor Anthology of Seventeenth-Century Verse.* Vol. 1. Garden City, NY: Doubleday & Co., 1969.

Melville, Herman. *Moby-Dick.* Ed. Harrison Hayford and Hershel Parker. New York: W. W. Norton & Co., 1967.

Milward, J. S., Ed. *Portraits and Documents: The Sixteenth Century.* London: Hutchinson, 1968.

Molina, Luis de. *On Divine Foreknowledge: Part IV of the Concordia.* Trans. Alfred J. Freddoso. Ithaca, NY: Cornell University Press, 1988.

Newman, John Henry. *An Essay on the Development of Christian Doctrine.* Ed. J. M. Cameron. Harmondsworth: Penguin Books, 1974.

Nichols, Fred, Ed. *An Anthology of Neo-Latin Poetry.* New Haven: Yale University Press, 1979.

Ockham, William of. *Predestination, God's Foreknowledge, and Future Contingents.* Trans. Marilyn McCord Adams and Norman Kretzman. 2nd ed. Indianapolis: Hackett, 1983.

Prudentius Clemens, Aurelius. *Prudentius.* Ed. and Trans. H. T. Thompson. 2 vols. Cambridge, MA: Harvard University Press, 1969.

Quevedo, Francisco de. *Obras completas*. Ed. José Manuel Blecua. Vol. I. Barcelona: Editorial Planeta, 1969.

Roberts, John R., Ed. *A Critical Anthology of English Recusant Devotional Prose, 1558–1603*. Pittsburgh: Duquesne University Press, 1966.

Scotus, John Duns. *Opera Omnia*. xx vols. Paris: Vivès, 1893.

——. *Philosophical Writings*. Trans. Allan Wolters, O.F.M. Indianapolis: Hackett, 1987.

Shakespeare, William. *Shakespeare's Sonnets*. Ed. Stephen Booth. New Haven and London: Yale University Press, 1977.

Sidney, Sir Philip. *The Poems of Sir Philip Sidney*. Ed. William A. Ringler, Jr. Oxford: Clarendon Press, 1962.

Southwell, Saint Robert. *The Poems of Robert Southwell, S.J.* Ed. James H. McDonald and Nancy Pollard Brown. Oxford: Clarendon Press, 1967.

Stevens, Wallace. *The Collected Poems of Wallace Stevens*. New York: Alfred Knopf, 1954.

Teresa de Jesús, Santa. *Obras completas*. Ed. Efren de la Madre de Dios, O.C.D. and Otger Steggink, O.Carm. 2nd ed. Madrid: Biblioteca de Autores Cristianos, 1957.

Terry, Arthur, Ed. *An Anthology of Spanish Poetry, 1500–1700*. 2 vols. Oxford: Pergamon Press, 1968.

Tertullianus, Florens Quintus Septimius. *Apologeticus*. Ed. and Trans. T. R. Glover. Cambridge, MA: Harvard University Press, 1931.

Thomas Aquinas, Saint. *Devoutly I Adore Thee: The Prayers and Hymns of Saint Thomas Aquinas*. Trans. and Ed. Robert Anderson and Johann Moser. Manchester, NH: Sophia Institute Press, 1993.

——. *Nature and Grace: Selections from the Summa Theologica of Saint Thomas Aquinas*. Ed. and Trans. A. M. Fairweather. Philadelphia: Westminster Press, 1954.

——. *Opuscula Philosophica*. Ed. Raymundi M. Spiazzi, O.P. Turin: Marietti, 1954.

——. *Quaestiones Disputatae*. 5 vols. 5th ed. Turin: Marietti, 1927.

——. *Summa Theologiae*. Cura Fratrum eiusdem Ordinis. 3rd ed. Madrid: Biblioteca de Autores Cristianos, 1964.

Thomas à Kempis. *The Imitation of Christ*. Trans. Richard Whitford, 1530. Rpt. New York: Pocket Books, 1953.

Vaughan, Henry. *Henry Vaughan: The Complete Poems*. Ed. Alan Rudrum. New Haven and London: Yale University Press, 1976.

——. *The Complete Poetry of Henry Vaughan*. Ed. French Fogle. New York: New York University Press, 1964.

——. *The Works of Henry Vaughan*. Ed. L. C. Martin. 2nd ed. Oxford: Clarendon Press, 1957.

Vega Carpio, Lope Félix de. *Obras poéticas*. Ed. José Manuel Blecua. Vol. I. Barcelona: Editorial Planeta, 1969.

——. *Obras escogidas*. Ed. Federico Carlos Sainz de Robles. 4th ed. 3 vols. Madrid: Aguilar, 1964.

Walton, Isaac. *Lives*. Intro. George Saintsbury. London. Oxford University Press, 1927.

Warnke, Frank, Ed. and Trans. *European Metaphysical Poetry*. New Haven and London: Yale University Press, 1961.

Zwingli, Ulrich. *The accompt rekenyng and confession of the faith of Huldrik Zwinglius.*

Trans. Thomas Cotsforde, Geneva, 1555. Facsimile Rpt. Amsterdam: Theatris Orbis Terrarum, 1979.

——. *Selected Works*. Ed. Samuel Macauley Jackson. Intro. Edward Peters. Philadelphia: University of Pennsylvania Press, 1972.

——. *Zwingli and Bullinger*. Ed. G. W. Bromiley. Philadelphia: Westminster Press, 1953.

SECONDARY SOURCES

Adams, Robert M. "Taste and Bad Taste in Metaphysical Poetry: Crashaw and Dylan Thomas." In *Seventeenth-Century English Poetry*. Ed. William R. Keast. New York: Oxford University Press, 1972, pp. 264–79.

Aers, David, Bob Hodge, and Gunther Kress. *Literature, Language and Society in England, 1580–1680*. Totowa, NJ: Barnes & Noble, 1981.

Allen, Don Cameron. *Image and Meaning: Metaphoric Traditions in Renaissance Poetry*. Rev. ed. Baltimore: Johns Hopkins University Press, 1968.

Anderson, James F. *The Bond of Being: An Essay on Analogy and Existence*. 1949. Rpt. New York: Greenwood Press, 1969.

Anscombe, G. E. M. and Peter T. Geach. *Three Philosophers*. Itahca, NY: Cornell University Press, 1961.

Asals, Heather A.R. *Equivocal Predication: George Herbert's Way to God*. Toronto: University of Toronto Press, 1981.

Bainton, Roand H. *Here I Stand: A Life of Martin Luther*. New York: New American Library, 1950.

Bald, R. C. *John Donne: A Life*. Ed. Wesley Milgate. New York and Oxford: Oxford University Press, 1970.

Balthasar, Hans Urs von. *The Glory of the Lord*, Vol. I: *Seeing the Form*. Trans. Erasmo Leiva-Merikakis. Ed. Joseph Fessio and John Riches. San Francisco: Ignatius Press, 1982.

Bangs, Carl. *Arminius: A Study in the Dutch Reformation*. 2nd ed. Grand Rapids, MI: Zondervan, 1985.

Bauer, Matthias. "'A Title Strange, Yet True': Toward an Explanation of Herbert's Titles." In *George Herbert: Sacred and Profane*. Ed. Helen Wilcox and Richard Todd. Amsterdam: VU University Press, 1995, pp. 103–17.

Bell, Ilona. "Revision and Revelation in Herbert's 'Affliction (I)'." *John Donne Journal* 3 (1984) 73–96.

——. "'Setting Foot into Divinity': George Herbert and the English Reformation." In *Essential Articles for the Study of George Herbert's Poetry*. Ed. John R. Roberts. Hamden, CT: Archon Books, 1979, pp. 63–83.

Benet, Diana. *The Secretary of Praise: The Poetic Vocation of George Herbert*. Columbia: University of Missouri Press, 1984.

Bennett, Joan. *Five Metaphysical Poets*. Cambridge: Cambridge University Press, 1964.

Bloch, Chana. *Spelling the Word: George Herbert and the Bible*. Berkeley: University of California Press, 1985.

Bloom, Harold. *Wallace Stevens: The Poems of Our Climate*. Ithaca, NY: Cornell University Press, 1977.

Boyle, Marjorie O'Rourke. *Rhetoric and Reform: Erasmus' Civil Dispute with Luther.* Cambridge, MA: Harvard University Press, 1983.

Broderick, James, S.J. *Robert Bellarmine: Saint and Scholar.* Westminster, MD: Newman Press, 1961.

Brown, Jonathan. *Velàzquez: Painter and Courtier.* New Haven and London: Yale University Press, 1986.

Calhoun, Thomas O. *Henry Vaughan: The Achievement of Silex Scintillans.* Newark: University of Delaware Press, 1981.

Carey, John. *John Donne: Life, Mind and Art.* New York: Oxford University Press, 1981.

Cathcart, Dwight. *Doubting Conscience: Donne and the Poetry of Moral Argument.* Ann Arbor: University of Michigan Press, 1975.

Cave, Terence. *Devotional Poetry in France, c. 1570–1613.* Cambridge: Cambridge University Press, 1969.

Chambers, A. B. "Christmas: The Liturgy of the Church and English Verse of the Renaissance." In *Literary Monographs.* Ed. Eric Rothstein and Joseph Anthony Wittreich, Jr. Madison and London: University of Wisconsin Press, 1975, VI.109–53.

——. " 'Goodfriday. 1613. Riding Westward': The Poem and the Tradition." In *Essential Articles for the Study of John Donne's Poetry.* Ed. John R. Roberts. Hamden, CT: Archon Books, 1975, pp. 333–48.

——. *Transfigured Rites in Seventeenth-Century English Poetry.* Columbia and London: University of Missouri Press, 1992.

Charles, Amy. *A Life of George Herbert.* Ithaca, NY, and London: Cornell University Press, 1977.

Chesterton, G. K. *Saint Thomas Aquinas: "The Dumb Ox".* 1933. Rpt. New York: Doubleday Image, 1956.

Chilton, P. A. *The Poetry of Jean de la Ceppède: A Study in Text and Context.* Oxford: Oxford University Press, 1977.

Christopher, Georgia B. "In Arcadia, Calvin . . .: A Study of Nature in Henry Vaughan." In *Essential Articles for the Study of Henry Vaughan.* Ed. Alan Rudrum. Hamden, Ct: Shoestring Press, 1987, pp. 170–88.

Cirillo, A. R. "Crashaw's 'Epiphany Hymn': The Dawn of Christian Time." *SP* 67 (1970) 67–88.

Clark, Ira. *Christ Revealed: The History of the Neotypological Lyric in the English Renaissance.* Gainesville: University Presses of Florida, 1982.

Coleridge, Samuel Taylor. *Coleridge on the Seventeenth Century.* Ed. Roberta Florence Brinkley. 1955. Rpt. New York: Greenwood Press, 1968.

Colie, Rosalie. *Paradoxica Epidemica: The Renaissance Tradition of Paradox.* 1966. Rpt. Hamden, CT: Shoestring Press, 1976.

Cressy, David. *Bonfires and Bells: National Memory and the Protestant Calendar in Elizabethan and Stuart England.* Berkeley and Los Angeles: University of California Press, 1989.

Cunnar, Eugene R. "Crashaw's Hymn 'To the Name Above Every Name': Background and Meaning." In *Essays on Richard Crashaw.* Ed. Robert M. Cooper. Salzburg: Institut für Anglistik und Amerikanistik, Universität Salzburg, 1979, pp. 102–28.

Davis, Elizabeth B. "Quevedo and the Rending of the Rocks." *Scripta Humanistica* 18 (1986) 58–72.

Davis, Walter R. "Meditation, Typology, and the Structure of John Donne's Sermons." In *The Eagle and the Dove: Reassessing John Donne*. Ed. Claude J. Summers and Ted-Larry Pebworth. Columbia: University of Missouri Press, 1986, pp. 166–88.

——. "The Meditative Hymnody of Richard Crashaw." *ELH* 50 (1983) 107–29.

Dawson, Christopher. *The Formation of Christendom*. New York: Sheed & Ward, 1967.

De Man, Paul. *Blindness and Insight*. Ed. Wlad Godzich. 2nd ed. Minneapolis: University of Minnesota Press, 1983.

Derrida, Jacques. *Dissemination*. Trans. Barbara Johnson. Chicago: University of Chicago Press, 1981.

——. *Mémoires for Paul de Man*. Trans. Cecile Lindsay, Jonathan Culler, and Eduardo Cadava. New York: Columbia University Press, 1986.

——. *Of Grammatology*. Trans. Gayatri Chakravorty Spivak. Baltimore: Johns Hopkins University Press, 1976.

——. *Speech and Phenomena and Other Essays on Husserl's Theory of Signs*. Trans. David B. Allison. Evanston, IL: Northwestern University Press, 1973.

Di Cesare, Mario A. and Rigo Mignani. *A Concordance to the Complete Writings of George Herbert*. Ithaca: Cornell University Press, 1977.

DiPasquale, Theresa M. "Ambivalent Mourning: Sacramentality, Idolatry, and Gender in 'Since she whome I lovd hath payd her last debt'." *John Donne Journal* 10 (1991) 45–56.

Duffy, Eamon. *The Stripping of the Altars: Traditional Religion in England c.1400–c.1580*. New Haven and London: Yale University Press, 1992.

Duncan, Joseph E. "Donne's 'Hymne to God my God, in my sicknesse' and the Iconographic Tradition." *John Donne Journal* 3 (1984) 157–80.

Elsky, Martin. "The Sacramental Frame of George Herbert's 'The Church' and the Shape of Spiritual Autobiography." *JEGP* 83 (1984) 313–29.

Empson, William. *Seven Types of Ambiguity*. 1930. Rpt. New York: Meridian Books, 1955.

Esch, Arno. *Englische Religiöse Lyrik des 17. Jahrhunderts*. Tübingen: Max Niemeyer Verlag, 1955.

Evans, Gillian R. "John Donne and the Augustinian Paradox of Sin." *RES* New Series, 33 (1982), No. 129: 1–22.

Ferry, Anne. *The "Inward" Language: Sonnets of Wyatt, Sidney, Shakespeare, and Donne*. Chicago: University of Chicago Press, 1983.

Fish, Stanley. *The Living Temple: George Herbert and Catechizing*. Berkeley: University of California Press, 1978.

——. *Self-Consuming Artifacts: The Experience of Seventeenth-Century Literature*. Berkeley: University of California Press, 1972.

——. *There's No Such Thing as Free Speech and It's a Good Thing, Too*. New York: Oxford University Press, 1994.

Flynn, Dennis. "The 'Annales School' and the Catholicism of Donne's Family. *John Donne Journal* 2 (1983) 1–9.

——. "Donne's Catholicism." *Recusant History* 13 (1975–76) 1–17, 178–95.

——. *John Donne and the Ancient Catholic Nobility*. Bloomington and Indianapolis: Indiana University Press, 1995.

Foucault, Michel. *The Order of Things: An Archeology of the Human Sciences.* New York: Random House, 1970.

Garner, Ross. *Henry Vaughan: Experience and the Tradition.* Chicago: University of Chicago Press, 1959.

Gates, Henry Louis. *Loose Canons: Notes on the Culture Wars.* New York: Oxford University Press, 1992.

Gilson, Etienne. *The Spirit of Medieval Philosophy.* Trans. A. H. C. Downes. New York: Charles Scribner's Sons, 1940.

Goldberg, Jonathan. *James I and the Politics of Literature: Jonson, Shakespeare, Donne, and Their Contemporaries.* Baltimore: Johns Hopkins University Press, 1983.

——. *Voice Terminal Echo: Postmodernism and English Renaissance Texts.* London: Methuen, 1986.

Green, Otis H. *Spain and the Western Tradition.* 4 vols. Madison: University of Wisconsin Press, 1966.

Greenblatt, Stephen. *Renaissance Self-Fashioning: From More to Shakespeare.* Chicago: University of Chicago Press, 1980.

Hageman, Elizabeth. "Calendrical Symbolism and the Unity of Crashaw's *Carmen Deo Nostro.*" *SP* 77 (1980) 161–79.

Halewood, William. *The Poetry of Grace: Reformation Themes and Structures in English Seventeenth-Century Poetry.* New Haven: Yale University Press, 1970.

Harman, Barbara Leah. *Costly Monuments: Representations of the Self in George Herbert's Poetry.* Cambridge, MA: Harvard University Press, 1982.

Hartman, Geoffrey. *Saving the Text: Literature, Derrida, Philosophy.* Johns Hopkins University Press, 1981.

Healy, Thomas F. "Crashaw and the Sense of History." In *New Perspectives on the Life and Art of Richard Crashaw.* Ed. John R. Roberts. Columbia and London: University of Missouri Press, 1990, pp. 49–65.

——. *Richard Crashaw.* Leiden: E. J. Brill, 1986.

Hester, M. Thomas. "Altering the Text of the Self: The Shapes of 'The Altar'." In *A Fine Tuning: Studies in the Religious Poetry of Herbert and Milton.* Ed. Mary A. Maleski. Binghamton, NY: MRTS, 1989, pp. 95–116.

——. "'Ask thy father': Rereading Donne's *Satyre III.*" *BJJ* 1 (1994) 201–18.

——. "'broken letters scarce remembered': Herbert's *Childhood* in Vaughan." *Christianity and Literature* 40 (1991) 209–22.

——. *Kinde Pitty and Brave Scorn: John Donne's Satyres.* Durham, NC: Duke University Press, 1982.

——. "'Let Me Love': Reading the Sacred 'Currant' of Donne's Profane Lyrics." In *Sacred and Profane: Secular and Devotional Interplay in Early Modern Literature.* Ed. Helen Wilcox, Richard Todd, and Alasdair MacDonald. Amsterdam: VU University Press, 1996, pp. 129–50.

——. "'let them sleepe': Donne's Personal Allusion in *Holy Sonnet IV.*" *PLL* 29 (1993) 346–50.

——. "*miserrimum dictu*: Donne's Epitaph for His Wife." *JEGP* 94 (1995) 13–29.

——. "'this cannot be said': A Preface to the Reader of Donne's Lyrics." *Christianity and Literature* 39 (1990) 365–85.

——. "The *troubled wit* of John Donne's 'blacke Soule'." *Cithara* 13 (1991) 16–27.

Hill, Christopher. *The Collected Essays of Christopher Hill.* Vol. I. University of Massachusetts Press, 1985.

——. *The World Turned Upside Down: Radical Ideas During the English Revolution.* New York: Viking Press, 1972.

Hirsch, David H. *The Deconstruction of Literature.* Hanover, NH and London: Brown University Press, 1991.

Hodgkins, Christopher. *Authority, Church, and Society in George Herbert: Return to the Middle Way.* Columbia and London: University of Missouri Press, 1993.

Huizinga, Johan. *Erasmus and the Age of Reformation.* Princeton, NJ: Princeton University Press, 1984.

Huntley, Frank L. *Bishop Joseph Hall and Protestant Meditation in Seventeenth-Century England.* Binghamton, NY: MRTS, 1981.

Hutchinson, F.E. *Cranmer and the English Reformation.* New York: Collier-MacMillan, 1962.

Itrat-Husain. *The Mystical Elements in the Metaphysical Poets.* Edinburgh: Oliver & Boyd, 1948.

Kemp, Anthony. *The Estrangement of the Past: A Study of the Origins of Modern Historical Consciouisness.* New York and Oxford: Oxford University Press, 1991.

Kerrigan, William. "The Fearful Accommodations of John Donne." *ELR* 4 (1974) 337–63.

King, James Roy. *Studies in Six 17th Century Writers.* Athens: Ohio University Press, 1966.

King, John N. *Reformation Literature: The Tudor Origins of the Protestant Tradition.* Princeton, NJ: Princeton University Press, 1982.

Lehman, David. *Signs of the Times: Deconstruction and the Fall of Paul de Man.* New York: Poseidon Press, 1991.

Levenson, J. C. "Donne's *Holy Sonnets* XIV." *Explicator* (March, 1953): Item 31.

Lewalski, Barbara K. *Donne's* Anniversaries *and the Poetry of Praise.* Princeton, NJ: Princeton University Press, 1973.

——. *Protestant Poetics and the Seventeenth-Century Religious Lyric.* Princeton, NJ: Princeton University Press, 1979.

Lewis, C. S. and E. M. W. Tillyard. *The Personal Heresy.* London: Oxford University Press, 1939.

Low, Anthony. *The Georgic Revolution.* Princeton, NJ: Princeton University Press, 1985.

——. *Loves Architecture: Devotional Modes in Seventeenth-Century English Poetry.* New York: New York University Press, 1978.

——. *The Reinvention of Love: Poetry, Politics and Culture from Sidney to Milton.* Cambridge: Cambridge University Press, 1993.

Lull, Janis. *The Poem in Time: Reading George Herbert's Revisions of* The Church. Newark: University of Delaware Press, 1990.

McCabe, Richard A. *Joseph Hall: A Study in Satire and Meditation.* Oxford: Clarendon Press, 1982.

McInerny, Ralph. *The Logic of Analogy: An Interpretation of St. Thomas.* The Hague: Martinns Nijhoff, 1961.

——. *Studies in Analogy.* The Hague: Martinns Nijhof, 1968.

Maddison, Carol. *Marcantonio Flaminio: Poet, Humanist and Reformer.* Chapel Hill: University of North Carolina Press, 1965.

Magliola, Robert. *Derrida on the Mend.* West Lafayette, IN: Purdue University Press, 1984.

Mahood, M. M. *Poetry and Humanism.* London: Jonathan Cape, 1950.

Malpezzi, Frances. "The Withered Garden in Herbert's 'Grace'." *John Donne Journal* 4 (1985) 35–47.

Marcus, Leah S. *The Politics of Mirth: Jonson, Herrick, Milton, Marvell, and the Defense of Old Holiday Pastimes.* Chicago: University of Chicago Press, 1986.

Marilla, E. L. "Henry Vaughan's Conversion: A Recent View." *MLN* 63 (1948) 394–97.

——. "The Religious Conversion of Henry Vaughan." *RES* 21 (1945) 15–22.

——. "The Secular and Religious Poetry of Henry Vaughan." *MLQ* 9 (1948) 394–411.

Marotti, Arthur. *John Donne: Coterie Poet.* Madison: University of Wisconsin Press, 1986.

Martz, Louis L. *From Renaissance to Baroque: Essays on Literature and Art.* Columbia and London: University of Missouri Press, 1991.

——. *The Paradise Within.* New Haven and London: Yale University Press, 1964.

——. *The Poetry of Meditation.* 2nd Ed. New Haven and London: Yale University Press, 1962.

Mazzeo, Joseph. "Modern Theories of Metaphysical Poetry." *MP* 50 (1952) 88–96.

——. *Renaissance and Seventeenth-Century Studies.* New York: Columbia University Press, 1964.

Miller, David Lee. *The Poem's Two Bodies: The Poetics of the 1590* Faerie Queene. Princeton: Princeton University Press, 1988.

Mirollo, James V. *The Poet of the Marvelous: Giambattista Marino.* New York: Columbia University Press, 1963.

Nania, John and P. J. Klemp. "John Donne's *La Corona*: A Second Structure." *Renaissance and Reformation* N.S. 2 (1978) 49–54.

Nelson, Lowry, Jr. *Baroque Lyric Poetry.* New Haven and London: Yale University Press, 1960.

Oberman, Heiko. *The Harvest of Medieval Theology: Gabriel Biel and Late Medieval Nominalism.* Cambridge, MA: Harvard University Press, 1963.

O'Connell, Patrick F. "'La Corona': Donne's *Ars Poetica Sacra*." In *The Eagle and the Dove: Reassessing John Donne.* Ed. Claude J. Summers and Ted-Larry Pebworth. Columbia and London: University of Missouri Press, 1986, pp. 119–30.

——. "The Successive Arrangements of Donne's 'Holy Sonnets'." *PQ* 60 (1981) 323–42.

——. "'Restore Thine Image': Structure and Theme in Donne's 'Goodfriday'." *John Donne Journal* 4 (1985) 13–28.

Ong, Walter J., S.J. "Wit and Mystery" A Revaluation in Medieval Latin Hymnody." *Speculum* 22 (1947) 310–41.

Pahlka, William H. *Saint Augustine's Meter and George Herbert's Will.* Kent, OH, and London: Kent State University Press, 1987.

Parrish, Paul. *Richard Crashaw.* Twayne's English Authors Series No. 299. Boston: G. K. Hall, 1980.

Pelikan, Jaroslav. *The Mystery of Continuity: Time and History, Memory and Eternity in the Thought of St. Augustine.* Charlottesville: University Press of Virginia, 1986.

Phelan, Gerald B. *St. Thomas and Analogy.* Milwaukee: Marquette University Press, 1948.

Pieper, Joseph. *Guide to St. Thomas Aquinas.* Trans. Richard and Clara Winston. 1962. Rpt. New York: Mentor-Omega, 1964.

Post, Jonathan F. S. *Henry Vaughan: The Unfolding Vision.* Princeton: Princeton University Press, 1982.

Raspa, Anthony. *The Emotive Image: Jesuit Poetics in the English Renaissance.* Fort Worth: Texas Christian University Press, 1983.

Ridley, Jasper. *Thomas Cranmer.* Oxford: Clarendon Press, 1962.

Roberts, John R., ed. *New Perspectives on the Life and Art of Richard Crashaw.* Columbia and London: University of Missouri Press, 1990.

Ross, Malcolm M. *Poetry and Dogma.* 1954. Rpt. New York: Octagon Press, 1969.

Sabine, Maureen. "Crashaw and the Feminine Animus: Patterns of Self-Sacrifice in Two of his Devotional Poems." *John Donne Journal* 4 (1985) 69–94.

——. *Feminine Engendered Faith: The Poetry of John Donne and Richard Crashaw.* London: MacMillan, 1992.

Sanders, Wilbur. *John Donne's Poetry.* Cambridge: Cambridge University Press, 1971.

Saussure, Ferdinand de. *Course in General Linguistics.* Trans. Wade Baskin, 1959. Rpt. New York: McGraw-Hill, 1966.

Scarisbrick, J. J. *The Reformation and the English People.* Oxford: Basil Blackwell, 1984.

Schoenfeldt, Michael C. *Prayer and Power: George Herbert and Renaissance Courtship.* Chicago: University of Chicago Press, 1991.

Seelig, Sharon Cadman. *The Shadow of Eternity: Belief and Structure in Herbert, Vaughan, and Traherne.* Lexington: University Press of Kentucky, 1981.

Sellin, Paul R. *John Donne and "Calvinist" Views of Grace.* Amsterdam: VU Boekhandel/Uitgerij, 1983.

——. *So Doth, So Is Religion: John Donne and Diplomatic Contexts in the Reformed Netherlands, 1619–1620.* Columbia and London: University of Missouri Press, 1988.

Shaw, Robert. *The Call of God: The Theme of Vocation in the Poetry of Donne and Herbert.* Cambridge, MA: Cowley Publications, 1981.

Sherwood, Terry. *Fulfilling the Circle: A Study of John Donne's Thought.* Toronto: University of Toronto Press, 1984.

——. *Herbert's Prayerful Art.* Toronto: University of Toronto Press, 1989.

Shuger, Debora Kuller. *Habits of Thought in the English Renaissance: Religion, Politics, and the Dominant Culture.* Berkeley/Los Angeles/London: University of California Press, 1990.

Simmonds, James D. *Masques of God: Form and Theme in the Poetry of Henry Vaughan.* Pittsburgh: University of Pittsburgh Press, 1972.

Singleton, Marion White. *God's Courtier: Configuring a Different Grace in George Herbert's Temple.* Cambridge: Cambridge University Press, 1987.

Smalley, Beryl. *The Study of the Bible in the Middle Ages.* 1952. Rpt. Notre Dame: University of Notre Dame Press, 1964.

Sparrow, John. "George Herbert and John Donne Among the Moravians." *BNYPL* 68 (1964) 625–53.

Stachniewski, John. "John Donne: The Despair of the 'Holy Sonnets'." *ELH* 48 (1981) 677–705.

Stanwood, Paul G. "Time and Liturgy in Donne, Crashaw, and T. S. Eliot." *Mosaic* 12 (1979), No. 2: 91–105.

Stein, Arnold. *George Herbert's Lyrics.* Baltimore: Johns Hopkins University Press, 1968.

Stewart, Stanley. *The Enclosed Garden: The Tradition and the Image in Seventeenth-Century Poetry.* Madison and London: University of Wisconsin Press, 1967.

———. *George Herbert.* Twayne's English Authors Series No. 428. Boston: G. K. Hall, 1980.

———. "Herbert and the 'Harmonies' of Little Gidding." *Cithara* 24 (1984) No. 1: 3–26.

Strier, Richard. "Crashaw's Other Voice." *SEL* 9 (1969) 135–51.

———. "History, Criticism, and Herbert: A Polemical Note." *PLL* 17 (1981) 347–52.

———. "Ironic Humanism in *The Temple.*" In *"Too Rich To Clothe the Sun": Essays on George Herbert.* Ed. Claude J. Summers and Ted-Larry Pebworth. Pittsburgh: University of Pittsburgh Press, 1980, pp. 33–52.

———. "John Donne Awry and Squint: The 'Holy Sonnets', 1608–1610." *MP* 86 (1989) 357–84.

———. *Love Known: Theology and Experience in George Herbert's Poetry.* Chicago: University of Chicago Press, 1983.

Summers, Joseph H. *George Herbert: His Religion and Art,* 1954. Rpt. Binghamton: MRTS, 1981.

Tayler, Edward W. *Donne's Idea of Woman: Structure and Meaning in The Anniversaries.* New York: Columbia University Press, 1991.

Taylor, Mark. *The Soul in Paraphrase: George Herbert's Poetics.* The Hague: Mouton, 1974.

Taylor, Mark C. *Erring: A Deconstructive A/Theology.* Chicago: University of Chicago Press, 1984.

Todd, Richard. *The Opacity of Signs: Acts of Interpretation: George Herbert's* The Temple. Columbia and London: University of Missouri Press, 1986.

———. " 'So Well Attyr'd Abroad': Background to the Sidney-Pembroke Psalter and its Implication for the Seventeenth-Century Religious Lyric." *TSLL* 29 (1987) 74–93.

Toliver, Harold. *George Herbert's Christian Narrative.* University Park: Pennsylvania State University Press, 1993.

Tuve, Rosemond. *A Reading of George Herbert.* Chicago: University of Chicago Press, 1952.

Veith, Gene Edward. *Reformation Spirituality: The Religion of George Herbert.* Lewisburg: Bucknell University Press. 1985.

———. "The Religious Wars in George Herbert Criticism: Reinterpreting Seventeenth-Century Anglicanism." *GHJ* 11 (1988) No. 2: 19–35.

Vendler, Helen. *The Poetry of George Herbert.* Cambridge, MA: Harvard University Press, 1975.

Vossler, Karl. *Poesie der Einsamkeit in Spanien.* 2nd ed. München: C. H. Beck'sche Verlagsbuchhandlung, 1950.

Wall, John N.. *Transformations of the Word: Spenser, Herbert, Vaughan.* Athens and London: University of Georgia Press, 1988.

Warnke, Frank. *Versions of Baroque: European Literature in the Seventeenth Century.* New Haven and London: Yale University Press, 1972.

Warren, Austin. *Richard Crashaw: A Study in Baroque Sensibility.* 1939. Rpt. Ann Arbor: University of Michigan Press. 1957.

Wedgewood, C. V. *The Thirty Years' War.* 1938. Rpt. Garden City: Doubleday & Co., 1961.

Weiner, Andrew. *Sir Philip Sidney and the Poetics of Protestantism.* Minneapolis: University of Minnesota Press, 1978.

Westfall, Richard S. *Science and Religion in Seventeenth-Century England.* 1958. Rpt. Ann Arbor: University of Michigan Press, 1973.

White, Helen C. *The Metaphysical Poets.* 1936. Rpt. New York: Collier Books, 1962.

White, James Boyd. *"This Book of Starres": Learning to Read George Herbert.* Ann Arbor: The University of Michigan Press, 1994.

Williams, George Walton. *Image and Symbol in the Sacred Poetry of Richard Crashaw.* Columbia: University of South Carolina Press, 1963.

Wilson, Michael. *The National Gallery.* London: Orbis, 1977.

Winburn, Martha. "The First Wesley Hymnbook." *BNYPL* 68 (1964) 225–38.

Winters, Yvor. *Forms of Discovery: Critical and Historical Essays on the Forms of the Short Poem in English.* Chicago: Swallow Press, 1967.

Wood, Chauncey. "An Augustinian Reading of George Herbert's 'The Pulley'." In *A Fine Tuning: Studies of the Religious Poetry of Herbert and Milton.* Ed. Mary A. Maleski. Binghamton: MRTS, 1989, pp. 145–59.

Woodhouse, A. S. P. "Nature and Grace in *The Faerie Queene.*" In *Elizabethan Poetry: Modern Essays in Criticism.* Ed. Paul Alpers. New York: Oxford University Press, 1967, pp. 345–79.

Wright, Terry R. "Through a *Glas* Darkly: Derrida, Literature, and the Specter of Christianity." *Christianity and Literature* 44 (1994) 73–92.

Young, R. V. "Derrida or Deity: Deconstruction in the Presence of the Word." In *Issues in the Wake of Vatican II.* Proceedings of the Eighth Convention of the Fellowship of Catholic Scholars. Ed. Paul L. Williams. Scranton: Northeast Books, 1985, pp. 105–20.

——. "'O my America, my new-found-land': Pornography and Imperial Politics in Donne's Elegies." *South Central Review* 4 (1987) No. 2: 35–48.

——. *Richard Crashaw and the Spanish Golden Age.* New Haven and London: Yale University Press, 1982.

Zim, Rivkah. *English Metrical Psalms: Poetry as Praise and Prayer, 1535–1601.* Cambridge: Cambridge University Press, 1987.

INDEX

Index